CW00709278

The Cambridge Companion to Richard Strauss

Richard Strauss is a composer much loved among audiences throughout the world, in both the opera house and the concert hall. Despite this popularity, Strauss was for many years ignored by scholars, who considered his commercial success and his continued reliance on the tonal system to be liabilities. However, the past two decades have seen a resurgence of scholarly interest in the composer. This *Companion* surveys the results, focussing on the principal genres, the social and historical context, and topics perennially controversial over the last century. Chapters cover Strauss's immense operatic output, the electrifying modernism of his tone poems, and his ever-popular lieder. Controversial topics are explored, including Strauss's relationship to the Third Reich and the sexual dimension of his works. Reintroducing the composer and his music in light of recent research, the volume shows Strauss's artistic personality to be richer and much more complicated than has been previously acknowledged.

Charles Youmans is Associate Professor of Music at Penn State University. He is the author of *Richard Strauss and the German Intellectual Tradition* (2005), and his articles and essays have appeared in *19th-Century Music*, *The Musical Quarterly*, the *Journal of Musicology*, and various edited collections.

The Cambridge Companion to

RICHARD STRAUSS

EDITED BY
Charles Youmans
Penn State University

CAMBRIDGE
UNIVERSITY PRESS

CAMBRIDGE UNIVERSITY PRESS
Cambridge, New York, Melbourne, Madrid, Cape Town, Singapore,
São Paulo, Delhi, Dubai, Tokyo, Mexico City

Cambridge University Press
The Edinburgh Building, Cambridge CB2 8RU, UK

Published in the United States of America by Cambridge University Press, New York

www.cambridge.org
Information on this title: www.cambridge.org/9780521728157

© Cambridge University Press 2010

This publication is in copyright. Subject to statutory exception
and to the provisions of relevant collective licensing agreements,
no reproduction of any part may take place without the written
permission of Cambridge University Press.

First published 2010

Printed in the United Kingdom at the University Press, Cambridge

A catalogue record for this publication is available from the British Library

Library of Congress Cataloguing in Publication data
The Cambridge companion to Richard Strauss / [edited by] Charles Youmans.
    p.   cm. – (Cambridge companions to music)
Includes bibliographical references and index.
ISBN 978-0-521-89930-7 (hardback) – ISBN 978-0-521-72815-7 (pbk.)
1. Strauss, Richard, 1864–1949–Criticism and interpretation.   I. Youmans, Charles Dowell,
1964– II. Title.   III. Series.
ML410.S93C36 2010
780.92–dc22
2010028672

ISBN 978-0-521-89930-7 hardback
ISBN 978-0-521-72815-7 paperback

Cambridge University Press has no responsibility for the persistence or
accuracy of URLs for external or third-party internet websites referred to in
this publication, and does not guarantee that any content on such websites is,
or will remain, accurate or appropriate.

For my parents

Contents

Illustrations

Music examples

Tables

Contributors

Günter Brosche served from 1981 to 2002 as Director of the Music Collection at the Austrian National Library. His scholarly publications include the *Richard-Strauss-Bibliographie* (1973), *Richard Strauss, Franz Schalk: Ein Briefwechsel* (1983), and most recently *Richard Strauss: Werk und Leben* (2008). Since 1975 he has been the General Secretary of the *Internationale Richard Strauss-Gesellschaft* (Vienna) and editor of the bi-annual *Richard Strauss-Blätter*.

James Deaville is Professor in the School for Studies in Art and Culture: Music, Carleton University, Ottawa. He has published extensively on Liszt, Wagner, and the New German School in (among others) *Journal of the American Musicological Society*, the *Journal of Musicological Research*, and *Notes*; co-edited *Peter Cornelius: Sämtliche Schriften*, and has contributed chapters to books published by Oxford, Cambridge, Routledge, Chicago, Princeton, Yale, Rochester, Ashgate, Continuum, and Boehlau.

Bryan Gilliam is Frances Fox Hill Professor in Humanities at Duke University. His books include *The Life of Richard Strauss* (Cambridge, 1999), *Richard Strauss's Elektra* (1991), and the edited volumes *Richard Strauss and His World* (1992) and *Richard Strauss: New Perspectives on the Composer and His Work* (1992). A study of Strauss's operas, *Rounding Wagner's Mountain: Richard Strauss and Modern German Opera*, is forthcoming from Cambridge University Press. Gilliam also serves as associate editor for *The Music Quarterly*.

Philip Graydon is currently Lecturer in Music at the Dublin Institute of Technology Conservatory of Music and Drama, having previously taught at the National University of Ireland, Maynooth, from which he received the degrees of B.A. and M.A. He received his Ph.D. from Queen's University Belfast with a dissertation on Richard Strauss's 1927 opera, *Die ägyptische Helena*. He has published articles on Strauss in *The Musical Quarterly* and the *Journal of the Royal Musical Association*, and is currently at work on a monograph on Strauss's mythological operas.

Wayne Heisler, Jr.'s interests lie in music of the late nineteenth through twentieth centuries, including art and popular traditions, and the intersection of music and dance. He is the author of *The Ballet Collaborations of Richard Strauss* (2009). Current projects include an essay on choreographies of Strauss's *Vier letzte Lieder*. Heisler is an Associate Professor of Historical and Cultural Studies in Music at The College of New Jersey.

James Hepokoski is Professor of Music at Yale University. He is the author or co-author of seven books and has written numerous articles on a wide variety of topics including Italian opera, Classical form, analytical hermeneutics, national identity, and modern and post-modern methodologies. His book, *Elements of Sonata Theory* (2006), co-authored with Warren Darcy, was the winner of the 2008 Wallace Berry Award from the Society for Music Theory. His most recent book is a selection of his essays from 1984 to 2008: *Music, Structure, Thought* (2009).

Raymond Holden was born in Australia in 1954; studied at Sydney, Cologne, and London; and has worked as a conductor, writer, and lecturer. He has performed with the Philharmonia Orchestra, the BBC Symphony Orchestra, the Orchestra of the Emilia Romagna, and the New Symphony Orchestra of London; has been published by Oxford, Cambridge and Yale University Presses; and has spoken at many of the world's leading universities and conservatoires. At present, he is finishing a major study of Strauss as a conductor and is Associate Head of Research at the Royal Academy of Music, London.

Originally from Copenhagen, **Morten Kristiansen** completed his doctorate in musicology at Yale University in 2000 with a dissertation on Strauss's opera *Feuersnot*, and now teaches music history at Xavier University in Cincinnati, Ohio. His work is focussed on Strauss's music and aesthetics around the turn of the century and has been published in *The Musical Quarterly*, *Richard Strauss-Blätter*, and *The Richard Strauss Companion*. He has a chapter in the forthcoming *Strauss Studies* for Cambridge University Press.

David Larkin completed his B.Mus. and M.Litt. degrees at University College Dublin and in 2007 was awarded his Ph.D. by the University of Cambridge. Formerly a research fellow funded by the Irish Research Council for the Humanities and Social Sciences, he is currently lecturing at the Sydney Conservatorium of Music (University of Sydney). His research interests and publications center on nineteenth-century German music, with particular focus on Strauss, Liszt, and Wagner, as well as issues such as intertextuality and composer–audience relations.

Jürgen May received his Ph.D. at the University of Bonn with a dissertation on early-seventeenth-century lute music. At the Beethoven-Archiv Bonn he worked on the edition of Beethoven's letters. Employed at the Richard-Strauss-Institut Garmisch-Partenkirchen since 1999, he is Senior Researcher of the *Richard Strauss Quellenverzeichnis* (catalogue of the sources of Strauss's works, established in October, 2009) and co-editor of the serial *Veröffentlichungen der Richard-Strauss-Gesellschaft*. May has published various articles on Beethoven and Strauss.

Alex Ross has been the music critic of *The New Yorker* since 1996. He has published *The Rest Is Noise: Listening to the Twentieth Century*, which won a National Book Critics Circle Award and the Guardian First Book Award, and *Listen To This*, a collection of his *New Yorker* writings. In 2008 he was named a MacArthur Fellow.

Michael Walter is Professor of Musicology at the Karl Franzens University of Graz, Austria; Head of the Department of Musicology; and Head of the Center for Cultural Studies. He has published widely on music history and the history of opera. Among his books are *Hitler in der Oper* (1995) and *Richard Strauss und seine Zeit* (2000).

Scott Warfield earned his Ph.D. at the University of North Carolina at Chapel Hill, where he wrote his dissertation on Richard Strauss's first tone poem, *Macbeth*. He contributed the chapter on Strauss's instrumental music and the bibliographic essay to *The Richard Strauss Companion* (2003), and his articles and reviews appear in *Fontes artis musicae*, the *Journal of Musicological Research*, the *Kurt Weill Newsletter*, MLA *Notes*, the *Nineteenth-Century Music Review*, and *Richard*

Strauss-Blätter. He is Associate Professor of Music History at the University of Central Florida.

Walter Werbeck is Professor of Musicology at the University of Greifswald, Germany. He received his Ph.D. from the University of Paderborn in 1987 with a dissertation concerning German modal theory in the first half of the sixteenth century. His *Habilitationsschrift* (1995) on Strauss's tone poems was published as *Die Tondichtungen von Richard Strauss* the following year. He is currently President of the *Internationale Heinrich-Schütz-Gesellschaft* and General Editor of the *Schütz-Jahrbuch* and the *Neue Schütz-Ausgabe*, and his main fields of research are the music of the early German Baroque and the life and works of Richard Strauss.

Susan Youens is the J. W. Van Gorkom Professor of Music at the University of Notre Dame. She is the author of numerous scholarly articles and eight books on lieder, including *Heinrich Heine and the Lied* (Cambridge, 2007), *Schubert's Late Lieder: Beyond the Song Cycles* (Cambridge, 2002), *Hugo Wolf and His Mörike Songs* (Cambridge, 2000), and *Schubert, Müller, and* Die schöne Müllerin (Cambridge, 1997). She is currently working on two books, one entitled *Schumann in the World* and *A Social History of the Lied.*

Charles Youmans is Associate Professor of Music at Penn State University. His book *Richard Strauss's Orchestral Music and the German Intellectual Tradition* was published in 2005. Other work has appeared in *19th-Century Music, The Musical Quarterly*, the *Journal of Musicology*, and various collections, including the forthcoming *Strauss-Handbuch* edited by Walter Werbeck. His current project is a monograph on the relationship between Strauss and Gustav Mahler.

Preface and acknowledgments

Three decades into the oft-noted "resurgence" of Strauss scholarship, taking him seriously is no longer remarkable. True, for Strauss to become the object of academic inquiry there had to be a rediscovery. Unshakably popular with the listening public, this all-too-likable composer was for many years simply ignored by scholars. But what seemed novel in the 1980s and 1990s has settled into normalcy; musicologists now routinely investigate Strauss with the same tools applied to Bach and Beethoven.

Not surprisingly, uncritical assumptions have faded away. Strauss's rejection of atonality is no longer an indictment. The sophistication of his intellect has been recognized, and indeed, documented. A fresh appreciation of the heterogeneity of early-twentieth-century musical modernism has cast his varied oeuvre in a different light. And musical developments during the last fifty years suggest that qualities long considered old-fashioned may have been among his most visionary. There is a new Strauss among us, then, a more complex figure with richer connections to his art and its history.

This sea change was already apparent in 1999, when the fiftieth anniversary of the composer's death elicited a spate of biographical reassessments. These publications alerted the broader public to work by a handful of Straussian musicological pioneers – most importantly Bryan Gilliam on one side of the Atlantic and Walter Werbeck on the other – and stimulated a second wave of scholarly interest now sufficiently large and diverse to be called a "community." The last ten years have seen over a dozen new Ph.D. dissertations on Strauss, a healthy series of international conferences and essay collections, and even the first article on the composer in the *Journal of the American Musicological Society*. With contributions from scholars representing six different nations and a wide range of methodologies, *The Cambridge Companion to Richard Strauss* is one more sign of the depth that now obtains.

Given the wealth of newly available information, there is every reason to introduce Strauss again to the general reader and undergraduate music student – the kind of enthusiast whose regular engagement with the music is one of the most important justifications for musicological research. The expectations of this reader account for the book's organizational plan. At the center stand new accounts of the major genres, with several chapters each for tone poem and opera, and separate treatments of the early works, lieder, and the beloved "Indian summer." This material is approached via three chapters on topics yet to be elucidated for the non-specialist: the musical life of late-nineteenth-century Munich, where Strauss came of age; the creative process by which the composer produced his works; and the promising but mostly forgotten (with a few notable exceptions) music of his first twenty years. Finally, the last section deals with important topics in the endless wrangling over this controversial figure: his place in the twentieth century, his love for musical borrowing, his relationship to the Nazi regime, his unapologetic treatment of music as a business, his character as a performer, and his curious tendency to write music about music.

In a detailed overview of Munich's diverse musical culture in the 1870s and 1880s, James Deaville clarifies the range of influences on an apprentice composer talented enough to succeed in any direction he chose. The impressive artistic substance of each respective camp, and the power of the personalities involved, goes a long way towards explaining why in his youth Strauss had already developed into something of a musical chameleon, paradoxically flexible long after being acknowledged as a "finished" professional musician. Walter Werbeck demonstrates, drawing on meticulous study of the surviving sketches, that Strauss continued to refine his creative methods well into his maturity – even after such masterworks as *Don Juan* (1888) and *Tod und Verklärung* (1889) – but also that by *Till Eulenspiegels lustige Streiche* (1895) he had arrived at a method that would serve him for the next fifty years. A similar finding-of-his-way is documented by Wayne Heisler, Jr. in a survey of Strauss's youthful output. The high quality of these pieces, attested not just by Heisler's analyses but by the facts of contemporaneous reception, is all the more striking given their stylistic variety; as in the technical realm of compositional process, the challenges of youth would coalesce into an idiosyncratic mature practice.

David Larkin too shows that for Strauss the phenomenon of the "overnight success," as we might be tempted to read *Don Juan*, emerged from struggle, specifically Strauss's need in *Macbeth* simultaneously to absorb and adapt the legacies of Liszt and Wagner. By the time of the second group of tone poems, considered by James Hepokoski with a level of sophistication appropriate to their content, the composer was actively pushing the orchestral genre to the breaking-point, in every musical respect but also in its long-standing Romantic capacity as a bearer of philosophical and spiritual content. And even as Strauss drove this side of his creative personality to its culmination, he was building momentum towards his principal creative outlet, opera. The triumph of *Salome* would mark the conclusion, as Morten Kristiansen explains, of an even more elaborate negotiation with the demands of tradition (a resolution that no other German composer would find in the twenty years after *Parsifal*).

The relationship with Hofmannsthal, which would produce Strauss's greatest creative triumphs, is shown by Bryan Gilliam to have flourished through a strange chemistry that saw superficial differences in personality and outlook enlivening deeper commonalities: devotion to the artistic themes of gesture, transformation, and the power of marriage and children to give life meaning. The cruel loss of Hofmannsthal, and then of Stefan Zweig, the poet best equipped to replace him, would prove endlessly disheartening to Strauss, but Philip Graydon confirms that these setbacks did nothing to weaken the composer's creative energies, or to discourage him from further operatic explorations even as he entered his seventies. In recent decades these later operas have experienced a slow but steady revival, much as is to be hoped for the songs considered in loving detail by Susan Youens, who reveals the myriad subtle beauties to be found in measure after measure of works that even confirmed Straussians can overlook. Such would not be the fate of the so-called *Four Last Songs* and *Metamorphosen*, in spite of their genesis in a period when Strauss claimed to be writing only "wrist exercises." Jürgen May discloses the full extent of Strauss's continuing productivity in this final period, however, establishing connections among the two celebrated works and the others, and arguing that all of them offer insights into his creative personality, however insistently he may have downplayed their significance.

If certain topics seem perennially at issue in the controversies swirling about Strauss, the surest way towards intellectual progress must be to resist oversimplification. What, for example, did he mean for the twentieth century? Alex Ross considers the full scope of possibilities, sharing new insights on the obvious connection to the Second Viennese group, but also efficiently surveying the enormously wide field of subtler influence – an impact that continues to be felt, consciously for some composers, even today. Günter Brosche reveals that the question of influence *on* Strauss is no less complex; not only is there much to be done in establishing the facts of Strauss's encyclopedic intertextuality, but the work of interpreting this deeply important creative practice has only begun. Nowhere is the avoidance of the easy answer more crucial for the historian than in the Nazi question, and Michael Walter provides an uncompromisingly forthright treatment, with source-critical observations informing a cautious piecing-together of Strauss's own perspective, offered from a standpoint equidistant from apology and accusation.

For a composer who so openly reveled in the practical activities of a musician, Strauss has enjoyed relatively little scholarly treatment of these aspects of his life. Scott Warfield takes up the widely, inexplicably ignored question of what was required for a young composer to compete in the music business in late-nineteenth-century Bavaria; whatever natural talents and interests Strauss possessed in this area, his mature practice was shaped in reaction to powerful forces that had to be confronted. The book on his character as performer remains to be written, but Raymond Holden indicates here both what would need to be considered and how it could be done. A desire to bring music closer to the authentic realities of human experience underlay Strauss's frequent and at times disconcertingly realistic treatments of sexuality, which Bryan Gilliam shows to have been integral to the philosphical agendas served by this music. Finally, my own contribution examines a practical question directly at issue in Strauss's works themselves: what factors might account for his life-long joy in using music to reflect on the very art of music, a tendency that despite its often playful character seems bound up with his deepest beliefs about the nature of the art.

In preparing this volume I have enjoyed the gracious support of Gabriele Strauss, who made available the resources of the Richard-Strauss-Archiv and granted permission to use material from the composer's sketchbooks. I am grateful also to Christian Strauss, for his kind offer of assistance during my most recent stay in Garmisch. At the Richard-Strauss-Insitut, Christian Wolf and Jürgen May were, as ever, wonderfully responsive to my many requests. It has been an honor to work with a superb roster of contributors, who gladly accommodated a tight schedule. Bryan Gilliam, my faithful *Doktorvater*, provided valuable advice and shouldered a double load of essays. The book has gained immensely from the involvement of Jürgen Thym, a scholar exquisitely sensitive to linguistic nuance, who readily put aside his own work to make these translations. In the fall of 2009 I had the pleasure to share drafts of the essays with an outstanding collection of graduate students – Alex Bainbridge, Peter Cirka, Himani Gupta, Chris Madden, Grace Myers, Hyun Joo Park, Heather Paudler, Christi Smith, Paul Sommerfeld, Mia Tootill, and Cynthia Weevers – who combed every page and made numerous improvements. Mia deserves special thanks for cheerful assistance of all sorts, especially with musical examples. At Penn State I had the benefit of several releases from teaching; for these and for general support I am grateful to Sue Haug, Director of the School of Music, and Marica Tacconi, my esteemed colleague in musicology and Director of the Institute for the Arts and Humanities. Amanda Maple, the university's omnicompetent music librarian, cleared up several difficulties with typical effortlessness. I owe a considerable debt of gratitude to Victoria Cooper, who initiated the project and maintained a keen interest throughout, and to Rebecca Taylor, whose efficient attentions made a complex process seem easy. I would also like to acknowledge the careful production work of Jamie Hood, and the countless improvements made by a knowledgeable and sensitive copy-editor, Robert Whitelock. And finally, my most heartfelt thanks go to Nancy, Frances, and Hannah, for their patience, enthusiasm, and encouragement.

Chronology of Strauss's life and career

1863	Franz Strauss, aged forty-one, marries the twenty-five-year-old Josephine Pschorr on August 29; Franz had lost a previous wife and daughter to cholera in 1854, and a son to tuberculosis in 1852.
1864	On June 11, Richard Strauss is born at 2 Altheimer Eck, Munich, adjacent to the brewery owned by his mother's family.
1865	In his capacity as first horn with the Court Opera, Franz plays in the premiere of *Tristan und Isolde*, under Hans von Bülow; he would also take part in the first performances of *Die Meistersinger von Nürnberg* (1868), *Das Rheingold* (1869), *Die Walküre* (1870), and *Parsifal* (1882).
1867	Birth of Strauss's only sibling, Johanna, on June 9.
1868	The young Strauss enjoys walking with his father to hear the band play at the changing of the guard on the Marienplatz, whistling the tunes as they return home; he receives his first piano lessons from August Tombo, harpist in the Court Orchestra.
1869	The family moves to its permanent home at 11 Neuhauserstrasse.
1870	Strauss produces his first two compositions, the "Schneiderpolka" ("Tailor's Polka") and "Weihnachtslied" ("Christmas Song"), written down by Franz; matriculates at Munich's Cathedral School; Franz Strauss named Professor at Munich's Royal Music Academy.
1871	First two visits to the opera, to hear *Der Freischütz* and *Die Zauberflöte*; at the carnival festivities at the Munich Odeon, Strauss joins the children's masquerade as a *Minnesinger* from *Tannhäuser*.
1872	Introduced to Ludwig Thuille (1861–1907) by Pauline Nagiller, a friend of Josephine Strauss; begins violin study with Benno Walter, concertmaster of the Court Orchestra and Franz's first cousin.
1873	Conducts Franz's orchestration of the "Schneiderpolka" at a carnival concert arranged by the Munich Philharmonic Association.
1874	Enters the Ludwigs-Gymnasium, Sendlinger Straße, Munich; his teacher writes that "there can be few pupils in whom a sense of duty, talent, and liveliness are united to the degree that they are in this boy"; an inheritance allows the family to purchase a Blüthner grand piano.
1875	Begins music theory studies with Friedrich Wilhelm Meyer (harmony, counterpoint, canon, fugue, form, basic orchestration).
1876	At a Pschorr family concert Strauss plays Weber's *Invitation to the Dance*.
1877	Completes a Serenade for Orchestra – the first work he orchestrated himself – dedicating it to Meyer; by now Strauss has produced some fifty compositions, mostly works for piano, songs, and chamber music.
1878	Beginning of friendship with Friedrich Rösch (1862–1925), close confidant, personal lawyer, musical colleague; advanced piano study with distinguished Munich pedagogue Friedrich Niest.

1879	Thuille moves to Munich to study at the Royal Music Academy, bringing to a close the rich correspondence between himself and Strauss during the former's 1877–9 stay in Innsbruck.
1880	Conclusion of training with Meyer; secret study of the score of *Tristan und Isolde*.
1881	First published work, the *Festmarsch* for large orchestra, Op. 1 (composed in 1876), dedicated to Georg Pschorr.
1882	Graduates from the Ludwigs-Gymnasium; enrolls at the University of Munich for the winter semester, 1882–3; accompanies his father to Bayreuth for the first performances of *Parsifal* (Strauss attends not the premiere but a later performance); visits Vienna, where he meets Hans Richter and Eduard Hanslick and plays the piano in a performance of his Violin Concerto.
1883	In December begins a three-month trip to Berlin, where he meets Hans von Bülow, Joseph Joachim, the concert agent Hermann Wolff, and the musicologist Philipp Spitta, among many other musical figures.
1884	Makes his conducting debut with Bülow's Meiningen Orchestra at the Munich Odeon on November 18, performing the Suite in B♭ major for Thirteen Wind Instruments, Op. 4.
1885	In September takes up the position of Court Music Director in Meiningen, as Bülow's assistant; succeeds Bülow on the latter's departure in November; befriended by the arch-Wagnerian composer and violinist Alexander Ritter (1833–96), a member of the Meiningen orchestra.
1886	Completes *Aus Italien*; moves to the Munich Court Opera as third conductor, working under Hermann Levi and Franz Fischer; in the spring, beginning of love affair with Cäcilie Wenzel, Court Actress in Meiningen.
1887	In August, meets his future wife, Pauline de Ahna (1863–1950), who becomes his vocal student.
1888	Completes *Macbeth* (first version; revised 1891) and *Don Juan*; prepares new production of Wagner's *Die Feen* at Munich, only to hand over the performances to the second conductor, Franz Fischer; first invitation to a Wahnfried soirée (the following summer Strauss would serve as rehearsal assistant at Bayreuth).
1889	Completes *Tod und Verklärung*; relocates to Weimar as Kapellmeister to the Grand Duke of Saxe-Weimar-Eisenach; Franz Strauss abruptly pensioned from the Munich Court Opera by means of a notice posted on a bulletin board; first extant letter to Dora Wihan, an early love interest whom Strauss had met in 1883.
1890	Conducts Ritter's one-act operas *Der faule Hans* and *Wem die Krone?* at Weimar.
1891	In May, hospitalized for life-threatening lung inflammation; growing intimacy with Cosima Wagner and family, marked by familiar *du* form of address with Siegfried Wagner.
1892	Conducts *Tristan und Isolde* at Weimar, in a *Nuancierung* designed to compensate for the orchestra's small size; in November departs for eight-month journey to Greece and Egypt to convalesce from severe lung ailment; immerses himself in Goethe, Schopenhauer, and Nietzsche, and completes the short score of his first opera, *Guntram*.

1893   Completes *Guntram* (premiere: May 10, 1894, Weimar).

1894   Returns to Munich as Kapellmeister; lukewarm reception of Weimar premiere of *Guntram*; marries Pauline on September 10, offering the Op. 27 lieder as a wedding present.

1895   Completes *Till Eulenspiegels lustige Streiche*; conducts *Tannhäuser* at the Bayreuth Festival; bitter disappointment at the negative reception of *Guntram*'s first Munich performance in November.

1896   Promoted to Hofkapellmeister at Munich; completes *Also sprach Zarathustra*.

1897   Completes *Don Quixote*; in collaboration with Ernst von Possart, revival of *Così fan tutte* at the eighteenth-century theater designed by Francois Cuvilliés in Munich's Residenz.

1898   Completes *Ein Heldenleben*; moves to Berlin as conductor at the Court Opera; with Rösch and Hans Sommer, begins planning a society for the protection of composers' rights.

1899   First meeting with Hugo von Hofmannsthal, at the Berlin home of Richard Dehmel.

1900   First letter from Hofmannsthal, offering the ballet *Der Triumph der Zeit*; to Eugen Spitzweg, his long-time publisher, Strauss declares that he will "never again hand over performance rights to a publisher."

1901   Completes *Feuersnot* (premiere: November 21, 1901, Dresden); elected president of the *Allgemeiner Deutscher Musikverein* (All-German Music Society).

1902   On the Isle of Wight without his family, Strauss conceives the idea for *Symphonia domestica*; back home, Pauline pens a letter threatening divorce after erroneously discovering "evidence" of an affair.

1903   Completes *Symphonia domestica*; with Rösch and Sommer, founds *Genossenschaft Deutscher Tonsetzer* (German Composers' Cooperative); awarded honorary doctorate from the University of Heidelberg.

1904   First American tour, with performances in New York, Philadelphia, Boston, Cleveland, Pittsburgh, Chicago, Milwaukee, Detroit, Cincinnati, Minneapolis, Washington, and other smaller cities.

1905   Completes *Salome* (premiere: December 9, 1905, Dresden); Franz Strauss dies at age eighty-three.

1906   The first Austrian performance of *Salome*, in Graz, is attended by Mahler, Puccini, Schoenberg, and (it is said) the young Adolf Hitler.

1907   *Salome* is banned from New York's Metropolitan Opera after one performance, at the behest of J. P. Morgan's daughter; Strauss suffers second major illness of his life, collapsing from exhaustion and weakness of the heart.

1908   Completes *Elektra* (premiere: January 25, 1909, Dresden).

1909   Turns down Schoenberg's *Five Orchestral Pieces* for performance in Berlin.

1910   Completes *Der Rosenkavalier* (premiere: January 26, 1911, Dresden); first appearance as conductor at the Vienna Court Opera, with *Elektra* (June 19); Josephine Strauss dies at the age of seventy-two.

1911   Devastated by the news of Mahler's death (May 18), Strauss declares that he will title his *Eine Alpensinfonie* "Der Antichrist."

1912	Completes *Ariadne auf Naxos* (premiere: October 25, 1912, Stuttgart).
1913	Beginning on March 30, three-week auto tour through Italy with Hofmannsthal.
1914	Travels to Paris to conduct premiere of *Josephslegende* with the Ballets Russes; on the eve of World War I, receives honorary doctorate from the University of Oxford.
1915	Completes *Eine Alpensinfonie*; founding of *Genossenschaft zur Verwertung musikalischer Aufführungsrechte* (Cooperative for the Exploitation of Musical Performance Rights, or *GEMA*).
1916	Completes revision of *Ariadne auf Naxos* (premiere: October 4, 1916, Vienna).
1917	Completes *Die Frau ohne Schatten* (premiere: October 19, 1919, Vienna); with Hofmannsthal, Max Reinhardt, and Alfred Roller, founds the *Salzburger Festspielhausgemeinde* (Salzburg Festival Society).
1918	At the conclusion of the war, after a brief stint as interim director of the Berlin Opera – which he calls a "nuthouse" (*Narrenhaus*) – Strauss reaches agreement on a contract with the Vienna State Opera.
1919	Becomes co-director, with Franz Schalk, of the Vienna State Opera.
1920	Tours South America with the Vienna Philharmonic to raise money for the financially strapped Court Opera; he would return in 1923.
1921	Travels again to the USA, conducting his tone poems, accompanying Elizabeth Schumann, and being broadcast on radio for the first time.
1922	First Salzburg Festival to feature musical performances (the 1920 and 1921 events having been devoted to Hofmannsthal's *Jedermann*), with Strauss conducting *Don Giovanni* and *Così fan tutte*.
1923	Completes *Intermezzo* (premiere: November 4, 1924, Dresden).
1924	Resigns Vienna post after Schalk's machinations (henceforth Strauss's principal income comes from guest-conducting engagements and compositional royalties); Franz Strauss marries Alice von Grab, who would become Strauss's faithful assistant and the caretaker of the Richard Strauss-Archiv until her death in 1991.
1925	Completes *Parergon zur* Symphonia domestica for Paul Wittgenstein; death of Rösch.
1926	Travels to Athens to consider sites for a proposed Strauss Festival Theater.
1927	Completes *Die ägyptische Helena*, which Hofmannsthal regarded as his best libretto (premiere: June 6, 1928, Dresden); birth of Strauss's first grandchild, Richard.
1928	Conducts the first Vienna performance of *Helena*, which he calls (in a letter to Pauline) "perhaps the greatest triumph of my life."
1929	Death of Hofmannsthal on July 15; in a letter to the poet's wife, a grieving Strauss declares "No one will ever replace him for me or the world of music!"; arranges Mozart's *Idomeneo* for the Vienna State Opera, stating that he will "personally answer for my impiety to the divine Mozart if I ever get to heaven."
1930	Deaths of Cosima and Siegfried Wagner; Strauss has Franz Werfel and Alma Mahler-Werfel to dinner, with what Alice calls "a lively discussion of Christianity."

1931   First contact with Stefan Zweig.

1932   Completes *Arabella*, despite the unfinished state of the libretto for the second and third acts (premiere: July 1, 1933, Dresden); birth of second grandchild, Christian.

1933   Appointed President of the Reich Music Chamber of the new National Socialist regime; after Toscanini withdraws from Bayreuth in protest at Nazi policies, Strauss takes his place in a move towards reconciliation with the Wagner family; meets Hitler and suggests that the new government offer financial support to the festival.

1934   Completes *Die schweigsame Frau* (premiere: June 24, 1935, Dresden); meets Hitler again at Bayreuth and asks for an extension of the thirty-year period of copyright protection.

1935   Letter to Stefan Zweig requesting (in vain) a secret artistic collaboration is intercepted and delivered to Goebbels; Strauss resigns his official post.

1936   Completes *Friedenstag* (premiere: July 24, 1938, Munich); conducts *Olympic Hymn* at the Berlin games; during the winter games at Garmisch, no official from the Nazi government visits Strauss at his home.

1937   Completes *Daphne* (premiere: October 15, 1938, Dresden).

1938   On *Kristallnacht*, Strauss's grandsons are beaten in Garmisch; Alice is placed under house arrest.

1939   Hitler and Goebbels attend festival performance of *Friedenstag* in Vienna; the following day, a two-hour conversation with Goebbels; Strauss writes to Heinz Tietjen and Heinz Drewes seeking protection for his *nichtarisch* daughter-in-law and grandchildren.

1940   Completes *Die Liebe der Danae* (dress rehearsal for canceled premiere, August 16, 1944; premiere: August 14, 1952, Salzburg); revision of *Guntram* performed in Weimar.

1941   Completes *Capriccio* (premiere: October 28, 1942, Munich).

1942   Zweig commits suicide in Brazil; Strauss approaches the gate of the concentration camp at Theresienstadt in his chauffeur-driven automobile, determined to visit Alice's grandmother, Paula Neumann, an octogenarian inmate, only to be turned away by incredulous guards.

1943   Destruction of the Munich Nationaltheater by Allied bombs; among the lost materials are the "model productions" of Strauss's operas made by Clemens Krauss.

1944   Goebbels's declaration of total war leads to cancelation of Salzburg premiere of *Die Liebe der Danae*, but not before a full dress rehearsal attended by Strauss and a full audience; Alice and her children are classified as "half-breeds, first class"; records some of his orchestral music with the Vienna Philharmonic.

1945   Completes *Metamorphosen*; Allies occupy Garmisch, but declare Strauss's villa off limits after he introduces himself to American soldiers as the composer of *Salome* and *Der Rosenkavalier*; Vienna State Opera destroyed; beginning of exile in Switzerland.

1946   Invited to the USA by Lionel Barrymore; copies Eichendorff's "Im Abendrot" into a sketchbook.

1947   Travels to London at the invitaton of Sir Thomas Beecham for final foreign tour; conducts *Don Juan, Burleske, Symphonia domestica*, waltzes from *Rosenkavalier*, and "God Save the King."

1948   Completes last four orchestral lieder; cleared by denazification tribunal.

1949   After a heart attack on August 15, Strauss dies in his Garmisch villa on September 8, two days before his fifty-fifth wedding anniversary.

1950   Pauline Strauss dies on May 13.

Abbreviations

Chronicle	Willi Schuh. *Richard Strauss: A Chronicle of the Early Years 1864–1898*. Trans. Mary Whittall. Cambridge: Cambridge University Press, 1982.
New Perspectives	Bryan Gilliam, ed. *Richard Strauss: New Perspectives on the Composer and His Work*. Durham, NC: Duke University Press, 1992.
Recollections	Richard Strauss. *Recollections and Reflections*. Ed. Willi Schuh. Trans. L. J. Lawrence. London: Boosey and Hawkes, 1953. Originally published as *Betrachtungen und Erinnerungen* (Zurich: Atlantis, 1949). The second and third editions (Zurich: Atlantis, 1957, 1981) include material not in the first edition or the translation.
Strauss and His World	Bryan Gilliam, ed. *Richard Strauss and His World*. Princeton: Princeton University Press, 1992.
Strauss/Hofmannsthal	Franz and Alice Strauss, eds. *The Correspondence between Richard Strauss and Hugo von Hofmannsthal*. Arr. Willi Schuh. Trans. Hanns Hammelmann and Ewald Osers. Cambridge: Cambridge University Press, 1980.

PART I

Background

1 The musical world of Strauss's youth

JAMES DEAVILLE

Born in Munich on June 11, 1864, Richard Strauss entered the world at a crucial time of change for the political and cultural environment in which he would develop as person and musician: three months earlier, Ludwig II had acceded to power over the Kingdom of Bavaria, while almost six weeks earlier, Richard Wagner had first arrived in Munich under the new king's aegis. That these related events did not have an immediate impact on Strauss in his earliest years does not diminish their ultimate real and symbolic significance for his life and career: he emerged as musician within a city where the revolution in music was a matter of public debate, especially to the extent that its progenitor Wagner directly influenced the monarch and indirectly had an impact on affairs of state.

Character of the city

However, of all German-speaking major cities, Munich may have been the least suited for artistic upheaval, given the nature of its institutions and the character of its citizens. In his study *Pleasure Wars*, Peter Gay paints a picture of a Munich that was hopelessly polarized, between the cultural offerings sponsored by the ruling Wittelsbachs and the middle class that preferred popular types of entertainment.[1] Notably absent during the reigns of Ludwig I, Maximilian II, and Ludwig II was a significant bourgeois involvement in the higher forms of art, which Gay attributes in part to what he calls the "habitual passivity" of Munich's *Bürger*,[2] formed by a nexus of the monarch's paternalist attitude towards his subjects and the residents' appetite for amusement. Ludwig I speaks from this position when he opined in 1842, "*opera seria* is boring, but the *Münchener* and their king love merry *Singspiele*."[3] Munich Intendant Karl von Perfall, writing as Theodor von der Ammer, takes a more cynical view of this attitude in his observation: "The Isar-Athenian is not and never was that which with greater refinement can be called artistic. He only possesses a great urge to amuse himself … Thus his theater visit is also only for the purpose of finding entertainment."[4] Edward Wilberforce's 1863 book *Social*

Life in Munich provides more detail about musical taste among the city's residents:

> To the people who frequent the concerts, the music seems only a second-
> ary consideration … The crowd at every concert is a matter of fashion
> and of custom. Most people go because the rest go; a great many because
> they hope to be spoken to by the king; a great many more because their
> husbands have gone to their clubs, and they have nothing to do at home …
> The excellence of the orchestra, and the presence of the court, makes these
> [Musical Academy] concerts the principal ones in Munich.[5]

Wilberforce proceeds to contrast this artificial, elaborately staged concert hall experience with the "natural" outdoor culture of Munich's
bourgeoisie:

> But we breathe a very different atmosphere from that of these gas-lit rooms,
> brilliant though the company, and brilliant the play, when we get out into
> the open air, to one of the many gardens about Munich. How pleasant it
> is to sit on a bench and listen to the music of some military brass band or
> society of instrumentalists![6]

Other nineteenth-century visitors similarly observed the city's two faces,
whether traveller Theodore Child in calling Munich a "dolorous and incon-
gruous patchwork,"[7] or an unnamed author in the opinion "Munich is the
most artificial of all the cities of this world,"[8] or when – more positively
reporting about the polarized artistic life there – Friedrich Kaiser remarked
how theater director Carl Bernbrunn "significantly obtained both the support of the fun-loving [*lebenslustig*] Munich public and the favour of the
royal court by staging … festivals."[9] Such assessments criticized the low
artistic tastes of the Munich *Bürger*, whose "beer culture" figured prominently in travelogues and memoirs by visitors to the city. Still, city guides
from the early 1860s could direct visitors to Munich's architecture and art
collections as unique in Germany, the legacy of Ludwig I and (to a lesser
extent) Maximilian II, even though Grieben's notes at the same time "the
pleasant [*gemüthlich*], yet at times coarse [*derb*] lifestyle."[10]

In this light it is interesting to observe how travelers from the United
States tend to judge the music offered in Munich's beer gardens favorably.
Indeed, a certain trope appears to exist in American travel memoirs about
central Europe: the visitor provides an extended description of Munich's
architectural and artistic wonders, and then briefly portrays the city's
beer culture and beer gardens, replete with a positive description of the
accompanying music (the same writers tend not to refer to either operatic or orchestral performances in Munich). This applies to such diverse
reminiscences as W. H. K. Godfrey's *Three Months on the Continent* (1874),

P. B. Cogswell's *Glints from over the Water* (1880), Curtis Guild's *Over the Ocean* (1882), and Theodore Child's *Summer Holidays: Travelling Notes in Europe* (1889).[11] It appears that these aspects of Munich culture particularly struck the American visitor, whether out of novelty or familiarity.[12]

This ongoing question of artistic sensibility among the city's residents inspired critic Theodor Goering to ask in 1888, "[I]s Munich a musical city?" His answer was equivocal: "He acknowledged the city's fine orchestras, choirs, soloists, and singers … but … though times were beginning to change, Munich was still essentially dominated by 'princely hobbies' rather than by musical tastes freely developed by the educated middle classes."[13] The "princely hobbies" involved cultivating the higher forms of musical expression – the opera and symphonic music – which did not encourage the development of large-scale municipal musical institutions. In fact, the Munich Philharmonic Orchestra only came into existence in 1893, and then as the Kaim Orchestra (the current name dates from 1924). Considerably smaller than court cities Berlin and Vienna, which respectively numbered 702,500 and 663,000 inhabitants in 1869 and supported lively musical scenes outside court, Munich (with its 170,000 residents) failed to develop a middle-class public for "high-status" musical events (opera, symphonic and chamber music) comparable to those in Dresden and Leipzig, for example.[14] Yes, citizens of Munich did attend such performances, but – as we have already discovered – they were just as, if not more, likely to participate in "low-status" entertainment, as also reflected in the limited number of concerts offered during the season (thus the primary professional orchestra, the Musikalische Akademie, presented eight to twelve concerts annually).

Institutions of musical life: overview

These limitations of the scene notwithstanding, members of the *Bildungsbürgertum* could hear opera, symphonic music, and the sacred repertory in Munich at a high level of accomplishment. The primary high-status public institutions of musical life during Strauss's youth were the Hofoper (the Court Opera, which performed at the Hof-Theater and the Residenz-Theater), the Musikalische Akademie (in the Odeon), and the Königliche Vokalkapelle, the first two employing the Hoforchester (Strauss's father Franz was a horn player with the orchestra from 1847 to 1889). The amateur orchestra called "Wilde Gung'l" came into existence in late 1864 (conducted by Franz Strauss from 1875 to 1896), in response to Joseph Gungl's eighteen-member *Kapelle*, which had established itself earlier that year at the Englisches Café. The Königliche Musikschule (1867–73, in 1874 reorganized as a state institution) provided concerts for the Munich community, while the Volkstheater presented operettas and ballet. Public presentations of chamber music did not prominently figure in the city's musical life during Strauss's formative years, but the nineteenth-century practice of music-making did continue to flourish in the homes and salons of Munich's *Bürger*. Needless to say, the city did not lack opportunities for hearing "popular music": in the 1867 edition of Grieben's guide to Munich and environs, author Adolf Ackermann indicates the city possessed over 300 beer houses and that at these and other *Vergnügungsorte* (entertainment venues) there was "music everywhere on an almost daily basis."[15] Daily at noon a parade with military music took place – a military band also played "every Weds. Evening 6–7 in the Hofgarten, and Sat. evenings by the Chinese tower in the English Garden."[16]

That the majority of the elite institutions stood under royal patronage – not only in name but also in deed – did leave a mark upon the musical life of Munich, ranging from the employment of musicians to the repertory performed at the Court Opera. After all, Franz Strauss remained in active court service for over forty years, during which time he developed a career and raised a family in the employ of the Wittelsbach monarchy. At the same time, the Bavarian kings of the nineteenth century exerted varying degrees of influence upon the selection of works for the Hof-Theater, the musical institution of the highest prestige in the city.[17] The operatic repertory cultivated after 1864 under Ludwig II proves that royal taste did not always take a conservative or (in the case of Ludwig I) popular direction, even though scholarly studies – including Willi Schuh's detailed account of Strauss's Munich years[18] – have neglected the more traditional operatic programming during the king's reign in the desire to foreground Wagner's contributions.

Indeed, the account by Schuh may well describe the domestic conditions under which the young Richard emerged as a musician, but his book (and other biographies that followed) fails to establish an adequate context for the composer's early development. Granted that Strauss would have been too young during the late 1860s and early 1870s to pay much attention to details of the city's musical life, let alone to understand the machinations at court, he did mature within a musical/cultural environment that – by his own admission – left a lasting mark upon the youth.[19] The milieu Strauss encountered was unique in Germany, with musical, cultural, and social polarities the order of the day: the conflict between Wagner/Ludwig II and the conservative musical establishment, the disparity between the tastes and character of the nobility/*Bildungsbürger* and the lower classes, and even the divide between "interior culture" (sites of privilege, whether the opera stage, concert hall, or domestic salon) and "exterior culture" (military music, music in the beer gardens, street music), with the church and its music serving as intermediary.

A closer study of the city's institutions of musical life and the individuals associated with them will provide an understanding of what it meant for Richard Strauss to be an aspiring musician in late-nineteenth-century Munich and, indeed, for a musician to develop in a central European city other than the leading centers of Berlin, Vienna, and Leipzig.

The Hofoper

After a long period of ascendancy during the seventeenth and eighteenth centuries, the climax of which many historians identify as the premiere of Mozart's *Idomeneo* in 1781, the Munich Hofoper went into decline in the early nineteenth century.[20] Not until Franz Lachner took over the musical leadership of the institution in 1836 – under Intendant Karl Theodor von Küstner – was the Munich Court Opera able to rise again to prominence. He improved the quality of performance and reformed the repertory, so that new works by Lortzing, Marschner, Flotow, Gounod, and Verdi received solid performances – Lachner also conducted the Munich premieres of *Tannhäuser* (1855) and *Lohengrin* (1858), despite his lack of sympathy for Wagner's music. In general, the Hofoper was quite active during Lachner's tenure, mounting over 100 performances per season.[21]

Musical scholarship has assumed that, with the arrivals of Ludwig II and Richard Wagner in Munich in 1864, the operatic scene there dramatically changed. Indeed, Wagner's ascendancy did lead to Lachner's eventual retirement, with Hans von Bülow briefly taking the helm. During the late 1860s, the Court Opera became the primary site for new Wagner productions, with the premieres of *Tristan und Isolde* (June 10, 1865) and *Die Meistersinger* (June 21, 1868), and the unauthorized first performances of *Das Rheingold* (September 22, 1869) and *Die Walküre* (June 26, 1870). None of these first performances would have influenced the very young Strauss, but it should be remembered that Wagner remained a staple in Munich after the initiation of the Festspielhaus in Bayreuth, with twenty-four performances in 1876 alone, twenty-three in 1877, and twenty-five in 1878 (including the individual evenings of the *Ring* cycle).

The scholar nevertheless is well advised to put these Wagner performances into a broader perspective. Thus in 1868, the Hofoper presented almost 120 full evenings of opera, mounting thirteen performances of Wagner (three of *Der fliegende Holländer*, one of *Lohengrin*, and nine of *Die Meistersinger*).[22] That same year, however, the stage offered Auber ten times (*Der erste Glückstag* five times, *Maurer und Schlosser* four times, and *Die Stumme von Portici* once),[23] Lortzing nine times (*Der Wildschütz* twice, *Zar und Zimmermann* twice, *Der Waffenschmied* twice, and *Die beiden Schützen* three times), Boïeldieu nine times (*Die weiße Frau* five times, *Rothkäppchen* twice, *Der neue Gutsherr* twice), Weber six times (*Der Freischütz* five times, *Oberon* once), Halévy six times (*Die Jüdin* three times, *Die Musketiere der Königin* three times), Meyerbeer four times (*Die Hugenotten* three times, *Robert der Teufel* once), Gounod twice (*Faust*) and Verdi twice (*Der Troubadour*). Other opera composers represented on the repertory of calendar year 1868 include Beethoven, Cherubini, Dittersdorf, Donizetti, Flotow, Gluck, Krempelsetzer, Lachner, Méhul, Mozart, Nicolai, Rossini, Schubert, Schumann, Spohr, and Zenger.

In other words, opera-goers during 1868 in Munich would have enjoyed a rather complete cross-section of European opera of the nineteenth century, at the rate of one performance every third evening – this level of activity made the Hofoper the leading high-status musical institution in Munich of the time.[24] Of course, the opera performances of the late 1860s and early 1870s would not yet have a real effect on the child and youth Strauss, but they do represent the music his father played and the repertory that Richard himself would eventually experience at the Court Opera. Jumping ahead one decade to the late 1870s, and Strauss's first serious engagements with opera in performance, we discover that the number of evenings devoted to opera did not significantly vary from year to year during that period, and the representation of composers from the past and the proportion of works from the various national "schools" remained relatively stable. The seasons ranged from approximately 120 to 140 performances, although 1881 featured 150 and 1883 over 160, so that the son of an orchestral musician would have had ample opportunity to become familiar with staged opera.

Moreover, the repertory was surprisingly diverse, especially considering that Wagner's shadow hung over the institution through both his influence upon Ludwig II and his intervention through conductor Hans von Bülow. Needless to say, Wagner's music dominated every season, with at least twice, if not three times the works by the second-most performed composers. For the entire period from 1868 to 1892, Perfall counted a total of 742 Wagner performances at the Hofoper, followed by Mozart (241), Weber (226), Lortzing (213), Verdi (170), Auber (160), Meyerbeer (136), Beethoven (135), Rossini (132), and Gounod (116).[25] It is enlightening to observe how large a role the works of Lortzing played, but even more interesting to consider the significant presence of Italian and French composers of the past and present, especially Meyerbeer, Gounod, and Verdi, none of whose operas Wagner felt was of artistic value.

Turning specifically to the theater's repertory from the period 1877 to 1883, the formative years for the young Strauss, one can note similar proportions among these leading composers, yet with some informative variants. For example, Auber was particularly well represented during these years, with twelve performances in 1877 (ten percent of the repertory),[26] while Meyerbeer's four main operas received thirty-four performances (*Die Hugenotten* accounting for over half that number) and Lortzing's five leading works fifty-eight performances between 1877 and 1883.[27] Both *Aïda* and *Carmen* entered the Munich repertory several years after their premieres – *Aïda* in 1877, *Carmen* in 1880 – but once on the program, they would play dominant roles for years to come: Verdi's opera opened with ten performances, the most for any one work in 1877, and the Hofoper consistently staged Bizet's work five times per year into the late 1880s. Other favourites during this period – operas that annually received multiple performances – include Adam's *Der Postillon von Longjumeau*, Auber's *Die Stumme von Portici*, Beethoven's *Fidelio*, Boïeldieu's *Die weiße Frau*, Gounod's *Faust*, Lortzing's *Der Waffenschmied*, Mozart's *Don Juan* and *Die Zauberflöte*, Rossini's *Wilhelm Tell* and *Der Barbier von Seville*, Schumann's *Manfred*(!), Verdi's *Der Troubadour*, all of Wagner's operas (including the individual evenings of the *Ring*), and Weber's *Der Freischütz*. Among new operas, the theater repeatedly staged the very successful *Das goldene Kreuz* by Ignaz Brüll (which Strauss himself would later conduct in Munich), *Der Widerspenstigen Zähmung* by Carl Goetz, *Die Folkunger* by Edmund Kretschmer, and the perennial favourite *Katharina Cornaro* by former Kapellmeister Franz Lachner.

Of course, just because he came into contact with an opera through the Hofoper does not mean that Strauss valued the work, then or at a later date: for example, Strauss famously attacked Gounod's *Faust*, calling its German success "one of the greatest blots of shame."[28] After his "conversion" to Wagner, Strauss by and large adopted the party line of the New German School in his tastes, although his repertoire choices for Weimar and Munich can be said to reflect the eclectic operatic programming of the Hofoper during the reign of Ludwig II. It was during those early, formative years, while his father's anti-Wagnerian position still held sway with the boy, that Strauss acquired an intimate knowledge of the standard repertoire of the time, as documented in his letters to Ludwig Thuille.[29] There the young Strauss reports at length to his friend about his (positive) impressions from such works as Auber's *Die Stumme von Portici*, Boïeldieu's *Die weiße Frau*, and Lortzing's *Zar und Zimmermann*.[30] Needless to say, Strauss was also able to obtain an early, close familiarity with those staples of the nineteenth-century German stage – the operas of Mozart and Weber's *Der Freischütz* – as a result of his exposure at the Hofoper. He may have come to maintain a musical and ideological allegiance to Bayreuth, but the foundations of Strauss's opera aesthetic were laid in the Court Opera of Munich.

Observing such opera conductors as Hans von Bülow (as guest), Hermann Levi, and Franz Wüllner also contributed to the young composer's musical training, whether they were conducting the standard repertoire or Wagner's operas. The audience member of the Hofoper not only benefited from its first-rate conducting, but also was able to hear some of the leading voices of the day on stage, which included sopranos Mathilde Mallinger (the first Eva) and Therese Vogl (the first Sieglinde), tenor Heinrich Vogl (the first Loge and Siegmund), and bass Kaspar Bausewein (the first Fafner and Hunding). Starting in the Lachner years, the orchestra for the opera (the Hofkapelle) maintained a high level of artistic accomplishment, which carried over into its concert activities (see below).

Musikalische Akademie

Established in 1811, the Musikalische Akademie was the symphonic arm of the Court Opera Orchestra, consisting of Hofoper performers and led by its conductor.[31] While not as prominent a Munich institution during Strauss's youth as the opera, the orchestra nevertheless maintained a season of subscription concerts in the Odeon, divided into two series of four-to-six concerts each, the first finishing by Christmas, the second occurring during the Lenten season. Strauss regularly attended the Musikalische Akademie concerts – in fact, his letters to Thuille more substantially refer to the orchestra concerts than to the opera performances, and in greater detail.

During his formative years, Strauss would have experienced the concerts under the direction of Hermann Levi (conductor 1872–96), who presented exemplary orchestral programs that reflected both his early, close friendship with Brahms and his strong support for the music of Wagner.[32] The 1864 season under the direction of Franz Lachner reflects the orchestra's conservative repertoire before the arrival of Bülow and Levi: five compositions by Lachner himself; four by Mendelssohn; three by Beethoven; two by Mozart, Schumann, and Spohr; and one by Bach, Cherubini, Haydn, and Schubert. The season featured four new works: Lachner's Psalm 63 and Orchestral Suite No. 2, J. J. Abert's *Columbus* Symphony, and Wilhelm Taubert's Overture to *Tausend und eine Nacht*.

By the time Strauss was regularly attending the Musikalische Akademie concerts – his father had been a member since 1847 – the program contents had dramatically changed. Writing to friend Thuille in March, 1878, the thirteen-year-old already expressed in some detail his opinions about visiting composer Saint-Saëns and his *Rouet d'Omphale*, which Levi had programmed in the second subscription concert beside Mozart's Symphony No. 38, three songs by Max Zenger from *Der Trompeter von Säckingen*, three duets by Schumann, and Mendelssohn's Symphony No. 3.[33] The other concerts of the Lenten series brought subscribers mixed programs of old and new compositions: Beethoven, Symphony No. 5; Brahms, Piano Concerto No. 1 and Symphony No. 1; Wagner, *Siegfried-Idyll*; Raff, Violin Concerto in A minor; Spohr, Overture to *Jessonda*.

The second series of the 1880–1 season is particularly noteworthy because it featured works by all three composers of the New German School (Berlioz's *Harold en Italie*, Wagner's *Siegfried Idyll*, and Liszt's *Orpheus*), which are balanced by the usual assortment of symphonies by Haydn, Mozart, and Beethoven, and by Brahms's *Variationen über ein Thema von Haydn*. This was also the series in which Strauss's Symphony in D minor received its premiere, while the first half of the season brought recent compositions by Raff (Symphony No. 9, *Im Sommer*), Dvořák (Slavonic Rhapsody), Svendsen (Swedish Rhapsody), and Goldmark (*Ländliche Hochzeit* Symphony).

Thus the resident of Munich could have heard some of the newest orchestral music at the Musikalische Akademie concerts, while enjoying the established figures from the Classical and Romantic eras. Not unlike the Opera, these concerts reveal a more mixed repertoire than the scholar might suspect – Levi programmed leading composers whatever their musico-political direction, which led to quite interesting juxtapositions – for example, Brahms and Wagner on the same night. It must be borne in mind that the post-1872 repertoire is more a product of Levi's personal predilections than of any pressure exerted by Ludwig II or Wagner, since friend Brahms received more performances at the Odeon than did Wagner, Liszt, or Berlioz. This situation in Munich is unique and should not be interpreted as characterizing orchestral symphonic repertoires in other major central European cities, which – with the exception of Weimar and similar New German "outposts" – tended towards more conservative concert offerings. As a result, however, it provided the young Strauss with a greater familiarity with the totality of recent central Austro-German orchestral composition (conservative and progressive) than he might have acquired in other cities, including Berlin and Vienna.

Wilde Gung'l

More important for Strauss – and possibly also for the citizens of Munich – was the amateur orchestra called "Wilde Gung'l," which took life in the year of Strauss's birth.[34] As Bryan Gilliam observes,

Towards the end of the 1870s Strauss demonstrated an increasing interest in orchestral music, probably linked to the fact that his father had taken over the so-called Wilde Gung'l Orchestra in 1875. This amateur orchestra, which Franz Strauss led until 1896, helped introduce Richard to the world of symphonic composition. He attended rehearsals and himself joined the ensemble in 1882 as a first violinist ... The Wilde Gung'l allowed Strauss to learn orchestration on a practical level.[35]

The ensemble's name derived from the conductor Joseph Gung'l (Gungl), who had established his *Kapelle* in Munich in 1864 (it performed lighter, popular musical fare). The amateur orchestra, Wilde Gung'l, formed later that year, as a "wild" offshoot of the professional ensemble. As the first professional musician to conduct the Wilde Gung'l, Franz Strauss is credited with elevating its repertoire and performance standards. However, the orchestra's modest size – about thirty players at the time – necessarily limited programming, which featured both smaller "high-status" symphonic works, and popular orchestral dance and salon pieces, including waltzes, gallops, polkas, and quadrilles by Franz himself. Given Franz Strauss's musical tastes, it is no coincidence that neither Liszt nor Wagner figured in the repertoire of the Wilde Gung'l during his long-term tenure as conductor. Even though he did not begin playing violin in the ensemble until late 1882, Richard Strauss undoubtedly attended performances and rehearsals well before that date, possibly as early as the mid 1870s, especially considering that his father "turned [the Wilde Gung'l] into a type of private orchestra."[36] During Richard's active participation, which extended until September, 1885 (with the exception of his Berlin visit of 1883–4), he would have played such works as Symphonies Nos. 93 and 98 by Haydn; Symphony No. 41 and arranged quartet movements by Mozart; Symphonies Nos. 1 and 2 and the *Prometheus* music by Beethoven; the *Rosamunde* Overture and the Overture "in the Italian style" by Schubert; the Overtures to *Abu Hassan* and *Preciosa* by Weber; the *Ruy Blas* Overture and selections from *A Midsummer Night's Dream* by Mendelssohn; a concert overture by Johann Nepomuk Hummel; various overtures by Cherubini, Auber, Boïeldieu, and Carl Gottlieb Reissiger (a favourite of Franz); selections from the opera *Die Folkunger* by Edmund Kretschmer; the "Triumphal March" from *Aïda* by Verdi; and Symphony No. 4 by Niels Gade.[37] This repertoire may have borne some similarity to that of the Musikalische Akademie in the selection of earlier composers (even though the Wilde Gung'l only performed their smaller works), but the differences between Franz Strauss and Levi become readily evident upon comparing their programming of recent concert music: for Levi, it included Wagner and Liszt; for Strauss, Verdi, Kretschmer, and Reissiger (who had died in 1859). It is interesting to contemplate whether the Wilde Gung'l would have programmed some of the earliest orchestral works by the young Strauss had his father not been the conductor, although those compositions certainly betray no influence from the New German School.[38] At the same time, Franz Strauss himself set a conservative tone through his repertoire selections for the Wilde Gung'l, which ironically was not at all musically "wild" in comparison with Gung'l's own ensemble, which often performed Wagner in popular venues (see below). The citizens and amateur musicians of Munich nevertheless did become more acquainted with standard works from the traditional genres of "Classical" and "light Classical" music through the concerts of the Wilde Gung'l. Above all, the young Richard Strauss would intimately experience these pieces through his performance, which would leave its mark upon him.[39]

Chamber music

Rather poorly served by professional chamber music ensembles and concert series in comparison with Berlin, Vienna, Hamburg, Leipzig, or even smaller cities like Basel and Weimar,[40] Munich nevertheless was able to maintain two primary groups, each with its own series that customarily took place in the Museuemssaal. Anonymous *Allgemeine Musikalische Zeitung* reviewer and Munich resident "Wahrmund" ("Word of Truth") commented in early 1882 on how welcome Hans Bussmeyer's chamber series was, "since we do possess a standing string quartet through Herr Walter and colleagues, but the rest of the extensive field of chamber music is otherwise cultivated only in private circles."[41] Reports in music journals from the time suggest that attendance numbers greatly varied for these concerts, which – taken together with the paucity of ensembles – reflects the city's problematic relationship with "elite" culture. However, we know of at least one young *Bürger* who participated in the city's chamber music institutions: as Schuh comments, "in addition to operas and symphony concerts, Richard regularly attended recitals by the Benno Walter Quartet and the Hans Bussmeyer Trio."[42]

That the offerings of these ensembles tended to represent either older music or a conservative style of direction is a factor of chamber music itself rather than a marker of local or regional taste. Neither Wagner nor Liszt cultivated the genre, which did not lend itself towards programmatic composition, and those colleagues who did – Karl Goldmark and Robert Volkmann, for example – occupied the fringes of the New German School. The chamber music concerts in Munich tended to program Brahms and Raff among living composers, whose music had already developed a following among the high-status public.

An overview of two representative seasons (from Strauss's formative years) should suffice to establish the repertoires of the Walter Quartet and the Bussmeyer Piano Trio.[43] For the 1877–8 season, Walter's quartet presented two quartets by Haydn and one by Mozart; Beethoven's Op. 18, No. 2 and Op. 135; Schubert's String Quartet in G; Schumann's Op. 41, No. 3; and Brahms's Op. 67. The six concerts of the 1881–2 season did not bring much change: the opening concert of the first series, on October 26, 1881, offered the residents of Munich Haydn's Op. 76, No. 4; Mozart's Clarinet Quintet; and Beethoven's String Quartet, Op. 95. The only instances of chamber music for the season that extended beyond these three composers were Schumann's Op. 41, No. 2; Mendelssohn's Op. 12; and Joseph Rheinberger's String Quartet in C minor, Op. 89. Although Walter's quartet gave the premiere of Richard Strauss's String Quartet in A on March 11, 1881, the programming was so Classically oriented that even the critic for the conservative *Allgemeine Musikalische Zeitung* complained.[44]

Bussmeyer's *Kammermusikabende* (chamber music evenings) presented in reality anything but trio concerts, since – despite a core of pianist (Bussmeyer), violin and violoncello – they featured chamber ensembles ranging from duets to a small orchestra. For the same two seasons of four concerts each, Bussmeyer presented more varied and current programming than Walter: in 1877–8, the audience heard Mozart and Beethoven (no Haydn), but also Lachner's Piano Quintet, Op. 39; Anton Rubinstein's Cello Sonata, Op. 18; and Saint-Saëns's Piano Quartet, Op. 41. The later season likewise featured the Saint-Saëns Piano Quartet, as well as his Piano Quintet, Op. 14 and a Piano Quintet, Op. 4 by Giovanni Sgambati, which certainly provided the audience with a glimpse of recent chamber music production, even though Brahms and his associates were largely absent from the programs.

In all, this scene meant that a *Münchner* like the young Strauss could only count on about ten concerts of professional chamber music annually during the late 1870s and early 1880s, a figure not at all comparable to the offerings of other central European cities. As "Wahrmund" remarked, the gap was in part filled by performances in private circles, which proliferated in late-nineteenth-century urban milieux. This activity was even more exclusive than attendance at public concerts, since it presumed either social status or ability as performer, and thus cannot be considered as typical of musical taste in Munich. Like select fellow residents, violinist Richard Strauss himself participated in quartet performances, every other Sunday afternoon in the residence of his cousin Carl Aschenbrenner, whose father was a counsel in the Bavarian Supreme Court. There he acquired a close familiarity with the standard repertoire of Haydn, Mozart, Schubert, and Beethoven quartets.[45] In this regard, Richard's early experiences of chamber music were unlike those of fellow *Münchner*, however, who may have played in informal circles, but generally possessed neither the talent nor the music that Franz Strauss could draw upon to gain first-hand familiarity with the more challenging pieces from the "Classical" canon.[46]

Königliche Musikschule

Originally called the Königliche Konservatorium für Musik (1846–65),[47] the Königliche Musikschule (now the Hochschule für Musik und Theater München) provided the citizens of Munich a source for chamber and orchestral music that augmented the city's public concert life. As William Weber has argued, conservatory programs reflect the musical tastes and practices of a place, while adopting a generally conservative repertoire[48] – the Königliche Musikschule is no exception, despite the participation of Wagner associates. Thus the Conservatory's *Musikabend* on March 11, 1878 brought movements from concerti and chamber works by Bach, Mozart, and Beethoven, and the *Musikabend* of March 29 (which Strauss critiques in a letter to Thuille)[49] featured an orchestral suite by Bach, concerto movements by Mozart and Beethoven, an overture by Haydn, an aria by Marschner, an opera quintet by Mozart, and a serenade by Karl Matys. It was only in the *musikalisch-dramatischer Abend* on April 6 that the audience would have heard more contemporary music, including vocal pieces by Engelbert Humperdinck, Philipp Wolfrum, and Anton Rubinstein. That larger works also figured in the public concerts of the Musikschule is evidenced by the *Musikabend* on March 29, 1882 in the Odeonssaal, at which the institution's combined forces performed the Mozart Requiem.[50] The quality of the conservatory concerts could not match that of the professional ensembles or even the Wilde Gung'l under Franz Strauss, yet it afforded the Munich *Bildungsbürgertum* one other venue for cultivating "elevated" taste.

Other concerts

Like any major city in central Europe at the time, Munich attracted its share of traveling virtuosi and staged the usual recitals by and benefit concerts for local artists. During the 1879–80 season, for example, such noted performers as Désirée Artôt, Hans von Bülow, and Anton Rubinstein made stops in the city, while recitals were given by Munich cellist Siegmund Bürger, violinist Walter, and coloratura soprano Henriette Levasseur. Moreover, the city's various vocal musical associations, whether the *Männergesangverein*

"Liederhort", the *Lehrer-Gesangverein* or the *Oratorienverein*, all offered annual concerts, while providing their members with the type of musical experience that the amateur orchestra Wilde Gung'l did for local instrumentalists. Again, it must be noted that, despite their quality, the number of these individual concerts stands behind that for comparably sized German cities, which became clear to young Richard upon his visit to Berlin. In a letter to Thuille from Berlin in March, 1884, he warned that "the lethargic air of Munich is your artistic death."[51]

Königliche Vokalkapelle

The Catholic Munich placed high value in an active church-music scene, which in the late nineteenth century manifested itself most visibly at the court church Allerheiligen. This was the home of the Königliche Vokalkapelle, which – although a product of the late eighteenth century – was thoroughly reorganized in 1864 and placed under the direction of Franz Wüllner.[52] Indeed, some commentators gave Wüllner credit for calling the Vokalkapelle into life and developing it to a high degree of accomplishment.[53] Above and beyond the ensemble's ecclesiastical responsibilities (which were considerable), Wüllner's Vokalkapelle annually offered a series of four concerts called "Vokalsoiréen,"[54] which used the Odeonssaal for its performances – after Wüllner left Munich in 1877, Rheinberger carried on his directorial practices, although the season was reduced to three concerts. The choir's concert repertoire embraced both sacred and secular compositions, the more recent offerings including works by Wüllner, Rheinberger, Lachner, and – for the 1881–2 season – Brahms, Schumann, Robert Franz, Philipp Scharwenka, and Woldemar Bargiel. One of the most interesting and varied of Rheinberger's Vokalkapelle concerts from the late 1870s and early 1880s took place on March 16, 1880, for which he programmed choral works by Palestrina, Hammerschmidt, Eccard, Liszt (*Ave Maria*), Vivaldi, Lachner (Psalm 25), Rheinberger (*Salve regina*), Bernhard Scholz (lied), Franz von Holstein (lied), Ignaz Brüll (chorus), Adolpha Le Beau (two choruses), Schubert (*Des Tages Weihe*), and Bargiel (Psalm 95). Despite Liszt's presence on the program, the Königliche Vokalkapelle was not a site for the performance of New German sacred music, which did not accord well with the conservatism of the Catholic region.

Indeed, the music performed by the Vokalkapelle at the Allerheiligenkirche for high church holidays like Easter and Christmas reflects the strong, almost reactionary influence of the Caecilian movement in Bavaria. For Holy Week of 1878, Rheinberger and his Vokalkapelle presented six works by Palestrina, three by Tomás Luis de Victoria, and one each by Jakobus Gallus and Orlando di Lasso, while also performing Caecilian-style music by nineteenth-century-Munich sacred composers Caspar Ett and Johann Caspar Aiblinger. The three separate performances on Good Friday consisted of a Passion and *Popule meus* by Victoria; a *Vexilla regis* by Aiblinger; a *Matutin*, *Benedictus*, and *Stabat mater* by Palestrina; an *Adoramus* by Giacomo Antonio Perti; and an *Adoramus* by Gregor Aichinger.[55]

The stark aesthetic contrast between this conservative repertoire in the churches and the Wagner cultivation of the Hofoper illustrates the polarized nature of musical life in Munich. Lacking the musical diversity encountered in other large central European cities, and under the direct cultural management of the reigning Wittelsbachs, the Bavarian capital offered its citizens and visitors strongly divergent musical experiences, between the elite institutions for opera and concerts on the one hand and "popular" music on the other. The *Bildingsbürger* seemed to aim for the high-status events, while at the same time enjoying the city's "beer culture" and its music.

"Popular" music in Munich

Despite the rising quality of the Court Orchestra, some of the best music in Munich was heard in the city's entertainment venues, whether the beer halls and gardens, cafés or taverns. As already observed, such sites represented the other side of musical taste in the culturally polarized Munich. However, it is particularly difficult to reconstruct the "popular-music" scene from Strauss's youth, since these daily concerts did not receive reviews in the local or the musical press. Pre-eminent among the ensembles was that of Joseph Gung'l, whose orchestra numbered between twenty and forty players according to the venue.[56] Gung'l's programming included the usual entertainment fare of waltzes by himself, Lanner, and the Strauss family, yet he also expertly presented more demanding works by Beethoven, Schubert, and – even – Wagner. Thus one American visitor could make the following remarks on the quality of Gung'l's performance and repertory: "The superb music which one may listen to here for a mere trifle is astonishing. I visited one of these gardens, where Gung'l's band of about forty performers played a splendid programme – twelve compositions of [Johann] Strauss, Wagner, Beethoven, Mendelssohn, and Gung'l."[57] As an unnamed critic in the *Allgemeine Musikalische Zeitung* of 1866 notes, Gung'l's intention was "to stimulate taste for symphonic music in less educated circles."[58] Thus, despite the maligned beer culture of Munich, those very drinkers were at the same time consuming music of some sophistication, at least at establishments where Gung'l's ensemble was performing.

It is certainly ironic that residents and visitors were more likely to hear Wagner's music at the Englisches Café and the Café National than at a Musikalische Akademie concert in the Odeon (and not at all at a Wilde Gung'l performance). Indeed, Gung'l conducted his orchestra on January 5, 1872 at a concert of the *Wagner-Verein* for the benefit of the *Nibelungen* performances – the program consisted of the prelude to *Lohengrin*; a vocal selection from Weber's *Oberon*; a violin concerto by orchestra member Fromm; the overture to *Tannhäuser*; the lieder "La Tombe dit à la rose" (as "Die Rose"), "Träume," and "Attente" (as "Die Erwartung") by Wagner;[59] Beethoven's Piano Concerto in C minor; and the *Kaisermarsch*.[60] The following passage by traveler Henry Bedford from 1875 may well overstate the case for Wagner at "low-status concerts" (using William Weber's designation), yet it does certainly argue for his music's popularity at the time:

> That Wagner's music is popular and that it is growing in popularity is obvious enough, at least in Germany, where it is best known. We do not remember a single programme at any of the many concerts we heard – and every German town as well as city has its nightly concert in one or more of its public gardens – wherein Wagner's music did not occupy a chief place, and was not listened to with the most attention, and received with the most applause. Those who cater for the public take good care to learn the public taste, and when conductors like Gung'l, Strauss, and Marchner[61] give but the second place to their own brilliant and showy compositions, and honour, as the popular favourite, so profound a thinker, and so severe a composer as Richard Wagner, we may be sure that the music of the new school is making its way, indeed has already made its way, into the hearts of the most musical people in Europe.[62]

Under such circumstances, it is unlikely that the young composer Strauss would not have had some experiences with performances of Wagner's music beyond the royal musical institutions and "high-status" musical events in Munich. How he responded to those compositions, probably in arrangements by Gung'l and others, is another matter, although Schuh does document the youth's positive response to *Lohengrin*.[63] At the same time, Gung'l's band or other such ensembles would have introduced to him the lighter repertory of dance music, particularly waltzes, at an age prior to his active participation in Wilde Gung'l – such contact with popular music would have been virtually unavoidable in Munich of the day, despite Strauss's famous remark, "under my father's strict tutelage I heard nothing but Classical music until I was sixteen."[64]

Music publishers

When the budding composer Richard Strauss sought to publish his early
works, it stood to reason that he would turn to the Munich company Joseph
Aibl, under the direction of Eugen Spitzweg. Munich was no important
center of music publishing, especially in comparison with Leipzig, Vienna,
and Berlin, so Strauss had little choice in the local market regarding his
best chance of finding a publisher for his first opus numbers (despite his
father's assistance). Aibl was the most established firm in the city, dating
back to 1824 and led by Eduard Spitzweg from 1836 to 1884, then by his
sons Eugen and Otto until 1904, when Universal bought the company.
Smaller music publishers in Munich included Theodor Ackermann, Falter
und Sohn (their catalogue acquired by Aibl in 1888), Halbreiter, Schmid
and Janke, and Steiner – Franz Strauss published a number of his compositions (Opp. 2, 7, 8, 9, 12) with Falter, although he also availed himself of Aibl
and Halbreiter for individual publications. However, other Munich composers of the 1870s and 1880s – Hans von Bülow, Franz Lachner, Joseph
Rheinberger, Franz Wüllner – chose Aibl above other Munich houses,
although they also prominently maintained ties with the leading houses in
Leipzig, Vienna, and Berlin, and with Schott in Mainz. This desire for publication outside Munich, in prestigious Leipzig, undoubtedly contributed
to Strauss's (successful) solicitation of Breitkopf and Härtel as publisher of
his Festive March, Op. 1.[65]

Of course, music itself would have been readily available in the Bavarian
capital. According to the *Bayerische Gewerbe-Statistik* of 1879 (based on
the census of 1875), the province was home to 826 music stores, with the
greatest concentration of them in Munich.[66] Studies have yet to be undertaken regarding the purchase of music in Munich (indeed, in any specific
market for the nineteenth century), but, given the continued expansion of
central European music publishing in the late nineteenth century, there
can be little doubt that music stores did a brisk business in Munich and –
with the well established network of individual publisher representation
and distribution throughout Europe[67] – the consumer there could likely
obtain any in-print music.

Music journalism

Munich did not produce any music journals of note during Strauss's youth,
but the major Leipzig publications of the time – *Neue Zeitschrift für Musik*,
Allgemeine Musikalische Zeitung, and *Musikalisches Wochenblatt* – did
cover the city's musical scene with irregular correspondence reports. In

general, these and other German-language music periodicals would have been available to residents of Munich through various avenues: individual subscriptions, purchase at music stores, and sharing of copies, whether personally or through *Lesesalons*.

More significant for the composers and performers of Munich was the daily press, and particularly the *Münchner Neueste Nachrichten*, which reviewed local operatic performances and concerts, including those of the Wilde Gung'l (music journals did not report on popular concert institutions). This paper generally reported favorably about Wagner and his music, which may well have had some influence on the Munich public – with a circulation of 25,000, it was the most read paper in the city.[68] More popular on the national scene was the *Allgemeine Zeitung*, "the first paper in Germany,"[69] which moved to Munich from Augsburg in 1882 and had been promulgating a strongly anti-Wagnerian and anti-Liszt position since the late 1860s. The other Munich-based newspapers, such as the *Süddeutsche Presse* and the *Volksbote*, occupied artistic and aesthetic positions between the two larger dailies. The young Strauss would have had contact with these papers, but, filtered through his father's aesthetics, it is difficult to determine what he might have derived from music reviews in the daily press other than its evaluations of his own music. In these reviews, especially those from the *Münchner Neueste Nachrichten*, he found modest encouragement for his early compositions.

Conclusions

The Munich of Richard Strauss's youth did not offer its citizens the musical scene that larger or even comparably sized German and Austrian cities could boast. The paternalistic Wittelsbachs maintained control over the city's three primary institutions for musical production: the opera, the symphony orchestra, and the sacred vocal ensemble (not to mention the Königliche Musikschule). This royal involvement in music undoubtedly hindered the development of municipal or private musical organizations that could have filled the gap between the elite offerings under the aegis of the court and the popular music scene that flourished in open-air venues, cafés, and beer halls. Not that the average *Bürger* objected to that culture, which accorded well with contemporary descriptions of the *lebenslustiger Bayer* and – more specifically – *Münchner*. However, such polarization between high- and low-status performances characterized the city's musical life, which also divided along the lines of progressive (i.e. pro-Wagner) and conservative (i.e. anti-Wagner) taste, a split that shaped more than just musical politics in the Bavarian capital.

At the same time, this study of Munich musical life between 1864 and 1883 has uncovered how a diverse scene could nevertheless unfold within such constraints, whether the varied offerings of the Hofoper from the German, French, and Italian repertories, including Wagner, Meyerbeer, Gounod, and Verdi; or Levi's mixed programming of old and new, conservative and progressive compositions for the Musikalische Akademie concerts; or even the range of music – from Johann Strauss to Richard Wagner – heard in popular entertainment venues, especially through the performances of Joseph Gung'l's ensemble. Richard Strauss may have grown up in a domestic and social milieu that cultivated high-status, conservative values in music, and yet we know he attended Levi's Musikalische Akademie, for example, and it is hard to believe that he did not pay call on Gung'l on occasion. Certainly the dominance of Wagner's figure in Munich – whether at the Hofoper or in the social networks of the time, and at that, for better or worse – prepared the young Strauss for his eventual conversion to the master's cause. And the acquired close familiarity with compositions of the eighteenth- and nineteenth-century musical heritage would put him in good stead for a future career as conductor (and composer).

2 Strauss's compositional process

WALTER WERBECK

TRANSLATED BY JÜRGEN THYM

Principles and methods

Richard Strauss was a composer who, like any other member of his profession, made a living from the sale and performance of his works. With the printing of his music he offered it to the public, and with performances he saw to the unfolding of its public life. Whatever preceded the completion of the scores was, according to Strauss, inconsequential. Granted, the genesis of his works was not just a private matter – many other people were involved, including friends, colleagues, librettists, publishers, proofreaders, copyists, and translators – but he did not believe it of interest to the general public.

On the other hand, Strauss was a composer who, like his great model Richard Wagner, wanted his audiences to understand his music. When working on tone poems, he did not shy from offering progress reports to newspapers,[1] nor from arranging publications in which musicians or journalists explained the programmatic content. (To be sure, Strauss was much more taciturn with his operas. Fearing that other composers might preempt him, he never divulged the subject matter of his operas while working on them.) As his success increased, Strauss found himself confronted, again and again, with questions pertaining not only to the content of his music – the poetic ideas of the works – but also to his method of composition. Surprisingly, he never refused to answer such questions, but readily responded to them. The student of Strauss's compositional process thus finds a wealth of useful texts, ranging from detailed answers to a questionnaire[2] from *c.* 1895 (reprinted several times in a paraphrased and abbreviated version) to a manuscript (dated by Willi Schuh "circa 1940") with the title *Vom melodischen Einfall* (*On Melodic Invention*).[3] In these writings Strauss laid out the essential musical elements that concerned him during the act of composing and explained in detail, albeit more rarely, his specific working methods.

At the outset, a few remarks on his music are in order. The invention of themes and their elaboration into larger complexes stood at the center of Strauss's compositional practice. In accordance with the late-nineteenth-century trend towards "brevity of the musical idea,"[4] Strauss emphasized again and again that what came to him initially were themes of two to four measures, and that the act of composing consisted of expanding these themes to eight, sixteen, or thirty-two measures. It has been reported that he likewise instructed his few composition students to develop a short melodic structure into "a larger melodic arch of sixteen to thirty-two measures."[5] Strauss's consistency is remarkable: over a period of nearly fifty years he advised composers to invent "Classical" themes with periodic metric structures. This tendency can be attributed first to his own Classical training, and second to the advice Brahms gave him in Meiningen[6] to shape his themes as eight-measure phrases according to the pattern of Schubert's dances. Naturally Strauss's enthusiasm for Mozart also played an essential role.

In comparison with thematic content (melody), other musical parameters receive noticeably less discussion in Strauss's statements about his working method. But in 1918, in a conversation passed on by Max Marschalk, the composer assigned harmony a major role. "[T]he disposition of harmonies extending over, say, a movement or an act" occupied him intensely; he applied "the greatest of care … in the choice of keys. I determine them for long stretches in advance, and finding the way to move from one to another is often quite labor-intensive."[7] Obviously Strauss still considered melody and harmony – the traditional principal categories of composition since the beginning of the eighteenth century – to be the most essential elements of his music. In contrast, his use of orchestral color – an aspect of his music traditionally emphasized as particularly innovative – is not mentioned at all in Strauss's statements.

In Strauss's working methods, spontaneous inspiration apparently played an essential role with short works such as songs. "Reading [the poem] gave rise to the musical inspiration. I immediately jotted down the song" – thus Strauss to Marschalk on his composition of Achim von Arnim's poem "Stern" ("Star") (TrV 237, 1).[8] Longer works, however, called for a different modus operandi. Strauss mentions this in an interview published shortly before his fiftieth birthday in the *Neues Wiener Journal*:

> My music notebook accompanies me all the time … and as soon as an appropriate motive occurs to me for a theme on which I am working at the moment, it will be recorded in my most faithful companion. The ideas I notate are only sketches to be elaborated later, but before I write down even the smallest of preparatory sketches of an opera, I am occupied with the text for six months. I dig in and study all situations and characters down to the smallest detail … From my notes I fashion sketches, which later are put together for a piano reduction; I make changes in the sketches and work through them four times – this is the most exhausting part of composition. What follows then – the orchestral score, the grand colorful elaboration – is for me relaxation, it refreshes me.[9]

This passage, besides referring to work on themes and with libretti, focuses especially on the aspect of a precisely calculating economy of composition. The composer, it seems, worked according to fixed rules and followed a detailed strategy of musical production. Because of this rationalized method of composition, Strauss's critics have tended to refer to him as a skillful but uninspired "fabricator" (*Macher*). Technique, as Theodor W. Adorno put it, "has become independent of what matters."[10] And Stefan Zweig got the impression that even inspiration came to Strauss like clockwork.[11] The sketches, however, many of which have been preserved, tell a different story.

Documentation of the compositional process

Strauss's description of his process of composing operas includes four stages: intensive study of the libretto; drafting of musical sketches; linking the sketches together in a particell (the term that, for brevity's sake, I will use instead of "piano score"); and, finally, the writing of the orchestral score. In instrumental works, the earliest stage, Strauss's "presketch planning,"[12] is omitted – that is, the habit of adding musical commentaries to libretti and copies of libretti even before the first musical sketches. Such commentaries could exist for printed or copied texts in the case of piano-accompanied songs, but a particell was not necessary in this case. The fundamental documents of any study of Strauss's compositional process are the sketches, and, in the case of larger, more complex works, the particell, which formed the basis for the orchestral score.

For Strauss the act of composition was finished with the completion of the particell (which he referred to not only as "piano score" [not to be confused with "piano reduction"] but also as "sketch").[13] Only when extending the study to include the process of orchestration (as we shall do below) does one need to consult the scores. The post-creative status of orchestration explains how Strauss could call this stage "relaxation" that "refreshed" him; the difficult work had been completed. Indeed, the fair copies of piano-accompanied songs, or orchestral scores, which Strauss wrote on the basis of the particell, are nearly always without mistakes: all traces of earlier troubles have been expunged. Their calligraphy communicates grace and elegance, in stark contrast to the hard work evident in earlier sketches. Richard Wagner may have been the model for planning the fair copies, especially the two-tiered work before the writing of the score.[14] Like Strauss, Wagner worked with individual sketches and a particell (the so-called *Orchesterskizze* or orchestral sketch) in preparing the score. And, like Wagner (especially after *Siegfried*), Strauss moved from sketches to particell as soon as possible, and he furnished the particell with sufficient detail so that the writing of the score did not cause any difficulties.

Two impediments, however, hamper the study of Strauss's compositional process on the basis of sketches and particells. First, the material has not come down to us in its entirety. The principal body of evidence is the 135 Garmisch sketchbooks, including several particells. The sources in Garmisch, however, constitute less than half of the original stock – a circumstance attributable to Strauss's casual attitude towards compositional drafts.[15] Once a work was completed, he considered all preparatory work superfluous. Granted, he preserved musical sketches, as a rule, but he also liked to give them away as presents: complete sketchbooks and particells, as well as single leaves removed, if necessary, from larger units. Occasionally, especially in the difficult economic times after World War II, Strauss used such manuscripts as a currency substitute. Separate notations on instrumentation were generally not preserved; they have come down to us only in exceptional cases. Any kind of statements about Strauss's compositional process and instrumentation on the basis of sketches need therefore to be qualified, as a matter of principle, by keeping in mind that the sources are not complete.

Second, Strauss scholars have studied the sources of compositional process only in isolated cases, on the basis of a few works or groups of works.[16] A complete systematic study remains to be written. In particular, we do not know how the young Strauss developed his method of composition in the crucial period of the mid 1880s. The first Garmisch sketchbook does not begin until 1886, and there are no sketches of the larger works composed earlier, with the exception of the Violin Concerto. Yet the materials for this latter work, together with the sketches for larger orchestral works following 1886, provide important clues concerning those years when the young composer, after a long search, finally found his own way. It appears that the development of an unmistakable musical language was closely linked to the development of a characteristic compositional method.

Compositional methods in the early works: the Violin Concerto

Important clues to how Strauss sketched in his early years are contained in the drafts for his Violin Concerto, jotted down in a mathematical exercise book by the seventeen-year-old schoolboy around the turn of the year 1881–2.[17] Here a brief remark on the handwriting is necessary. Thus far, unfortunately, neither the handwriting nor the musical script of the young Strauss have been studied in detail. Judging from letters of Strauss to Ludwig Thuille that have been published in facsimile,[18] one can conclude that the handwriting of the composer underwent drastic changes after 1879, and it probably was no different with his musical script – the illustrations in the 1999 catalogue (showing examples from before 1874 and from 1880) at least suggest such an interpretation.[19] We do not know exactly when, how, and why Strauss's writing style changed. Schuh remarked that "the strictly controlled and consciously painstaking way of composing" began "in the fall of 1878."[20] In 1880 Strauss wrote his First Symphony, taking up the largest instrumental genre of his time and (in his own assessment) leaving behind the phase of small-bore composition. It is conceivable that in these circumstances he not only changed his handwriting but rethought his compositional methods. In any case, the sketches to the Violin Concerto already show the handwriting and style of notation of the following works, and they hint at working methods that Strauss did not fundamentally alter in subsequent years. For example, in the illustration on p. 6 of the catalogue, Strauss notates on two staves the music of mm. 190–221 from the first movement. He jots down essential elements of the music, melodic parts, and harmonies, and, by way of abbreviated or written-out instrumental notations, he lays out the orchestration. It seems that the draft served as the foundation for the score (the role that would later be played by the particell), even though it functioned at the same time as a sketch. As is shown on p. 5 with the notation for mm. 168–89,[21] Strauss crossed out an initial sketch for mm. 177–80, and on p. 6 there are improvements in the figurations of the violin. Typical for Strauss's method of sketching is the use of abbreviations: for example *bis*, meaning "twice" (p. 5 at the beginning), or *1–4 in Moll* (p. 6), by which Strauss meant a repetition of mm. 191–4, now in G minor.

All things considered, the draft of the Violin Concerto serves the functions of both the later sketches and the later particells: it is a document of composition and, at the same time, a preparation for the score. We do not know whether additional sketches preceded the draft, nor do we know whether Strauss was already differentiating between sketches and particell by the time he was seventeen. Worth noting are a few deviations from the score (e.g., the violin figures in the solo cadenza); even after completing the draft, Strauss changed some details. Finally, two additional observations: in the violin cadenza Strauss notates fingerings – proof that he was not only familiar with the technique of playing the violin but also with orchestral instruments in general; and if, as seems clearly the case, he drafted the music during classes at school, then already in these early years he was not dependent on a piano for composition.[22]

Compositional methods in mature works: sketches

After the Violin Concerto, Strauss's compositions for large orchestra and for chamber ensemble became increasingly complex. Without doubt sketches did exist for works as substantial as the two Symphonies, *Wandrers Sturmlied*, the First Horn Concerto, the Piano Quartet, and the *Burleske*. But nothing is known about such materials thus far – the Garmisch sketchbooks begin with the work on *Aus Italien* (1886). We can conclude with a reasonable amount of certainty that from 1896 Strauss separated sketch and particell into two compositional stages. For that reason I will first describe only the sketches, followed by the particells.

We do not know when Strauss started to use the sketchbooks typical for him: small notation booklets, mostly in oblong format. The first Garmisch sketchbook of this type carries the number 4 in Trenner's list, but since Strauss himself gave this item the heading "Skizzen I," it indeed could have been the first "real" sketchbook.[23] The date is approximately 1897; Sketchbook "II" also originated in this year – indeed, as Strauss noted, on September 10, his third wedding anniversary. Such precise dates of sketches or sketchbooks are unfortunately rare; an exact chronology of Strauss's sketches has been, and still is, an urgent necessity for Strauss scholars.

Before using the booklet that he labeled I, Strauss drafted his music (aside from what appears in the math exercise booklet) either on single sheets that later were bound together (Trenner's Sketchbook 1 is such a collection) or in an upright sketchbook (Trenner 2) that possibly was bound together by Strauss himself. But even after small-format sketchbooks became the norm, Strauss still sometimes used individual sheets to write down sketches of any kind; of those sheets presumably only a few have come down to us (such leaves could have been cut out of sketchbooks).

Strauss sketched his music mostly in pencil. But there are also ink sketches, and those drafts do not necessarily follow the pencil sketches in terms of chronology. A clear differentiation between pencil sketches for early drafts and ink sketches for later stages of composition develops only gradually.

Musical sketches

The entries in the sketchbooks can be divided generally into musical sketches and verbal texts. Concerning the musical sketches, the following can be said:

First, when Strauss sketches music, he focuses exclusively on the essential constituent parts of the composition: theme/motive/melody and harmony.

Example 2.1   Sketchbook 1, p. 47: *Don Juan*, mm. 53–6, harmonic skeleton

Example 2.2   Sketchbook 1, p. 49: *Don Juan*, mm. 52–5, passagework in the strings

He drafts on two staves (rarely on fewer, and even less often on more than two staves), producing one-voice motives or themes, two-part skeletons or polyphonic passages (concentrated as a rule on just a few main voices), and themes with harmonic progressions (the most common type), but sometimes only chord progressions and series of sounds. What he sketches – whether horizontal or vertical events – can, in general, lay claim to thematic significance. In other words, Strauss's sketches confirm the impressions gained from his statements cited earlier: his compositional work involves the traditional main elements of music – melody and harmony.

Second, he generally omits what seems to him superfluous: meter, clefs, key-signatures, and indications for instrumentation (e.g., timbre), articulation, dynamics, and tempo. Such details about which he was certain could be left out of the sketches without causing problems. Surprisingly, one searches mostly in vain for sketches of the typical Straussian figurations that imbue his music with its characteristic élan. However strongly such figurations set the tone in his scores, during the creative process they were clearly of secondary import. The ornamentation of his music was for Strauss a process comparable to orchestration: it gave the music its characteristic décor, but it did not count as musical substance and thus was not fixed until the writing of the score. Exceptions do exist, in cases where the figurations have particular import, as in *Don Juan*, mm. 52ff. Here Strauss first sketched the most important material, the harmonic successions in the woodwinds, then followed two pages later with a draft of the fast string passages. Both drafts are already very close to the final version (Examples 2.1 and 2.2).

Third, composition is sometimes easy, sometimes difficult for Strauss. Unsuccessful passages are crossed out, or Strauss abandons a sketch and

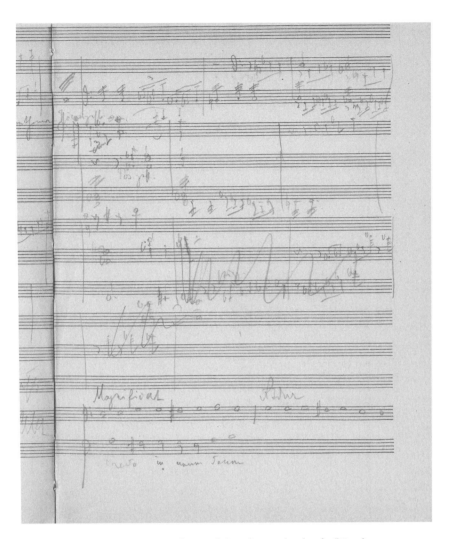

Figure 2.1 Sketchbook 2, pp. 71–3: *Also sprach Zarathustra*, sketches for "Von den Hinterweltlern."

starts afresh: either on the same stave or system, on the next, or sometimes on a different page. As in the Violin Concerto, literal repeats are abbreviated with *bis* and measures that appear later in a different context are marked *vi-de* or with other symbols or numbers. Evidently Strauss encountered major difficulties only rarely, but he was noticeably less at ease with sections in slow tempo (for example in *Tod und Verklärung* or *Ein Heldenleben*) than with fast passages.

Strauss's working method may be shown briefly in the earliest surviving sketches to *Also sprach Zarathustra* in Sketchbook 2 (Figure 2.1). On the page preceding the example (p. 70) he had sketched only the Nature motive (c′–g′–c″) in triple meter and then mm. 428–30 of the upper voice

Figure 2.1 (cont.)

of the violins. On p. 71 begins an extended draft of the music after the introduction. At the beginning of the top of the upper system, he writes out mm. 22 and 23 as in the final version. (Since the bass motive in m. 23 is derived from the A♭ major theme of the *Hinterweltler* ["backworldsmen"], it is likely that the theme had been already drafted in sketches that did not survive.) Then he sketches m. 24 – with a bass rhythm of two quarter notes followed by a half note instead of the final version's quarter note followed by a dotted half – and m. 25, again almost completely identical with the final version. Measure 26 is notated in a system of three staves; as in a particell, indications for instrumentation appear in the upper and middle staves – perhaps a spontaneous idea for a combination of brass

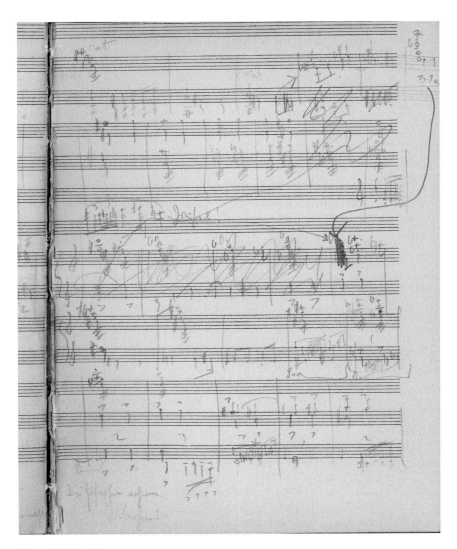

Figure 2.1 (cont.)

instruments. But Strauss kept only the stopped trombones, replacing the stopped horns with bassoons and the continuous F minor tremolo in the bass with an eighth note with rests. For mm. 29–30 Strauss first sketched a harmonic progression from F minor to A♭ minor. What he later called the *Sehnsuchtsmotiv* ("motive of longing") was to appear in this key for the first time in its distinct form; at the end the tone E♭ was marked with a fermata. Then the sketch stops. Strauss notated, at the bottom of the page, two Gregorian themes – a Magnificat verse and a Credo intonation – and the indication *Asdur* (A♭ major). In this way he clarified that these themes were to be incorporated in the A♭ major sphere of the *Hinterweltler* theme and that the A♭ major music could begin after the fermata.

But Strauss was not satisfied with the simple harmonic progression from F minor via A♭ minor to A♭ major. He crossed out the A♭ minor measures, so that the *Sehnsuchtsmotiv* would not to be too closely connected with the *Hinterweltler* harmonies. On the next page we find an improved version, one that was to be of major significance for the entire piece: the exposition of the *Sehnsuchtsmotiv* in B minor. (Two systems later Strauss explicitly writes the word *Sehnsucht* above the motive.) Thus was born the harmonic conflict between the tonalities of C and B that is central to *Zarathustra*. The motive now ends on D♯ (the same pitch as before, enharmonically), two Credo intonations ensue, and then the A♭ major theme can begin. Strauss's remark *Asdur, etc.* at the beginning of the third system confirms that the theme had been drafted before and was to be incorporated at this point.

To help keep track of musical fragments, Strauss began with Sketchbook 4 to supply numbers to sketches related to each other. That practice was especially helpful when pieces from separately sketched sections were pasted together – for instance in *Don Quixote*, a tone poem for which Strauss sketched individual "episodes" without knowing whether they would make it into the final version. Later, however, Strauss abandoned the practice of numbering sketches.

Fourth, in general we can distinguish between continuity drafts and individual sketches. Continuity drafts notate more or less extended sections in one stroke. Often Strauss succeeds with them right away – as for instance on the first page of sketches for *Till Eulenspiegel* (Figure 2.2). Granted, the slow introduction has not been conceived; the piece was to begin in a fast tempo (which however is not indicated in the sketch) with the clarinet theme (mm. 46ff. of the final version).[24] Strauss needed two attempts to find the correct metric position of the horn; the first try was abandoned after four measures. But then the knot unraveled: the music from m. 6 to m. 45 was jotted down at one fell swoop.

Strauss did not always succeed in producing such quick and sure drafts, and many times did not intend to; the sketching practice with *Don Quixote* mentioned earlier is a case in point. Thus we frequently encounter fragmentary sketches: short passages from different sections of a piece. Some of these are passages where Strauss got stuck in his continuity drafts; in others he picks up material already drafted in order to add more detail or try out thematic combinations. Often in such sketches, themes or motives are jotted down that Strauss invented for a specific composition but for which there was not yet a definitive position. They can be inventions of his own as well as quotations. The Gregorian melodies in *Zarathustra* belong in this category (Strauss used only the first five tones of the Magnificat verse, but the complete Credo intonation). Another example is the "doubt" motive

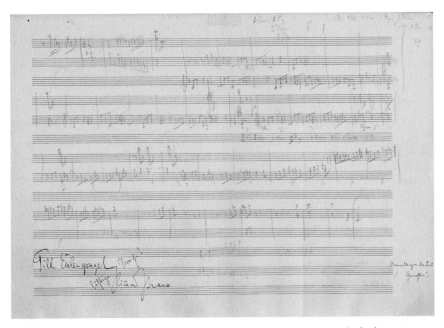

Figure 2.2 Sketchbook 3, p. 17: *Till Eulenspiegels lustige Streiche*, continuity draft of opening.

notated in the middle of p. 73 of Sketchbook 2 (Figure 2.1), which Strauss liked so much that shortly thereafter he included it in the sketches. (In the end this motive was introduced much later, *fortissimo* in the trombones, at the end of *Von den Freuden- und Leidenschaften* ["Of joys and passions"], mm. 150–3.) Strauss also wrote out a *Lebenstrieb* ("Urge to life") motive and a theme labeled *niedrige Leidenschaften* ("base passions"), but he used only the former.

In his sketches Strauss did not restrict himself to themes for compositions he was working on at that moment. "Sometimes a theme comes to me," he said in an interview of 1902,[25] "and later I discover the poetic vestment for it." In other words, sometimes he notated motives as a stockpile without knowing whether and when he might use them. Occasionally Strauss sought inspiration by way of such notations.[26] In some sketchbooks he established lists of such themes.[27]

Fifth, we earlier considered the emphasis Strauss placed on thematic invention and the elaboration of short motives to longer periods of eight, sixteen, or thirty-two measures. Sketches documenting such a compositional process are rare in the manuscript sources before 1900 – presumably an indication that Strauss had no particular difficulties in these years with the elaboration of themes. He sketched his themes, in general, within continuity drafts, on which he worked for a considerable time, as shown for instance by the *Liebesszene* ("Love Scene") in *Ein Heldenleben* (mm.

288ff.): no fewer than ten pages of Sketchbooks 4 and 5 are devoted to this section. The difficulties have less to do with metric issues than with motivic divisions; for instance, Strauss needed several attempts until he found the continuation of the theme in m. 296. Still, the evidence suggests that Strauss thought in regular metric units: a sketch of more than sixty measures for a *Freundschaftstanz* ("Dance of Friendship") in 6/8 meter in D major (Sketchbook 4, Sketch 19, pp. 34–7)[28] shows Strauss thinking exclusively in eight-measure segments.

Finally, when Strauss sketched songs, he focused completely on the vocal part, usually with the complete text added (or with sporadic gaps). Again, the melody dominates. Remarkably, several songs (e.g. Op. 15, Nos. 2 and 3) are sketched a whole tone higher than they appear in the final version. The sketches are sometimes significantly different – harmonically, melodically, and rhythmically – from the fair copies. The piano part is only rarely indicated; sometimes Strauss drafts the prelude (for instance for Op. 17, No. 5), sometimes only the postlude (Op. 17, No. 6). Even the harmonic support for the melody can be left out entirely or present only in rudiments; the chromatic bass progression of Op. 19, No. 4 (Sketchbook 1, mm. 27–30, p. 40) is an exception. We have to assume that as a rule these sparse jottings were enough for Strauss. However, we cannot rule out – especially given the incomplete state of the song sketches – that there were other drafts before the respective fair copies. In any case, the dates given in Franz Trenner's work list for the genesis of the songs refer only to their fair copies, and tell us nothing about how long Strauss took to compose the songs.

Textual sketches

Time and again Strauss entered textual annotations in the sketches of his instrumental works. Generally they provide indications of harmony and form, as well as, for the tone poems, of the program. The comments can range from merely a word (often abbreviated) to longer passages. Indications of dynamics, tempo, and instrumentation are rare – again confirming the impression that such parameters were not counted by Strauss as musical substance, however strongly they shape his music.

The language of these texts is characteristic. Strauss either uses musical-technical terms (e.g. "C dominant," "development," and "intensification"), or he mixes musical terms with programmatic indications (in the drafts of the tone poems). The latter texts have a dual function: on the one hand, the composer names specific compositional strategies on the basis of individual sketches; on the other, he ascertains the particular connection between these strategies and the program. When we find in the sketches for *Tod und Verklärung* a text such as "at the end of the introduction the dreams become restless, but dynamics intensify only a little,"[29] Strauss assigns a sketch to a specific position in the program; at the same time, he uses the comment as a concrete instruction to himself (to hold back the dynamics in spite of the growing restlessness of the music).

Strauss's texts can be divided into several groups depending on position and content. A first group includes texts that belong to the notational sketch in which they are located. They consist mostly of names for motives, indications of keys, and remarks pertaining to structural function. In the process of composing, Strauss gives himself reminders of how to proceed with his work – how to fashion junctures, how to connect sketches notated non-contiguously, and how to revise drafts. A second group consists of texts that fit the sketches to which they belong, but that refer at the same time to larger structural sections.

A last group is particularly remarkable. In texts placed at the beginning of longer works or sections, Strauss laid out, often at considerable length, the structural and, if necessary, programmatic plan of all the music to follow. The concept of the finale of the Violin Sonata (jotted down in Sketchbook 1 at the beginning of the respective drafts) is envisioned as follows:

> Violin sonata, last movement, first theme E♭ major, second theme area
> [*Seitensatz*] E♭ major with scherzando motive leading to middle theme in
> C major, this theme without cadence combines with the first theme in C
> major and finally moves to A♭ major, secondary theme as cantilena with
> scherzando as a brief development; then middle movement in E♭ major
> slides into the principal theme, which concludes the movement in brilliant
> 6/8 meter.[30]

For a piece of chamber music, as here, the only "program" is a structural plan. But for a tone poem such as *Don Juan*, Strauss, after sketching the first theme, combines the formal plan (motives, keys, function of sections) with programmatic cues:

> from then on ~~wild and jovial~~ the pleasure theme as C sharp major can-
> tilena, interrupted by the violas when the first Don Juan theme suffers
> exhaustion, initially both sound together, with a bold leap he jolts the first
> theme to the dominant of C, then a frivolous theme ensues in a wild hustle
> and bustle, merry jubilation is interrupted by sighs of pain and pleasure,
> then development, always fortissimo and greatest intensification suddenly
> a sobering-up, desolate English horn, love and pleasure themes sound
> confusingly, interrupted by new spells of longing and pleasure, finally
> a new love motive ensues very enthusiastic and gentle, then suddenly
> another eruption of the first theme, grand (?) dashing coda, tempestuous
> conclusion.[31]

In his preliminary planning, Strauss treated both works structurally in a similar way. There are several themes, a development, and a brilliant tempestuous conclusion. He succeeded in realizing these plans, however, only in the finale of the Violin Sonata. The structural conception of the tone poem was to be drastically changed.[32]

Particells

Straightforward particells have come down to us only since *Guntram*. We do not know whether they existed for earlier works. There is evidence (of which more below) speaking against particells for, say, *Macbeth*, *Don Juan*, or *Tod und Verklärung*. In any case, Strauss tried out the use of a particell with *Guntram* and subsequently continued the practice. With his next tone poem, *Till Eulenspiegel*, however, it was not easy for him to distinguish between sketch and particell. A clear distinction between the two stages of composition emerges in the tone poems only with *Also sprach Zarathustra*.

Work on sketches and particells was not always linked to particular notational formats. *Guntram* and *Feuersnot* were written down in oblong particells, while *Also sprach Zarathustra*, *Don Quixote*, *Ein Heldenleben*, and the *Alpensinfonie* were sketched in upright particells.[33] The particell of *Till Eulenspiegel* is contained on separate leaves in oblong format that later were bound together, and the (unfortunately incomplete) particell of *Symphonia domestica* is part of the contents of Sketchbook 8.

Strauss's particells have a dual function: they represent the final stage of composition proper, and they serve as blueprint for the fair copy of the score. In the first function, they are documents of the compositional process; in their second role, they provide information about Strauss's method of orchestration.

To begin, a few remarks on the first function:

First, particells are the first continuity drafts of a given work from beginning to end. Passages that are not contained in the sketches are notated in the particell.

Second, in general, the particell contains much more information about the composition than sketches. By using at least two and frequently three staves continuously, Strauss was able to record many more voices. Indications of articulation and dynamics, however, continue to be rather sparse. Even figurations (melodic decorations) are often only hinted at. In many such instances Strauss did not come to a final decision until the writing of the score.

Third, all particells of the tone poems have, to some extent, the character of a sketch. While working on the particells, Strauss continued to sketch – in other words, to compose. He used the particell to sum up and review the material sketched thus far. (That is the reason why, for instance, he occasionally jotted down in the particell for *Zarathustra* the page numbers where the passage at issue could be found in the sketchbook.) When there were difficulties – when the connections did not fit, when the formal functions did not develop properly, when harmonic progressions needed to be changed, etc. – then the particell became a sketch, until Strauss was satisfied and able to continue the work with the existing drafts. The sketch character of the particell is particularly strongly pronounced with *Till Eulenspiegel*, but in his other tone poems Strauss often rejected and revised certain passages at this stage. Moreover, even after the completion of the particell the composition itself was occasionally subject to revision. For instance, *Also sprach Zarathustra* began in the particell with a sustained perfect fifth in the horns (C–G); in the third measure the organ pedal and double basses were to sound their sustained C and the bass drum was to perform a roll (it is possible that Strauss indicated a tremolo also for the first measure; see Figure 2.3).[34] And sometimes Strauss included in the particells of his tone poems additional programmatic clues that he did not transfer to the score, such as the remark *fromme Schauer* ("pious shiver") at the beginning of the third system.

Orchestration

We now come to the second function of the particell, its role as immediate precursor to the orchestral score. Strauss wished not only to write his scores cleanly and clearly but also to arrange the staves as efficiently as possible: i.e., not to have any blank staves and, in the case of sparsely orchestrated passages, to have several systems on one page. That required a considerable amount of planning before writing any one page of the score, and many traces of this preparation can be found in the particells.

Scott Warfield has observed that Strauss's scores up to *Tod und Verklärung* were not optimized.[35] During these years, Strauss always notated one system per page, showing all staves required for the piece even when they were not needed. This can be seen in the facsimile of the autograph score of *Tod und Verklärung*, where one also finds the entire instrumentation notated at the beginning.[36] He changed this practice only with *Guntram*, where on the first page there are several systems and no indication of the complete instrumentation. The new method had several advantages, but it required working from a particell.

Beginning with *Guntram*, Strauss prepared to write a page of a score by first jotting down how many systems with how many staves were needed,

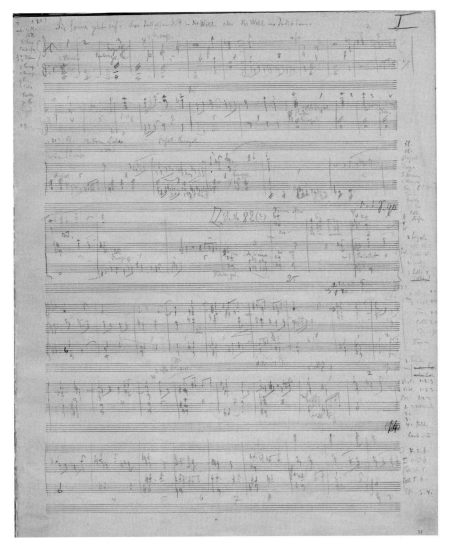

Figure 2.3 Sketchbook 3, p. 31: *Also sprach Zarathustra*, particell of opening orchestration.

and then calculating whether the number of staves allowed a second system on the page. For that purpose he recorded, at the appropriate places in the particell, the orchestration and the staves needed: he notated the instruments, one below the other, in abbreviations, beginning with the woodwinds and concluding with the strings (either, as in the case of *Till Eulenspiegel*, between the staves of the particell, or, more frequently, in the margins – see Figures 2.2 and 2.3). This shorthand can be found for the first time on a leaf of the sketches for *Don Juan* (Sketchbook 1, p. 48), but it was used systematically in the particells of *Guntram*, *Till Eulenspiegel*, *Also sprach Zarathustra*, *Don Quixote*, and *Ein Heldenleben*.

Because his orchestra became constantly larger, Strauss decided, beginning with *Symphonia domestica*, to perform these calculations on separate sheets rather than in the particells. Only a few such leaves are extant, but they are important documents for studying the process of orchestration.[37]

Once the instrumentation and number of systems per page had been decided, Strauss, in order to use the space optimally, calculated the number of measures per system and counted the measures continuously in the particell.[38] Only when this was done could the writing of the score page begin. As Josef Gregor has testified, Strauss notated one measure at a time from top to bottom and then drew the measure line.[39]

Such a modus operandi required an astonishingly sure grasp of each measure of his orchestral score. For the first page of the *Eulenspiegel* sketches, a rudimentary draft of the first forty-or-so measures sufficed as a particell; additional preparatory work was not necessary (Figure 2.2). However, miscalculations occurred frequently – either Strauss forgot instruments or he misjudged the length of measures. For the beginning of the *Zarathustra* score, for instance, Strauss reckoned in the upper left margin on one stave for three oboes, a stave each for the E♭ clarinet and B♭ clarinets, a stave for three bassoons, and one for contrabassoon; then two staves each for four horns, four trumpets, and trombones and tuba together; one stave each for timpani and bass drum; two staves for organ; and five for strings (Figure 2.3). That adds up to twenty staves, but Strauss jotted down "(21)" – either miscalculating, or including a stave for the cymbal (missing in the list of instruments). And there was another oversight: instead of a tuba he used a third trombone (which however did not affect the number of staves). For the second page of the score, which began after nine measures on the first page with the antepenultimate measure of the particell's first system, Strauss jotted down the number of staves under the second system "(21) Fl. 5.–6. Horn 2 Tuben" and below that "(24)": meaning that in addition to the twenty-one staves required for the first page, three more staves were needed for the second: one each for flutes, two additional horns, and two tubas.

Even when Strauss strictly observed the order of compositional phases from sketches via particell to score, he did not have to complete one phase before beginning the next. *Zarathustra* again provides a good example. Having begun the first sketches presumably in June or July, 1895, he started work on the particell on December 7 of the same year, at a time when some material remained to be sketched. He wrote the first page of the score on February 4, 1896, the birthday of his wife, before the particell (and thus the process of composition) had been completed. Thus it seems that for a while Strauss worked simultaneously on the sketches, the particell, and the score of the tone poem. On July 17, 1896 the particell was completed; only five weeks later, on August 24 (at 4 p.m.), did Strauss put finishing touches on the score.

Strauss's compositional process in opera

The compositional modus operandi that Strauss developed in the years up to 1900 served him for the rest of his life. All the evidence gathered thus far supports this hypothesis, even though not all sketches and drafts have been studied carefully. In particular, for his major works he produced sketches and particells, as had been his habit since *Guntram*. Although the relationship between voices and orchestra as well as dramaturgical conciseness were central in the composition of operas (the genre that dominated his work beginning with *Salome*), Strauss did not change his methods of sketching music, developing it into particells, and, finally, committing it to a precisely planned score. Moreover, the documents reveal that composition was not always easy for Strauss; on the contrary, he occasionally had to struggle for a satisfactory final product.

In place of the early structural and programmatic plans of his instrumental works, we encounter in his operas, as noted before, commentaries written into the libretti. Strauss notated motives, melodic lines (using letters or pitches, sometimes already with rhythmic shapes), rhythmic ideas (rendered with rhythmic symbols above individual syllables), keys (ranging from chords and brief ornaments to key areas for longer stretches), tempi, meter, harmonic functions and progressions, instruments, formal functions, and caesuras. Important examples have been discussed in the recent Strauss literature.[40] Keys seem to play a special role throughout; frequently even the first indications hold good in the final product. Melodic inspiration, unlike key, does not appear to have had a dominating role in Strauss's initial creative process when composing an opera – at least as far as these marginal comments in the libretti reveal.

But it may be doubted whether the notations that Strauss jotted into his libretti on first reading (and that were so admired by Karl Böhm and other contemporaries)[41] were indeed immediate inspirations. Without question Strauss began thinking about the music of an opera as soon as he knew the subject matter or plot. Keys, motives, and perhaps also themes were drafted before he had read a line of the text. The melody of the concluding duet of Octavian and Sophie in *Rosenkavalier* was already composed without knowledge of the text, and he had to ask Hofmannsthal to adjust the text to the pre-existing melody.[42] In other words, Strauss was already creatively prepared when reading a libretto; he was immediately able to determine the rough tonal disposition as well as important motives because he had carried them in his head for a long time. But of course some rhythmic and melodic ideas may have been recorded as spontaneous inspirations – in which case he was able to rely on his experiences as a composer of lieder.

All things considered, the originality of Strauss's ideas is as astonishing as the diversity of his music. Such an immense and diverse œuvre was possible because Strauss understood how to compose with extreme calculation. With his happy combination of profound musical expressivity and the utmost rationality in production, he far surpassed even his great model Richard Wagner.

3 Maturity and indecision in the early works

WAYNE HEISLER, JR.

Writing in 1931, music critic Max Steinitzer opined, "Under the general title 'The Unknown Richard Strauss,' radio broadcasters ... would find enough rich and rewarding material for an hour of piano music, as well as lieder, chamber, orchestral, and choral music."[1] Steinitzer had been a reliable advocate for Strauss, whose stature by the 1930s was downgraded from that of a pioneer of modernism to a figurehead for Germany's late-Romantic musical past. Steinitzer found in the margins of this composer's oeuvre unfamiliar works of surprising variety that stood to offer fresh insights on him – specifically, music from the early part of Strauss's career, before his international emergence with the tone poems *Don Juan* (1888) and *Tod und Verklärung* (1888–9).

Steinitzer's proposed radio program never hit the airwaves, and for the most part the diverse music of Strauss's youth and young adulthood has remained little known. Several factors account for the obscurity of Strauss's early works. First, many of them were not published until the last quarter of the twentieth century, and hence were rarely performed or recorded. (Of course, the fact that there were few performances and recordings of this music placed little demand on its publication.)[2] Second, the truism that Strauss's compositions prior to his tone poems were but a training ground is not unfounded: clearly, the young composer cycled through genres, forms, and styles rather than settling into an individual voice. Employing characteristically imaginative language, musicologist Richard Specht effectively summed up the reception of Strauss's pre-tone-poem compositions when, in 1921, he equated the String Quartet in A, Op. 2 (1880) with a wax statue transmitting "the voice of a deceased beloved over a gramophone," a simile Specht repeated in regard to the more ambitious but still "impersonal" Symphony No. 2 in F minor, Op. 12 (1884), which he experienced as "a symphonic phonograph recording of the voice of a Romantic composer."[3] In fact, Strauss's autumnal reminiscences on his early career have contributed to the view of a young composer who despite having attained a certain level of maturity – the breakthrough *Don Juan* was already his Op. 20 – remained indecisive. Strauss's account began by detailing his initial emulation of the Austro-German masters of "absolute" music (Haydn, Mozart, Beethoven) under the sway of his conservative father, renowned horn player Franz Strauss. Thereafter, Strauss outlined the path he took via Mendelssohn and Schumann to Brahms (influenced by the conductor, pianist, and composer Hans von Bülow), before his "conversion" by composer and philosopher Alexander Ritter to the New German School (Liszt and Wagner, with bows to Berlioz).[4]

In this chapter I survey Strauss's compositional output from the 1870s through the mid 1880s, and draw on recent scholarly literature as well as writings from the composer's lifetime. Since the early 1990s, the dominant trend in Strauss scholarship has been to identify continuity across his output, especially in relation to the post-World War I compositions. The voice that opened the door for the early works, though, was that of pianist Glenn Gould, who regarded Strauss as "among the most contrapuntal minded of composers" and discussed in one breath the youthful Symphony No. 2 and the late *Metamorphosen* (1945) for 23 Solo Strings.[5] Gould's comparison of such seemingly incompatible compositions implies that the consistency in Strauss's oeuvre was not totally eclipsed by its range or variety, an impression that is supported *within* the body of early works, too. In the late 1880s Strauss clearly underwent a transformation (his self-proclaimed "conversion"), one that is usually located in the "symphonic fantasy" *Aus Italien*, Op. 16 (1886). Still, the change was gradual and not total: Strauss never broke completely with his musical pasts, as witnessed by continuities in his technique, style, and aesthetics from the 1870s through the 1880s and beyond. With an eye towards softening the divide between the young, "absolutist" composer and the programmatic one of the breakout tone poems, I highlight the multiple influences and traditions that made themselves felt in the early works, which were, above all, the training ground for the diversity that would become Strauss's trademark. Ultimately, I will return to *Aus Italien* and the question of when Richard Strauss became "Richard Strauss."

Aspiring composer (1870–1882)

Strauss's first compositions date from 1870, when he was barely school age: the "Schneiderpolka" ("Tailor's Polka") for piano, and a "Weihnachtslied" ("Christmas Song") on a text by Christian Friedrich Daniel Schubart, the writer best known in latter-day musical circles for Schubert's setting of his poem "Die Forelle" ("The Trout"). In subsequent pieces from the early 1870s, witness is borne to Strauss's precociousness by the range of genres and forms he undertook. A piano student since the fall of 1868, the child composer produced a variety of short works for that instrument, including the lost Sonatinas No. 1 in C and No. 2 in E (both *c.* 1873). Song, too, was an important component of Strauss's formative musical environment; for example, his aunt Johanna Pschorr was a singer and the dedicatee of many of his youthful lieder. Following the aforementioned "Weihnachtslied," Strauss's earliest lied settings included poems by Emanuel von Geibel ("Herz, mein Herz" ["Heart, My Heart"]) and Ludwig Uhland ("Einkehr" ["Stay at the Inn"] and "Winterreise" ["Winter Journey"]).

Among early pieces conceived for family and friends in domestic and social circles, Strauss wrote choral works, too, such as "Der weisse Hirsch" ("The White Deer") for alto, tenor, and bass with piano (*c.* 1871), also on a poem by Uhland. Around the age of ten, Strauss dabbled with composing chamber music, including the incomplete *Zwei kleine Stücke* (1873) for violin and piano, doubtless resulting from violin lessons with his father's cousin Benno Walter that had begun the previous year, and an unfinished *Quartettsatz* (1875). Strauss's first aspirations to compose for orchestra also date to the early 1870s in the form of an overture for a *Singspiel* entitled *Hochlands Treue* (*Highland Loyalty*, 1872–3).

Were it not for the objections of his father, who believed that training solely for a career as a composer was too uncertain an investment in the future, Strauss would have enrolled in Munich's Hochschule für Musik upon completion of his primary schooling. Instead, from 1874 to 1882 Strauss pursued a general education at the Ludwigs-Gymnasium while continuing music study privately. In addition to lessons on piano and violin, he began taking instruction in music theory and composition with the conductor Friedrich Wilhelm Meyer in 1875. Meyer was an accomplished, if conservative musician, and Richard clearly benefited from the disciplined lessons – Gilliam has convincingly argued that Meyer's conservatism is what led a traditionalist like Franz Strauss to entrust him with his son.[6] Within a year of beginning his studies with Meyer, Strauss composed a *Festmarsch* in E♭ for orchestra, which, when published in 1881, became his Op. 1.

Conventional wisdom holds that the first decade of Strauss's endeavors as a composer was a period of filial loyalty, expressed through his devotion to his father's beloved Austro-Germanic triumvirate: again, Haydn, Mozart, and Beethoven (but not late Beethoven!). As is evident in two of Strauss's student compositions, the Piano Trio No. 1 in A (1877) and Piano Trio No. 2 in D (1878), his Classical allegiances served his ever-growing proficiency in harmony, counterpoint, Classical form, and writing for specific instruments. Composed in a day-and-a-half in December, 1877, the First Trio was conceived and initially performed as a three-movement work, but soon thereafter Strauss added a minuet movement to be performed *ad libitum*.[7] That Strauss was still but a student, albeit a talented one, is apparent from his handling of sonata form in the inaugural movement of the Trio

No. 1. Strauss tackled the exposition with textbook faithfulness in terms of tonal–harmonic design and thematic contrast. The development, however, betrays some awkwardness. Devoted exclusively to a theme derived from the main theme of the exposition (treated imitatively by the piano, violin, and cello in turn), this development is disproportionately brief for a sonata-form movement but too extensive for a sonatina. Following one statement of the theme by each instrument, the ensemble comes together on a dominant chord that tips unceremoniously into the recapitulation. From a harmonic standpoint, the most daring passage of the First Trio is in the ternary Adagio movement in E major: at the height of a *B* section that tonicizes F♯ major (V of V), Strauss accomplished a modulation to the remote key of E♭ major in just three bars, and then returned to the tonic via a mere four-bar transition back to the *A* section. In a February 6, 1878 letter to the composer and theorist Ludwig Thuille, his closest childhood friend, Strauss recounted how his uncle Anton Knözinger, a judge and public prosecutor who also played cello (hence the Trio's dedication to him), was "quite delighted" with this relatively daring harmony.[8]

If Strauss's First Trio was steeped in the world of Haydn and Mozart, the Trio No. 2 in D of the following year suggests that early Beethoven was a model. The proportions are now larger: the Second Trio was intended as a four-movement work from its inception, and the first movement includes an expansive development section. Strauss's increased imagination and daring are revealed by the transformation from minor to major tonic (B minor to B major) in the Andante. The final movement, in ternary form, is the Second Trio's longest – perhaps too long and too serious for a piece of domestic chamber music by a teenage composer – an example of what Specht identified as the youthful Strauss's "eagerness to emulate the great masters" and an "aptitude for assimilation" in his early works.[9]

The range of Strauss's earliest childhood compositions grew under Meyer's tutelage. Beyond the two piano trios, Strauss continued to produce vocal music, such as the *Zwei Lieder* (1876) for unaccompanied SATB with texts by Joseph von Eichendorff, also the poet of Strauss's unaccompanied *Sieben Lieder* (1880) for the same forces. Moreover, the late 1870s saw his first foray into dramatic music. In 1876 he planned two operas: *Ein Studentenstreich* (*A Student Prank*) and *Dom Sebastian*, both of which yielded only unfinished overtures. More developed plans were hatched for a *Singspiel* on Goethe's *Lila* in 1878, but Strauss only completed a soprano aria (for the character of Almaide).

Strauss's endeavors in the realm of chamber music during his years at the Gymnasium resulted in his second published work, the String Quartet in A, Op. 2 (1880), followed shortly thereafter by the *Fünf Klavierstücke*, Op. 3 and the Piano Sonata in B minor, Op. 5. Nevertheless, it was Strauss's works for orchestra in the early 1880s that attest most strongly to his early maturity – or at least his quest for maturity. Strauss completed his Symphony No. 1 in D minor in the fall of 1880, optimistically designating it as his Op. 4. (It remained unpublished until a century later, while that opus number was reassigned to the Suite in B♭ for Thirteen Wind Instruments, commissioned by Bülow in 1884.) Jürgen Schaarwächter has highlighted the indebtedness of Strauss's Symphony No. 1 to a growing list of composers beyond Haydn and Mozart, including, of course, Beethoven, but also Mendelssohn and Schumann. Moreover, Schaarwächter has identified points of similarity between Strauss's First Symphony and works by Brahms, Bruckner, Dvořák, Tchaikovsky, and even Wagner.[10] Although the precise sources of Strauss's inspiration remain debatable, it is significant that in 1880 the young symphonist was already beginning to migrate from his father's esteemed classics to the late Romantics in terms of harmony, thematic development, and orchestration.

Following the premiere of Strauss's Symphony No. 1 by Munich's amateur Wilde Gung'l orchestra in spring, 1881, a critic for the *Münchner Neuesten Nachrichten* offered high (if qualified) praise: "The symphony … shows considerable competence in the treatment of the form as well as remarkable skill in orchestration. It must be said that the work cannot lay any claim to true originality, but it demonstrates throughout a fertile musical imagination, to which composition comes easily."[11] Formal proficiency, high orchestral aptitude, imagination without originality: these observations can serve as a précis of Strauss's student compositions, including his next major work, the Violin Concerto in D minor, Op. 8. The concerto's premiere in Vienna in December, 1882, with Walter as soloist and Strauss accompanying with his own piano arrangement, occurred during the composer's first tour – his international debut. In Classical three-movement concerto form, Strauss's Op. 8 features once again the eclecticism that is a calling card of his early style, and an augury of his full maturity. Commentators drew comparisons with other violin concertos in the German repertory at the time, especially Beethoven, Mendelssohn, and Bruch. In a 1901 essay, Erich Urban noted the composer's growth in the Violin Concerto, which he experienced as a mixture of Classical influences, together with Mendelssohn, but also Weber and (again) Wagner, particularly in the Lento movement.[12] Steinitzer, too, singled out the slow movement, in which he claimed to be able to identify "at least fifteen good composers, French ones, too."[13]

Here, it is appropriate to call attention to a leitmotif in the reception and assessment of Strauss's compositions from the early 1880s: his lack of expression, accounting for the perceived weakness of his slow movements generally. Urban, who wrote enthusiastically about the Violin Concerto overall, reserved criticism for what he experienced as the too-long melodic lines of the Lento movement,[14] implying a lack of authentic feeling on Strauss's part (the downside to the admixture of different composers' styles, Classical and Romantic, that both Urban and Steinitzer heard). In relation to Strauss's Symphony No. 1 we have already seen charges of a mechanical technique, which, while impressive from such a young musician, seemed to be an end rather than a means. Ernest Newman's comments from 1908 elaborate on this view of early Strauss, and locate the proverbial fault line in his allegedly inexpressive slow movements:

> The general impression one gets from [Strauss's early] works is that of a head full to overflowing with music, a temperament that is energetic and forthright rather than warm ... There is often a good deal of ardour in the writing, but it is the ardour of the intellect rather than of the emotions. Though he is sometimes dry, he is scarcely ever dull; the dryness is a personal tang; it suggests a sinewy young athlete's joy in his own energizing and in his freedom from anything like excess of feeling ... [W]herever the youthful Strauss has to sing rather than declaim, when he has to be emotional rather than intellectual, as in his slow movements, he almost invariably fails.[15]

Newman did not doubt the sincerity of Strauss's early works, and his explication reminds us that the young composer did not compose them with the benefit of hindsight. Put another way: the teenage Strauss already regarded himself as a legitimate composer, technically and expressively. Conversely, the mature Strauss is often thought of as a composer who gravitated naturally towards and shone in moments of lyricism and "excess of feeling" – qualities, however, he had to learn.

While Strauss's early career is commonly divided between "absolute" music on the one hand and his embrace of the programmatic aims of the New German School in the late 1880s on the other, the poetic side of his musical personality was not wholly absent from the student works. For example, from 1882 to 1884 Strauss completed a set of five piano pieces entitled *Stimmungsbilder* (*Moods and Fancies*), Op. 9, which fall in line with the tradition of Romantic character pieces. Steinitzer saw these as a highlight among Strauss's early compositions, singling out No. 1, "Auf stillem Waldespfad" ("On the Silent Woodland Path") and No. 4, "Träumerei" ("Reverie") as worthy of Schumann in terms of their lyricism and the creation of a musico-poetic atmosphere, respectively.[16] The remaining movements are "An einsamer Quelle" ("Beside the Lonely Spring," No. 2), "Intermezzo" (No. 3), and "Heidebild" ("On the Heath," No. 5). Rather than being motivated by formal and technical prowess as Strauss seemed to have been in his Symphony No. 1 and Violin Concerto, the touches employed in pieces such as "An einsamer Quelle" with its delicate, omnipresent thirty-second-note triplets now represent a means to an expressive, programmatic end. Along with the early vocal music, then, the *Stimmungsbilder* serve as a reminder that this young composer was already inspired by extra-musical content, particularly images from nature, thus foreshadowing the pivotal *Aus Italien*.

Breaking away (1882–1884)

In 1882, Strauss completed his studies at the Gymnasium and enrolled at Ludwig-Maximilians-Universität in Munich. This decision was influenced by his father's urging for Richard to prepare for a viable profession in the event that his vocation as a musician be less than successful. Strauss only stuck it out for the winter semester at the university, after which he committed to a career in music for good.

By any measure, Strauss's Serenade in E♭ for Thirteen Wind Instruments, Op. 7 (1881) marked his professional arrival point. Scored for two flutes, two oboes, two clarinets, four horns, two bassoons, and contrabassoon (or tuba), the Serenade was the first composition by Strauss to meet the approval of Hans von Bülow. Eugen Spitzweg, Strauss's first publisher, had, in fact, sent the Op. 9 *Stimmungsbilder* to Bülow (along with the *Five Piano Pieces*, Op. 3) for an assessment, but the latter rather coldly assessed Strauss as "*Not a genius* in my most sincere belief, but at best a talent."[17] All the same, in February, 1884 Strauss met Bülow, who was so impressed by the Op. 7 Serenade that he invited its composer to conduct it in a concert with the Meiningen Orchestra on their November tour stop in Munich. The Serenade, a single movement in sonata form, was arguably the most inspired and original of Strauss's compositions to date, owing in part to the modest proportions of the genre, but also to his fluency in scoring winds. That Strauss dedicated Op. 7 to his composition teacher Meyer suggests both a commemoration of his formative years and a mature leave-taking of them.

Rather than derailing his musical aspirations, Strauss's brief time at university saw him composing feverishly. During the period from 1882 to 1883, he completed such substantial works as the Sonata for Cello and Piano, Op. 6 and a Concert Overture in C minor, as well as the Horn Concerto No. 1, Op. 11, which arguably suggests his future orientation towards program music and is one of the earliest of Strauss's works to maintain a position in the repertory of major orchestras up to the present day. Clearly a tribute to his father (but dedicated to the Dresden horn player Oscar Franz), the concerto represents the payoff for his careful mastery of form and earlier struggles with thematic development. In an analytical discussion of the work, Norman Del Mar characterized the horn's introductory fanfare as a *Naturmotiv* (nature motive). This descriptor is consistent with the composer's programmatic designation of the work as a *Waldhornkonzert* – i.e., referring to the older, valveless French horn, even though the concerto can only be played on a modern instrument (Strauss wrote the solo part for an F horn). Del Mar also outlined the unifying function of the fanfare, first as "a framework enclosing the two long and free cantilenas which comprise the first movement," and then as the seed for the principal theme of the final movement, in which it is "transformed into 6/8 rhythm."[18] Other examples of such thematic transformation include a short hunting-horn motive, played tutti in the first movement and transferred in various guises to the accompaniment, including that of the middle Andante movement, where it serves as the germ for the triadically based theme itself. Moreover, the interrelationships between themes have implications for the form of the Concerto. The layout of its three movements conforms to the Classical fast–slow–fast framework; beyond that, the formal outlines of the individual movements are fuzzy. Not in a clear-cut sonata form, the opening Allegro is rhapsodic, while the three movements are continuous. What many commentators have found to be most striking and prescient, however, is the closing Rondo, which is cyclic in its recall of the principal theme from the first movement. Steinitzer described this event as "poetic … like a solemn dream."[19] Indeed, in light of the programmatically suggestive *Waldhorn* atmosphere and cyclic finale, Del Mar rightly noted that the "thematic metamorphosis" in this concerto "predate[d] by some three years Strauss's adoption of Lisztian methods under the influence of Alexander Ritter."[20] This observation implies that, rather than being converted suddenly to program music, Strauss was receptive to Ritter's ideas because he had already dabbled in compositional procedures that had technical and aesthetic grounding in the New German School.

Not even a year had passed following his departure from the university when Strauss embarked on what was to be a pivotal experience, personally and professionally: a nearly four-month residency (from December, 1883 through March, 1884) in Berlin, the political and cultural center of Germany. During this trip, the nineteen-year-old Strauss cultivated beneficial social relationships and made the acquaintance of important figures in the musical world. Of the many people he came into contact with on his journeys, there was one who exerted an almost lightning-bolt impact on the maturing composer, all the more acute given its swiftness: Brahms.

Infatuation (1884–1885)

Over the period of a few months in early 1884, Strauss heard Brahms's Third Symphony on four occasions. Strauss's rapidly changing perception of this piece is nothing less than remarkable, as documented by his reports to Thuille. Initially bothered by the "lack of clarity" and "wretched" and "unclear" scoring of Brahms's Third,[21] he declared two months later, after a concert at which Brahms himself conducted the symphony and appeared as soloist in his own Piano Concerto No. 1, that "Brahms's No. 3 [is] not only his finest symphony, *but probably the most important that has ever been written*" (my emphasis). Strauss went on to elaborate on the "colossally fresh and dashing first movement," the "very pretty" Andante, and the "dashing last movement, with just a hint of the daemonic." What he found most impacting, however, was the third movement, "the most delightful little minuet I've heard in a long time … it's all of a piece and the ideas are wonderfully pretty." "I'm beginning to get very attached to Brahms as a whole," Strauss concluded to Thuille, because "he's always interesting and very often really beautiful as well."[22]

Thus began the period that Strauss would later characterize as his *Brahmsschwärmerei* ("infatuation with Brahms").[23] In a seminal essay, R. Larry Todd argued that, "From his study of Brahms, Strauss found reinforcement for certain conservative features of his own music written before the 1885 conversion: its reliance on traditional forms and genres … its use of thick, contrapuntal textures, its general preference for double-wind orchestration – in short, its awareness of and close relation to the mainstream tradition of nineteenth-century German 'absolute' instrumental music."[24] Three of Strauss's compositions from the mid 1880s that have long been associated with Brahms are the Piano Quartet in C minor, Op. 13 (composed 1883–4); *Wandrers Sturmlied* (*Wanderer's Song to the Storm*) for six-part choir (SSATBB) and orchestra, Op. 14 (1884); and the *Burleske* for piano and orchestra (1885–6). Before turning to these works, however, it is necessary to focus on Strauss's Symphony No. 2 in F minor, Op. 12 – a turning point in his transition from student to professional composer and Brahmsian.

Strauss began the composition of his Second Symphony in Munich, before the trip to Berlin, completing the second movement (the Scherzo) in June, 1883, and the first movement after it, in October. The finale was finished in Leipzig on December 5, 1883, en route to Berlin, while the third movement (Andante cantabile) was still a work in progress when he arrived in the German capital, completed soon thereafter on January 25, 1884. Strauss's largest composition to date, the Symphony No. 2 reinforced the positive impression of the earlier Op. 7 Serenade on Bülow, who promoted the symphony enthusiastically. Premiered by Theodor Thomas in New York in December, 1884, and thus gaining Strauss international exposure beyond Bülow's circle, the symphony was performed in 1885 in Cologne and then Meiningen – a concert that the composer himself conducted at the debut of his appointment there (see below) – as well as Milan (1887, again with Strauss at the podium), Amsterdam (1892), and London (1896).

Mostly predating his "infatuation" with Brahms, Strauss's Symphony No. 2 has been seen as the apotheosis of his engagement with the Romantics: commentators from Steinitzer and Specht to Del Mar and Schaarwächter have cited Beethoven, but also Schumann and Mendelssohn, as models. (Steinitzer went so far as to characterize Strauss's indebtedness to the latter two composers as a "quotation or a portrait sketch," i.e., of Mendelssohn in the first and second movements, and Schumann in the second, third, and fourth.)[25] But Arthur Seidl, in his biographical sketch of 1896, also located in Strauss's symphony traces of Brahms's influence by way of the "construction, the organic fashioning of the individual movements," which he felt was formative for the subsequent tone poems.[26] By "organic fashioning," Seidl meant the close relationships between themes, which appear to develop gradually out of small ideas: e.g., the first two measures of the first-movement theme, which expand out to generate the next two measures, as well as the interrelationships between themes, such as the intervallic and rhythmic parallels between the first and second principal themes of the first movement. As we have seen, Strauss's new focus on development as a generative device and his mining of relationships between themes were also apparent in the Horn Concerto No. 1 from the previous year. Are these additions to Strauss's technical arsenal to be taken as early, pre-"conversion" Lisztian influence, akin to "thematic transformation," or as a kind of Brahmsian "developing variation," which then, to paraphrase Todd, was buttressed by an immersion in Brahms? It is more realistic to see in shades of gray rather than in black and white: Strauss's thematic-developmental procedures represent his exploration and assimilation of multifarious techniques and styles, in which he found justification and models in composers of various stripes. Whether or not he was being strictly "Brahmsian" or "Lisztian" would have been beside the point; Strauss had not been, and never would be, any such purist.

In light of the perceived similarities with Brahms (among others) in Strauss's Symphony No. 2, it is important to note that when Brahms heard the younger composer conduct it in 1885, he did not acknowledge hearing *himself* in Strauss's music. "Quite charming … Young man, take a close look at Schubert's dances and practice inventing simple eight-bar melodies … There's too much thematic trifling in your symphony; all that piling-up of a large number of themes on a triad, with only rhythmic contrast between them, has no value whatever."²⁷ Recalling that Strauss's favorite movement from the Third was the "delightful little minuet," the least contrapuntally and thematically dense, the older master's feedback seems canny.

Although Strauss's subsequent works such as *Wandrers Sturmlied*, the Piano Quartet in C minor, and the *Burleske* do not represent a literal application of Brahms's gentle but firm advice effectively to "lighten up," several of Brahms's compositions obviously served as models for Strauss. *Wandrers Sturmlied* is set to a 1772 poem by Goethe, a *Sturm und Drang* work marked also by Classical references, including the structure of a Pindaric ode (strophe, antistrophe, epode). Strauss set only the strophe, in which a wanderer-artist faces a storm and appeals to Genius for protection; having weathered the tempest, the wanderer "hovers over water, over earth, god-like." Strauss heard a likely model for this work, Brahms's *Gesang der Parzen* (*Song of the Fates*, 1883), at a performance in Leipzig in early 1884, in a program that also included the latter's Symphony No. 3. Likewise set to a text by Goethe, the *Gesang* shows a range of musical parallels with Strauss's *Sturmlied*, including key (D minor), a six-part chorus (but two altos in Brahms versus two sopranos in Strauss), comparable orchestral forces, and, as illuminated by Todd's analysis, a similar descending tetrachord referencing a lament, also employed in Brahms's *Nänie* (1881) for chorus and orchestra. Interestingly, this reference also has a parallel in the Good Friday spell (*Karfreitagszauber*) in Wagner's *Parsifal*, which Strauss heard on his first trip to Bayreuth in the summer of 1882.²⁸

Strauss's Piano Quartet in C minor is an example of his growing reputation in the mid 1880s; it was awarded first prize in a quartet competition sponsored by the Berlin *Tonkünstlerverein* (Society of Composers). Like the *Wandrers Sturmlied*, the Quartet bears comparison to several works by Brahms in the same genre, two examples being his Op. 25 No. 1 in G Minor and Op. 60 No. 3 in C minor, as well as his Piano Quintet in F minor, Op. 34. But among Strauss's Brahmsian works, the most provocative is his *Burleske* in D minor for piano and orchestra, a single-movement sonata form, the composition of which overlapped with his tenure in Meiningen as Assistant Court Director of Music (first under Bülow, then alone) from 1885 to 1886. (The *Burleske*'s premiere was delayed until 1890, in Eisenach, with Eugen d'Albert as soloist, because Bülow declared the piece to be unplayable.) With its formidable virtuosity and thematic-developmental technique, the *Burleske* has precedents in Brahms's two piano concertos. But if in the Piano Quartet there is, as Newman described it, "a quite new note … an unaccustomed emotion" fired by Strauss's exposure to Brahms, the *Burleske* represents a more momentous milestone, in which "the face of the Strauss we all know [from the tone poems] keeps peeping out of the heavy Brahmsian hood like the face of Till Eulenspiegel from under the hood of the monk."[29] Newman connected the *Burleske* to Strauss's impending conversion to program music, but Bryan Gilliam made more explicit the significance of this work. Citing Brahms, but also allusions to Wagner's *Die Walküre* (the opening storm) and *Tristan* (the chord), Gilliam designated the *Burleske* as "one of the earliest pieces to use the historical canon as a source of parody." This canon includes Liszt, of course, whose transcendent virtuosity might in Strauss's rendering be experienced at times as hollow, *too* pyrotechnic. Perhaps Bülow's allegation of an affront to the piano in the *Burleske* can be interpreted as the occasional "peeping out" of Strauss-as-Till. "Strauss, the fledgling modernist, had struck out on his own,"[30] asserted Gilliam; indeed, Strauss's reworking of pre-existing music (parody) in a manner that is at turns reverent, sardonic, or ambiguous, foreshadowed his tone poems *Don Juan* and *Till Eulenspiegel*, but also works of his full maturity, such as the operas *Der Rosenkavalier* and *Ariadne auf Naxos*.

"Richard Strauss"

That Brahms, Liszt, and Wagner would overlap in Strauss's music in the 1880s, and continue to do so in varying technical and aesthetic degrees, highlights what I have argued is Strauss's most singular and enduring trait: his reliance on an array of composers and traditions. To cite but two examples: the composition of the Sonata for Violin and Piano, Op. 18 (1887) intervened between *Aus Italien* on the one hand and the tone poems *Macbeth* and *Don Juan* on the other; and the period in which Strauss composed the family of historically retrospective *Ariadne* works, 1911–16, also saw the completion of such diverse scores as his last tone poem *Eine Alpensinfonie*, the exoticist-symbolist ballet-pantomime *Josephslegende*, and the neo-Romantic opera *Die Frau ohne Schatten*.

It is fitting to approach the end of Strauss's early works with his first published collections of lieder, a genre with which he had been active from the very beginning. In 1885, Strauss composed and published the *Acht Gedichte aus* Letzte Blätter *von Hermann Gilm* (*Eight Poems from* Last Leaves *by Hermann Gilm*), Op. 10. Dedicated to the tenor Heinrich Vogl, a principal singer at the Munich Court Opera for whose voice these "real tenor songs"[31] seem to have been conceived, the Op. 10 set exhibits a level of cohesiveness within and among songs that is exceptional among Strauss's lieder. It includes "Zueignung" ("Dedication") and "Allerseelen" ("All Souls' Day"), which are among his most famous songs. The *Fünf Lieder*, Op. 15, composed in tandem with Op. 10, are a more typical hodgepodge, although four of the five songs draw on the work of a single poet, Adolf Friedrich von Schack (the first in the set is a translation of a madrigal by Michelangelo). As with Strauss's oeuvre in general, variety and unity are not mutually exclusive states; rather, there is unity in this composer's reliable diversity. The *Sechs Lieder von A. F. v. Schack*, Op. 17 (1885–7), including what is arguably Strauss's most famous song, "Ständchen" ("Serenade"), suggest once more an integrated approach.

In his detailed discussion of Strauss's lieder, Del Mar referenced a number of composers whose presence is felt in Opp. 10, 15, and 17, including, of course, Brahms, in the brief coda of "Die Zeitlose" ("The Meadow Saffron"), Op. 10 No. 7, and the instrumental postlude to "Nur Muth!" ("Only Courage!"), Op. 17 No. 5; and also Hugo Wolf in the harmonic daring of "Die Georgine" ("The Dahlia"), Op. 10 No. 4, or the "freer, more declamatory idiom" of "Nichts" ("Nothing") and "Die Verschwiegenen" ("The Discreet Ones"), Op. 10 Nos. 2 and 6, respectively. Moreover, Del Mar noted the melodic resemblance of "Die Nacht" ("Night"), Op. 10 No. 3 to such disparate sources as the Prize Song from Wagner's *Die Meistersinger* and the love duet in Gounod's *Faust*,[32] not to mention Schumann's "Mondnacht." While the determination of precise models is often subjective, Strauss's lieder offer clear examples of a composer who relished diversity, among and within genres and opuses.

It was in 1886, the year in which Strauss completed the Op. 17 lieder, that he traveled to Italy for the first time, a trip that followed his five-month tenure in Meiningen and preceded his three-year post as third conductor at the Munich Court Opera. The immediate musical outcome of the Italian journey was *Aus Italien*, capturing Strauss's efforts to communicate his impressions and feelings of such places as the Campagna, the ruins of Rome, the beach at Sorrento, and folk life in Naples (the latter somewhat incongruously built upon Luigi Denza's then-popular tune "Funiculì, funiculà"). In *Aus Italien*, Strauss was looking forward and back: back to pedigreed Classical forms, albeit through a modified lens befitting a "symphonic fantasy" – slow introductory movement, Allegro con brio, Andantino, Allegro molto – while at the same time anticipating his impending turn away from "absolute" music to the programmatic. The composer's experiences at Meiningen pointed towards such a crossroads. On the one hand, *Aus Italien* is dedicated to Bülow "with deepest honor and gratitude"; on the other, it was also in Meiningen that Strauss became acquainted with Alexander Ritter, whom he cited, along with his father and Bülow, as a profound musical influence.

Specht's declaration that, in *Aus Italien*, we encounter "the real Richard Strauss for the first time" (particularly in the Sorrento movement),[33] suggests that this work is prescient not just of Strauss's conversion to Liszt and

Wagner, but also of his post-conversion wrangling with Romantic meta-physics in the 1890s under the sway of Nietzsche. Glossing on the phil-osopher, Romain Rolland regarded the 1886 Italian trip (and subsequent trips to Italy, Greece, and Egypt in 1892 when the composer was recover-ing from pneumonia and pleurisy) as fostering nostalgia in Strauss that "penetrated his music, in which one feels one of the most tormented souls of deep Germany and, at the same time, an unceasing yearning for the col-ours, the rhythms, the laughter, the joy of the South."[34] In *Aus Italien*, then, the presence of a program might be viewed as a superficial harbinger of the composer that Strauss was becoming. This "symphonic fantasy" marks once more the emergence of competing aesthetic urges that he would nego-tiate in the decades to come – indeed, for the remainder of his life.

PART II

Works

4 The first cycle of tone poems

DAVID LARKIN

"The Mannheim orchestra was very struck and astounded by the leap from my F minor Symphony to *Macbeth*," reported Strauss after a rehearsal of the latter work in January, 1889.[1] This astonishment is not to be wondered at: there is a profound stylistic gulf between the staid Classicism of Strauss's Second Symphony (which the orchestra performed under the composer's direction in October, 1885) and his first tone poem with its corrosive dissonances, structural freedoms, and, most obviously, its overt reference to extra-musical subject matter. In the interim, Strauss had been converted to a "totally new way" of composing, one inspired by Liszt and Wagner.[2] While some of his earlier works display high levels of technical assurance, it was not until the first cycle of tone poems – *Macbeth* (1887–8, rev. 1891), *Don Juan* (1888), and *Tod und Verklärung* (1888–9) – that Strauss found a fully original voice. These three works mark the beginnings of an interest in poetic music that would dominate his output until the final decade of his life and would earn him widespread fame, even notoriety, throughout the German-speaking lands and beyond.

The heir to Liszt and Wagner

When Strauss took up his first professional engagement as assistant conductor to the gifted if irascible Hans von Bülow in October, 1885, he could not have foreseen how significantly this position would change his life. At that time, Strauss was in the grips of what he later called his *Brahmsschwärmerei*, a juvenile passion for Brahms, and shortly after arriving at Meiningen he met his idol, who encouraged him and gave him valuable advice. Yet this was not the encounter that Strauss would later describe as the "greatest event of the winter in Meiningen." This accolade was reserved for his acquaintance with a far less renowned figure: Alexander Ritter, then a violinist in the orchestra.[3] The importance of Ritter's contribution to the young composer's development was acknowledged by Strauss in one of his earliest autobiographical accounts, adding this lengthy aside to the tabular chronology for 1885:

> Acquaintance with *Alexander Ritter*, who made me – I had been strictly
> Classically trained until that point, having grown up with only Haydn,

Mozart, Beethoven, and having just arrived at Brahms by way of Mendelssohn, Chopin, and Schumann – into a confirmed *musician-of-the-future* after years of affectionate efforts and teaching, in which he disclosed the music-historical importance of the works and writings of Wagner and Liszt. I owe to him alone my understanding of these two masters; he put me on the way that I now walk independently. He introduced me to Schopenhauer's doctrines.[4]

Ritter, himself a minor composer, had been a pupil of Liszt and had married Wagner's niece, factors that explain his fanatical enthusiasm for the two leaders of the so-called New German School. Over the course of that winter, Strauss's indoctrination began, and it continued when both men relocated to Munich in fall, 1886. In one sense, Ritter's impassioned advocacy was only the catalyst that aroused Strauss's latent sympathies for "progressive" music: ever since his secret study of *Tristan* at the age of seventeen, Strauss had been ambivalently fascinated by Wagner, in spite of his conservative training and the fulminations of his deeply anti-Wagnerian father. So while Ritter had not a tabula rasa to work on, he certainly deepened his young protégé's knowledge of the Wagnerian repertory, and firmly grounded Wagner's aesthetic project in Schopenhauer's philosophy, something that would complicate Strauss's Wagner reception in the 1890s.[5] So far as can be established, Strauss's acquaintance with Liszt's music was minimal before Ritter took him in hand, but he quickly became convinced of its merits and remained a life-long enthusiast.

The progress of Strauss's musical realignment between 1886 and 1888 is difficult to chart with any exactitude, given the scantiness of the evidence. His decision to join the progressive *Allgemeiner Deutscher Musikverein* in March, 1887 – a society dedicated to the promotion of new music that had been founded under Liszt's auspices in 1859 – is one straw in the wind.[6] The clearest intimation of his changing compositional orientation is *Aus Italien*, the "symphonic fantasy" he wrote in 1886 after a visit to Italy. Described by the composer as his "first step towards independence," this work still adheres to the four-movement pattern he would later abjure, but marks a decisive step towards the tone poem on several fronts.[7] Most obviously, it marks Strauss's earliest venture into programmatic orchestral composition: the individual movements are given titles – "In the Campagna," "Among Rome's Ruins," "On the Beach at Sorrento," and "Folk Life at Naples," respectively – which can be related to the music to a greater or lesser extent.[8] The overt tone-painting of wind, waves, and bird cries in the third movement attracted much attention, to the evident chagrin of the composer, who strenuously argued that "the content of my work [is] the *feelings* aroused at the sight of the splendid beauties of Rome and Naples, not *descriptions* of these."[9]

Still more significant in Strauss's mind, to judge from his remarks, were the innovations of form and structure in *Aus Italien*. A couple of days after the premiere, he stated that the work "departed in almost every respect from the conventional symphony, i.e. from sonata form."[10] This claim is at most partially true – the "Rome" movement, in particular, is clearly in sonata form, as Strauss's later analysis confirms – but even as an aspiration, it is indicative of the direction of his thought.[11] Over the course of time, Strauss's initial enthusiasm for the work faded, and he came to a more even-handed estimation of its innovations. In the last decade of his life, he referred to *Aus Italien* as his "first hesitant effort" to implement a new compositional agenda, which he described as follows: "New ideas must search for new forms – this basic principle of Liszt's symphonic works, in which the poetic idea was really the form-shaping element, became from then on the guiding principle for my own symphonic work."[12]

Strauss's views on form, poetic idea, and the relationship between the two received detailed articulation in a lengthy letter he wrote to Bülow in August, 1888, effectively a manifesto for his new compositional bent. For reasons of tact, he refrains from criticizing Brahms, even though by now he was thoroughly disenchanted with his former idol. Similarly, Strauss avoids controversial appeals to Liszt or Wagner; instead he invokes Beethoven's indisputable authority for his new direction (the connection between Beethoven and the New Germans was something he repeatedly emphasized elsewhere). Citing Beethoven's overtures and his oeuvre in general as "unthinkable without the stimulus of a poetic subject," Strauss maintains that "inspiration by a poetical idea, whether or not it be introduced as a program" is vital to the creation of "a work of art that is unified in its mood and consistent in its structure." The musical-poetic content he wished to convey was incompatible with "ternary sonata form," whose ubiquity in symphonic composition he challenged, noting that even Beethoven had departed from it "where for a new content he had to devise a new form." Instead of slavishly adhering to this outworn formula, Strauss claimed that it was "a legitimate artistic method to create a correspondingly new form for every new subject, to shape which neatly and perfectly is a very difficult task, but for that reason the more attractive." In consequence, there could be no more "purely formalistic, Hanslickian music-making," and "no symphonies."[13] To other correspondents he was less restrained, inveighing against the irredeemable aridity of the symphony: "Away with the barren four-movement formulaic entity, which has sprouted no new content since [Beethoven's Ninth Symphony]."[14] His vehement condemnation of absolute music ("art fabrication," "possible for anyone only moderately musical") ran parallel with his veneration of program music ("real music!", "true art").[15] Such outspoken, radical views merely confirm the new direction of Strauss's thought, which had by that time already found more practical expression in his first symphonic poems.

Macbeth: **Strauss's vaulting ambition**

If *Aus Italien* was still a "bridge," then with *Macbeth* and *Don Juan* Strauss felt he had entered onto his own "totally individual path."[16] The symphonic poem, which had been associated with "advanced" composition ever since its invention at the hands of Liszt, was an obvious choice of genre for one who claimed to be "a young musical progressive (of the most extreme left)."[17] For publication, Strauss tended to give his works the label *Tondichtung* (tone poem) in preference to Liszt's title, but in his correspondence he uses both designations indiscriminately.[18] While the two terms are thus demonstrably cognate, that should not be taken to imply that Strauss's conception of the genre was identical to Liszt's: far from it, in fact. At one point in the gestation of *Macbeth*, Strauss claimed that he was working on a sort of symphonic poem, "but not in the manner of Liszt" (*nicht nach Liszt*).[19] This cryptic remark on one level signals Strauss's wish to distance himself from Liszt's homophonic textures in favour of a richer, more polyphonic approach.[20] Another important distinction between the two has been noted by John Williamson: where Liszt's works are mainly focussed on character depiction, Strauss's involve the representation of dramatic events.[21] The following excerpt from a letter to Ludwig Thuille shows how important this approach was for Strauss, one that he claimed was partly taken in Liszt's *Faust* Symphony:

> The real dramatic action happens first in Mephisto, and this is really also the first "symphonic poem"; the two great figures of Faust and Gretchen are by contrast so complicated, that their *representation* as well as dramatic development in a single movement was not at all possible for him [Liszt]. Hence as exposition the two greatest mood pictures ever written (the Faust movement does admittedly also have some development) and the real dramatic complexity in Mephisto.[22]

Whatever its merits as an analysis of Liszt's oeuvre, the idea that the symphonic poem is of its nature imbued with dramatic development seems to have had regulative force for Strauss. As such, his tone poems can also be seen as sites of engagement with Wagner's ideas, a fusion of Liszt's invention with elements of music drama. The trajectory of Strauss's career, in which a period mainly given over to symphonic music was succeeded by one focussed on writing for the stage with relatively little overlap between the two, has further encouraged the identification of proto-operatic traits in his tone poems. Writing after *Salome* and *Elektra* had appeared, Rudolf Louis had the benefit of hindsight when commenting upon the increased realism, even visuality, of Strauss's approach to program music in comparison to Liszt:

> Strauss's unique and personal strength [is] that he has developed the ideal, elevated gestures of the tonal language of Liszt into a gestural language of great specificity, that undertakes quite seriously not only to interpret the events of an external plot in tone (by revealing the music that is latent in them), but to *draw* them until they are recognizable to the inner eye.[23]

While observations such as these are true for Strauss's orchestral oeuvre as a whole, matters are more equivocal in the case of his first tone poem, *Macbeth*. The question of how this piece relates to its Shakespearean source is still a subject of debate. Some interpret the work as no more than a character portrait of Macbeth himself: "the music tells us almost exclusively about the hero," wrote one reviewer after the premiere in 1890.[24] This was the approach taken by Liszt, who "invented musical equivalents of Hamlet and Faust as the archetypes which, half released from the poetic works themselves, they had in the meantime become in the general European consciousness."[25] Like his precursor, Strauss tended to choose characters with strong symbolic resonance – figures such as Macbeth, Don Juan, Till Eulenspiegel, Don Quixote – as the eponymous heroes of his tone poems. However, in the case of the latter two works at least, he went beyond finding musical analogues for the personalities involved and explicitly depicted a series of incidents involving those characters. By contrast, the scantiness of the paratextual clues in *Macbeth* would seem to indicate more modest ambitions. Strauss gave labels to two themes, "Macbeth" (m. 6) and "Lady Macbeth" (m. 64), the latter accompanied by a brief extract from her first soliloquy ("Hie thee hither ..." [I.v.12–17]).[26] Where later works are supplied with a more detailed poetic preface or section titles, Strauss's first tone poem does not give much overt encouragement to those who might wish to see it as a musical enactment of the plot of Shakespeare's play.

Recently, writers such as James Hepokoski have convincingly argued that establishing the extent of the relationship between a symphonic poem's music and its declared poetic subject is part of the remit of the listener-interpreter rather than an immanent property of the work itself.[27] Thus plausible scenarios can be devised that build on these minimal clues to construct an interpretation of the music alongside the events of Shakespeare's play. And for those who hold to the "play" theory, there is some empirical evidence on which to draw. In 1887, Strauss played the work through for Bülow, who strongly objected to its original conclusion, a D major march of Macduff: "It was all very well for an *Egmont* overture to conclude with a

Example 4.1a *Macbeth*, mm. 6–13

Example 4.1b *Macbeth*, mm. 324–30

triumphal march of Egmont, but a symphonic poem *Macbeth* could never finish with the triumph of Macduff."[28] While Strauss did accept this argument and pruned the Macduff element down to a few off-stage fanfares (mm. 538–41), it nonetheless seems that he had attempted to encapsulate the broad course of the play into his tone poem. Scott Warfield has argued that after the revisions, the work was "refocused exclusively on the psychological states of Macbeth and his accomplice, Lady Macbeth, instead of the more specific events of Shakespeare's drama."[29] True, there is no Birnam Wood, no Banquo, nothing that unambiguously suggests the three witches.[30] However, Macbeth himself undergoes profound development across the course of the five acts, from pusillanimous Thane to paranoid tyrant and, as such, any character-based tone poem will of necessity follow the narrative trajectory. Such is the case here, with the music depicting a gradual descent into turmoil in the latter half of the tone poem. The unraveling of the hero can be heard in the distorted echoes of the "Macbeth" theme later on (Examples 4.1a and b). Lady Macbeth, initially portrayed as a manipulative inciter of her husband, is subsequently reduced to mere interjections (Examples 4.2a and b), while a subordinate idea, sometimes interpreted as her goading her husband to murder (mm. 83–4), becomes ever more prominent, in keeping with the increasing bloodiness of Macbeth's actions and his independence from her direction.[31] Other musical signifiers that can easily be associated with elements of the plot include the fanfare-based march (mm. 260–1) as an emblem of royalty,[32] and the

Example 4.2a *Macbeth*, mm. 67–70

Example 4.2b *Macbeth*, mm. 387–8 (woodwind only)

irregular, jagged chords fading into silence as an unmistakable symbol of death (mm. 509–15). Not without cause did Strauss subtitle the work *nach Shakespeares drama*.

In many ways, *Macbeth* is a bold statement of intent on Strauss's part. The harmonic language he employs here is difficult, deliberately so: Strauss was proud of having written dissonances so corrosive that they could "devour each other."[33] The abrupt harmonic changes in the "Macbeth" theme (Example 4.1a) evince a desire to shock, to break with convention, and are deliberately jagged in comparison with the effortless modulatory freedom he demonstrates in later works. Perhaps the ambitions of the composer, who wished with one stroke to assume the mantle of heir to Liszt and Wagner, were not so dissimilar to those of the eponymous character. And just like Macbeth, Strauss might be seen to have overreached himself somewhat, even if the consequences were less calamitous. The protracted series of revisions that delayed its publication until after the appearance of *Don Juan* testifies to the difficulties he had in acclimatizing himself to this new style.[34] Even when he was finally satisfied with the content and structure of the work, he continued to tinker with the instrumentation.[35]

The work as we know it today takes sonata form as its point of departure, and subjects it to a variety of what may be described as "deformation procedures."[36] A short, testosterone-driven fanfare leads into the bi-partite expositional space with radically contrasted masculine (D minor) and feminine (F♯ minor) theme groups. This is followed by a double episode in B♭, first (m. 123) a lyrical song that becomes increasingly agitated and leads to some form of catastrophe (m. 242), followed by the regal march idea (unusually, in triple time). Measure 324 clearly marks a restart of some kind, with the failed restatements of the "Macbeth" theme and subsequent deployment of the second-group "goading" idea (and the signal omission of Lady Macbeth herself). In Hepokoski's reading, mm. 324–535 form a distorted "recapitulatory space," with the preceeding episodes (mm. 123–259 and 260–323) replacing the usual development section.[37] The practice of making a brief, recognizable recapitulatory allusion before deviating is also found in later tone poems, where it provides an important point of orientation for the listener, and thus synecdochically replaces a complete, dramatically redundant recapitulation.[38] Strauss's approach here thus closely matches his description of the *Faust Symphony* (for him, essentially an expanded symphonic poem): once the personae have been introduced in the exposition, the real dramatic action takes over. After Macbeth's "death," a slow, sinuous section with disembodied recollections of earlier themes ensues (mm. 515–58); this is initially supported by a long dominant pedal and only resolves to the tonic at m. 536. The somber mood is hardly mitigated by the perfunctory final crescendo with which the work closes, itself a reference back to a similar gesture at the opening.

Of all Strauss's tone poems, *Macbeth* was the least successful in the concert hall.[39] Ultimately, the public's affection was won not by the overt violence of this work, but by the unique blend of machismo and seductiveness in *Don Juan* and those that followed. Bülow commented that "for the time being the witches' servant is still not of equal significance to the witchmaster."[40] While Strauss's later works are arguably more accomplished and certainly have aroused more affection, nonetheless with *Macbeth*, which was appropriately dedicated to Alexander Ritter, the essential elements of his future practice are already in place.

Don Juan: a bolt from the heavens

"The idea of *élan* itself, music as curve, implies a fall from the heights; what was thrown by the composing hand must sink abruptly in a meteoric arc. This was the almost visual form of Strauss's first authentic work, *Don Juan*; never again did he achieve the same unity of program, thematic content, and formal development."[41] Although he is numbered among Strauss's sharpest critics, Adorno's essays on the composer are highly insightful, and never more so than in this penetrating description of *Don Juan*. Strauss's second tone poem launches itself with apparently inexhaustible vim and vigor, the stratospherically climbing violins in the opening bars emblematic of "the breakaway mood of the 1890s," as Dahlhaus famously described it.[42] The sheer swagger of this über-masculine portrayal of the libidinous hero outdoes even the prelude to Act III of *Lohengrin*, surely an inspiration. And yet, this rocketing, boundless vitality ultimately consumes itself and plummets to earth. At the end of the work, after many vicissitudes, matters appear be driving inexorably towards an emphatic peroration: yet at the very peak of dynamic intensity, Strauss brutally cuts away from the climactic dominant. After a tense *Generalpause* (m. 585) the music subsides in a series of quiet subdominant shudders onto the tonic minor. Explanations for this shocking reversal have naturally been sought in the subject matter. For his tone poem, Strauss drew on a version of the Don Juan story by Nikolaus Lenau, which ends with the death of the protagonist in a duel. In fact, Juan deliberately casts aside his rapier, having come to the realization that his imminent victory is worthless: "My deadly enemy is given into my power / But this too is tedious, as is life itself."[43] This existential angst differentiates Don Juan from literary prototypes such as Goethe's Werther or Byron's Manfred, whose self-sought deaths are Romantic responses to unfulfilled love or unexpiated guilt rather than undertaken out of sheer disgust with life.

Although there would seem to be a satisfying marriage of musical and dramatic plots at this point, Strauss never indicated any such extensive parallels between his music and Lenau's "dramatic scenes." In fact, his sketches reveal that at one stage in the gestation of the work he envisaged a "big daring coda, stormy ending."[44] Moreover, the three excerpts from the poem included in the Preface to the published score reveal aspects of Don Juan's philosophy and mood rather than touching on specific events. In conjunction with the associations of the title, these verses would enable listeners to situate the changes in mood and emotion within an appropriate frame of reference, but Strauss refrained from pointing up any more detailed correspondence to extra-musical events. The questions of how much audiences need be told and how best this information might be conveyed occupied Strauss throughout his career as a tone poet. Like other composers of program music, Strauss was caught between conflicting positions. On one side was his conviction that music was ineffable, that its central expressive poetic content transcended verbal explanation, as the following 1889 remarks attest:

> [A] piece of music which has nothing truly poetic to convey to me – the sort of content which can be properly represented *only in music*, that *words* may be able to *suggest, but no more than suggest* – in my view a piece like that is anything you care to call it, but not that most poetic of arts, capable of the highest expression: music.[45]

Over fifty years later, Strauss's belief in the self-sufficiency of music was articulated still more strongly when he claimed that "[a] poetic program may well suggest new forms, but whenever music is not developed logically from within, it becomes *Literaturmusik*."[46] In other words, Strauss believed that the musical coherence of a work should not have to be shored up by appeals to the extra-musical, to verbal explications. And yet, this focus on poetic content was in Strauss's mind not incompatible with the illustration of specific dramatic events. The series of torrid love affairs in *Don Juan*, for instance, was irresistible to one aware of his talents for depicting the erotic.[47] He was pragmatic enough to recognize that greater success could be achieved if the connection between his music and the extra-musical element were spelled out unequivocally. In later years he would attempt to solve this dilemma by authorizing the production of an explanatory book-let by a third party. This ensured that audiences had a crutch on which to lean, while the arm's-length distance between artwork and explication allowed Strauss to preserve deniability in the face of hostile criticism. The widespread practice of relating *Don Juan* to the events of Lenau's poem ultimately stems from one such guide written by Wilhelm Mauke dating from 1897.[48]

Even before this appeared, Strauss was obliged to defend himself on the charge of excessive attention to events in this work. Cosima Wagner gently reproached her young protégé (whom she was grooming for future Bayreuth stardom) for allowing his intellect to rule his feelings. He was guilty, in effect, of failing to adhere to Wagner's dictum that a symphonic musician should "look away from the incidents of ordinary life … and sub-limate whatever lies within it to its quintessential emotional content."[49] In response, Strauss pleaded that naïve composition of the sort practiced by Mozart, Haydn, and Schubert was impossible in his day, given interven-ing developments, and so artists had to engage both intellect and emo-tion in the task of creation, with the latter quality predominating in all "true" musicians.[50] Wagner's widow was not alone in sensing a departure from Wagnerian orthodoxy in *Don Juan*: Engelbert Humperdinck called it a "breach with Romanticism," and contrasted it with *Tod und Verklärung*, which for him marked "a perceptible return to Liszt and Wagner."[51]

Like *Macbeth*, *Don Juan* poses its share of formal problems for the ana-lyst. From a *Formenlehre* perspective, there are elements of rondo, son-ata, and the multi-movement symphony to be found, brought together in an idiosyncratic fusion. In his celebrated article on the work, Hepokoski makes a case for an initial rondo-like structure, which mutates into a son-ata offshoot after a pivotal central double-episode (mm. 197–307), and he provides convincing hermeneutic justification for this shift (the once-careless seducer cannot cast off his latest inamorata as before; he too has

been changed by the affair).[52] However, without denying the rondo (or rit-
ornello) tendencies of the opening, it might still be read as a sonata exposition, with a masculine first theme in E major (mm. 1–40), transition, and
lyrical second theme in B major (mm. 90–148, preceded by its dominant in
m. 71).[53] Thus far, indeed, it could hardly adhere more blatantly to the common nineteenth-century expositional archetype, even though the second
group avoids clear cadential demarcation and instead drifts towards E
minor (m. 148) before dissolving. The reappearance of the Don Juan (first
theme) music in m. 169, the element most strongly suggestive of rondo,
might be interpreted as initiating the second rotation in sonata form, i.e.
the development. It quickly gives way to the aforementioned double episode, in G minor (m. 197) and subsequently G major (m. 232). The latter
section has something of the character of a lyrical slow movement, with
the music becoming almost totally becalmed at this point. Suddenly, a
new idea breaks through: a C major *Heldenthema* (m. 314) rings out in the
horns. This crucial moment gives renewed momentum to the form, and
also confirms the significance of the E–C tonal polarity in the work (this is
present from the beginning, with the very first chord actually a C_3^6 sonority,
quickly subsumed within an E major horizon). A jaunty and carnivalesque
episode, commonly related to the masked ball in Lenau's poem, starts in
m. 351, and assumes the function of a scherzo in the subcutaneous multi-
movement design. The music becomes increasingly hectic and strenuous
and (in anticipation of the ending) builds to a climax before collapsing into
a ghostly pianissimo (m. 424). Against a mysterious, shimmering backdrop,
distorted fragments of themes associated earlier with various female characters are heard. The pedal B underpinning these reminiscences is given
new focus from m. 457, which initiates a retransition to the recapitulated
first theme (m. 424, curtailed). In place of the lyrical second theme, Strauss
then reprises the resplendent *Heldenthema* (m. 510). However, as it is spun
out, the manly bravura of the latter is suffused with the impassioned sweep
of the "original" second group. The music makes a strong perfect authentic
cadence in E major at m. 466 (exactly equivalent to that which closed the
first theme in m. 40), before the final crescendo and derailment.

The foregoing description will have given some idea of complexities of
the dialogue between Strauss's music and various formal archetypes, but
such an approach can only take us so far in understanding the music. The
more dynamic aspects of this score, in particular the wave-like surging of
the musical surface, have been explored by Walter Werbeck in his study of
Steigerung (intensification) technique across the set of tone poems.[54] These
propulsive gestures may either lead into, or (as in *Don Juan*) develop out
of a thematic statement, a prime example being the overlapping extensions
which emerge from the recapitulated *Heldenthema* (Example 4.3).

Example 4.3 *Don Juan*, mm. 536–43

This type of surging writing that whips the music into a frenzy is one of Strauss's most noticeable stylistic fingerprints, and is central to the élan that Adorno identified in the work. The hectic, intense emotionality also contributes to its enormous popularity. *Don Juan* marks a major breakthrough for Strauss as a composer, but historians such as Dahlhaus have accorded it greater significance still, seeing in its opening notes the dawning of "musical modernism."[55]

Tod und Verklärung: striving for the ideal

It was in the aftermath of the successful premiere of *Don Juan* that Strauss opened negotiations with his publisher for bringing out *Tod und Verklärung*, his "best and most mature work." In the course of the letter, he announced, "I will probably shortly abandon absolute music in order to seek my salvation in music drama."[56] This apparently sudden decision to move into stage composition was in fact not an impulsive one: Strauss had begun the libretto for what would be his first opera, *Guntram*, as early as August 26, 1887, which makes it coeval with *Macbeth*.[57] Strauss's initial focus on the tone poem may therefore be regarded as a sublimated opera-wish, a strategy allowing him to work in an appropriately "advanced" genre while he readied himself to take up Wagner's mantle. This intermediate focus on programmatic symphonic composition certainly had the benefit of equipping the fledgling dramatist with a musical language that could convey moods, images, and even events almost synaesthetically to an audience.

A few perceptive critics were able to deduce Strauss's nascent operatic ambitions from hearing *Tod und Verklärung*. Hanslick, for one, felt that "the nature of his talent really points the composer in the direction of music drama."[58] In a similar vein, a writer in the *Chicago Daily Tribune* was moved to remark: "the idea frequently is suggested from Herr Strauss's work, if it is to follow in the free and fanciful path taken in this instance, that opera is a field in which he would best devote his energies."[59] These responses were partly elicited by the nature of the program. For the first time, Strauss moved away from the world of literature and invented his own scenario, which was turned into a prefatory poem by Ritter. Since his music was not based on a pre-existent literary work, Strauss could not rely on established associations to supplement whatever clues he gave his audiences. The title does indicate a well-marked archetype, but not content with this, the poem describes in close detail a series of events befalling the dying man. Strauss summarized the main thrust of the program in a letter some years later:

> About six years ago [i.e. 1888] the idea occurred to me to represent in a tone poem the death of a person who had striven for the highest ideal-istic goals, therefore probably an artist. The sick man lies in bed asleep, breathing heavily and irregularly; agreeable dreams charm a smile onto his features in spite of his suffering; his sleep becomes lighter; he wakens; once again he is racked by terrible pain, his limbs shake with fear – as the attack draws to a close and the pain subsides he reflects on his past life, his childhood passes before him, his youth with its striving, its passions, and then, while the pain resumes, the fruit of his path through life appears to him, the idea, the Ideal which he has tried to realize to represent in his art, but which he has been unable to perfect, because it was not for any human being to perfect it. The hour of death approaches, the soul leaves the body, in order to find perfected in the most glorious form in the eternal cosmos that which he could not fulfil here on earth.[60]

The first version of the poem, written for the premiere, was revised and expanded shortly afterwards to mirror the tone poem still more closely, and in this second incarnation was published with the score.[61] From his study of the sketches, Werbeck dismisses the idea that there was anything as fixed as a libretto predating the composition. Many central concepts – among them struggle, death, and eventual transcendence – were present from the beginning, but their precise order and format only emerged during the compositional process.[62]

The virtuosic representation technique Strauss had honed in earlier tone poems was here put to the task of vividly realizing the content. Twenty-first-century listeners might hear in the non-linear unfolding of time in *Tod und Verklärung* and the use of flashbacks analogies to Tarantino-style filmic procedure rather than traditional opera, although it could be argued that Strauss was building on Wagner's propensity for *narrating* past events in his music dramas. The absence of a stage realization allowed him to move seamlessly between present and past. The first brief foray into the mind and

Example 4.4 *Tod und Verklärung*, mm. 13–20

memories of the protagonist illustrates how cleverly these changes of perspective are accomplished (Example 4.4). Having initially painted a picture
of the dying sleeper by means of the offbeat string palpitations and heavy
chordal tread, Strauss freezes on a D♭$^4_2$ chord that is sustained across five
bars by means of ethereal harp arpeggios. The warm woodwind melodies
pitched against this backdrop emphasize the scene's separateness from the
grim deathbed scene. When the opening music resumes, it takes up from
where it left off as if there had been no interruption, surely implying that
the parenthetic flashback took place outside the normal temporal frame.[63]

Tod und Verklärung thus marks an advance over *Don Juan* in its hyper-
realism, but in other areas it is arguably less bold. Gustav Brecher went so

Example 4.4 (cont.)

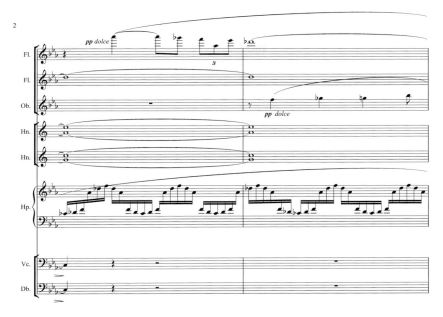

far as to call it "the only 'reactionary' one of all Strauss's works, both in the metaphysical nature of its program and in the fact that the music abides in the Lisztian-Wagnerian style."[64] *Tod und Verklärung*, with its message of hope and redemption through suffering, is certainly sharply differentiated from *Don Juan*, with its physicalism and nihilistic ending. Such stark contrasts occur repeatedly in Strauss's oeuvre and serve to refute the supposition that his own ideological stance can be straightforwardly decoded from his music. The *per ardua ad astra* plot of the later tone poem is certainly one with many precedents in the works of Liszt and Wagner. The idea of posthumous artistic vindication informs Liszt's *Tasso: Lamento e trionfo*, a commemoration of the sufferings and eventual triumph of the poet. The parallels between *Tod und Verklärung* and *Tristan* are even more striking: like Isolde's final scene, entitled "Verklärung" by Wagner, Strauss's conception of "transfiguration" eschews the religious overtones associated with this concept in favor of a secularized version.[65] The final quatrain of the *Tod und Verklärung* poem includes the patently *Tristan*-esque final line, establishing a deliberate intertextual reference to the music drama Strauss worshiped above all others:

> Aber mächtig tönet ihm
> Aus dem Himmelsraum entgegen,
> Was er sehnend hier gesucht:
> Welterlösung, Weltverklärung![66]

Example 4.4 (cont.)

But mightily there sounds to him
Coming from the broad expanse of heaven
What he yearned and searched for here:
World-redemption, world-transfiguration!

Musical references to *Tristan* abound as well: the famous "gaze" motive
is cited at one point (Example 4.5), in conjunction with that *echt-Tristan*

Example 4.5 *Tod und Verklärung*, mm. 268–70

Example 4.6 *Tod und Verklärung*, mm. 160–4

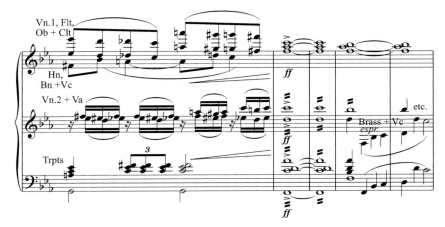

sonority, the half-diminished seventh chord. Another incidence of this sonority comes earlier in m. 161, as the climax chord before the first adumbration of the "Ideal" theme (Example 4.6). More generally, the musical language that Strauss adopts in his third tone poem has also been described as a return to "the more trodden paths of the truly chromatic style of Liszt and Wagner."[67] It certainly is audibly contrasted with *Don Juan*, which sounds ebulliently diatonic despite the plethora of accidentals.[68]

Further intertextual possibilities are opened by the key scheme of *Tod und Verklärung*, which follows the C minor→major path familiar from Beethoven's Fifth Symphony, Liszt's *Faust* Symphony and *Tasso*, and many other works besides.[69] Strauss himself playfully speculated that it might have stemmed from "the musical need – after *Macbeth* (begins and ends in D minor), *Don Juan* (begins in E major and ends in E minor) to write a piece that begins in C minor and finishes in C major! Who can tell?"[70] The overall shape of the tone poem does in fact recall the end-weighted, struggle-to-victory trajectory of Beethoven's Symphony and the aforementioned works of Liszt. One of the principal means of creating this sense of goal-directed progress here is the gradual unfolding of the "Ideal" theme, first presented in mm. 163–4 (Example 4.6), and in ever more complete versions in mm. 320ff. (A♭ major), 334 (A major), and 355 (D♭ major), before it is stated in full harmonic plenitude in the transfiguration section proper (m. 430 in C major).[71] This same process of "becoming" is replicated throughout the work: what is usually identified as the main thematic idea in the Allegro section (m. 96) marks the culmination and end-point of the preceding music, rather than initiating a new section. In *Don Juan*, by comparison, the *Steigerung* develops out of, rather than leads to, a thematic idea. Thus the overall shape of each composition as a whole is in some way replicated by the shapes outlined locally on the musical surface.

This ongoing process of teleological genesis co-exists with a formal outline that has been read as a conflation of sonata and multi-movement elements. The final version of the poem is laid out in four discrete portions, each of which connects to major divisions in the score. Lines 1–14 describing the sleeping invalid and his dreams equate to mm. 1–66, an introductory Largo section in which various leitmotifs of crucial significance are first presented. Lines 15–22 describe the artist's waking agonies and correspond to mm. 67–185, which initiate the main Allegro action. It acts as a sonata exposition and simultaneously functions as the first movement of the composition as cycle: Dahlhaus has identified on this micro-level an introduction (m. 67), thematic statement (m. 96), development-like area (m. 101), and reprise (m. 147).[72] Matters are whipped into a frenzy as the fever reaches a crisis at the musical climax signaled by the aforementioned *Tristan* chord and first appearance of the "Ideal" theme (mm. 161–4). The third and longest portion of the poem (lines 23–58) describes his delirious memories of childhood and youth, his vain struggles to achieve his Ideal, and then his final paroxysm and death. The music for this section conflates development and recapitulation portions of the form, the latter signaled by a very abbreviated recall of material from the introduction and exposition (mm. 364–94). Matters seem to be heading towards the same *Tristan*-chord climax as before, but instead it all dissolves onto an insubstantial diminished seventh as the artist dies to the sound of a tam-tam (m. 395). From this point onwards, there is an inexorable, incremental build-up over a tolling ostinato, leading to the complete statement of the Ideal theme. This expansive Moderato (mm. 395–499), related to the final quatrain of the poem (59–62), is at one and the same time a coda and a final movement that recapitulates two of the most significant themes from earlier in the work.

The valedictory tone of this final section might be interpreted as Strauss's farewell to symphonic composition, now that his own Ideal – music drama – was within reach. To some extent, his first cycle of tone poems did serve as prolegomena to his operatic ventures: his fusion of the Lisztian symphonic poem with deeper psychological and dramatic elements anticipates his approach to stage composition. However, whatever their role in Strauss's overall development, these three works are hugely significant artworks in their own right. By 1889, Strauss had established himself as an exciting new voice within the tradition of Liszt and Wagner, and had written at least two masterpieces that would ensure his undying fame.

5 The second cycle of tone poems

JAMES HEPOKOSKI

Things suddenly deprived of their supposed meaning, of the place assigned to them in the so-called order of things … make us laugh. In origin, laughter is thus of the devil's domain. It has something malicious about it (things suddenly turning out different from what they pretended to be), but to some extent also a beneficent relief (things are less weighty than they appeared to be, letting us live more freely, no longer oppressing us with their austere seriousness).[1]

For those connoisseurs in the mid and late 1890s who were tracking the latest developments of musical "progress" (*Fortschritt*) in Austro-Germanic art music, there was no doubt. The most innovative orchestral works of the decade were the tone poems of the young modernist, Richard Strauss. Debated everywhere in these circles were the four stunners that comprise his second cycle of tone poems, each of which outflanked its predecessor in extremity and provocation: *Till Eulenspiegels lustige Streiche* (1894–5), *Also sprach Zarathustra* (1896), *Don Quixote* (1897), and *Ein Heldenleben* (1897–8). (A later work, *Symphonia domestica* [1902–3], not considered in this essay, may be regarded as an extension to this cycle, as might *Eine Alpensinfonie* [1915], for which Strauss jotted down a few sketches as early as 1899, considerably before taking up the work in earnest over a decade later.) For listeners today, becoming acquainted with their narrative programs along with a basic history of their composition is a simple task. Such background information is well known and widely available. The more pressing issue is to orient ourselves to the larger artistic purposes that motivated these works in the first place.

While these compositions persist in the repertory as spectacularized historical landmarks, one cannot reduce them only to their initial shock-value or still-ringing sonic thrills. They are also multifaceted in their implications, approachable from several different angles. On the one hand, as pro-institutional works they were intended to attract notice within an elite symphonic tradition. On the other hand, as splashy manifestos they also struck a pose of overturning that tradition's sober pieties through iconoclastic *lèse-majesté*, raffish parody, and, at times, nose-thumbing ridicule. They both sustained and undermined the institution. In this respect they were resounding emblems of the high-strung *Nervenkunst* that was sweeping a new-generational wave of modernism through all of the European arts. From another perspective the second-cycle works could be grasped autobiographically: Strauss as impish Till, as world-smashing Zarathustra, as mad and illusion-ridden Quixote, as himself qua composer. Or one could assess them careeristically: the entrepreneurial Strauss manufacturing sensational artistic merchandise towards the goal of unabashed self-promotion. Or technically: Strauss as avant-garde wizard of huge-ensemble orchestration and polyphony; as brilliant pastiche-coordinator of multiple compositional styles in the service of wide-ranging, ad hoc representations; as masterly conjurer of precise images and narratives; as harmonic and textural alchemist whose effects range from the calm or lush to the unbridled and chaotic; as composer-craftsman with an unparalleled sense of emancipation from the constraints of Classical symphonic form.

The conversion to Nietzscheanism

At the bottom of it lay Strauss's collapse of faith in the metaphysical view of music, with which he had probably never been entirely comfortable.[2] Strauss's "full-blown personal crisis"[3] emerged two or three years after the completion of the first cycle of tone poems and came to a head during the period that saw the completion and premiere of the opera *Guntram* (1892–3). By this time he had acquired a distaste for any naïve claim that music was a sacramental conveyor of altruistic, spiritual truths. This was the Schopenhauerian/Wagnerian view promoted not only at Bayreuth but also by his once-persuasive former mentor Alexander Ritter. Instead, breaking with Bayreuth's Cosima Wagner in an anti-Schopenhauerian letter from March 1, 1893, he began to embrace the antimetaphysical, anti-Christian, and self-affirming iconoclasm of Nietzsche and distance himself from the doctrine of *Willensverneinung*, the ascetic, self-renouncing denial of the Will so prized by Ritter.

With his reading of *Human, All Too Human, Beyond Good and Evil*, and *Thus Spoke Zarathustra*, a philosophical line was crossed.[4] Strauss was on his way to constructing a new musical aesthetic, capable, he thought, of reinvigorating German composition. The second tone-poem cycle provided a series of endorsements of a Nietzsche-fueled conception of music. "Gott ist tot," Nietzsche had written in 1882 and 1883.[5] In these tone poems from the later 1890s the god that Strauss declared dead was the overinflated musical *doxa* of the age, the bowed-head faith in music as a bearer of a mystical, redemptive content. Those metaphysical beliefs – phantoms, self-deceptions – were now to be sloughed off, laughed away, replaced with an embrace of the joyous physicality of the earth and the creative assertion of the unbound self. Music was still important as a human statement, a grand personal and cultural achievement, but it was no longer to be believed in as a bearer of world-transcendence.

To those musical idealists who grasped what the composer was doing, this was nothing short of apostasy. While in Strauss's hands the grand pillars of the Austro-Germanic symphonic temple remained standing, that temple was now desacralized, no longer the home of a god.[6] Strauss's reorientation projected a novel, often misunderstood style of modernism into art music. It participated in what Max Weber would later call the "disenchantment of the world" (*Entzauberung der Welt*), the falling-away of faith-based illusions. In the face of this matter-of-fact demythologizing, other modernist styles less eager to dispense with a hyper-elevated conception of music – even when more obviously dissonant – can seem outdated, clinging to an unsustainable aesthetics of self-absorption and inwardness, propped up with heavy-handed moral assessments. In that celebratory release from the encumbrances of austere seriousness lay the heart of the Strauss-tone-poem controversies that would dominate not only the 1890s but most of the next century as well.[7]

The dismayed Ritter saw all this coming in January, 1893, almost two years before the composer started to work on *Till*, writing in a concerned letter to Strauss: "What alone of Wagner has survived in you? The mechanics of his art. But to use this art for the glorification of a worldview that directly contradicts the Wagnerian is not to *build upon* Wagner's achievement, but: *to undermine it*."[8] The original listeners of Strauss's second cycle were presented with a sense of disorienting incongruity. Abundantly present were the splendor, orchestral power, and technical alliance with "musical progress" that they had associated with the redemptive claims of Schopenhauerian and Wagnerian metaphysics. And yet those associations were rendered inaccessible with these desacralized musical programs and displays, so eager to slap the face of that tradition.

It was not only a matter of flamboyant exhibits of pictorialism nor of the adoption of more detailed musical narratives, now outlined for audiences in instructive program notes by Strauss-authorized commentators (Wilhelm Mauke, Arthur Hahn, Wilhelm Klatte, Friedrich Rösch).[9] The composer had also chosen the programs as anti-idealistic affronts. They could hardly have been more deflationary in implication. While the instantly popular *Till Eulenspiegel* could be viewed by the naïve as a harmlessly *völkisch*, *gemütlich* tale, its deeper, "esoteric" program, noted in 1896 by its pro-Nietzsche dedicatee (and friend of Strauss), Arthur Seidl, was anti-institutional, a mocking rebellion against established rigidities. Here in *Till* we should recognize that "a superior spirit interacts with the external world … 'Épater le bourgeois!' War against all apostles of moderation, against the old guild of the merely virtuous and comfortable, against all good middle-class folk and secure 'schools of abstinence.'"[10] Celebrating gleeful destruction for its own sake and culminating in Till's seizure, trial, and (unsuccessful) execution by scandalized social authorities, these anarchic romps were veiled metaphors for the new, antimetaphysical music that Strauss was inaugurating.

Also sprach Zarathustra, the hypertrophic companion-piece to *Till*, was more explicit. Here Strauss turned the tables on the prevailing conviction that both absolute and program music could harbor deep philosophical truths: if the musical public wished to believe in musical philosophizing, why, then, he would give it to them. In this act of purposefully hyperbolic overreaching, he wrote immensely conceived music "freely after Nietzsche" (*frei nach Nietzsche*), loosely conjuring up selected ideas from a literal book of philosophy, or at least from a literal philosopher, since one issue has always been the degree to which the tone poem adheres to the narrative specifics of Nietzsche's *Zarathustra*.[11] From certain perspectives this was a *reductio ad absurdum* flung back at the tradition's face. Doubling the outrage, it was an atheistic philosophy that sought to ridicule and annihilate earlier, sentimentalized pieties – above all, Christianity and its morality of body-denying self-sacrifice. In its place was an *Übermensch* titanism repeatedly ushered in by a recurring disgust (*Ekel*) with the past coupled with a hearty, profane laughter that flooded away that past's burdensome illusions. "I should believe only in a God who understood how to dance," wrote Nietzsche in *Zarathustra*. "My devil … was the Spirit of Gravity – through him all things are ruined. One does not kill by anger but by laughter. Come, let us kill the Spirit of Gravity."[12]

If *Till* and *Zarathustra* could be construed "esoterically" as complementary works, opposite faces of the same coin – comic and serious, antihero and hero – so too could the next pair, *Don Quixote* and *Heldenleben*. In 1898 Strauss claimed to have conceived them as "direct pendants" to one another, with *Heldenleben* providing the context for an interpretation of *Quixote*.[13] However we interpret this remark, it is clear that selecting Cervantes's character as a topic served as another parody of an entrenched tradition within program music. Representative masculine heroes – strivers, achievers – were common fare in symphonic poems and other illustrative music. *Quixote* alluded to and deflated this tradition. This hero was no Prometheus, no Tasso, Dante, Hamlet, or Faust – not even a Macbeth or a Don Juan. Rather, he was a deluded dreamer drawn off the track of sanity by too much reading of chivalric novels, foolishly believing in the pursuit of imagined ideals, and Strauss illustrated him to appear as preposterous as possible. Youmans has elaborated the suggestion that the implied "knight" (*Ritter*) in this set of variations for cello and orchestra on a theme "of knightly character" (*ritterlichen Characters*) was none other than Alexander Ritter, the young Strauss's pious mentor, alluded to here as a stand-in for all believers in the metaphysics of music, the position of which

Strauss had once, in vain, tried to convince himself.[14] And yet for all of the musical hijinks and sensational mockery, the musical caricature is streaked with a wistful, "if only" flavor, as if Strauss were bidding a tender farewell to a once grand idea that never was and never could be true. As has been observed, such sentiments may be found more than once in the second-cycle works, at times surfacing as an aching nostalgia for the simplicity of the old illusions and their comforts. Even as he adopted Nietzscheanism as the leading edge of his tone-poem manifestos, it was neither absolute nor uncompromising. Mists of old-world sentiment continued to linger, and from time to time he appears to have questioned the thoroughness of his recent conversion and, disillusioned, to have wished only for withdrawal and peace.[15]

Raising the deflationary stakes to their utmost, Strauss now, in *Ein Heldenleben*, parodied another cherished aspect of the romantic-hero stereotype: not the elevated literary topic this time, as in *Quixote*, but rather the image of the masculine artist-creator. Here the broad target was the conception of the composer as a Promethean figure: the *Eroica*-propelled, Beethoven-through-Wagner legacy. In a calculated act of staged egoism Strauss now lionized himself as the tone poem's subject. He thus isolated a linchpin doctrine of the tradition and pushed it across any normative line of self-restraint. More to the point, he situated himself not in any idealized metaphysical empyrean but in the flat, everyday world that fluctuated between the careerist production of musical goods within the strife-torn marketplace of carping critics and the bourgeois concerns and erotic pursuits of personal-domestic life. Such a maneuver challenged at its core an aesthetic culture that, at least since Schiller, had insisted upon the purified separateness of art from the affairs of this world – the aesthetic sphere conceived as an emancipatory realm of freedom. *Symphonia domestica*, composed about five years later, would be an even more outrageous successor to the *Heldenleben* assault, depicting the ordinary concerns of a typical day in the Strauss household.

Like the other second-cycle tone poems, *Ein Heldenleben* offers multiple, sometimes contradictory implications co-existing in tension. Its aim was not entirely destructive. On the contrary, in this self-aggrandizing display one may perceive a performative act of personal affirmation, a quasi-Nietzschean heroic deed promulgated under the aegis of a new aesthetic regime. This is obvious in its demonstration of an undeniably formidable musical accomplishment, a sonic presence meant to astonish at every turn. At the same time this is tongue-in-cheek music writ large. Its very orchestral grandiosity plays into this contradiction. The more ostentatious the musical apparatus, the more disproportionate is the gap between the physical splendor of sound and the banal everydayness of what is claimed to be represented. It is not merely the piece's concept that launches a siege on cherished aesthetic convictions; it is also its performative enactment on the concert stage, the resonant physicality of its acoustic effect on audiences.

Music and historical progress

Particularly in its original 1890s context, the music conjured up in these second-cycle tone poems was astounding. Immense, hyper-rich worlds of sound were made to appear and disappear with a frictionless ease and magic that took one's breath away. Driven by audacity and nerves, the sheer exhibitionism of it all was an essential part of its claim to represent the *ne plus ultra* of modern practice. Central to the enterprise was a continual display of a technological complexity that overrode past limits of taste and technique. Moreover, the coolness and calculating mastery of the hand that set all this into motion gave the impression that the works were being produced as if to show objectively (or, as some came to suspect, cynically)[16] what could now be done with modern textural, harmonic, and orchestral resources. The result was analogous to a public demonstration of the latest wonders of newly manufactured industrial equipment capable of serving modern needs more productively.

The progress claimed by the supporters of such music was sometimes recast as a simple fact of reality, a correlate of the age's technological advances. Writing in 1896, Arthur Seidl asserted that *Eulenspiegel* had displayed an "empirical progress in the analysis of the life of the soul, from the differentiation of the feelings to the laying-bare of the nerves."[17] For Hans Merian (in a trenchant commentary on *Zarathustra* from 1899) the essence of Strauss's modernism lay in his unswerving embrace of program music and overt pictorial effects.[18] The mere conveying of abstract feelings in music, so characteristic of early decades in the century, had now been overtaken by representations of clear images. Prior "architectonic fetters" and traditional compositional "rules" had yielded to the modern world of coloristic pictorialism. "These days," insisted Merian, "program music is a fact." As a result, "modern composers can express more complicated ideas than could the older masters." This new music was "poetry" [*Dichtung*] "in a higher sense … [and yet] it still remained, in all cases, music above all."[19]

"Music above all." Such remarks remind us that for all of the programmatic and philosophical interests driving these tone poems, Strauss was also pursuing musical issues of thematic construction, harmony, texture, orchestration, and form. This point plunges us into discipline-specific matters of craft that are difficult if not impossible to simplify. Not only did these works have to be composed, measure-by-measure, but each measure, each phrase, each larger section was also to respond to the musical urgencies and debates of the day. Here we confront these works' specifically musical qualities, professionally wrought and situated at every moment within an ongoing symphonic tradition. Technical concerns of expertise and originality are features that no commentator should downplay. Strauss invited his keenest listeners to savor musical details at their most specialized, set forth at the far end of over a century-and-a-half of theoretical and formal development.

Other composers noticed these things at once. Strauss's local and long-range effects served as a sourcebook for contemporary and later composers to imitate and extend: daring compositional ideas, innovative instrumental effects, swashbuckling melodic arcs, sudden chromatic slippages and tonal jolts, exploratory or shocking dissonances, overt depictions of eroticism, nervously busy and stratified polyphony, radical and sophisticated structural deformations. One cannot overstate this point. It is the larger part of the Strauss legacy, a musical counterpart to the aesthetic revolution that he was introducing into the turgid institution of art music. This is one reason why thumbnail descriptions of these pieces fall so short of conveying the plenitude and complexity that burst forth from virtually every page. No brief essay – and certainly not this one – can do justice to the countless details of musical and historical significance here. At best one might provide a sampler of a few musical features to serve as a spur to a more adequate examination of this music.

Aspects of musical style

Strauss's arsenal of hypermodern techniques ranged freely in the second cycle, stirring up controversy in their wake. Foreshadowing many of the practical concerns of film-music composers of the subsequent century, his style is best characterized as a mixture of different historical styles. To be sure, all of these works are shot through with unmistakable Strauss signatures: incandescent, prolonged dominant-seventh chords, $^6_4$ arrival-chord epiphanies, orchestrationally resonant chord-spacing, and so on. But what was most new to the later 1890s was his willingness to dip his musical brush into any number of stylistic paint-pots to produce ("objectively") the image-impression or mood-effect for which each moment called. In Strauss one encounters a manipulation of different styles evoked from a cool distance, summoned up as if in quotation marks, apart from an aesthetic commitment to any of them. This was a departure from the historical metanarrative of internal consistency and organic development still being pursued as a virtually moral imperative by other composers of the time. Coupled with the decentering of the authority of any single aesthetic narrative, this abundance of concurrently available style options resonated with the ever-emerging marketplace modernity of the age.

Morten Kristiansen has characterized Strauss's embrace of pluralism as an example of the era's interest in *Stilkunst* (an art of styles): the adoption of a stylistic volatility that alluded, as needed, to differing, connotatively marked historical identifiers. This *Stilkunst* embraced the "juxtaposing [of] contrasting styles inside of works," a purposely adopted "aesthetic of constant change" fully consistent, Kristiansen argues, with the "contemporary zeitgeist," a tightly coiled "culture of nerves" (*Nervenkultur*), and an obsession with rapidly shifting psychological states that several literary, artistic, and musical critics saw arising at the turn of the century.[20] Leon Botstein, similarly, has noted Strauss's detached "fragmentation," his "stylistic extraction and appropriation" of past practices, and his "disregard for consistency" as central features of the composer's style, one that might even be interpreted as a prefiguration of late-twentieth-century postmodernism.[21]

The quintessential Strauss might be recognized in any number of characteristic procedures and sounds: the composer returned to the same set of personalized topoi in each work, probably seeking in each case to surpass his earlier examples of them. The most obvious of these is the production of a self-enclosed scene of ironized wit, linked with an amusing narrative incident indicated in the program, that sometimes precipitates a sudden disorder or climactic calamity at its end. Often riddled with sonic gimmicks and historical style-allusions, such scenes seek to demonstrate how precise the pictorial capabilities of "progressive" music could be. *Till* is a succession of such tableaux. Much of its counterpart, *Don Quixote*, followed suit as an over-the-top pictorial extravaganza – windmill, sheep, penitents, coarse peasant girl, imagined ride through the air, the boat that capsizes. While somewhat more abstract in illustration, often depicting general conditions rather than narratives, many sections of *Zarathustra* and *Heldenleben* are underpinned by similarly illustrative aims. In the former, for instance, we encounter the hymn-singing of the soon-superseded *Hinterweltler* and, later, the probing scientists fugally examining a single three-note object from all angles, systematically turning it over and over in learned, academic fashion. In the latter we have the finger-pointing disapprovals of sniping critics, the hero's patiently repeated amorous advances (tried in various keys) to a skittish *des Helden Gefährtin* (solo violin) before she yields, and the immediately succeeding central battle with his ideological foes.

Another Straussian earmark is the ultra-lush love scene, a creamily scored sound-sheet of erotic bliss. Here the most direct model was the oboe-led, G major ("third mistress") episode from his own *Don Juan* (mm. 232–309). While *Till* and *Zarathustra*, occupied with other matters, do not feature extended passages along these lines, *Quixote* and *Heldenleben* do, replete with soaring melodies and provocative contrapuntal interiors. Quixote's F♯ major Dulcinea-Idyll (mm. 332–*c*. 371, beginning six bars before rehearsal no. 36) and the Hero's prolonged G♭ major, *mässig lang-sam* – marking the conquest of the *Gefährtin*, and beginning with one of Strauss's most luxuriantly surging ⁶₄s of arrival and the broadly spanned *Thema der Siegesgewissheit* ("Certainty-of-conquest theme," mm. 288–369) – provide touchstone illustrations. (Another, even more extravagant, occupies the vast center of *Symphonia domestica*: the potent erotics of cre-ativity, the onset of *Schaffen und Schauen* – Adagio, m. 600 [rehearsal no. 55] – eventually proceeding into more graphically construed sexual activ-ity.) Related to this sonorously gratifying topos is a mood of affectionate gentleness, especially in introductions and valedictory epilogues for his ironized heroes, notably Till, Quixote, and himself: winsome framings of their personalities and lovable quirks. Or his penchant for mock-pastoral episodes replete with ovine or *ranz-des-vaches* double-reed circular-ities: with chipper alertness in *Zarathustra* (mm. 435ff., rehearsal no. 26, shortly after the onset of the C major *Tanzlied*); with high parody in the sheep scene of *Quixote* (Variation II); and attaining a much-desired, per-sonal island of rest near the end of *Heldenleben* (m. 828 [rehearsal no. 99]), soon tipping into the hero's concluding *Vollendung*, or withdrawal from the world.

Strauss's harmonic language is riddled with cavalier shifts of tonal implication – casual chromatic twists – within melodic contexts that might otherwise have led us to expect a more straightforward diatonicism. The insouciance of his short-range glides from one tonal world to another can give the impression of an arbitrary sense of local key, a weakened tonal force capable of being slid from anywhere to anywhere else with the wave of a compositional wand. The opening seventeen bars of *Don Quixote*, three successive D major images of the knight, provide a much-noted illus-tration (Example 5.1). Considered seriatim, the three melodic modules give us the succession: largely normative, odder, oddest. Measures 1–4 (the hero's "knightly character," Arthur Hahn tells us)[22] are diatonic, leading a sprightly initial impulse into an expanded cadential progression (featuring a savory, sustained I⁶₅ in m. 3), concluding with a straightforward D major perfect authentic cadence at m. 4 (I:perfect authentic cadence [PAC]). The example's second module, mm. 5–12 ("the principal duty of the knight, to honor and protect his lady"), is more extravagant. Built on an exagger-ated, *grazioso* bowing and swooping, it is a parody of a parallel period. Here the sentential antecedent swerves outlandishly (m. 7) to an imperfect

Example 5.1 *Don Quixote*, mm. 1–17

authentic cadence a diminished fifth away, on A♭ (♭V:imperfect authentic cadence [IAC]!, m. 8), while the consequent reverses the tritonal deviation as though nothing unusual had happened, returning to the tonic D to conclude with a I:PAC in m. 12. (As Youmans remarks, such a D–A♭–D tonal course "lets us know [at once] that the protagonist is at the very least a strange bird.")[23] Even more eccentric is the codetta punctuation-tag in mm. 13–17 ("the dream-prone man, to whom even the simple appears as something dreadfully complex"), whose effect, however, seems like the solemn equivalent of "This I vow," or perhaps a self-crossing before one rises at the end of a prayer. (Strauss will later use this heartfelt module to furnish a lovingly valedictory end to the tone poem.) Here the chromatic chords slip liquidly from a "*Tristan*" half-diminished seventh (m. 13) through a succession of "forbidden-parallel" major–minor sevenths, heedless of normative voice-leading, in which a single "V^7" sonority (sometimes with augmented-sixth implications) is moved up and down by half-steps (with a melodically contoured upper voice) before settling on a deliciously gratifying I:PAC at m. 16.

Those of Strauss's critics who were accusing the composer of going too far sometimes pointed to his cacophonous dissonances. In turn, Strauss went out of his way to guarantee that each work would have its own "outrageous" moments, as if goading his opponents into denouncing the scandal. While these passages were invariably produced for pictorial purposes (moments of extremity or uproarious chaos), they became important forerunners of the twentieth-century emancipation of the dissonance. In 1896 Seidl noted that the multiple *fortissimo* soundings of the *Halt!* dissonances in the midst of the fever-delirium of *Tod und Verklärung* (trombones, tuba, and timpani, mm. 270–1, 278–9, 282–3, 287–8) had shocked some and been denounced as an "empty boxing of the ears" (*eitel Ohrgeschinder*).[24] Successors in the second cycle were forthcoming. Till's upsetting of the marketwives provides an obvious example (mm. 133ff.), as does the madly climactic illustration of his chase and capture by the authorities (mm. 500–73). In *Zarathustra* we have the celebrated bichordal fade-out conclusion, juxtaposing C (or perhaps an incomplete French sixth built above C) and B major – alluding to earlier C–B juxtapositions within the work and provoking an endless string of commentaries and explanations. *Quixote* is riddled with splashy dissonance-upsets, as the unhinged knight charges and routs one thing after another. Moreover, the work's introduction (Quixote's descent into delusion) drives to a climactic *telos* of bichordal madness, tritone-based dissociations representing a fractured consciousness (Example 5.2). Following Quixote's imagined transformation into a D minor knight-of-steel-resolve (trumpets and trombones, mm. 109–12, a determined, taut-muscled variant of the head-motive from m. 1), Strauss hurls the harmony, triple-*fortissimo*, first into a $B\flat^7$ sounded against an incomplete E^7, mm. 112–16 (with inner "resolutions" to what amounts to an extended stack of thirds, or an $E\flat^9$ chord, mm. 113, 115), then into a repetitively jammed, incomplete A^7 (V^7 of the ensuing D minor) against $E\flat^7$, mm. 117–20. In *Heldenleben* there is the central battle-scene (*Des Helden Walstatt*, beginning with off-stage, call-to-arms fanfares at m. 369 [rehearsal no. 42]), that occupies most of the developmental space,

Example 5.2 *Don Quixote*, mm. 109–22

unleashing a manic tableau goaded onwards by the militaristic prodding of snare drum and percussion (m. 434).

Apart from such Straussian fingerprints, the tone poems (especially the post-*Till* ones) are marked by a self-promoting grandiosity in orchestral size, length, and sonic splendor. In *Zarathustra*, *Quixote*, and *Heldenleben* Strauss pursued a sonorous and structural massiveness exceeding prior limitations. Within individual tableaux this often claimed by sheer fiat a liberated monumentality uncontainable by mere convention – a declaration that the "new man" celebrated by Nietzsche has been forcefully emancipated beyond the norms.

The famous, C major opening of *Zarathustra* – a blazing illuminated initial too well known to need citing here – provides an illustration in terms of absolute *Klang* (sonority). One likely candidate for its immediate model would be the closing three or four bars of Liszt's *Les Préludes*: a similar, C major fanfare-paroxysm of orchestral sound. But what Liszt had placed at the end as the ecstatic, cadential *telos* of a heroic life, Strauss situated at the beginning, with an immensely augmented orchestra (including contra-bassoon and low-rumbling organ) and a much-expanded time-span. It is as if Liszt's programmatic hopes (old romantic illusions) were only starting-points for the new antimetaphysical philosophy. From another perspective in its acoustic references to an emerging overtone-series from raw sound, Strauss's opening recalled the *creatio ex nihilo* openings of Beethoven's Ninth Symphony and Wagner's *Das Rheingold* – there, in both cases, an initial creative stirring; here, an ego-centered conquering of sonic territory. The underlying conception remained: starting from natural overtones, the acoustic emergence of sound, then of music. In *Zarathustra* Strauss recast the idea as a three-gesture event. Over a deep, resonant C pedal funda-mental, one first hears two flaring sonic-convulsions: the major-to-minor one, an initiating surge not yet capable of sustaining its overtone-frame, is at once strengthened into a more stable minor-to-major complement. Each is responded to by elemental triplet-pounding in the timpani. These raw-acoustic phenomena are followed by the great moment of continu-ation: the thrilling leap into "music" with the subdominant chord, m. 15. This is a musical shock beyond mere acoustics, proceeding harmonically into the sonically unprecedented *Klang*-cadence at m. 19. Considered as a whole – in formal terms – this famous opening is shaped as a colossal sen-tence: two briefer, complementary gestures (*aa′*, mm. 5–8, 9–12), the sen-tence's presentation modules; followed by a more expansive continuation (*b*, mm. 13–21).[25] At the same time, the opening measures are packed with a complex of programmatic references. In 1896 Arthur Hahn identified the opening î–ŝ–ŝ in the unison trumpets as an elemental *Natur-Thema* (a world as yet without humans) as well as "something mysterious, unfathom-able, a great, unsolved riddle," while in 1899 Hans Merian agreed, referring to its "elemental Being" also as the "World-Riddle … Nature the Sphinx that gazes upon us with empty, starless eyes." This "Nature theme" or "world-riddle," however, comes to us from a Nietzschean world.[26] It is not too extravagant to propose that the three rising notes, here and especially later in the tone poem, may also be underlaid with *Gott ist tot*, the proclam-ation of a godless, purely physical nature eventually to be embraced as such by the liberated superman.

Or consider the opening statement of *Ein Heldenleben* (Example 5.3), the initial presentation of *Der Held* ("the hero"), not surprisingly in Beethoven's *Eroica* key of E♭ major. (The intended connection between the two works is obvious enough.) Once again, in terms of thematic

Example 5.3 *Ein Heldenleben*, mm. 1–19

format this is a large-scale sentence (*aa′b*, mm. 1–2, 3–4, 5–17) – or, more accurately, a sentence-chain, in which each successive continuation (*b*) is itself shaped as a sentence, beginning with another *aa′*-type presentational unit.[27] (Strauss often favored the thematic shapes of sentences and sentence-chains in these works.) Typical also is the enormously wide range and registral disposition of the melody, leaping over and through multiple octaves with unconfined heroic strides and sharp-angled, whiplash twists, commanding broad expanses of musical space. Nor is the hero to be contained by the diatonic traditions of any single tonality. While the statement begins and ends in E♭, the theme momentarily breaks free of these shackles with the accented, quasi-whole-tone descent at m. 7;[28] returns to E♭ by mm.

8–10; stretches upward, sequentially, to a hyperintense E major sonority (E♭ "arbitrarily" pulled up a half-step); then returns to a cadential $^6_4$ in E♭ at m. 13 to pursue a florid and decisive cadence in that key. The ever-moralistic Adorno cited the seemingly "wrong notes" F and C in the melody at the end of m. 3 as an illustration of what he regarded as Strauss's careless composition, marked by an "imprecision of details." The perceived problem was that those two pitches do not belong within the implied E♭ chord. "Their effect is to obscure: they are designed to blur the pedantry of the surrounding chords: in the *élan* of the theme, the individual notes become irrelevant as opposed to the irresistible whole." As Adorno assessed it, like so many other effects in Strauss, they seemed to produce only irresponsible "jet flame" effects over banal and commonplace chords.[29] To be sure, such free melodic dissonances are characteristic of Strauss as modernist. But there is no reason to suppose that they were casually written. Not only do the non-chordal tones reinforce the image of the hero's irrepressible character, but this fleeting deviation away from normative pitches is also soon succeeded, as part of an intensifying pattern, by the two more telling escapes from E♭ diatonicism mentioned above.

Illustrative program and musical form

Essential to the production of programmatic musical scenes is an assumed generic contract between composer and listener whereby musical ideas are agreed to be mappable onto aspects of specific characters or situations: let motives A, B, and C represent narrative-images X, Y, and Z. Without an initial agreement to accept this principle of musical metaphor, the tone-poem premise collapses. To suggest that it might be appropriate to listen to these works as absolute music or that they are adequately comprehensible in terms of pure music alone is to blind oneself to the historically controversial and witty aesthetic game that the tone poems are playing. Once the central musical signifiers for each work are grasped, it becomes a simple matter to follow their recurrences and transformative adventures. Hence the importance of the initially published, authorized guidebooks from the 1890s, which not only provided listeners with the broad outlines of the intended narratives (while still leaving much to the imagination) but also decoded the various motives. Still, the official explanations are only starting-points for more advanced inquiries. Are they truly reliable or only safe public statements? Do the explanations themselves need to be decoded? What might they have suppressed, ignored, glossed over, or sanitized? What are their larger "esoteric" implications? While composing the works did Strauss have these (or other) labels in mind?[30]

From the perspective of the signifying motives, one aspect of the musical form may be construed as purely narrative: tracing the linear adventures of a single masculine identity (or, in *Zarathustra*, an inexorable ruling idea) marked by a cluster of recognizable attributes and put through a paratactic series of different environments or adventures. Under these lights the poetic form of the story, with its own climaxes and denouements, may be taken to be a sufficient guarantor of linear graspability apart from any allusion to more traditional formal prototypes. This may be the way that most of Strauss's non-professional listeners have heard these pieces – as musically narrated, engaging tales. At the heart of this lies the familiar technique of thematic transformation: mood- and situation-reshapings of easily recognized pitch- and contour-shapes. While this (Berlioz-, Liszt-, and Wagner-influenced) technique is so obvious that it requires no extended commentary here, it is nonetheless central to our experience of these works: how many ways can Strauss refashion individual ideas?

Example 5.4 shows five instances (of many) from *Till Eulenspiegel*. The opening four bars of prologue (5.4a), Mauke tells us, sought to depict the onset of the telling of a narrative, *Es war einmal ein Schalksnarr* ("Once upon a time there was a knavish fool").[31] Recast into 6/8 meter and accelerated in tempo, the same initial pitches soon become one of Till's central identifiers, the *arger "Kobold"* ("wicked 'goblin'") motive (5.4b), the *lustig* sign of the irrepressibly teasing prankster.[32] The onset of the marketwives incident begins with a new transformation of the idea, m. 113, led off with carefully tentative, *piano* mutterings in the bass (5.4c), as if Till were tiptoeing unobserved into a social scene that he will soon disrupt (*Wartet auf, ihr Duckmeister!* ["Just wait, you fainthearts!"]). Examples 5.4d and 5.4e are taken from the "Pastor" scene, Till disguised as a sober minister entering with a dignified (Brahmsian) hymn (m. 179). In 5.4d (mm. 187–9) we are informed that we are to recognize Till by this mischievous bass-line figure, representing his "big toe" sticking out from under his robe, while in the immediately following 5.4e we are apparently to sense Till's high-pitched, smug complacency (m. 195, solo violin) just before he begins to shiver with fears about his own mocking of religion (mm. 196–201). Similar examples could be multiplied throughout not only *Till* but also all of the other tone poems. (As suggested in Examples 5.1 and 5.2 above, the transformations of the opening bar of *Don Quixote* – the primary image of the knight – are also noteworthy.)

The task of uncovering the musical principles that govern the large-scale architecture of each of these compositions is more difficult. As is also common in Strauss's earlier tone poems, each of the four works furnishes us with a narrative succession of individualized, contrasting tableaux, well stocked with reappearing, reshaped motives. To what degree are the

Example 5.4a–e *Till Eulenspiegels lustige Streiche*, opening idea and transformations

consecutive musical scenes, grouped together, dialogically relatable to any of the traditional *Formenlehre* patterns as handed down to the late nineteenth century? In no case does the paratactic succession outline a familiar pattern in familiar ways.

When the tableaux-contrasts include matters of tempo and character, as they customarily do, it is inviting to try to grasp the entire complex as alluding to the traditional four-movement plan: opening movement, slow movement, scherzo, and finale. As Steven Vande Moortele has recently noted, this much-noted "integration of elements of multi-movement patterns into single-movement designs was a constant concern of many composers of the nineteenth century." Citing familiar examples ranging from Beethoven and Schubert through Liszt, Strauss (*Don Juan*, *Heldenleben*, and *Domestica*), Schoenberg, and others, Vande Moortele redubbed this format "'two-dimensional sonata form': the combination of sections of a sonata cycle and movements of a sonata form at the same hierarchical level in a single-movement composition … the projection of a sonata form onto an entire through-composed sonata cycle."[33] Dahlhaus had termed this a "multimovement form within a single movement"; for William S. Newman the structure had been a "double-function sonata."[34] Some caveats are pertinent: the concept of a rapid scherzo is to be understood freely; and "movements" need not coincide with the standard zones of a sonata, though the "finale" impression sometimes begins with the onset of a recapitulatory space. The multimovement aspect of the two-dimensional idea is significant and introduces its own set of interrelated issues. Analysts, for example, have had differing views on its applicability and clarity of demarcation in each piece. Nevertheless, the concept is elementary, and that feature will not be pursued here.

More problematic is the other side of the double-function issue: the potential dialogical relationship of each tone poem's entire tableau-sequence, programmatically inflected, to any of the institutionally sanctioned musical formats, even as they had been modified by the end of the century. To what extent might we justifiably perceive implied allusions, however transient or free, to the procedures of once-normative sonata form, sonata-rondo form, theme and variations, and so on? The challenge is to perceive the formal clues that Strauss gives us along the way and then flexibly to imagine how and for which purposes he might have wished us to regard the ongoing succession as potentially in dialogue (or not) with any of a number of these conventional structural formats. Now marketing himself as a brash modernist and Nietzschean "free spirit," Strauss's characteristic approach was to provide gestures towards one or more of these formats (thereby claiming himself as a participant within an honored tradition on whose accrued cultural distinction he was capitalizing) but simultaneously to stage such reassurances as generationally out of date through a transgressive emancipation from their normative constraints. What one encounters is an audacity of conception that explodes definitional aspects of the forms from within. The first two of the tone poems are perhaps the most formally innovative, and it is with these two that we shall spend the most time.

The title-page of *Till Eulenspiegel* famously declares that the work is disposed *in Rondeauform* (though *nach alter Schelmenweise*, "in the old roguish manner"). Heightened by the antique spelling of "rondo" (an insider's wink of the eye), the reference to an institutionally orthodox form declares an intention to conform to formal behavior that the work delights in shattering. This is no ordinary rondo within which predictable recurrences of a generally stable refrain-theme are separated by contrasting episodes. Instead, once past the brief, initial introduction of Till, the remainder of the piece unspools a paratactic string of adventure-episodes, within which the "rondo" elements, the Till-identifiers, are constantly present and threaded throughout. Thus the "rondo" themes and the episodes are simultaneously present: a strikingly modernist idea, appropriate for Strauss's narrative predilections. From this perspective one can also read the successive episodes as differing adventure-cycles of the same rondo-ideas. This circular or helical aspect – one rotation of the generative ideas cycling into the next – can be regarded as an instance of what I have elsewhere called *rotational form*: successive presentations of similarly ordered, often-transforming material, including the possibility of free variants, expansions, and modular omissions.[35] At the same time, one can perceive droll gestures towards the "good behavior" of a *sonata*-rondo in the large-scale arrangement. Not long after the episode in which Till mocks the academic philistines, we re-encounter the familiar solo-horn motive (m. 429, twelve measures after rehearsal no. 28), an obvious reprise of the opening (m. 6) and a telling signal that invites us to understand the moment as the launch of a potentially well-mannered recapitulation. Not surprisingly, what follows is the most disruptive, unleashed music in the work, a "recapitulation" torn to shreds at every stage, even while several of the motives from earlier in the piece do manage to resurface, albeit transformed, in the expected order. In sum (and engaging with Strauss's "rondeau" paratext), the work's tableau-succession may also be grasped as an extreme sonata-rondo deformation. It maintains a transgressive dialogue with the norms of a sonata-rondo, whose typical, "textbook" procedures and options are to be kept in mind as a benchmark by the listener, even as the piece regularly and brazenly violates those norms – mocks them – as a manifesto of modernist liberation.[36]

This liberation is more aggressively proclaimed in *Also sprach Zarathustra*, whose large-scale organization and programmatic implications are more puzzling than those of the other three works. The structure of *Zarathustra* superimposes a number of principles. One of them, the tonal conflict between the tonalities of C and B, suggesting the irreconcilability of nature and humankind, has been so frequently discussed that it need not be rehearsed again here. Instead, we can focus on another important structural procedure: that of the staging of a process of persistent overcoming, whereby each major section (or section-pair) begins forthrightly but is allowed to flourish only so far before encountering a field of dissolution or an outright rejection. The resulting disintegration leads to another rebirth-cycle of similar materials on a higher level of human emancipation from superstition and naïveté. Each cycle (or cycle-pair) presents reconceived transformations of the germinal motives of the piece. From this perspective the form is freely rotational, with each rotation-tableau replacing its predecessor and aspiring to a higher philosophical status. In addition, the

Example 5.5a *Also sprach Zarathustra,* "Nature"

Example 5.5b *Also sprach Zarathustra,* "Reverent shudder"

Example 5.5c *Also sprach Zarathustra,* "Longing"

Example 5.5d *Also sprach Zarathustra,* "Of the afterworldsmen"

Example 5.5e *Also sprach Zarathustra,* "Of joys and passions"

Example 5.5f *Also sprach Zarathustra,* "Disgust"

successive cycles are connected in such a manner as to suggest here and there a tangential, free dialogue with aspects of sonata form, while never concretizing its realization of that traditional format.

The famous introduction, Rotation 1, lays out some of the most fundamental motives of the piece (Example 5.5a–c) and is the referential,

Example 5.5g *Also sprach Zarathustra*, "Ideal" theme

Example 5.5h *Also sprach Zarathustra*, "Dance" theme

generative source for many of the variants and expansions found in the later rotations: the colossal material being of Nature, the C major Î–5̂–8̂, also posing a world-riddle to be faced by humanity (5.5a); the cowering human response in the muted low strings, a "reverent shudder" (*ein andachtsvoller Schauer*; 5.5b); and the embryo of humankind's B minor "Longing theme" (*Sehnsuchts-Thema*), the urge to inquire and understand (5.5c). A fearful and primitive response in the muted horns, representing blind religious faith (Strauss underlaid it with the words *Credo in unum deum*), leads to the first of four successive rotation-pairs (double rotations, or eight rotations in all). These may be designated as Rotations 2a–b, 3a–b, 4a–b, and 5a–b. In each pair the first half (a), the positive tableau, presents a temporary solution to the world-riddle, superseding prior stages but decaying or proving insufficient at its end. In the second half (b), the negative tableau, we find a distorted commentary on the wreckage or destruction of the insufficient solution proposed in the first, along with a reorientation and preparation for the next stage to come. The initial pair, Rotations 2a and b, is concerned with religious faith and its loss: *Von der Hinterweltlern* ("Of the afterworldsmen"), whose theme, Example 5.5d, smooths out the shudder of Example 5.5b; and *Von der großen Sehnsucht* ("Of the great longing"), expanding on the "Longing" motive, Example 5.5c, then proceeding to a sharp Nature critique (*Gott is tot!*, Î–5̂–8̂) of any attempt to continue the religious life.

We are soon thrown into Rotations 3a and b, *Von der Freuden- und Leidenschaften* ("Of joys and passions") and *Das Grablied* ("Song of the grave"). Of these, the stormy and feral "joys and passions," locking onto an earnest C minor (Example 5.5e) and representing a stirringly youthful, religion-free embrace of the "stream of life," is eventually blocked from further progress by the first statement of the important motive of "Disgust" (*Ekel*) sounded *fortissimo* in the trombones (Example 5.5f). The ensuing *Grablied*, a zone of stark dissolution (with some recurrences of the Nature motive) surveys the damage in spectral and mysterious, proto-expressionistic textures.

Rotations 4a and b comprise *Von der Wissenschaft* ("Of science") and *Der Genesende* ("The convalescent"), which itself subdivides into two parts separated by the emphatic, full-force return of the Nature motive on C (recalling the opening of the work) and a hyperdramatic grand pause. *Von der Wissenschaft* presents us with the slow Science fugue – an image of dry rationality, the academic scrutiny of the Nature motive – soon spinning into a more animated recurrence of B minor longing that immediately sprouts a new, clearly aspirational continuation, the B major "Ideal theme" (*Weise des Ideals*), as Hans Merian dubbed it in 1899 (Example 5.5g).[37] In turn this triggers a first, anticipatory glimpse of the new man-to-come, Zarathustra, in the dotted-rhythm "Dance theme" (*Thema des Tanzes*; Example 5.5h), and this unexpected vision provokes dizzying recurrences of the Disgust motive. The vehement first part of "The convalescent" depicts the violent unspooling of belief in scientific rationality – the fugue – in the face of Being and Nature itself. It builds to a blindingly climactic, open-fifth return, on C, of the $\hat{1}$–$\hat{5}$–$\hat{8}$ Nature motive, the persistently unsolved riddle, triple-*fortissimo*, in the full orchestra.[38] And then … an astonishing silence. (This long pause responds to a parallel moment of physical collapse in Nietzsche's own *Der Genesende* section, from Part 3 of the book, in which Zarathustra, overwhelmed by an epiphany of the abyss of material Being, "fell down like a dead man and remained like a dead man for a long time," only to be granted, upon reawakening, the hidden secret of eternal recurrence: "Everything goes, everything returns; the wheel of existence rolls forever.")[39] "The convalescent" restarts on a low-register, leaden B minor triad and is soon extracted from this pitch-black lethargy (stirred by the contrary urges of Longing and Disgust) to enter unexpectedly into a new lightness of being marked by Nietzschean laughter. This is the throwing-off of weights, the dismissal of the Spirit of Gravity. Even the Disgust motive is now lightened into humor. Urged onward by forward-pointing citations of the Longing and Dance themes, the music enters an exalted and prolonged corridor leading into what is to be celebrated in the next rotation-pair: the new, antimetaphysical human being.

Rotations 5a and b, "The dance song" (*Das Tanzlied*) and "The night-wanderer's song" (*Das Nachtwandlerlied*), draw together and recast in radical transformations the principal motives of the piece (those from Example 5.5). Promised as a final revelation, the exaggeratedly trivial, popular-style opening of the "The dance song" – Strauss's riskiest wager in the piece – comes as a shock. What may strike some as an anticlimactic purveying of C major cabaret-*Kitsch* must have been intended instead to convey the audacity of the new lightness, along with a mock-pastoral sense of peace and expansiveness released through the shrugging off of tradition. This new aura of liberation is confirmed several minutes later by an affirmationally exuberant re-sounding and peroration of the Dance theme. The remainder of the "Dance song" moves through further stages of thematic transformation that eventually coalesce around colossal intensifications of the Longing motive, driven through various tonal areas (often lurched onto as violent tonal shocks), seeking but never cadentially attaining its resolution into C major. This inability to close cadentially, an ecstatically immense "almost," is central to the tone poem's philosophical agenda of non-closure in a new world shorn of faith and definitive answers. It pushes the music into a vertiginous zone of mounting decay. At the moment of its *Götterdämmerung*-like collapse, a convulsive triple-*fortissimo* marked also with the first of the "midnight" bell-strokes, we merge into Rotation 5b. "The night-wanderer's song" concludes the work in two phases: a prolonged *diminuendo* from this negative crest; and a slow, B major fade-out epilogue grounded in a return of the Ideal theme, suggesting humanity's persistent dream of proceeding further, into an uncharted future. At the end it dissolves away with the famous C–B ambiguity.[40]

How are these rotations related, if at all, to any notion of sonata form? The sonata idea persists as a much-weakened shaping principle that is alluded to at various referential stations of the work but is never carried out in any easily explained way.[41] Rotations 1 and 2a–b can be initially construed as an extended, multisectional introduction, particularly since Rotation 3a, "Of joys and passions," sounds much like the onset of a sonata exposition. On the other hand, central material is also set forth in Rotations 1 and 2a–b, which are in some important senses expository as well, and if Rotation 3a is to be construed as the primary-theme marker of a just-launched exposition, that exposition is soon aborted (with the arrival of the Disgust motive and entry into the *Grablied*), failing to produce a secondary theme proper. Rotation 4a–b, "Science" and "Convalescent," may be interpreted as occupying an episodic developmental space – a procedure familiar from Strauss's earlier tone poems. "The dance song," Rotation 5a, suggests the onset of a freely transformed recapitulation (though it is at first based on materials from Rotations 1 and 2a–b), while Rotation 5b, "The night-wanderer's song," devolves into an epilogue-coda. Complicating the whole matter, though, are not only important tonal factors but also the seeming lack of a properly situated secondary theme. In the "recapitulatory" Rotation 5a, the Longing theme, associated earlier in the work with B minor, seeks a sonata-like apotheosis-transformation into C major (which it does not fully attain). This can suggest that at least here that theme is taking on aspects of one type of late-nineteenth-century secondary-theme behavior. It may be that

Strauss invites us to imagine that the Longing theme, in its disparate and scattered placements earlier in the work, has been aspiring to become a secondary theme within a sonata form. (The Ideal theme, similarly, may be one of its most transformed mutations.) In *Zarathustra* the sonata idea, only dimly discernible at best, functions largely as a remembered vessel, an antique container demonstrated via occasional allusions as inadequate to hold these massive new contents.

The "fantastic variations on a theme" of *Don Quixote* present us with conflicting impressions. On the one hand, aspects of its paratactic structure are obviously similar to those of *Till* and *Zarathustra*: what we find is the familiar Straussian string of leitmotivically interrelated, illustrative tableaux through which the protagonist is made to advance. In this case, as with *Till*, the whole is framed by an extended introduction (Quixote falling into madness and deciding to set out on his quests) and an epilogue-"finale" (the knight's death) that recycles, as a concluding valediction, a portion of the music of the introduction. On the other hand, it is difficult not to conclude that the ordering of these tableaux is freer, more arbitrary, than those of its predecessors: could not some of the interior adventures be reordered without significant effect on the whole? More to the point, unequivocal allusions to the normative indicators of sonata form are now absent. Strauss was now asking his audiences to conceptualize the episodic whole under the looser category of theme and variations.[42] Most significantly, there is no *rappel à l'ordre* provided by any sense of recapitulation-onset – a crucial moment of strong articulation in the preceding two tone poems and in those of the first tone-poem cycle. This purposeful lack makes any retrospective identification of a deformational exposition impossible. Or nearly so. The structural problem is that even while the successive-chapter architecture of the whole seems to preclude the relevance of the sonata concept, Strauss did stock the work with some characteristic thematic types that in a more logically ordered world might have been used for sonata or sonata-deformational purposes. Thus the Quixote theme (especially in the solo cello as it restarts the theme after the introduction, four measures before rehearsal no. 13, m. 122) – or, if one prefers, the Quixote/Sancho complex – strikes one as a potential "masculine-protagonist" primary theme, just as the ideal "Lady" or "Dulcinea" theme (for example, at rehearsal no. 17, m. 170) sounds as though it could have been deployed as a generically standard "feminine-redemptrix" secondary theme. But it may be the point that in this crazed Quixote-world recognizably sonata-like themes are discursively scrambled in ways that cannot be assimilated into cogent sonata-logic. The sonata-form background-concept is present only in its absence or unattainability. To the extent that one might wish to entertain this idea, we may conclude – once again – that even the arbitrary thematic organization and sectional design in *Quixote* contribute via negation and disorientation to the larger programmatic idea governing the whole.[43]

While *Till*, *Zarathustra*, and *Quixote* show us a Strauss moving ever further away from allusive references to a historically enervated sonata concept, *Ein Heldenleben* surprises by turning once again, more explicitly, to that format. But this is no mere retrenchment. On the contrary, the return to a more clearly sonata–deformational practice can seem transgressive in a larger sense, as if it had been deployed to demonstrate the new-world hero's right to reconceive a venerable tradition as audaciously as possible. Invading and conquering the old "Classical" lands on modern terms: this seizure of old ground, replete with pitched battles for control against persistent militias of resistance, motivates the architectural design of *Heldenleben*. The familiar sonata stations are there not as passive nods to tradition but rather as highlighted signposts that mark off, zone-by-zone, which conventional features of the form are being conceptually overpowered at any given moment as one self-enclosed tableau is succeeded by another.

This is not to say that all of the sonata aspects of this hypertrophic work are self-evident. The twenty-minute exposition, for instance (mm. 1–368), comprises four contrasting tableaux: the entry of the masculine hero (E♭, mm. 1–117);[44] the hero's initial struggles with his opponents (*Des Helden Widersacher*; mm. 118–c. 191); the wooing of "The hero's feminine companion" (*Des Helden Gefährtin*; m. 192, three measures after rehearsal no. 22); and a subsequent love scene marked by the wide-spanning "Certainty-of-conquest theme" (*Thema der Siegesgewißheit*; m. 288 [rehearsal no. 32]–368, now settling into and concluding in a sustained G♭ major). That we are to regard the *Gefährtin* and *Siegesgewißheit* music as occupying a "feminine" secondary-theme space seems likely,[45] but what about the preceding *Widersacher* tableau? Is that the first part of a double secondary theme of differing contrasts, as some have suggested?[46] Or is it a tableau standing in for a more traditional transition away from the primary theme? Or might it be better regarded, as I prefer to think, as an interruption in the sonata form – a distractive parenthesis-episode that the heroic composer is obliged to bear and confront: the petty objections of nitpicking critics? The developmental space (m. 369, rehearsal no. 42; *Des Helden Walstatt*) is given over to distant calls to battle followed by the unrestrained furor of combat. While there can be no doubt that the recapitulatory space proper is launched only with the enormous structural downbeat and *fortissimo* reprise of the opening music at m. 631 (rehearsal no. 77), its tonic E♭ had been set in place several bars earlier (m. 616), as a non-normative tonic preparation (proclaiming an ecstatic victory) for the recapitulatory re-entry of the all-vanquishing hero. And the recapitulatory space from this point onwards is totally reconceived as a celebration of achievement, marred only by recurring, interruptive spats with the not-yet-pacified remnants of old-guard criticism and moving inexorably towards the eroticized pastoral-vision of a satisfied (but surely temporary) withdrawal from the struggle.

But withdrawal is hardly the lasting impression provided by these four aggressive tone poems considered as a group. All four were locked in joyous battles with the symphonic traditions and expectations of the 1890s, particularly as institutionalized in the agendas of Austro-Germanic conservatories and universities, along with those of the partisan press. To remind ourselves of those contextual battles is the first step in reawakening the often-disturbing implications harbored in this music. Naïvely to enjoy these works is profoundly to misconstrue them. Far better to grasp how riddled they are with provocation and challenge: in Strauss's renunciation of the ideology of absolute music (orthodox "musical logic") in favor of a modernist embrace of an intensely detailed program music ("poetic logic"); in his irreverent deflations of the elevated topics that had nourished art music's metaphysical fantasies for decades; in his attraction to the atheistic, "free-spirit" laughter of Nietzscheanism; in his disquieting intermixture of symphonic high purpose and boisterous sonic sprees; in his easy acceptance of the concept of symphonic music both as an esteemed craft that sustained his conception of high culture and as a frankly commodified product to be introduced into the urban-modern marketplace of art. Most unsettling of all, perhaps, is the impression of total control and *Übermensch*-ease with which young Strauss, striding into the arena as pure ego, had set this scandalous gigantism into motion.

Strauss's tone poems were the most significant and influential orchestral works of their decade. The controversies that they aroused continued to unfold throughout most of the twentieth century, even as the art-music project was falling into a decline in social relevance, challenged by more commercially viable musical sectors in rapidly changing times. Throughout it all these pieces remained formidable staples of the concert and recorded repertory. Not only were they championed as personal vehicles by influential star conductors, but they also served as exhibition-pieces for virtuoso orchestras competing with each other in increasingly meticulous, razor-sharp performances. Their continued attraction among the broad musical public surely had little to do with any prolonged reflection on the quasi-nihilism that they had once been advancing, nor with any adequate grasp of the complexities of their musical contents. They appealed, more superficially, as repertory objects offering a seductive immediacy of rich instrumentation along with massively grand, climactic deliveries. Here one could experience orchestral glamour. And orchestral glamour sold tickets. By the second half of the century this led seamlessly into the "living stereo" market (discs of the tone poems as demonstrations of proudly owned, high-tech woofers and tweeters), followed not long after by such appropriations as the popular-culture ubiquity of that Kubrickian extract. In not a few scholarly quarters the tone poems were regarded as unsuitable material for serious treatment and research. It has only been in the past two decades that these tone poems – the first and second cycles along with *Symphonia domestica* and *Eine Alpensinfonie* – have been reopened for significant discussion and a much-needed rethinking. One senses that new debates about them have just begun.

6 Strauss's road to operatic success: *Guntram, Feuersnot,* and *Salome*

MORTEN KRISTIANSEN

The years from the completion of his first opera *Guntram* in 1893 to that of *Salome* in 1905 were pivotal to the career and aesthetic development of Richard Strauss: his operatic fortunes changed from failure to success, his creative focus from tone poem to opera, his philosophical allegiance from Schopenhauer to Nietzsche, and his aesthetic orientation from relative epigonism to assertive independence. The thread that connects these three dissimilar works is their implicit or explicit critique of Wagner. During the final decades of the nineteenth century Wagner's musical style and dramatic themes became the baseline against which all new works were measured, and critics typically referred to Wagner's successors as "epigones" because of their uninspired imitation of the older master.[1] The idealistic, quasi-Schopenhauerian themes of Wagner's works – especially redemption through love, Christian compassion, renunciation, and physical versus ideal love – appeared with limited variations and in diluted or superficial form in the serious operas of Strauss's most prominent colleagues, such as Wilhelm Kienzl (1857–1941), Felix Weingartner (1863–1942), Eugen d'Albert (1864–1932), Max von Schillings (1868–1933), and Hans Pfitzner (1869–1949). In this feebly obedient context Strauss's early operas stand out as radical documents. Although Strauss identified himself as a Wagnerian, this adherence became limited to musical style and principles: a huge, colorful, polyphonic, and dominant orchestra; an intricate web of leitmotifs; chromaticism; and placing drama above purely musical concerns. Aesthetically, however, Strauss progressed from pseudo-Wagnerian to anti-Wagnerian during the 1890s, and achieving independence of Bayreuth helped him become the only German opera composer of his time to emerge successfully from Wagner's shadow.

Guntram (1893)

Given his awe of Wagner's music dramas, Strauss had no desire to enter into competition with them, but Alexander Ritter (1833–96), his mentor from the mid 1880s until 1893, who had brought him into the fold of the programmatic composers and introduced him to the writings of Schopenhauer and Wagner, convinced him to confront this challenge and even supplied the subject matter.² Opting to write the libretto himself, a sine qua non among committed Wagnerians at the time, Strauss began working on the text in 1887 and did not finish until 1892 while on an extended trip to Egypt and Greece to recover from pleurisy.³ As we shall see, *Guntram* is very much a product of Wagnerian idealism, but with a few subtle yet crucial differences that alienated Bayreuth insiders, most notably Alexander Ritter, and initiated Strauss's ideological maturation.

As the opera begins we meet Guntram and his mentor Friedhold, members of a thirteenth-century German brotherhood of *Minnesinger* (the "champions of love") who disseminate their Christian message through music, as they minister to peasants brutally oppressed by the evil Duke Robert. When Guntram is invited to the court after preventing the suicide of Robert's compassionate wife Freihild, his powerful "peace narration" nearly provokes a rebellion, and he kills Robert in self-defense. Freihild now schemes to free the jailed Guntram, but before he can escape Friedhold arrives and demands that Guntram appear before the brotherhood for judgment. Refusing to submit, Guntram explains that he did the right thing for the wrong reasons (jealousy of Robert, and sinful physical attraction to Freihild), then breaks his lyre in disillusionment with the brotherhood's idealistic aims and pronounces his pivotal new credo: "Only the atonement of my choice can expiate my guilt; my spirit's decree governs my life; my God speaks to me only through myself!" Guntram now explains to Freihild that only their mutual renunciation will allow him to find redemption through solitary reflection and rejection of all worldly matters, then leaves her to assume her new role of benevolent ruler.

Receiving just five performances during 1894 to 1895 before falling into oblivion (four in Weimar, only one in Strauss's home town of Munich), *Guntram* was a resounding failure. Critics mostly noted the work's extensive imitation of Wagner (characters, plot, language, musical style) and enjoyed pointing out the specific Wagnerian sources of certain leitmotifs, or the fact that Guntram had 160 bars more to sing than Tristan.⁴ One conservative critic, who no doubt preferred the earlier Wagner of *Tannhäuser* and *Lohengrin*, deplored the fact that Strauss appeared to have taken Wagner's most advanced compositional techniques one step further: "In this opera Richard Strauss has written a score which in complexity, polyphony, tormented and tearing harmonies, nerve-whipping dissonances, new orchestrational effects, disturbing rhythm, and finally physical and spiritual demands on the endurance of the singers' throats, leaves *Tristan* far behind."⁵ At the opposite extreme, Ernest Newman claimed in hindsight that *Guntram* was at most five percent Wagner, showing the problematic nature of assessing Wagner's precise influence on Strauss – a question that has yet to be addressed in detail.[6] Although highly imitative of Wagner – the opening clearly recalls that of *Lohengrin*, for example – the music draws on the full range of Wagner's operas and also contains distinctly un-Wagnerian passages (a chord sequence with perfect intervals in parallel motion, for example), thus prefiguring the diverse mix of styles that would come to characterize Strauss's operas.[7]

It was the ideological dimension of *Guntram*, however, that had tremendous repercussions for Strauss's career. In most respects the opera falls in line with contemporary music drama; the Schopenhauerian themes listed above – redemption, renunciation, Christian compassion, and physical versus ideal love – are all central to the work. Nonetheless, Strauss treated the first two in a somewhat unconventional manner, revealing his discomfort with Wagnerian idealistic orthodoxy. In the works of Wagner and his epigones the male protagonist stereotypically achieves redemption through the compassionate sacrifice, and usually death, of the female protagonist (Senta in *Der fliegende Holländer* and Elisabeth in *Tannhäuser*, for example). Strauss places Guntram's redemption outside the opera as a future event, and Freihild does not have to sacrifice herself. Although Guntram claims to need her renunciation in order to achieve redemption, he also makes it abundantly clear that he alone is the master of his own destiny, and that solitary asceticism and renunciation of worldly concerns constitute his path to redemption. Likewise, Guntram's arrogant dismissal of the idealistic brotherhood and his insistence on self-determination were a new twist, which critics almost unanimously blamed on Nietzsche, whose increasingly popular writings had made "individualism" a buzzword of the age.

This is precisely how Ritter interpreted the ending, which caused an irreparable rift between Strauss and his Wagnerian mentor in 1893 about a year before the Weimar premiere. Ritter had approved wholeheartedly of the original denouement, in which Guntram submits to the authority of the brotherhood and embarks on a pilgrimage to the Holy Sepulchre, but the revised ending filled him with horror and elicited a long, passionate letter imploring Strauss to undo the change.[8] Calling the revision his most deeply painful experience of the last decade, Ritter wondered if Guntram had been reading Stirner, or Nietzsche's *Beyond Good and Evil*; accused Guntram of being immoral and un-Christian; doubted whether anything except the mechanics of Wagner's art remained in Strauss; and advised Strauss to consult Schopenhauer and Wagner on the "correct" Bayreuth ideology.[9] Strauss defended himself in matching detail and even asked his friends Friedrich Rösch and Ludwig Thuille to locate support for his position in Schopenhauer, showing just how seriously he took the ideological underpinnings of his first opera and how much he wanted to placate Ritter to save their friendship.

What is most remarkable about the allegation of Nietzsche's influence, however, is that the opera was in fact more faithfully Schopenhauerian than any by Wagner or Strauss's contemporaries.[10] Most composers of the late nineteenth century appear to have known Schopenhauer only through Wagner's (distorting) operas and writings, meaning that hardly any of them had actually read the philosopher's long *magnum opus, The World as Will and Representation* (1818, revised 1844). Understandably, they were content to know the headlines: Schopenhauer's elevation of music to a privileged status for its ability to represent the "Will" (the central metaphysical force in the universe), and the philosopher's finding that through art one could "deny the Will" (transcend our egoistic desires, a moral imperative essential to redemption). Unlike most composers, however, Strauss studied Schopenhauer's work in detail, and there he learned (in Books III and IV) that art can only serve as a temporary denial of the will, whereas saintly asceticism and isolation constitute the true path to permanent redemption. Thus, Guntram appears to act out this philosophy: by breaking his lyre he rejects music as a redeeming force, and by retreating into solitary reflection in order to atone for the physical desire that led to murder he follows the precise road to redemption recommended in *The World as Will and Representation*. We might argue, then, that *Guntram* exposes the ignorance of Wagner and his epigones, who conveniently ignored Schopenhauer's reservations about art. To Ritter, however, who had high hopes for Strauss as standard-bearer of Wagnerian ideals, the revised ending amounted to nothing less than heresy, and their relationship remained strained until Ritter's death in 1896.

In spite of the opera's Schopenhauerian orthodoxy, its ending became associated specifically with Nietzsche. Given the fact that, as Roy Pascal has noted, before 1918 "Nietzsche stands above all as the champion of personal liberation and personal fulfillment, as against parental and social authority, mass movements and ideological systems," it was only logical for commentators lacking philosophical expertise to make this connection.[11] Among contemporaries, only Eugen Schmitz appears to have noticed that Guntram's ascetic, Christian goals were incompatible with Nietzsche's ideas.[12] Significantly, Strauss's own retrospective comments associated Guntram's defiant insistence on being the agent of his own redemption with Nietzsche's critique of Christian dogma:

> When during my stay in Egypt I became familiar with the works of Nietzsche, whose polemic against Christianity was particularly to my liking, the antipathy which I had always felt against a religion which relieves the faithful of responsibility for their actions (by means of confession) was confirmed and strengthened. Ritter could never quite forgive me for

the renunciation of society (Third act, Guntram–Friedhold scene) when Guntram judges himself and abrogates the right of the community to punish him.[13]

Although Strauss claimed in his response to Ritter's letter that he had been reading only Wagner, Goethe, and Schopenhauer in Egypt, we know that he had read Nietzsche's *Beyond Good and Evil* no later than two months after writing the letter, making his claim less than credible.[14] Also noteworthy are the criticisms of Schopenhauer that Strauss entrusted only to the diary he kept in Egypt. Among other philosophical liberties, he reversed the goal of the will from denial of our desires to "consciousness of desire" and "affirmation of the body," developing a very un-Guntram-like interest in sexuality that would emerge powerfully in his next opera.[15]

In spite of the clear difference between the personalities of Strauss and Guntram, the opera is convincingly autobiographical with respect to Wagnerian discipleship. Strauss's friend Arthur Seidl, for example, identified Guntram with Strauss, Friedhold with Ritter, and the brotherhood with Bayreuth in his review of *Guntram*, and there can be no doubt that Bayreuth insiders (such as Ritter) perceived the work as a thinly veiled rejection of Wagnerian idealism.[16] Five decades later Strauss pinpointed the beginning of his compositional autonomy (i.e., from Bayreuth) as the third act of *Guntram*, noting that "the road was clear for unimpededly independent work."[17] After the Schopenhauer crisis of *Guntram*, Strauss had purged metaphysical concerns from his system, continued to pursue his interest in Nietzsche, and had alienated Bayreuth entirely by 1896. When Ritter wondered if anything of Wagner had remained in Strauss besides the "mechanics of his art," he was on the right track; although Strauss continued to consider himself a Wagnerian, this no longer meant idealism but musical technique. Although *Guntram* liberated Strauss from Bayreuth, however, it would take one more opera before he achieved complete independence.

Feuersnot (1901)

Although Gustav Mahler told Strauss that he considered *Guntram* the most important, perhaps the *only* important opera since Wagner's *Parsifal* (1882), the work so utterly flopped that a less thick-skinned composer would have given up opera for good.[18] Despite the abject failure, Strauss continued to search for suitable operatic subjects, and the success of his tone poems and a prestigious Kapellmeister position in Berlin as of 1898 had given him the necessary confidence. When he came across the Flemish legend *The Extinguished Fire of Audenaerde* about a rejected lover's revenge on his town, he decided to do the same to Munich, the city that had caused him a host of problems with superiors, colleagues, orchestra, and press, and most notably had handed his first opera an embarrassing defeat.[19] Resolved to work for the first time with a librettist, Strauss chose the like-minded Ernst von Wolzogen (1855–1934), a multifaceted writer who had left Munich for Berlin just a few months after Strauss and would found the Berlin *Überbrettl* ("Superstage") cabaret there in 1901. Wolzogen had an even stronger motivation for revenge on Munich, having been evicted from his own literary society following a failed revival of Shakespeare's *Troilus and Cressida* in 1898. This trauma, along with other points of compatibility – pronounced individualism, rejection of Bayreuth idealism, interest in Nietzsche – made him the ideal partner for the project. As a predominantly comic opera with an unusual admixture of fairy tale and music drama, *Feuersnot* was also the outcome of Strauss's search for a subject that would contrast with *Guntram* and serve as an antidote to the tragic pathos of typical post-Wagnerian opera.[20]

Set in the small-town milieu of medieval Munich on Midsummer's Day, the one-act opera opens with a group of children collecting firewood for the traditional bonfire and the villagers gossiping about the mysterious loner Kunrad living in the house of his evicted master, an old sorcerer. When the children reach his house and the townsfolk tease him about forgetting Midsummer, Kunrad spontaneously dismisses the unspecified readings that had confined him to his gloomy house, waxes enthusiastic about sunlight and life itself, and proceeds to help the children tear his house into pieces to be used in the bonfire. This sudden exuberance culminates in a scandalous act: Kunrad publically humiliates the mayor's beautiful daughter Diemut by kissing her without her consent. When she appears to soften to his advances later on, she has actually led him into a trap that leaves him hanging mid-air in a basket on his way to Diemut's window, exposed to the ridicule of the townsfolk. In response, Kunrad summons the magic of his master, the old sorcerer, and extinguishes all light in the city (*Feuersnot* meaning fire deprivation or emergency). After reaching the balcony on his own he explains his actions in a pompous address, in which he establishes himself as the sorcerer's heir, rebukes the people for evicting his master and for mocking his love for Diemut, and announces the astounding condition for restoring fire to the city: Diemut must surrender her virginity. The town cheers on as she obliges him, and a brief afterglow duet finishes the opera.

Although *Guntram* liberated Strauss from Bayreuth, Wagner is at the very center of *Feuersnot* even if Strauss seemingly cannot decide between homage and rejection. The most obvious connection is the small-town setting on Midsummer's Day, derived directly from Wagner's comic opera *Die Meistersinger von Nürnberg*. Kunrad's embrace of life beyond his house closely resembles Walther's decision to leave his castle to investigate the life of Nuremberg in *Meistersinger*. Later in the opera a word-play confirms that the old sorcerer evicted from Munich is in fact Wagner, while his apprentice Kunrad is Strauss himself. Finally, the Wagnerian themes of love and redemption play obvious roles in *Feuersnot*: the archaic term *Minnegebot* – or "love's decree" – the higher calling of love that Diemut supposedly violates, refers directly to Wagner's transcendent notion of love, and Diemut literally redeems the city through her sacrifice as many Wagnerian heroines had done before her. When Kunrad (alias Strauss) scolds the Munich people for evicting his master (alias Wagner) and installs himself as his avenger and heir, he is aligning himself with his idol and presenting himself as Wagner's musical apprentice.

This apparent homage breaks down on closer examination, and the Nietzschean conception of Kunrad is the primary agent of this reversal, beginning with the demolition of his master's house – Strauss's symbolic yet paradoxical rejection of his own Wagnerian heritage. Kunrad's impetuous kiss suggests that he considers himself above common morality, or what Nietzsche called "herd morality," and his individualistic independence and arrogant demeanor establish him as a sort of *Übermensch* bordering on caricature. Kunrad clinches this Nietzschean interpretation when he calls himself "too good for virtue" in his address and delivers it on the balcony while literally looking down on the townsfolk. Strauss, who considered this monologue the essence of the opera (the rest being merely "amusing padding"), wrote to the conductor before the premiere to ensure its rudely arrogant delivery, and dubbed himself a "naughty Nietzschean" in a letter encouraging Cosima Wagner (of all people) to see *Feuersnot*.[21]

Kunrad's Nietzschean allegiance has profound implications for the Wagnerian themes of love and redemption. Although he appears to be defending Wagner's metaphysical conception of love by punishing Diemut's affront to "love's decree," Kunrad's emphatically physical adaptation inverts Wagner's *Minne* by making it entirely down-to-earth and intensely egocentric rather than elevated and selfless. Along the same lines, Wagner's favorite notion of redemption through love undergoes a satirical subversion. While in the stereotypical Wagnerian redemption the female protagonist sacrifices her life to redeem the male protagonist in a noble act of compassion, Diemut agrees to have sex with Kunrad in order to redeem the city only after being blackmailed and subjected to intense peer pressure. In spite of establishing himself as Wagner's successor, then, Kunrad (alias Strauss) becomes a "modernized," Nietzschean, anti-Wagnerian antihero.

Ernst von Wolzogen shared Strauss's private desire to debunk Wagner's metaphysical notions of love and redemption. Like Strauss, he remained committed to the Bayreuth cause until the mid 1890s and then withdrew his support on ideological grounds. As the half-brother of Bayreuth fanatic Hans von Wolzogen he had direct access to Wahnfried, but after attending the premiere of Wagner's *Parsifal* in 1882 he realized that his instinctive rejection of the concept of redemption through love stemmed from his distaste for the Christian redemption through the agency of a Savior, the very aspect of Christianity that Nietzsche had inspired Strauss to dismiss and that *Guntram* dramatized. Also like Strauss, Wolzogen believed in sexuality as a central source of artistic inspiration, and we know that he viewed *Feuersnot* as an expression of this idea, although his literary works reveal a prudishness that contradicts his free views on sexuality and points to Strauss as the source of the opera's sexual directness.[22]

Not surprisingly, most critics blamed the opera's burlesque "*Überbrettl* tone" on Wolzogen's now infamous Berlin cabaret, which had opened in January, 1901, almost a year before the *Feuersnot* premiere on November 21.[23] Many of them found it difficult to distinguish parody from sincerity, a recurring complaint in writings on Strauss, owing to the absence of clear "markers" in the music.[24] A few conservative commentators recorded extreme reactions to the work. Ernst Otto Nodnagel accused Strauss of "playing with art" and saw in *Feuersnot* nothing short of "the end of music," and Strauss's friend and fellow composer Max von Schillings wrote to a friend that he cried bitterly after the premiere owing to Strauss's betrayal of the idealistic, Wagnerian cause.[25] The most perceptive assessment came from Eugen Schmitz, who noted the modern qualities of the opera – satire, sexual freedom, Nietzschean ideas – and Strauss's collaboration with contemporary efforts to emerge from the Wagnerian "redemption fog."[26]

When some reviewers observed a lack of stylistic unity in *Feuersnot* (another recurring complaint about Strauss's music), they were noticing an early instance of Strauss's modern stylistic principle of changing styles both between and within works, one I have labeled *Stilkunst* ("style art").[27] Thus, *Feuersnot* employs at least three very different styles: a simple and popular style for the opening scene and the children's choruses, a heavier style derived from music drama for some of Kunrad's scenes and the love duet, and several sumptuous waltzes. Strauss also incorporated direct musical quotations from Wagner and *Guntram* that reinforce the effect of stylistic pluralism. Moreover, contrasting styles or moods often last just a few bars each, creating a "nervous" feeling. This amounts to a direct reflection of the splintering of contemporary culture into multiple directions, and the "nervousness" that featured prominently in cultural and artistic debates around the turn of the century. What facilitated Strauss's *Stilkunst* as a "consummate wearer of masks," to use Leon Botstein's expression, was his modern detachment from his subjects, an objective aesthetic that diverged significantly from most post-Wagnerian, intimately confessional music (although *Feuersnot* hardly appears "objective" with Kunrad representing Strauss himself, the presence of Strauss's autobiographical persona has little to do with intimate confessions or deeply held beliefs).[28] In *Feuersnot*, then, Strauss embraced a modern stylistic principle, lampooned Wagnerian idealism through a down-to-earth inversion, and incorporated contemporary issues such as satire, sexual freedom, and Nietzschean philosophy.

Salome (1905)

As he had done with *Guntram*, Mahler called *Salome* "one of the greatest masterpieces of our time," but since he was writing to his wife this time, we need not question his sincerity.[29] Embracing modern literature by setting a recent play by Oscar Wilde, Strauss increased the level of dissonance and chromaticism dramatically, pushed the size and coloristic capabilities of the orchestra to new extremes, and, according to one contemporary observer, went beyond Wagner and "disposed of those antiquated gods of ideology."[30] Although Strauss had no interest in the literary "decadence" that Wilde epitomized, the writer's published pronouncements that "no artist has ethical sympathies," "art is the most intense mood of Individualism that the world has known," and "[the artist] stands outside his subject" found a strong resonance in Strauss's own distaste of ideology, and his espousal of individualism and of distance between creator and creation.[31] Written in French in 1891 and first performed in Paris in 1896, Wilde's *Salomé* had its German premiere in 1901, and by the time Strauss saw it in Berlin in November, 1902 he had already read it and decided to use the play for his next opera, thereby setting a drama that was brand-new from a German perspective and one that became hugely popular in Germany. Rather than writing his own libretto or collaborating with a librettist as in *Guntram* and *Feuersnot*, he chose to set the play directly with abbreviations and minor alterations, and thus pioneered what Germans call *Literaturoper*.[32] The premiere in Dresden on December 9, 1905 turned the opera into an overnight sensation that eventually financed Strauss's villa in Garmisch.

Since the late nineteenth century witnessed a veritable cult of Salome,[33] Wilde's choice of subject was not surprising, but he changed the biblical story (Matthew 14:1–12, Mark 6:14–29) and its many later variants to focus exclusively on Salome: he added her fatal attraction to John the Baptist, transferred the demand for his head from her mother Herodias to Salome herself, and has her killed at the end.[34] The one-act opera opens with the ominous conversation of soldiers and servants during a banquet at Herod's palace, and we hear Jochanaan's voice (Wilde and Strauss used John's Hebrew name) from the cistern in which Herod has imprisoned him. When Salome leaves the banquet, she is intrigued by the voice from below and sweet-talks the captain in charge (who is in love with her) to bring Jochanaan up from the cistern. Although he rudely insults her and Herodias, she develops an incurable physical attraction to him, but he rejects her and returns to his underground prison (meanwhile the captain has committed suicide without her noticing it). Herod and Herodias now appear with the court, and his obsession with Salome causes Herod to promise her whatever she desires if she will dance for him, which she does. In return, she demands Jochanaan's head on a silver platter, and receives it in spite of Herod's desperate protests. When an extensive monologue to the severed head culminates in her kissing the lips, Herod orders her killed.

Predictably, the controversial opera elicited a great variety of reactions, which we may divide into a few categories: moral outrage and the inevitable trouble with censorship, evaluation of musical features, the perceived disparity between the styles and characterizations of Strauss and Wilde, and the contentious issue of Salome's transfiguration and redemption. The biblical source of the story notwithstanding, an opera featuring the severed head of a Christian saint as the object of intense physical passion was guaranteed to cause moral outrage. Berlin critic Leopold Schmidt, for example, considered the final scene "the most disgusting ever to be shown on stage," and blamed the sensationalist modernism of Strauss, "leader of the musical left."[35] It is well known that Strauss's friend Romain Rolland asked Strauss why he wasted his talent on an inferior text, which Rolland considered "nauseous and sickly," but it is less recognized that Rolland had the protagonist of his novel series *Jean-Christophe* voice an even more frank critique of the opera: "A masterpiece … I should not like to have written it … An Isolde who is a Jewish prostitute … Strauss is the genius of bad taste."[36] Needless to say, the audacious blend of religion and perversity caused problems with censorship, official or voluntary. Thus, the Metropolitan Opera in New York performed *Salome* just once in 1907 and did not restore it until 1933, Vienna blocked it until 1918, and the London premiere in 1910 only took place after censors had turned "a lurid tale of love and revenge into a comforting sermon that could have been safely preached from any country pulpit" and the bloody head had been replaced by a cloth with no head under it.[37]

Contemporary comments on the music of *Salome* focused on harmony, orchestration, nervousness, and authenticity of emotional expression.

A typical statement on the dense polyphony and extreme chromaticism came from Richard Batka, who considered *Salome* a radical continuation of *Tristan* and *Parsifal* and quipped that "the pure triad is administered like medication – only one teaspoonful every half hour."[38] Strauss later remarked that the contrast between Herod and Jochanaan led him to bitonality, and scores of commentators have cited the infamous clash of an F♯ major triad with a dominant-seventh chord on A sixteen bars from the end.[39] Strauss's protean handling of orchestral color, on the other hand, was universally lauded even though the gigantic orchestra (including seven percussionists, heckelphone, organ, and harmonium) had required the Dresden opera house to remove two rows of seats and shorten the stage for the premiere. Lawrence Gilman's observation that "the alphabet of music is ransacked for new and undreamt-of combinations of tone" is typical.[40] Along with the volatile harmonic language and kaleidoscopic color changes, the rapid-fire shifts of style or mood – intensified since *Feuersnot* – contributed to the widespread identification of "nervousness" in the music. Otto Roese, citing historian Karl Lamprecht's reduction of contemporary culture to the common denominator of nervousness or excitability, saw turn-of-the-century society mirrored on stage, especially in the edgy Herod.[41] Strauss's father, famously, likened the music to having maybugs in his pants.[42] The majority of commentators perceived in this music a conspicuous lack of genuine emotional expression, a deficiency observed in most of Strauss's works. Gilman, for example, called the music "incurably external" and noted its lack of true substance, and Mahler, though impressed with the opera, considered it a work of superficial virtuosity and felt repelled by "Strauss's coldness of temperament."[43] Thus, Strauss's contemporaries sensed a clear, disconcerting contrast between this music, and more deeply felt and confessional "Romantic" music, a distinction that is difficult for modern audiences to appreciate.

Other perceived differences included the dissonance between the overall styles of Wilde and Strauss and between their respective characterizations of the two protagonists. Many critics noted that the (Germanic) power and high pathos of Strauss's music contrasted inappropriately with Wilde's subtle and refined "decadence" – Batka, for example, would have preferred less Wagner/Isolde and more Wilde – and others remarked that Strauss had revised Wilde's characterization of Jochanaan and Salome.[44] Whereas Wilde made his Saint John pompous, menacing, insulting, and decidedly unsaintly, Strauss ennobled him through a diatonic, quasi-hymnic style that delighted some and bored others. While one early reviewer saw Jochanaan's style as more suitable for huntsmen's choruses in older operas than for Wilde's intimidating figure, Rolland discerned that this was in fact the agnostic composer's unconvincing attempt at creating a religious figure.[45] Strauss's lack of empathy with Jochanaan is well known from comments to Rolland and Stefan Zweig, in which he called the saint an imbecile and a clown but also explained his setting: "Only because I have already caricatured the five Jews and also poked fun at Father Herodes did I feel that I had to follow the law of contrast and write a pedantic-Philistine motif for four horns to characterize Jochanaan."[46] Along similar lines, most observers heard in Strauss's unsuitably beautiful music for Salome the sympathetic qualities of humanity and compassion allegedly lacking in Wilde's portrayal of perversity incarnate, and many singled out Salome's final monologue as especially out of character. Thus, Gilman noted that the saccharine, vulgarly sentimental music created a mood of noble rapture rather than one of barbaric abandon (and Joseph Kerman, infamously, called the ending a "sugary orgasm").[47] A little-known comment from Strauss to Franz Schreker elaborates on his deliberate alteration of Wilde's protagonists in favor of musical contrast: "If you consider the characters of this play, they are really all perverted, and in my opinion the most perverted of them all is – Jochanaan. If I had composed it the way the author probably intended it, from where would I have taken the contrasts I need as a musician? Thus, I elevated Salome to a human sphere of emotions and moved Jochanaan in a religious, sublime direction."[48]

This elevation and the obvious parallel with the end of Wagner's *Tristan* (monologue to dead object of love followed by the singer's own death) have caused commentators from the premiere to the present day to interpret the opera along Wagnerian lines – Salome being transfigured and/or redeemed by her love-death (*Liebestod*) – in spite of the obvious differences (necrophiliac desire versus metaphysical love, brutal execution versus mystical death). While Salome's redemption through divine love was unproblematic to Roese, Schmidt needed to fall back on Strauss's lineage: "The composer of *Guntram* … coming from the school of Wagner and supporting the theory of redemption, also saves this daughter of sin. He must, or he could not have set her to music."[49] Rudolf Louis's sarcastic remarks tacitly admitted that a redemption opera would now be outdated: "Even Richard Strauss … pathfinder to the land of the future, has really just heated up the old stew and written a drama of 'redemption'? One should imagine that all 'modern' people … would rise up to protest … the one stigma that in his own eyes must be the most hideous of all: that of unmodernity."[50] At the opposite end of the spectrum, Gilman found the notion of Salome's transfiguration "as a kind of Oriental Isolde" ridiculous, and Schmitz saw in *Salome* the sharpest possible contrast with Wagner's idea of a woman's redemptive love."[51] Significantly, interpreting *Salome* as an extreme physicalization of

Isolde's metaphysical love would be entirely consistent with the inversion of Wagnerian ideology in *Feuersnot*.

More recent studies of *Salome* have explored issues of race, gender, and sexuality. Agreeing that Strauss invited audiences to hear the work as an opera about Jews (*Judenoper*), Sander Gilman and Anne Seshadri offer divergent interpretations of its racial politics.[52] According to Gilman, Strauss deliberately encouraged audiences to construe *Salome* in the context of overlapping stereotypes of Jewish sexuality and incest, homosexuality, and perversion – a combination that appealed to the Jewish avant-garde left and branded Strauss himself as perverted. Seshadri focusses on Salome's perceived transfiguration, arguing that it represents assimilation of Jews into German society through erasure of Jewish difference. Touching on the concept of the gaze, studies by Lawrence Kramer, Linda and Michael Hutcheon, and Carolyn Abbate locate Salome in contradictory positions along the continuum between empowerment and subjugation.[53] While Kramer believes the opera to affirm the dominance of masculine power and the gaze, Hutcheon and Hutcheon – invoking contemporary female stereotypes such as childishness, hysteria, asexuality, and pubescent insanity – view Salome as controlling the gaze, empowered by the dissonance between pathology and youthful innocence. Abbate, on the other hand, argues that "Strauss *rejects* the notion of operatic music as objectifying gaze … and coaxes the listening ear into occupying a female position, by *erasing* any sense of male authorial voice."[54] Along with the polarized perceptions of Salome's redemption, these studies demonstrate that Strauss, although often accused of superficiality, created a heroine of sufficient depth and complexity to support highly divergent interpretations.

Coda

Within a span of twelve years, Strauss's operatic fortunes had progressed from humiliating fiasco to outright triumph, and he had become a dramatic composer above all. The Schopenhauerian orthodoxy of *Guntram* was interpreted as a Nietzschean individualism that alienated Bayreuth and set Strauss on an independent path. *Feuersnot* brought revenge on Munich while embracing 1890s culture and inverting Wagnerian ideology. And *Salome* humanized a perverse princess and pushed religion aside in a decidedly un-Wagnerian tragedy. Surely, the most remarkable aspect of this sequence of operas is its apparently paradoxical attitude to Wagner: untroubled adaptation and continued development of his musical style and principles coupled with irreverent deflation of his Romantic metaphysics. In the "Attempt at a Self-Criticism" written for the 1886 edition of

The Birth of Tragedy (1872), Nietzsche reiterated his call for un-Romantic music: "the great Dionysian question mark ... endures still, also with respect to music: what would music have to be like to be no longer of Romantic origin, like German music – but *Dionysian?*"[55] Strauss, given his Nietzschean leanings and the overtly maenadic rapture of Salome, eventually answered the call.

7 The Strauss–Hofmannsthal operas

BRYAN GILLIAM

The collaboration between Richard Strauss and Hugo von Hofmannsthal was one of the greatest composer–librettist relationships of all time, spanning nearly three decades until the poet's untimely death in July, 1929. It was an artistic association at the level of Verdi–Boito or Mozart–Da Ponte but, unlike these two earlier librettists, Hofmannsthal had a successful and independent career as a writer of some of Austria's finest lyric poetry, and his plays remain in the repertoire of German-speaking theater. Before setting Hofmannsthal's *Elektra* to music, Strauss had worked with various authors and various texts (those by himself, Ernst von Wolzogen, and Oscar Wilde). But with Hofmannsthal he collaborated on six operas, a series interrupted only by *Intermezzo* (1924). The partnership with Hofmannsthal also initiated an association with Austrians for all his future operatic collaborations: Stefan Zweig, Joseph Gregor, and Clemens Krauss.

Much has been made of the differences between Strauss and Hofmannsthal, the German and the Austrian, and these contrasts in personality, literary tastes, and artistic views are quite true. The famous photograph taken by Strauss's son, Franz, is one of two men standing together outside the composer's villa in Garmisch around the time of *Der Rosenkavalier*. Strauss, wearing walking breeches, with a cigarette in his left hand and a walking stick in his right, looks directly into the camera, while Hofmannsthal – nearly a head shorter – stands holding a horizontal umbrella, wearing a hat covering his eyes, awkwardly staring away from the camera in the direction of Strauss.

This very photograph adorns the front cover of the Cambridge edition of their correspondence, and what might be visually left to the imagination is filled in with great detail in those published letters dating from 1900 to 1929.[1] Time and again Hofmannsthal expresses offense at Strauss's abruptness, his lack of intellectual insight, his pettiness, and his apparent coolness and seeming absence of empathy. For Strauss the act of composition, of creating art, was as natural as breathing, something he did every day, while, for Hofmannsthal – the temperamental Viennese – creation required special circumstances, whether it be the weather or a particular frame of mind. These two antithetical modes of thinking and work constantly collided in this published record of their artistic endeavors.

Composing was not only as natural as breathing for Strauss, but was as important for the life of his artistic being, and the moments of greatest tension in their collaborations were when he had to wait for Hofmannsthal's text. As late as their last collaboration, *Arabella* (1932), the poet once pleaded: "Please don't rush me, *everything* that is any good comes to me only through concentration. I depend on *ideas*, even for small things on which the essence often hangs."[2] Moreover, Strauss did not shy from criticizing weak drafts; responding to an early version of *Ariadne auf Naxos* in 1911, Strauss remarked, "this bit must soar higher … harness your Pegasus for a little longer."[3] Despite their differences and their lack of social friendship (including Hofmannsthal's aversion to Strauss's wife, Pauline), they recognized each other's talents well enough to create an unsurpassed body of twentieth-century German opera.

More important than appreciating their differences is knowing their deeper commonalities, which unfolded as their relationship continued and intensified. These mutual themes began with the centrality of gesture as a primary carrier of meaning, then the importance of transformation (*Verwandlung*) as a path from the self to the social, and – within the realm of the social – marriage and children as the links binding generations. Indeed, their first extended conversation, in Paris (March 6, 1900), concerned ballet and inspired a dance scenario (*The Triumph of Time*) that Hofmannsthal sent the composer eight months later.[4] Strauss politely rejected the plan as he was working on a ballet of his own (*Kythere*) based on Watteau's *Embarquement pour Cythère*, which he had seen at the Louvre while in Paris.[5]

A first encounter: *Elektra*

As a young man, Hofmannsthal was already known in Viennese literary circles as a poetic prodigy, who gained fame under the pseudonym "Loris." A precocious youth fluent in many languages, with a deep sensitivity to literature, and a remarkable facility as a poet, he went beyond the normal stereotype of prodigy. His lyric poetry betrayed a maturity that seemingly could only be based upon years of life experience. When Hofmannsthal was introduced to Viennese literary society at the Café Griensteidl, at age seventeen, figures such as Hermann Bahr, Richard Beer-Hofmann, and Arthur Schnitzler accepted him not as an amazing talent but as a literary equal.

At the same time, Hofmannsthal was also engaged in the world of Greek myth, inspired by Nietzsche's *Birth of Tragedy*, believing that through myth a society might be modernized, or reinvigorated, by asserting Nietzsche's tragic Dionysian. Negating the idealized, neo-Socratic mid-nineteenth-century notions of Greek tragedy inspired the young writer to rework Euripides' *Alkestis* (1893), and though there were some other unfinished mythological projects around this time as well, the only successful venture into Dionysian tragedy was *Elektra* (1903). Through gesture, Hofmannsthal found the central expressive force in this play, the first major work after his so-called "language crisis" at the turn of the century.

During this period of crisis, the young lyric poet came to reject the insular poetry of his day, and in an essay, the so-called "Chandos Brief" (1902), Hofmannsthal suggests that words alone fail to penetrate to the core, to the inner essence of things, falling short of explaining human actions and motivations. He found the answer in gesture: where words are indirect, gesture is immediate, and where language is impure, gesture is undiluted. *Elektra* was a great success, and Strauss, having seen a production in 1905, was overwhelmed by the work's power and its potential for music. The composer was riveted by this Freudian interpretation of Sophocles's tragedy, expressed in a steadily rising tension culminating in Elektra's dance after her father's murder has finally been avenged. Struck by this crescendo of action, he contacted Hofmannsthal for permission to use his text.

Elektra (1908) was not really a collaboration, for after composer and playwright met on February 22, 1906 in Berlin, Strauss received permission from a delighted Hofmannsthal to use his text as he saw fit. Strauss's experience in unilaterally cutting and shaping Oscar Wilde's *Salomé* served him well with Hofmannsthal's text, and, with great speed, he created a remarkable libretto. Hofmannsthal once likened his play to a "taut chain of heavy massive iron links," and, indeed, *Elektra* is remarkably concise, made even more compact after Strauss's reworking, which cut nearly half of the dialogue, eliminating extraneous characters, and focussing on the triangular relationships of a mother (Clytemnestra) and her two daughters (Elektra and Chrysothemis). This extraordinarily succinct play, even more condensed in its operatic form, combines concentrated action and structural clarity with stark imagery, which as an opera make for the most potent one-act stage work Strauss had yet composed.

Tension steadily rises as each scene segues into the next with increasing momentum. The only notable break is the arrival of Orestes, a scene cut severely by Strauss. Thereafter, Hofmannsthal goes right to the murders: first Clytemnestra, then Aegisthus. In short, what Hofmannsthal creates, in terms of dramaturgical structure, is a monumental arch spanning from the introduction to the finale. This symmetrical arrangement appealed greatly to Strauss, whose reductions strengthened this sense of balance.

If *Elektra* is performed less often than *Salome*, the explanation lies with Strauss's most difficult soprano role. The singer is on stage for every scene save the first, and she must do constant sonic battle with a tumultuous orchestra, which proudly displays a young post-Wagnerian's leitmotivic abilities. The shape of the opera is that of an arch, the keystone being the scene between Elektra and her mother Clytemnestra. It is the tensest scene of any work by Strauss and certainly the most daring in terms of its hyper-chromatic harmonic language. Years later Strauss was embarrassed that much of the singing was "handicapped by instrumental polyphony," and he later suggested – tongue placed firmly in cheek – that it should be conducted like Mendelssohn: "fairy music."[6]

Genuine collaboration: *Der Rosenkavalier*

It was not the world of Mendelssohn but of Mozart that would inspire his next opera, *Der Rosenkavalier* (1910), a work set in the eighteenth century. It represented his first collaboration with Hofmannsthal, and though the libretto bears an intentional resemblance to Da Ponte's *Marriage of Figaro* it conflates a wide range of sources, and it combines comic elements with others of considerable profundity. Musically, Strauss opted for a language beyond *Salome*'s sinuous chromaticism and *Elektra*'s torturous dissonance, and, indeed, *Der Rosenkavalier* represents a stratification of various musical styles.

In this "comedy for music," the stylistic disunities are there for all to hear, but no longer are they so abruptly bandied about as in *Feuersnot* – rather critically layered in harmony with Hofmannsthal's text and worldview, which saw a society (Maria Theresa's Vienna) as an "alliance of past generations with later ones, and vice versa."[7] Thus, though *Der Rosenkavalier* is set in the 1740s, we hear allusions to the Viennese Classical style of the 1780s, the riper sounds of the 1860s and 1870s, and a chromatically enervated diatonicism of 1910. Strauss, accordingly, made musical alliances with Mozart, Johann Strauss, Jr., Wagner, and Italian opera, while Hofmannsthal made textual connections with, among other sources, Molière, Beaumarchais, Da Ponte, Wagner, Shakespeare, and – for the levée scene – even the visual world of Hogarth. These simultaneous non-simultaneities, a "harmony of contrasts," in Hofmannsthal's words, became a central common ground for poet and composer as they emerged as the young century's great collaboration.

The Marschallin demonstrates this worldview on a personal level, and with her other name, Marie Thérèse, we are reminded that there is a sociopolitical dimension to letting go and making new unions, as Carl Schorske once noted: "There is something elegiac about the whole opera, but it is also rich in history that is now being put to new purposes. The problem of

the passing of the aristocracy to the zweite Gesellschaft [ennobled bour-
geoisie] in turn must learn to yield power to the new forces of democracy
in the twentieth century."[8] Thus, Strauss's sonic signifiers index the world
of Austria on the threshold of its idiosyncratic Enlightenment, the escapist
waltz idiom of post-*Ausgleich* Austria, and the contemporary sounds of a
Habsburg empire on the verge of war and collapse.

On multiple levels, *Der Rosenkavalier* is an opera about time and transformation. In the very opening lines of the opera ("What you were, what
you are – that nobody knows, that no one can explain."), Octavian transforms the verb "to be" from the past to the present tense. In Act I the Baron
Ochs boasts to Octavian (disguised as "Mariandl") that he is "holy Jupiter
in his thousand manifestations," but Octavian himself is the one who takes
on various transformations throughout the opera: as the Marschallin's adolescent lover, as her chambermaid, as a rose cavalier, and – by the end – as
a wiser young man.

To Hofmannsthal, the miracle of life is that an old love can die, while a
new one can arise from its ashes. Yet in this transformation, which requires
us to forget, we still preserve our essence. How is it that – in the same
body – we are what we once were, now are, and will become? That is life's
great mystery, and, in one way or another, the theme permeates most of
Hofmannsthal's work. The Marschallin ponders this enigma in her poignant monologue towards the end of Act I, one of the opera's musical and
literary highlights. Beyond the monologue, *Rosenkavalier*'s delightfully
anachronistic nineteenth-century waltzes, the magical Act II Presentation
of the Rose, and the sublime final trio of Act III remain some of Strauss's
best-loved music. Yet their popularity, independent of the opera, has also
overshadowed the theatrical brilliance of this first modern stage work by
Strauss. It premiered in Dresden on January 26, 1911 when Strauss and
Hofmannsthal had already begun work on a new operatic project. Strauss,
the lover of contrasts, had found his ideal librettist.

Experimentation, clashing personalities, and *Ariadne auf Naxos*

Ariadne auf Naxos (1912/1916), like *Rosenkavalier*, is a remarkably modern theatrical piece, which in its historicism exploits an established canon
as a source of parody. The opera forges a new relationship between composer, performer, and audience, for without the audience's knowledge of
works from the recent and more distant past, parody cannot function. If
in *Rosenkavalier* Strauss alludes to the style of other composers, *Ariadne*
quotes specific musical works: Harlekin's song ("Lieben, Hassen, Hoffen,

Zagen") is based on the opening theme of Mozart's A major Piano Sonata, K. 331, and the melody of the Nymphs' trio ("Töne, töne, süße Stimme") comes from Schubert's *Wiegenlied* ("Schlafe, holder, süßer Knabe"). Although Zerbinetta's famous coloratura aria makes no direct quotations, Strauss's letters to Hofmannsthal make it clear from the outset that he looked to Bellini, Donizetti, and others as stylistic models.

Earlier letters to Hofmannsthal also show that Strauss initially failed to understand this unique mixture of comedy and tragedy, much to the annoyance of his librettist. For the first time in the collaboration, these opposing personalities – the sensible Bavarian, the sensitive Viennese – clashed. The composer required a concrete notion of what musical moments lay in the libretto, and he outlined them for Hofmannsthal as best he could:

(1) Recitative and aria for Ariadne;
(2) Harlekin's song;
(3) Zerbinetta's coloratura aria;
(4) Male quartet for Harlekin and company, becoming a quintet with Zerbinetta;
(5) *Buffo* male trio ;
(6) Finale: Naiad's warning, duet of Zerbinetta and Ariadne (concluding with Bacchus' entry), love duet (Ariadne and Bacchus), final ensemble.

But Strauss still needed to understand this work better; he found it difficult to compose for abstractions, for stylized figures. Hofmannsthal fulfilled the composer's wishes in a remarkable letter of mid July, 1911, which – following Strauss's suggestion – was published shortly before the premiere:

> What [*Ariadne*] is all about is one of the straightforward and stupendous problems of life: fidelity; whether to hold fast to that which is lost, to cling to it even in death – or to live, to live on, to get over it, to transform oneself, to sacrifice the integrity of the soul and yet in this transmutation to preserve one's essence, to remain a human being and not to sink to the level of beast, which is without recollection.[9]

Hofmannsthal finally articulated a topic that resonated with the composer, emphasizing the theme central to the previous opera: that of transformation on its various levels. Through Ariadne's love, Bacchus is transfigured, and Ariadne, who longs for death as she awaits the unfaithful Theseus, is herself transformed by embracing Bacchus and accepting life. Thus, we return to the theme of a new love (Ariadne's love for Bacchus) rising from the ruins an old one (her love for Theseus). This quality of relinquishing while embracing is thematically derived from the Marschallin in *Der Rosenkavalier*.

The work's original conception was a play or prologue (Moliére's *Le Bourgeois gentilhomme*) to be followed by the opera *Ariadne auf Naxos*, which itself juxtaposed the worlds of *opera seria* and *commedia dell'arte*.

The experiment fell short, and the entire work was revised by 1916: the play then became a lively operatic Prologue, presenting a behind-the-scenes view of the operatic stage, followed by the Opera itself. The work's juxtaposition and fragmentation of elements (for example, the everyday world of the Prologue versus the loftier Opera) foreshadow works that would not emerge until the 1920s. *Ariadne* offers a complex amalgam of contrasting literary and musical styles that, at face value, appear to undermine the overall coherence of the work.

In the hands of lesser artists, creating effective bridges for these jarring contrasts would have no doubt proved an impossible task. Strauss's characteristic penchant for juxtaposing the trivial and the exalted made him the ideal match for Hofmannsthal's chief aim in *Ariadne*, namely to "build on contrasts, to discover, above these contrasts, the harmony of the whole."[10] Taken together, the two versions of *Ariadne auf Naxos* embody transformation, and its implicit harmony, on various levels: from the allomatic *Verwandlung* of Bacchus and Ariadne on the narrative plane and then, conceptually, from the thirty-minute experiment transformed to a full-fledged one-act opera, at once stylized and human.[11] Hofmannsthal later remarked that the opera's greatest strength was rooted in that Austrian tradition of mixed elements (heroic mythology, French Baroque, and *commedia dell'arte*) all fused together in music. Though neither poet nor composer entirely agreed on *Ariadne* and its meanings, they nevertheless created their finest mythological opera, a work where music and text integrate as in no other opera by Strauss. It is a remarkable amalgam of style and substance, tragedy and comedy, economy and surfeit, all held together by a phantasmagoric sonic surface not surpassed by any of his operas to follow.

Hofmannsthal once reminded Strauss that opera had always been a *Gesamtkunstwerk*; Wagner had simply revisited a concept that was as old as opera itself: "since its glorious beginning, since the seventeenth century and by the terms of its fundamental purpose: the rebirth of the *Gesamtkunstwerk* of antiquity."[12] Indeed, Hofmannsthal believed that Wagner's project was less a renewal than a deformation of the original concept of a meta-art through synthesis, and the modern response should be its very opposite: set numbers instead of "endless melody," disunities instead of a totality, Greek myth instead of Teutonic legend, and by extension a Latin response to the Germanic impulse.

By returning to antiquity, removed from the dark tragedy of *Elektra*, Hofmannsthal created in *Ariadne* a thoroughly un-Wagnerian opera libretto, with musical gestures, ensembles, modes of singing, and the like built into the text, remaining unsynthesized. So sure was Hofmannsthal about the relationship between words and music that he added numerous musical annotations in the margins of his manuscript to help guide the composer, who responded positively and directly. Hofmannsthal had fully learned the craft of writing a libretto, and he had hit upon a theme that preoccupied poet and composer over the next decade. The theme was not Wagnerian redemption, but rather a "transformation through love" made manifest in marital relationships.

Opera and marriage: *Die Frau ohne Schatten* and *Die ägyptische Helena*

Strauss's next three operas, *Die Frau ohne Schatten*, *Intermezzo*, and *Die ägyptische Helena*, form a triptych of marriage operas, flanked by Hofmannsthal with an autobiographical *opera domestica* written by the composer himself. *Die Frau ohne Schatten* was, in fact, originally intended to follow *Rosenkavalier*; Strauss wanted to follow his "comedy for music" with a weightier subject. But *Ariadne*, the "interim work," soon became a major preoccupation (and source of frustration) in the years following *Rosenkavalier*. In early 1914 Hofmannsthal returned to his metaphysical fairy tale, and Strauss began composing the opera later that year. *Die Frau ohne Schatten*, with its rich orchestration, dense polyphony, and intricate symbolism is Strauss's most complex stage work, yet in many ways it is also his most personal. Though the subject concerns the shadowless Empress's search for humanity, the subplot of the Dyer, his wife, and their troubled marriage touched Strauss more deeply than any other aspect of the plot. His own marriage was troubled during this time, and Hofmannsthal may well have sensed their domestic friction when he suggested that the Dyer's Wife could be modeled "in all discretion" after Strauss's.[13]

Of the three operas, *Die Frau ohne Schatten* stands out with its narrative structuring around two different marriages between three worlds: the invisible, spiritual realm of Keikobad; the glittering, semi-mortal kingdom of the Emperor; and the noisy, prosaic world of humanity (Barak and his loved ones). The Empress "stands between two worlds," according to Hofmannsthal, "not released by one, not accepted by the other."[14] Daughter of the omniscient Keikobad, the Empress has been captured by the Emperor first while she was in the form of a gazelle, and then frozen in human form having lost her magic talisman. She has no human relationship with her husband, and is little more than a trophy (his "prey of all prey"), a sexual object as is made clear by the Nurse: "At first light he slips from her, when the stars appear he is there again. His nights are her day, his days are her night."

The immortal world of the Empress is one of constant bliss, but one lacking human passion. In order to attain mortality (to give and receive human love) she must accept the totality of the human condition: pain, death, and sacrifice. In short, to feel the fire of human passion, she must accept life's shadow, and ultimately life's risks. The Empress, whose heart is as pure yet as transparent as crystal, ultimately refuses to take the shadow (the humanity) from the mortal Barak's wife, putting the Emperor's life at risk. Through a leap of faith – recalling Ariadne's own risk-taking – she attains a shadow of her own.

The comparison between Pauline Strauss and the Dyer's Wife rings true, for despite earlier independent fame as a singer she was increasingly known as the composer's wife. The Dyer's Wife, who – out of frustration and vanity – would give her shadow to the Empress, wants more than mere marriage to Barak, the cloth dyer. She wants an identity beyond her marriage; unlike her husband, she has no name save being identified as his wife. In their different ways, the Empress and the Dyer's Wife learn something that Elektra can never know: that in order to attain humanity one must admit a responsibility to the past, present, and future of that humanity. Such an accountability, according to Hofmannsthal, can happen through marriage and the creation of a new generation.

Hofmannsthal, no doubt, offered Strauss a host of challenges in this most complex, heavily symbolic libretto that he ever wrote, but it would be a fallacy to suggest that Strauss failed to understand it. The composer's concern was not so much that Hofmannsthal's ideas be made clear to him than that his ideas become clear to an opera-going audience. He found that sense of clarity by locating the personal in this admittedly dense text. By looking into his own heart, he discovered the elusive flesh and blood he needed by taking Hofmannsthal's metaphysics of love and translating it into a palpable human conflict. Strauss took a high-minded libretto and tethered it compellingly to earth, to the opera stage and orchestra pit, exploiting a range of musical timbres, styles and forms: aria, duet, quartet, hymn, chorus, extended orchestral interludes, and instrumental solos.

Die Frau ohne Schatten, though finished in 1917, was not premiered until 1919, after the end of the Great War. By 1916, Strauss had already grown weary of late Romanticism and wrote to Hofmannsthal that this opera should be "the last Romantic opera. Hopefully you will have a fine, happy idea that will definitely help set me out on the new road."[15] For his new opera, Strauss would go that road alone; Hofmannsthal was at first appalled by the composer's idea for an *opera domestica*, though he expressed a liking for it after seeing it staged. Strauss's path led to *Intermezzo* (1924), a two-act, autobiographical sex comedy that again featured Pauline as a model for the leading female role. The work was based on a real-life incident where

Pauline mistakenly accused her husband of philandering while on tour. Strauss called his work a "bourgeois comedy with symphonic interludes" and firmly believed that he had established a new type of opera (*Spieloper*) for the twentieth century (an opinion that Schoenberg would share).[16]

By the time of *Intermezzo*, Strauss had been in Vienna for three years as co-director of the State Opera, though his closer proximity to Hofmannsthal, who disliked personal contact with Strauss and his wife, drew them apart. Indeed, it was not until 1924 that they resumed collaboration on a major project, the two-act *Die ägyptische Helena* (1927), completing Strauss's trilogy of marriage operas and, in doing so, returning to the world of Greek mythology. The approaches of this trilogy may have differed (fairy tale, comedy, mythology), but the theme remained the same: marriage, fidelity, trust, and – most important – forgiveness.

By stressing the importance of marital fidelity, by seeing this important domestic relationship not as confining but rather as a source for creativity, Strauss and Hofmannsthal stood apart from *fin-de-siècle* Austro-German culture, where such an institution was presented as middle-class, mundane, even deadening. We know from Strauss's own experience that his marriage was anything but mundane. Pauline, singer and daughter of a general, inspired countless lieder (many of which she sang in concert), as well as tone poems (such as the "hero's companion" in *Ein Heldenleben*) and operas (the Dyer's Wife in *Die Frau ohne Schatten* and Christina in *Intermezzo*). Encouraged by *Intermezzo*, Strauss declared to Hofmannsthal (albeit facetiously) his desire to become the "Offenbach of the twentieth century."[17] Hofmannsthal in turn was heartened by Strauss's continuing interest in the lighter vein and suggested a mythological operetta based on the story of Helen of Troy. The subject would be ideal for a lighter orchestra, one without the dense "Wagnerian musical armor," allowing for the voices to shine.[18]

In a certain sense, *Die ägyptische Helena* was their first and only *bel canto* work, Helena being one of Strauss's greatest soprano roles. Indeed, from the very outset, even as Hofmannsthal began devising the scenario, the poet had particular singers in mind: Maria Jeritza, Richard Tauber, and Alfred Jerger. Owing to issues financial and contractual, none of these singers sang in the premiere, which took place in Dresden in 1928. Moreover, *Helena* may have been *bel canto* in conception, but it never achieved the lighter world of *La Belle Hélène*. There are, to be sure, fanciful, satirical touches in Act I: a singing, omniscient shell; mischievous elves; and the like. But despite the Offenbachian concept, the result was, as Hofmannsthal predicted, "bound to be Richard Strauss in the end." And, indeed, the score is no less complex and demanding than *Die Frau ohne Schatten*.

But was Strauss entirely to blame? Perhaps the poet was, himself, projecting a bit, because – in the end – the text is pure Hofmannsthal.

By Act II satire takes a decided back seat to more serious matters, when Hofmannsthal brings into sharper focus those familiar themes of memory, marital fidelity, and the restoration of trust. Because of a magic potion, Helena's husband, Menelas, believes his wife to be innocent of infidelity. As much as she would like to, Helena cannot live with her husband if he remains under the spell of amnesia, even though she knows full well that he might kill her if the spell is broken.

Thus, like Ariadne, Helena gives herself to death, risking her life by offering her husband, Menelas, the potion of remembrance (allowing him to recall her infidelity). With this act of courage she is transformed and, in turn, transforms her husband, for the jealous Menelas is finally able to resolve the good and bad in Helena – and in him. Reborn, he accepts her: "Ever the same, ever new."

What links the Hofmannsthal mythological libretti is that critical moment when the title character (Ariadne, the Empress, Helena, Danae[19]) takes a potentially fatal risk and is thereby forever changed. "Transformation is the life of life itself," Hofmannsthal declared, "the real mystery of nature as creative force. Permanence is numbness and death. Whoever wants to live must surpass himself, must transform himself: he has to forget. And yet all human merit is linked with permanence, unforgetfulness, constancy."[20] For Hofmannsthal, this paradox was life's greatest enigma, and the poet believed it was explored with greatest poignancy in *Die ägyptische Helena*, his favorite and last completed opera text for Strauss.

Arabella: an untimely conclusion

Strauss's and Hofmannsthal's final collaboration, *Arabella*, would prove to be another matter, for it remains one of the most successful late-Hofmannsthal operas. *Helena* failed to satisfy Strauss's desire for an operatic comedy. He believed that, though *Rosenkavalier* had been his high water mark, he still had within him the ability to write another Viennese comedy, but without *Rosenkavalier*'s "mistakes and *longueurs*." *Arabella* marks a return to Vienna, but a Vienna of the 1860s, of the so-called *Ringstrasse* period with the Austrian capital on the verge of decline, and, thus, it shares more textual similarities with Hofmannsthal's *Der Schwierige* than with *Rosenkavalier*.

In constructing his libretto, Hofmannsthal returned to two earlier works: an unfinished play called *Der Fiaker als Graf* and a short story entitled "Lucidor." The play provided setting and atmosphere (especially the Fiaker ball), but the essence of the story came from "Lucidor," which, however, focussed more attention on Arabella's sister, Lucile – Zdenka in the opera – than Arabella herself. Strauss did not mind the fact that there were two sopranos; he had taken much pleasure in composing music for such paired voices as Ariadne–Zerbinetta, Empress–Dyer's Wife, and Helena–Aithra, but in all of these cases the title role was clearly articulated. Strauss, therefore, sent back Hofmannsthal's first draft asking that Arabella be given a soliloquy to close Act I, and Hofmannsthal's solution satisfied the composer.

So pleased was Strauss that he immediately sent a telegram of congratulations on July 15, 1929. This euphoria was sadly interrupted by tragedy. Two days earlier, Hofmannsthal's son had shot himself and, on the 15th, Strauss's librettist suffered a massive stroke while preparing for the funeral. His collaborator and artistic inspiration of two decades never opened the telegram. Strauss, profoundly shaken, was too distraught to attend the funeral (Franz and his wife Alice represented him at the ceremony in Vienna), but he sent a moving letter of sympathy from Garmisch to Hofmannsthal's widow: "This genius, this great poet, this sensitive collaborator, this unique talent! No musician ever found such a helper and supporter. No one will ever replace him for me or the world of music!"[21]

For the first time in his life, the sixty-five-year-old Strauss – who had such resilience through so many setbacks – seemed unable to emerge from depression. The normally stoic, reserved composer suddenly burst into unrestrained tears while reading aloud from Hofmannsthal's text to Elisabeth Schumann and her husband Carl Alwin, who were paying a condolence visit to Garmisch the day after the poet's death. Over the ensuing months Strauss came to feel increasingly isolated, even disoriented, convinced that his career as an opera composer had come to an end.

But Strauss was a lifetime believer in "liberation through work," and he escaped grief and impasse by doing just that, determined to set the text to Acts II and III just as Hofmannsthal had left it, the inherent dramaturgical weaknesses notwithstanding. As various commentators have noted, there are some minor changes – made for purely musical reasons – in the libretto. Despite the textual shortcomings, especially the abrupt ending of Act II, Strauss created an opera of compelling lyricism and poignancy. For once, Hofmannsthal was able to avoid the heavy psychological elements that had pervaded *Die Frau ohne Schatten* and had also worked their way into *Die ägyptische Helena*, which, we recall, had been intended as mythological operetta. *Arabella*, though not an operetta, certainly has the atmosphere of the lighter genre: a mysterious Croatian count, an Act II ballroom scene, the coloratura Fiakermilli, and sexual intrigue.

Strauss almost entirely succeeds in avoiding the dreaded "Wagnerian musical armor," with a light, conversational style reminiscent of *Intermezzo*, interspersed with soaring lyrical moments often infused with the flavor of

Croatian folk music. The famous Act I duet between Arabella and her sister, Zdenka, literally quotes a South Croatian folk song, as does the Act II duet between Arabella and her future husband, Mandryka. But the greatest moment of all is the final scene of the work, which opens with a downward sweep in the orchestra in a musical gesture recalling Strauss's lied "Allerseelen." Arabella, who has been falsely suspected by Mandryka of infidelity, is now vindicated, and descends the staircase to offer her betrothed a pure glass of water. It is a gesture based on folk custom yet, despite this act of premarital submission, Arabella is a character fully in control of her fate throughout the opera. She is "an entirely modern character" according to Hofmannsthal, and, indeed, in the final line of the piece she informs Mandryka that she can only be herself: "Take me as I am."

Hofmannsthal's continuing influence

While at work on *Arabella*, Strauss made the acquaintance of Stefan Zweig through his publisher, a mutual friend. The ultimate result was an operatic collaboration, *Die schweigsame Frau*, based on Ben Jonson's play, *The Silent Woman*. It remains Strauss's only comic work in the authentic *opera buffa* tradition, with its shades of Donizetti's *Don Pasquale*. As the published letters show, this was the happiest collaboration Strauss had ever experienced, for he now had a librettist of high quality who, years younger than Hofmannsthal, was remarkably deferential. The collaboration, officially at least, was also the shortest, given that Zweig, a Jew, had no future in Nazi Germany, which after March, 1938 included Austria.

Zweig offered his friend Joseph Gregor, a major theater historian in Vienna, as a replacement, with the promise to work with him behind the scenes if necessary. Indeed, the first Gregor opera libretto, *Friedenstag*, was conceived by Zweig who, as their published correspondence shows, provided significant hands-on assistance, as he did for Gregor's next opera, *Daphne*, as well. Though Zweig knew about Gregor's third libretto, begun in 1938, *Die Liebe der Danae*, it is doubtful he had any input, as he emigrated to London shortly after the Austrian *Anschluss*. Gregor claimed to have shown Strauss his own scenario for *Danae*, but the one Strauss wished to compose was based on a draft by Hofmannsthal from 1920.

We recall that, following the Great War, Strauss was tired of serious opera, in the wake of his grandiose *Die Frau ohne Schatten*, and he sought to move in an entirely different direction. Hofmannsthal's scenario *Danae; or, The Marriage of Convenience* was his response, a mythological operetta that conflated two myths: Danae's visitation by Jupiter in the guise of golden rain, and the legend of Midas and the golden touch. But there were too many insurmountable problems in dramaturgy and staging – even more than the preceding *Frau ohne Schatten* – and *Danae* was soon forgotten. Ultimately, *Die ägyptische Helena* would be Hofmannsthal's mythology for Strauss, though, as we have seen, not the light mythology originally envisioned.

In 1938, as Germany readied for another war, Strauss found himself in a similar state of mind to the one he had been in during the aftermath of the previous world conflict. He still wanted to compose that Offenbach-like mythology, and his friend, Willi Schuh – a music critic – had an answer. He reminded the composer of Hofmannsthal's 1920 scenario, and Strauss soon put Gregor to work fashioning a libretto from it. Though Gregor had already crafted a libretto from another person's scenario (Stefan Zweig's *Friedenstag*), this more ambitious project, with its fragile satire and complex dramaturgical demands, proved a far more overwhelming task. With much diligent work by librettist and composer, and much outside advice, a satisfactory libretto was forged.

The language of this text may be that of the prosaic Gregor, but the fundamental ideas still belong to Hofmannsthal, the very ones that appealed to Strauss throughout his lifetime in such works as *Ariadne auf Naxos, Die Frau ohne Schatten* and *Die ägyptische Helena*. First and foremost is the mixture of myth with the mundane world of everyday life and the exploration of purely human relationships within a mythological context. Jupiter is king of the gods, but he feels unfulfilled and, indeed, is envious of mortal love. At the end, like the Marschallin at the close of *Rosenkavalier* Act III, he blesses the love between Danae and Midas.

An important, and related, second theme is that of love, trust, and fidelity, which – according to Hofmannsthal – comprise the triangular essence of marriage. In all of the above-mentioned Hofmannsthal operas that essence is highlighted through the principal female character, who must make a vital choice putting herself at risk. Ariadne must choose between existing in numb grief or attaining new life and transformation by, paradoxically, reaching out potentially to death (she believes Bacchus to be Hermes, the god of death). At the very moment the shadowless Empress (in *Die Frau ohne Schatten*) refuses the shadow (the humanity) of the mortal Dyer's Wife, putting the Emperor's life in jeopardy, she attains a shadow of her own. Helena risks her life by offering her husband, Menelas, the potion of remembrance, and in doing so she is transformed.

This is the context for the great confrontation ending Act II of *Die Liebe der Danae*. Danae must choose between Jupiter and Midas, who has lost his golden touch and must return to a life of poverty. "Choose me," asks Jupiter, "I offer you a temple of gold!" "Choose me," begs Midas, "I offer you the greatest gift of all: a loving, faithful heart!" Given the choice of immortal life on Olympus or marriage to a Syrian donkey driver, she takes the latter; Jupiter, who had tried to lure her away, renounces all earthly things and, after blessing the union of Danae and Midas he returns to Olympus. Following the dress rehearsal in Salzburg (1944), after which the Festival was closed for the duration of the war, Strauss suggested that the "sovereign gods of Olympus" should have called him up as well.

This final work, with its roots in Hofmannsthal, shows Strauss's unique ambivalence towards Wagner. On the one hand, allusions to the *Ring* abound, with a Wotan-like Jupiter (obsessed by gold) in what Willi Schuh called a "Greek-*Götterdämmerung*." But Strauss's project was both to pay homage to Wagner and to find a detour around Bayreuth's metaphysical mountain. For all these apparent tributes, there are departures as well: a Greek, not a Teutonic, setting; a redemption not just through love but mortal marriage; a stage work whose continuity depended less on *Sprechgesang* than clear musical numbers, including some of Strauss's most impressive coloratura; and musical-stylistic contrasts as sharp as any other Hofmannsthal-based opera.

As an opera composer, Strauss's life-long desire was to distance himself from the aura of Wahnfried, without protest but with an artistic integrity and an originality that would assure his stage works a firm position in the operatic literature and in German musical culture. Hugo von Hofmannsthal, with his idea of an alternative to Wagner's *Gesamtkunstwerk* and his insistence that the operatic libretto might regain a sense of independence, was essential to Strauss's important project.

Strauss and Hofmannsthal were at one in rejecting a musically privileged synthesis of the arts proposed by Wagner under the philosophical umbrella of Schopenhauer. Hofmannsthal, in particular, maintained that divergent forms could be coherently harmonized or interwoven, but they should never be homogenized, which as a process – shown by Wagner – favored music above all else. A perusal of their letters shows that, even though Strauss intellectually realized this difference between Hofmannsthal's heterogeneous harmony and Wagner's disingenuous synthesis, his librettist repeatedly found it necessary to remind him of it from *Rosenkavalier* through *Arabella*.

Commentators outside Strauss studies, in German literature and in music history, have generally concluded that the relationship went on too long. For literary purists, Strauss siphoned off precious energy that Hofmannsthal should have applied to more worthy projects in the realm of spoken theater. For the equally pure high modernists in music, for whom the ideology of stylistic teleology trumped any significant discussion of contextual disciplines such as history, literature, and aesthetics, Hofmannsthal led Strauss in the wrong direction, first with *Der Rosenkavalier*, then with further affronts to the march of music history.

Even Norman Del Mar, whose three-volume survey of Strauss's works remains a major monument, felt obliged to conclude: "Nevertheless the suggestion cannot be avoided that in outstaying its original purpose the collaboration actually reached the point of doing harm to Strauss, who lost his initiative and with it his position of pre-eminence in the avant-garde of contemporary composition." These words have a strange ring in a new century, for they only make sense within an understood, if unarticulated, worldview that prized technical "progess" above all else. Strauss's view that music should not be at odds with its audience diverged significantly from the ethical tone set by some of the more strident supporters of the New Music. It was "self-evident" that Strauss's failing was being a tonal composer in an atonal era. For those who saw Strauss's canonical works as only those that purportedly answered the demands of history, Hofmannsthal led the composer away from the revered avant-garde.

What was the "purpose" of their relationship? Del Mar does not answer, though one suspects that part of that purpose was to maintain a position among the avant-garde, something in which neither ever expressed any interest. Indeed, one might well ask what the purpose of any composer–librettist collaboration might be. The simple answer is to create great, successful, and lasting music theater; surely that was Strauss's and Hofmannsthal's bottom line. Curiously, during the time in which Del Mar wrote his three-volume masterpiece (1962–72), contemporary opera was in a serious crisis, with few successful and lasting new works. Pierre Boulez's iconoclastic response to the crisis was simply to suggest burning down all the major opera houses in a kind of *Götterdämmerung* to cleanse the genre of impurities acquired over the centuries, especially the most recent one.

But opera as a viable, contemporary genre did come out of crisis, though not in the way the high modernists might have predicted. The master narrative of musical style as an inevitable, evolutionary process, one that responded less to the text than to its own historical materials, put impossible restrictions on opera composers. It is no coincidence that, as contemporary opera came out of its crisis in the eclectic 1980s, there was a simultaneous rebirth of interest in the later operas of Strauss, especially those with texts by Hofmannsthal.

A retrospective glance at their body of work shows a mutual purpose at every level. One purpose was to create a new repertoire of German opera for the twentieth century as Wagner had done in the nineteenth. The idea of a *Gesamtkunstwerk* – more a utopian goal than a final achievement for Wagner – would have to be redefined and the concept of "music drama" rejected, which Strauss had already done in his parody of that genre, *Salome*. With Hofmannsthal, the libretto gained unprecedented stature in German opera, first as *Literaturoper*, with Strauss's setting of Hofmannsthal's play, then with their first collaboration *Der Rosenkavalier: Comedy for Music in Three Acts by Hugo von Hofmannsthal*, where the librettist's name is part of the very title.

Dance is what first brought them together, and though they did not collaborate on Hofmannsthal's original ballet scenario, *Elektra* offered Strauss manifold opportunities for gesture and dance, even waltz, culminating in that maenadic moment at the end when the title character dances herself to death. Where the waltz was self-destructive in *Elektra* it was the topos for the socially binding in *Der Rosenkavalier*. "We should consider every day lost on which we have not danced at least once," Nietzsche reminds us in *Also sprach Zarathustra*, "and we should call every truth false which was not accompanied by at least one laugh."[22] Thus, Strauss's assertion that Johann Strauss, Jr. was the "laughing Genius of Vienna" should not be assumed as light-hearted or patronizing. Nietzsche at his most anti-Wagnerian also reminds us that Wagner swims and floats, but does not dance. Thus Strauss and Hofmannsthal used dance throughout their operas as a response to Wagner, as the signifier for artists free of metaphysics.

Finally, the common purpose is to be found in transformation, a theme predating Hofmannsthal in *Death and Transfiguration* (1890) and post-dating their relationship in the *Metamorphosen* (1945). Whether it surfaces in the guise of a boy turned into a rose cavalier, the transfiguring love of Ariadne and Bacchus, an Empress attaining humanity, Helena's and Menelas's marital rediscovery, or Arabella finding her womanhood, transformation means attaining a higher level, embracing the community of human beings, and, indeed, the very continuity of life.

8 Opera after Hofmannsthal

PHILIP GRAYDON

Introduction

"Your manner has so much in common with mine; we were born for one another and are certain to do fine things together." "You're Da Ponte and Scribe rolled into one."[1] Richard Strauss rejoiced in working with his longest-serving librettist, the Austrian man-of-letters Hugo von Hofmannsthal, and the feeling was mutual. Theirs, the most successful collaboration in twentieth-century opera, was predicated on mutual, professional respect, notwithstanding the natural conflict befitting of two creative artists already giants in their respective fields. *Elektra* (1908), the first of seven operas that helped to redefine the genre for the new century, set the template for a series of works unique as much for the pellucidity of their scoring as for the sheer depth of their libretti. Each partner recognized their commonality as much as those qualities that made them essentially different: Hofmannsthal's sage-like insight into twentieth-century humanity perfectly matched Strauss's candor, penchant for parody, and groundbreaking stylistic pluralism.

One can well imagine Strauss's grief at the sudden death of his colleague, confidant, and friend on July 15, 1929. While preparing to inter his son, who had committed suicide two days previously, Hofmannsthal suffered a fatal stroke. Too upset to attend the funeral, Strauss sent his son Franz and daughter-in-law Alice to Vienna, conveying a moving letter of condolence to the poet's widow, Gerty, with the following tribute: "This genius, this great poet, this sensitive collaborator, this unique talent! No musician ever found such a helper and supporter. No one will ever replace him for me or the world of music!"[2] Strauss grieved too for the unfinished libretto of *Arabella*, on which Hofmannsthal had worked right up to his death. The normally impassive composer burst into uncontrolled tears when reading aloud from the text for conductor Carl Alwin and soprano Elisabeth Schumann, who had called to Garmisch to offer their condolences the day after Hofmannsthal's death.[3] Bereft of his muse, the distraught and disoriented sixty-five-year-old concluded that his career as an opera composer was at an end. Yet despite his fears, the 1930s would be his most prolific decade in operatic output (see Table 8.1), as well as one of the most tumultuous periods in his personal and professional life.

Table 8.1 *Strauss's later operas* sans *Hofmannsthal.*

Title	Librettist	Composed	Premiere
Intermezzo	Richard Strauss	1918–23	Dresden, November 4, 1924
Die Schweigsame Frau	Stefan Zweig	1933–5	Dresden, June 24, 1935
Friedenstag	Joseph Gregor	1935–6	Munich, July 24, 1938
Daphne	Joseph Gregor	1936–7	Dresden, October 15, 1938
Die Liebe der Danae	Joseph Gregor	1938–40	Salzburg (final dress rehearsal for cancelled premiere), August 16, 1944; Salzburg, August 14, 1952
Capriccio	Clemens Krauss and Richard Strauss	1940–1	Munich, October 28, 1942

Intermezzo

Though titled "Opera after Hofmannsthal," this chapter must nonetheless begin with *Intermezzo*, composed to a libretto penned by Strauss himself and completed in the early 1920s during a five-year hiatus in his creative partnership with Hofmannsthal. This interim period saw significant refocussing on the part of the composer in light of post-war concerns, exemplified by a renewed interest in dance and attendant collaboration with other artists (such as choreographer Heinrich Kröller).[4] While practical and artistic reasons may also account for this temporary break, by 1918 Strauss had become disenchanted with large-scale post-Romanticism as epitomized by their previous opera, *Die Frau ohne Schatten* (1917). With its sprawling allegory, heavy symbolism, and often agitated counterpoint, this work represents, on the one hand, the apogee of post-Romanticism and, on the other, the irrelevance of that legacy for proponents of the anti-Romantic attitude that soon prevailed in post-war German art and society. As early as 1916, Strauss approached his librettist with the idea of "an entirely modern, absolutely realistic domestic and character comedy."[5] With Hofmannsthal completely averse to the whole concept, Strauss would have to traverse this "new road" alone.[6]

Premiering in Dresden on November 4, 1924 under conductor Fritz Busch, Strauss's *Intermezzo* – subtitled a "Bourgeois Comedy with Symphonic Interludes" – emerged as the first major post-war German opera. Drawing on an earlier incident in Strauss's private life concerning a case of mistaken identity, a supposed affair, and attendant marital difficulties, the work plays on dramatic conventions implied by the Baroque operatic genre of its title. Yet while Strauss would elsewhere call it a *Spieloper*, it nonetheless stands as the creative highpoint of the period *sans* Hofmannsthal.

Completed in 1923, *Intermezzo* underwent a long gestation, having been contemplated in germinal form by Strauss in 1911.[7] Rebuffed by Hofmannsthal, Strauss followed his librettist's advice and sought out play-wright Hermann Bahr instead. In 1908 Bahr had produced *Das Konzert*, a three-act domestic comedy featuring a distinctly Straussian musician on constant tours while his wife remained at home (perhaps unsurprisingly, the play was dedicated to Strauss). While delighted with Bahr's play, Strauss would be disappointed by his efforts for the opera, especially his watering-down of the autobiographical elements, and his overblown dramaturgy.[8] As a consequence, Strauss enclosed a series of sketched-out scenes that he labeled "almost like cinematic pictures" in a letter to Bahr of January 1, 1917, where the music was to be the "carrier," and the text merely a source of "catchwords" to sustain the action.[9] By July, overwhelmed by the composer's whims, Bahr suggested to Strauss that he himself write the libretto.[10]

Now immersed in his first solo operatic project since *Guntram* (1893), Strauss believed the new, fully fledged "conversational" style of vocal writing in *Intermezzo* to be so novel that he appended a Preface to the score reflecting his experiences as an opera conductor.[11] In particular, he stressed the importance of aiming for an ideal balance between singer and orchestra in conducting his later operas (referring here to *Salome* and *Elektra*), helped in no small part by clear articulation on the part of singers and strict observation of often varied dynamic markings on the part of individual orchestral groupings and, indeed, individual instruments. Acknowledging that such precision was not guaranteed in the hands of less attentive conductors, Strauss explained how in *Ariadne* and *Die Frau ohne Schatten* he sought to improve overall transparency and intelligibility, claiming that now, in *Intermezzo*, he had refined the "symphonic element" to such a degree that it could do nothing to impede the "natural conversational tone, culled and copied from everyday life."[12] In its passage from the prosaic to the (momentarily) profound, *Intermezzo* presents the listener with a panoply of vocal styles such as spoken dialogue, *secco* and *accompagnato* recitative, and aria. Strauss in his Preface particularly emphasized the fusion of these styles, in quasi-improvised dialogue that he termed "absolute naturalism."[13] By focussing on the conversational, Strauss presciently intimated, midway through his career as opera composer, that the genre's future lay in further such refinements.

Although *Intermezzo* can be firmly placed within the trilogy of "marriage operas" found in Strauss's oeuvre, it differs fundamentally from those that frame it – *Die Frau ohne Schatten* (1917) and *Die ägyptische Helena* (1927) – by its emphasis on *Alltäglichkeit*, the realistic world of quotidian existence over the mythical and the symbolic. Aware of its originality,

Strauss commented at the end of the *Intermezzo* Preface, if a little self-deprecatingly: "By turning its back on the popular love-and-murder interests of the usual opera libretto, and by taking its subject matter perhaps too exclusively from real life, this new work blazes a path for musical and dramatic composition which others after me may perhaps negotiate with more talent and better fortune."[14] Notwithstanding its autobiographical basis, the two-act *Intermezzo* foreshadows later *Zeitopern* by Hindemith (*Neues vom Tage*, 1929) and Schoenberg (*Von heute auf morgen*, 1930) in its presentation of a compelling slant on bourgeois culture in the fledgling Weimar Republic.[15] Thus, in a way, Strauss's idiosyncratic modernism did indeed blaze a trail of sorts for his younger contemporaries, given that Schoenberg's *Zeitoper* (composed to a text by his wife, Gertrude) also featured the use of a telephone. It is worth remembering how Schoenberg's later defence of Strauss as "one of the characteristic and outstanding figures in musical history" – made in the aftermath of World War II and the latter's reprehensible stint as president of the Nazi *Reichsmusikkammer* – drew specific attention to Strauss's 1923 opera: "Works like *Salome*, *Elektra*, *Intermezzo* and others will not perish."[16]

Strauss's bid to present *Intermezzo* as "entirely drawn from real life"[17] was apparent from its very opening. Eschewing the formalities of an overture (as also, for example, in *Salome*), Strauss propelled his audience into the epicenter of the Storch (alias Strauss) household in his serving up a slice of domestic life *chez* conductor husband, Robert (Richard) and wife, Christine (Pauline) (Example 8.1). In making Christine the central character (she appears in no fewer than ten of the total thirteen scenes), Strauss thus used this role not only to illustrate the diversity of vocal styles mentioned in his Preface but, more pointedly, to demonstrate how their application could heighten dramatic expression. As a result, Christine uses speech for conversation on the telephone, giving orders to the servants, and reading from the newspaper; dry recitative for business affairs; and *arioso* when entertaining the affections of the duplicitous young baron, whose interest in her is spurred only by the opportunity for financial gain. Vocal lyricism is reserved solely for her moments of contemplation beside the fire, bed-time wishes for her son, and the concluding duet in which she and Robert are reunited.[18] In fact, lyricism in general is confined mostly to the "symphonic interludes" of the work's subtitle, into which the brief cinematic scenes segue, with their provision of a commentary on the action leading some later commentators to class them as quasi-symphonic poems.[19]

For most contemporary critics *Intermezzo* represented a return to form for Strauss, and reviews teemed with language applied to the *Zeitopern* of the later 1920s: *Gusto der Welt*, *Alltagsprosa*, *Milieuechtheit*, and *nüchterne Sachlichkeit*.[20] While later observers have highlighted the opera's more

Example 8.1 *Intermezzo*, mm. 1–4

traditional elements, such as Strauss's trademark representational use of keys and thoroughly tonal harmonic language,[21] these dovetail with striking novelties: its everyday setting, repudiation of idealism, and vocal-stylistic naturalism. Thus, Strauss's *Intermezzo* represents the post-war, early *Zeitoper* by virtue of its conception as a piece of music theater specifically designed not for the *Oper*, but for the *Schauspielhaus*. In fact, Strauss articulated as much in its Preface, advising that the opera be given in a small theater with a capacity of under a thousand where singers should avoid traditional operatic gestures. *Intermezzo* may require a special type of singer-actor, but it was essentially designed as a *Kammeroper* for the 1920s. Moreover, when Strauss spoke of "blazing a path," he may also have meant creating a more viable form of opera for production in the harsh economic reality of Weimar Germany.

"A born comic opera"

Despite rough spots in the second and third acts of *Arabella*, Strauss decided to press on without tampering with Hofmannsthal's text. But finishing the opera proved to be no easy task; minor projects aside, it took until October, 1932 to complete the score. Strauss's despondency at having lost his treasured collaborator was somewhat assuaged during 1931 when he was put in touch with the Austrian writer Stefan Zweig through the publisher Anton Kippenberg. Urged on by their intermediary, Zweig sent Strauss two proposals in late October: an overly ambitious multimedia pantomime, and "a cheerful lively *Spieloper*" based on Ben Jonson's *Epicoene; or, The Silent Woman* (1609). Choosing the latter, Strauss could hardly contain himself upon receiving Zweig's preliminary outline: "enchanting – a born comic opera – a comedy equal to the best of its kind – more suitable for music than even *Figaro* or the *Barber of Seville*."[22]

Eventually named *Die schweigsame Frau*, the opera was the composer's first and only work in full *buffo* mode. Like Donizetti's *Don Pasquale* (1843), it features a cantankerous old bachelor (in this case, a retired sea-dog appropriately named Sir Morosus) who is tricked by friends and relatives. Pining after a world without noise and, as a result, resolutely anti-music (he disinherits his nephew Henry for joining an opera troupe), Morosus is persuaded to seek the hand of a silent woman in marriage. Settling on a seemingly ideal companion in the form of Timida (alias Henry's wife Aminta, the troupe's coloratura soprano), Morosus is horrified to discover that his "silent woman" is actually an intolerable virago as she whoops up a terrible racket. After a mock divorce hearing, Henry and Aminta admit to the whole sham and Morosus, though initially enraged, forgives all in contentment.

With its almost unbroken parlando, *Die schweigsame Frau* picks up where *Intermezzo* left off in terms of vocal style, though with even less by way of lyricism. Replete with witty allusions to Italian opera, the score sees Strauss in unbridled form, reveling in having found the ideal successor to the late Hofmannsthal. But his joy was short-lived. The completion of the three-act libretto on January 29, 1933 was followed two days later by Hitler's appointment as German Chancellor, though initially neither Strauss nor Zweig recognized the consequences for their collaboration. While *Die schweigsame Frau* was cleared by Nazi censors in time for its premiere in June, 1935, Strauss's special relationship with a Jewish artist was doomed – a reality that he was slow to accept. The composer's position was complicated particularly by his role as president of the *Reichsmusikkammer*, a "troublesome honorary office" (as he called it) which, in a heated letter to Zweig, he claimed to be "miming":

> Do you believe that I am ever, in any of my actions, guided by the thought that I am "German" …? Do you believe that Mozart composed as an "Aryan"? I know only two types of people: those with and those without talent. The people [*das Volk*] exist only for me at the moment they become

audience. Whether they are Chinese, Bavarians, New Zealanders, or
Berliners leaves me cold. What matters is that they pay the full price for
admission.[23]

Zweig never received the letter, as it was intercepted by the Gestapo. The
political backlash resulted in Strauss being forced to resign his post, thereby
intensifying the uneasy and often treacherous relationship between the
aged composer and the Nazi government – a situation further exacerbated
that fall by the passing of the Nuremberg Laws, which stripped Strauss's
Jewish daughter-in-law and two grandsons of their basic rights as citizens
of the Reich. For *Die schweigsame Frau*, the aftershock was just as abrupt;
premiering a week after the letter's interception, it was summarily canceled
after just four performances.

"Day of Peace," *Daphne*, and *Danae*

Zweig had been intensely aware just how untenable his collaboration with
Strauss was for some time before the axe finally fell. By April, 1935, he had
suggested writers Rudolf Binding, Robert Faesi, and Alexander Lernet-
Holenia as viable alternatives, but Strauss rejected them all outright. Such
was likewise the case when Zweig suggested Joseph Gregor, a respected
Austrian theater historian and budding playwright, but after six weeks of
concerted prodding by Zweig, and an assurance that he would vet everything Gregor produced, Strauss reluctantly acceded to a meeting on July 7.
According to Gregor, he showed the composer six proposals from which
Strauss picked three as "the working program for the next four years was
established."[24] While Gregor's comment betrays an element of rose-tinted
hindsight, it seems reasonable to speculate that the four-year "program"
included Strauss's next three operas (*Friedenstag, Daphne*, and *Die Liebe
der Danae*).

To declare that Strauss remained indifferent towards Gregor's work
throughout their collaboration would be an understatement; even prior
to their meeting, he was all too aware of the latter's limitations, lambasting
Gregor's sketch for a libretto on Calderon's *Semiramis* as "a philologist's
childish fairy tale" in a letter to Zweig of May 17.[25] Strauss's frustration
was compounded further during the summer of 1935 as he labored over
Gregor's reworking of Zweig's *Friedenstag* text, leading the composer to
postpone operatic projects temporarily and to seek consolation in Goethe
and Rückert instead. Having set Rückert's poetry in the a cappella double
chorus *Die Göttin im Putzzimmer* earlier that year, Strauss returned to it for
the *Drei Männerchöre* which, along with two incomplete choral sketches,

are crucial to an understanding of Strauss's tortured state of mind during this period. As Bryan Gilliam has shown, the incomplete sketches – "Friede im Innern" ("Inner Peace") and "Sühnung" ("Reconciliation") – particularly mirror Strauss's antipathy towards German politics and his fear of imminent war, leavened by a hope of finding some form of inner peace.[26]

By fall, 1935, Strauss was ready to resume work on *Friedenstag*, having accepted that his collaboration with Zweig was over, and that his immediate future lay with the hapless Gregor (whom Zweig promised to assist incognito). Set at the end of the Thirty Years' War and based on the Peace of Westphalia in 1648, the main action centres on the citadel of a beleaguered town headed by a Commandant determined to hold out against approaching forces from Protestant Holstein. A call for surrender from a delegation from the town is politely but firmly rejected by the uncompromising Commandant; although he agrees to fire a "signal" to open the town gates, the signal will be for his men to obliterate the citadel and its inhabitants. The Commandant's wife, Maria, then enters alone, bemoaning the destruction wrought by war and extolling the promise that future peace would bring in direct contrast to her militant husband. With distinctly topical political overtones *Friedenstag* concludes with resolution between the military opponents and is even crowned by a *Fidelio*-style, C major choral finale as the former enemies join together in a paean to peace.[27]

Though cut from the same cloth as the choral compositions that immediately preceded it, and completed during a period of acute instability in the composer's private life, the starkly somber tone of *Friedenstag* is nonetheless unsettling. Veering between Mahler and Kurt Weill at its opening, its musical references to the march idiom – particularly Mahler's Sixth Symphony and Bach's *Ein' feste Burg* – reveal a tangible measure of ironic distance between Strauss and the martial aspects of his subject, though Maria's lyrical entreaty for peace serves to provide temporary respite midflow. Completed in 1936 and premiered in July, 1938, *Friedenstag* vanished off the radar with the outbreak of war, and productions since 1945 have been few and far between. More scenic cantata than opera, when revived it has tended to appear in concert form; however, with no fewer than three recordings over the last two decades, the work would seem to have a future.[28]

Strauss's collaboration with Gregor continued with *Daphne*, another one-act opera, originally conceived as a companion-piece to *Friedenstag* in an integral double-bill. Having recently viewed a lithograph of Apollo and Daphne by Theodor Chasseriau, Gregor began to fashion a libretto centering on Chasseriau's portrayal of Apollo as amorous romantic and Daphne as chaste innocent, ending with Daphne being transformed into a laurel tree (as described in Ovid's *Metamorphoses*). Sending the first draft (with

Zweig's criticisms enclosed) to Strauss in early September, 1935, Gregor was advised by the composer to expunge a loquacious Zeus-figure and an unworkable Medusa ballet and focus instead on the virginal Daphne. While Gregor eventually followed this advice, he was continuously subjected to Strauss's often scathing remarks. Lambasting Gregor's "schoolmasterly *Weltanschauungs*-banalities" and his "not particularly felicitous imitation of Homeric jargon," Strauss was unashamedly forthright throughout the process: "I am naturally sorry that I hurt your feelings. The surgeon's saw also hurts, when it is used without anesthetic."[29] With much outside assistance from Zweig, Strauss, and the conductor Clemens Krauss – whose increasing artistic association with Strauss would culminate in collaboration with the composer on *Capriccio* – Gregor revised his text three times before Strauss was ready to compose.

By early spring, 1937, though, Strauss reached an impasse. In a conscious bid to link *Daphne* with planned companion-piece *Friedenstag*, Gregor had written a tedious choral finale in which all the voices would celebrate Daphne's transformation. Thoroughly unconvinced, Strauss consulted his friend Krauss, who pointed to the absurdity of assembling characters on stage to sing to a tree. Instead, Krauss suggested that the composer "close the piece with the visible transformation [of Daphne] and the gradual transition of human language into the [wordless] voice of nature."[30] As the composer wrote in a letter to Gregor of May 12, 1937: "After Apollo's *Abgesang* no human being but Daphne must appear on stage, no Peneios, no solo voices – no chorus – in short, no oratorio."[31] For Strauss, the visual effect of this closing scene was paramount: "In the moonlight, but still fully visible – the miracle of transformation occurs: *only with orchestra alone*! At most Daphne might speak a few words during the transformation, which turn into stuttering and then *wordless* melody!"[32] The theme of transformation, transfiguration, and metamorphosis was one that ran through Strauss's music from the tone poem *Death and Transfiguration* (1890) through the *Metamorphosen* (1945); it was of enduring interest to Hofmannsthal also, featuring in almost all the poet's libretti for Strauss.[33] Recalling and simultaneously inverting the trend instanced in *Ariadne auf Naxos* – where Ariadne is transfigured through her love for Bacchus – and *Die Frau ohne Schatten* – where a shadowless Empress is transformed into a mortal being through a profound act of humanity – the human Daphne is immortalized by Apollo as the eternal voice of nature. With its luminescent orchestration and ethereal vocalise, the raiment of this closing scene captures perfectly the autumnal glow of late-period Strauss opera.

While Gregor's original plan for joining *Friedenstag* and *Daphne* by interlinked choral finales was scrapped, the notion of performing them successively lasted for a time, and it was in this form that the latter opera was premiered in Dresden in October, 1938 under its dedicatee Karl Böhm. Though the night was a success, the inordinate length of the evening's proceedings (nearly four hours, bar one intermission) led to *Friedenstag* and *Daphne* parting company. The most distinguished of the three Gregor works, *Daphne* has also benefited from an upsurge in interest in recent years, as a reappraisal of Strauss's late operas by critics and public alike continues apace.

Strauss's final collaboration with Gregor was on a similarly mythological subject, if of a lighter hue. Reminded by Willi Schuh of an incomplete draft sketched by Hofmannsthal around 1920 entitled *Danae; oder, Der Vernunftheirat* [*Danae; or, The Marriage of Convenience*], Strauss asked Gregor to revive this conflation of two myths: Jupiter's visit to Danae disguised as golden rain, and the tale of Midas and the golden touch. Though Gregor had already shown Strauss his own *Danae* scenario in 1936, it was Hofmannsthal's draft that sparked the composer's creative imagination some two years later. The demands of Hofmannsthal's text, an ironic satire based on Austria's post-war position, far exceeded Gregor's meager talents, but a libretto finally came to fruition with the aid of others (namely Zweig, Krauss, and opera producer Lothar Wallerstein).

The opera *Die Liebe der Danae* was described by its creators as *heitere Mythologie* ("cheerful mythology") – with the German invasion of Poland on September 1, 1939 and the formal outbreak of World War II a few days later, Strauss was in dire need of diversion. By September 7 he began scoring Act I, convinced that *Danae* would be his last opera. Perhaps predictably, "cheerful" turned to serious amidst crises both personal and political. Ever industrious despite his advancing age, Strauss completed the score of his veritable *opera semiseria* in June, 1940.

Almost three hours in duration, *Die Liebe der Danae* is as demanding of its audience as it is of its producer and cast. In the four queens (Jupiter's former lovers), the opera includes vocally demanding parts for comparatively minor roles as well as its principals. Indeed, the title role (which was tailor-made for Krauss's wife, soprano Viorica Ursuleac) calls for a particular type of singer capable of quietly sustaining notes in the upper tessitura (a fine example being "Nimm denn Gold" at the end of the final act, as Danae – renouncing money and power for love – thanks Jupiter for "the curse that was really a blessing," giving him in gratitude a comb from her hair as her last item of value). In a similar fashion, the Wotan-like Jupiter – who had tried to tempt Danae away from an earthly existence – requires a baritone of suitably Wagnerian dimensions, most notably in the monologue "Maia Erzählung," where he enthuses about his early love for the spring goddess Maia, before blessing the union of Danae and Midas and taking leave of the world.

Determined that *Die Liebe der Danae* would receive a post-war (and thus likely posthumous) premiere, Strauss forbade such an event until at least two years after an armistice. However, after much badgering by Clemens Krauss, the composer reluctantly agreed to a Salzburg first performance in 1944, only to see that opportunity disappear upon the declaration of "total war" by Propaganda Minister Joseph Goebbels on August 1. Through the auspices of the Salzburg Gauleiter, Goebbels did permit rehearsals for the new opera to continue, but on the proviso that no actual production would follow. At the final dress rehearsal, before an invited audience on August 16, 1944, the spectacle of a resigned Jupiter returning to Olympus at the opera's end obviously struck a chord with the eighty-year-old Strauss, who, after the dress rehearsal, ventured that perhaps the "sovereign gods of Olympus" should have called him up too. Turning to the Vienna Philharmonic, he mused: "maybe we will see each other again in a better world."[34] Events global, political, and personal had impacted greatly on the resilient composer, as the normally stoic Strauss was overcome with a rare public display of emotion.

Despite its multiple collaborators, *Die Liebe der Danae* still manages to evoke Hofmannsthal, primarily though its tripartite emphasis on marriage, fidelity, and memory, which recalls *Die Frau ohne Schatten* and, in particular, *Die ägyptische Helena*.[35] But the links between *Danae* and *Helena* run deeper still, especially given their mutual origins in the early 1920s in the context of societal and cultural ruin tempered by the possibility of restoration.[36] When, in a speech to the audience at the 1944 *Danae* dress rehearsal, Strauss bewailed that western culture (*abendländische Kultur*) was at an end,[37] it was clear that the aged composer no longer held the aspirations of renewal embedded in the opera's core.

Ton oder Wort?

As ever, Strauss found consolation in work, now with an opera far removed from mythological grandeur. In fact, its origins reached back to the relative stability of 1934 and to Zweig, who discovered an eighteenth-century libretto entitled *Prima la musica e poi la parole* (*First the Music and Then the Text*) by Giovanni Battista Casti while researching in the British Museum. Set to music by Antonio Salieri, this theatrical *divertimento* was first performed in the Orangery at Schönbrunn outside Vienna in 1786 alongside Mozart's *Der Schauspieldirektor* (*The Impressario*). Whereas Mozart's comedy dealt with the practicalities of opera production, the Casti–Salieri work was concerned with opera's inbuilt tension between music and words – externalized by its inclusion of a composer and his poet as characters – and it was on this premise that Strauss conceived *Capriccio* (1941), a *Konversationsstück* ["conversation-piece"] *für Musik*. While one can detect both the spirit and the letter of *Ariadne auf Naxos* in its broad outlines, *Capriccio* represents a true *terminus ad quem* in terms of Strauss's trajectory as opera composer. If *Ariadne* presents its audience with an opera within an opera, *Capriccio* stands as meta-opera – an opera about the very nature of the genre, observed in the round. Given its experimental mold, it is not surprising that Strauss pitched his one-act debate about words and music at connoisseurs rather than the regular opera-going public.

Prodded into action by Zweig (who supervised from the wings) Gregor approached Strauss with a text fashioned on the Casti libretto in June, 1935. With his usual condescension, Strauss dispensed with Gregor's effort and the idea was shelved. By 1939, however, Strauss had asked Gregor to revive his plan, only to reject the first drafts as "dialogue which does not correspond to my taste in either form or content."[38] "I don't want to write another 'opera' at all," Strauss complained to Clemens Krauss: "I want something extraordinary, a dramaturgical treatise, a theatrical fugue … [N]ot lyricism, not poetry, not emotional vapourings; rational theatrical dialogue … dry wit."[39] It soon became clear to Strauss that Gregor was neither suitable for, nor capable of, collaboration on the "little discussion opera," and Krauss, who advised Strauss towards swift dispensation with Gregor's services and another solo effort on the composer's part *à la Intermezzo*, was soon enlisted as collaborator.

Set in a chateau near Paris during the so-called *Querelle des bouffons* ("War of the Bouffons") of the mid eighteenth century, *Capriccio* presents an intensification of the debate over the respective merits of French and Italian opera by hypostasizing the particular virtues possessed by words and music and their multivalent interrelation. With respect to its historical setting, Strauss luxuriates in the recreation of this milieu as filtered though his own experience as inveterate man-of-the-theater. Thus, we find musical quotations from Gluck, Piccinni, and Rameau, and textual allusions to Metastasio, Pascal, and Ronsard, mixed with musical self-references to *Ariadne*, *Daphne*, and the 1918 song-cycle, *Krämerspiegel* (*The Artist's Mirror*) – a triadic grouping tellingly book-ended by works that dwell on the realization and reception of artistic creativity.

The cast is comprised almost entirely of symbolic characters: composer Flamand (music), poet Olivier (words), La Roche (stage direction), and a Count and Countess (patrons). Both poet and composer are in love with the young widowed Countess Madeleine and, over the course of a day, try in turn to win her heart, primarily by respective recitation (by Olivier) and musical setting (by Flamand) of a sonnet excerpted from a play written by Olivier, intended for performance by the actress Clairon and the Count

under La Roche's direction.[40] But the Countess is unwilling to choose
between Olivier and Flamand, despite her attraction to both. As the conversation progresses, Flamand and Olivier resolve to write an opera on the
events of the day (the opera that any audience viewing *Capriccio* are thus
beholding), with the ending decided by Madeleine's definitive choice.

As Bryan Gilliam observes, the last of the thirteen scenes in *Capriccio*
catalogues the end-point of the sonnet's journey upwards from colourless
baritonal oration by the Count to poetic recitation by its "author" Olivier,
before continuing via a musical setting by the composer Flamand (tenor)
through to the *ne plus ultra* afforded by the Countess's soprano voice.[41] The
celebrated final scene is introduced by an orchestral prelude (the so-called
"moonlight music," based on the eighth and last song of *Krämerspiegel*); here
the piano original is replaced by the plaintive strains of the horn against a
gently undulating string background, consequently adding to the nostalgic
character of the opera as a whole (Example 8.2).[42] At the final curtain, the
Countess is faced with an ultimate choice between the composer and the
poet: to decide, in effect, between music and words. As if the audience need
be in any doubt, the sheer beauty of the opera's close – a monologue show-
casing Strauss's favourite instrument, the soprano voice – surely provides
the answer. But the effect left one important contemporary observer at least
curious. Upon finishing work on the opera, Krauss enquired as to a further
collaboration on the part of the composer, to which Strauss declared: "Isn't
this D flat major [final scene] the best summation of my theatrical life's
work? One can only leave one testament!"[43]

Conclusion

Subtitled "A Conversation-Piece for Music," *Capriccio* should lead full-
circle to *Intermezzo* in any considered précis of the late operas. Devoid of
Hofmannsthal's trademark psychological complexity, Strauss's characters
in these two operas display an earthy realism heightened by speechlike
vocal writing that looked back to *Ariadne auf Naxos* while (in the case
of *Intermezzo*) anticipating and (in the case of *Capriccio*) contextualiz-
ing the achievements of *Die schweigsame Frau*. *Daphne* and *Danae*, on
the other hand, signaled both a return to Greek mythology and a new
emphasis on clarity, lyricism, and transparency evident in the composer's
vocal and orchestral writing. In terms of their musical language, Strauss's
late operas chart the gradual refinement of a harmonic idiom predicated
on an enriched, chromaticized tonality whose utilization remained fresh
from work to work, yet uniquely Straussian in its deportment. As the
most important German opera composer of the first half of the twentieth

Example 8.2 *Capriccio*, final scene, rehearsal no. 258

century, Strauss wore that particular mantle with a palpable degree of confidence.

Yet with the wisdom of maturity came a certain wistfulness on the composer's part: a yearning for the certainties of the past against the backdrop of an unsure present. While anachronistic, ahistorical reminiscences from his own works and those of other composers – including seemingly arbitrary allusions to often mutually discrete musical eras – had long been part of Strauss's compositional stock-in-trade,[44] the late operas are marked by an increase in self-identification that accentuates their retrospective tone.

Though self-identification is present in Strauss's music from the early orchestral works onward (either covertly, as in *Don Juan* and *Zarathustra*; or overtly, as in *Heldenleben* and *Symphonia domestica*), the *sans-* and post-Hofmannsthal operas evidence a figure making the transition from mid-life to old age – and, by extension, artistic maturity to mastery – through the conduit of his creative impulse. Thus, the very personal identification felt by Strauss with Barak the Dyer in *Die Frau ohne Schatten* became sub-limated in the virtual self-casting plainly apparent in *Intermezzo*, with the security offered by domesticity as much a desideratum for Morosus in *Die schweigsame Frau* as it was for the maintenance of Strauss's strict, self-imposed work ethic. The ardor of youth in remembrance of past glories propels Apollo and Jupiter, respectively, in *Daphne* and *Danae*, even if such fleeting backward glances offer only temporary distraction from resigna-tion to fate in the former, and departure from the mortal world in the latter. Though modeled on the Austrian theater director Max Reinhardt, the fig-ure cut by La Roche in *Capriccio* is clearly semi-autobiographical – from the dictatorial posturing to his uncharacteristically serious monologue in Scene ix, where he laments the state of modern drama (and, by implication, modern music): "Where is the masterpiece that speaks to the hearts of the people …? I cannot discover it, although I keep on searching … They make fun of the old and create nothing new."

While it signaled a fitting end to Strauss's career as opera composer, *Capriccio* was followed by a remarkable return to instrumental compos-ition in a series of works he wryly dubbed *Handgelenksübungen* – musical "wrist exercises" for the purposes of keeping the hand supple. Despite specifically leaving this corpus of music without opus numbers, Strauss counted them among his best instrumental works. Displaying an economy of means and a character of utterance at once nostalgic and ebullient, the late works take up where the wordless conclusion to *Daphne* and, in a more visual sense, the on-stage string Sextet at the start of *Capriccio*, leave off – as witness to the noumenal world of pure sound.

9 "Actually, I like my songs best": Strauss's lieder

SUSAN YOUENS

If readers should perhaps take Strauss's statement to the great singer Hans Hotter with a barrel of salt,[1] given the composer's primary dedication to opera, it is nevertheless true that, from beginning to end, he wrote songs.[2] He lived around singers his entire life, after all; in his boyhood, he heard his aunt Johanna Pschorr – a gifted amateur mezzo-soprano – sing, and his father Franz Strauss played the horn in orchestral performances with some of the best singers of the day. Later, Richard's wife Pauline de Ahna was an accomplished professional soprano at the time of their marriage. In fact, Strauss began composing songs when he was a mere six-and-a-half years old: the earliest of thirty-two youthful songs without opus numbers, "Weihnachtslied" ("Christmas Song") on a poem by Christian Friedrich Daniel Schubart (the poet of Schubert's "Die Forelle"), was composed in 1870. There are gems to be found in this repertory composed before Strauss deemed his songs publishable; we discover, for example, that his love of Ludwig Uhland's poetry began early with such sensitive songs as "Die Drossel" ("The Thrush"), while "Der müde Wanderer" ("The Weary Wanderer") on a poem by August Hoffmann von Fallersleben is another worthwhile creation.[3] Nine other early songs are now lost, including a cluster of five lieder composed in the early 1880s; how one wishes that "Mein Geist ist trüb" ("My Soul is Dark") on a poem by Lord Byron would surface, and we could see what the conjunction of the great British Romantic poet and the twenty-year-old composer produced in this, his only setting of that poet. Thereafter, Strauss would compose 158 songs between 1885 and his death in 1948, songs that range from single-page miniatures ("Die Zeitlose" ["The Meadow Saffron"], Op. 10, No. 7 on a poem by Hermann von Gilm zu Rosenegg) to the operatic expansiveness of "Die Liebe" ("Love"), Op. 71, No. 3 on a text by Friedrich Hölderlin, which unfurls to thirteen pages in length. His "last rose," as he called it, was the song "Malven" ("Mallows"), for soprano and piano on a poem by the Swiss poet Betty Wehrli-Knobel, composed on November 23, 1948, some nine months before his death on September 8, 1949. In other words, songs are the book-ends on either side of his life.[4] If the lied was not his chief *métier*, it was of great importance at crucial periods in his life, and there is considerable variety to be found here.

But only a smattering of early songs from the 1880s and 1890s, along with an even scantier selection of works from Strauss's "middle years" and the immortal *Vier letzte Lieder* at the end of the composer's life, are standard fare in most singers' repertories. "Die Nacht" ("Night"), Op. 10, No. 3; "Allerseelen" ("All Souls' Day"), Op. 10, No. 8; "Ständchen" ("Serenade"), Op. 17, No. 2; "Breit' über mein Haupt" ("Unbind Your Black Hair over My Head"), "Schön sind, doch kalt die Himmelssterne" ("Beautiful but Cold Are the Stars in the Sky"), and "Wie sollten wir geheim sie halten" ("How Could We Have Kept Secret"), Op. 19, Nos. 2–4; "Du meines Herzens Krönelein" ("You, the Diadem of My Heart"), Op. 21, No. 2; "Morgen!" ("Tomorrow!"), Op. 27, No. 4; "Traum durch die Dämmerung" ("Reverie at Twilight"), Op. 29, No. 1; and "Freundliche Vision" ("A Pleasant Vision"), Op. 48, No. 1: any recital-goer will have heard these songs many times over. They deserve their status as "chestnuts" – who would not love such an exquisite thing as "Traum durch die Dämmerung"?[5] – but their ubiquity, coupled with the composer's occasional descent into post-"Ride of the Valkyries" noise-noise-and-more-noise, have led many to condemn Strauss's songs as inferior to those of Brahms, Wolf, and Mahler.

It cannot be denied, I think, that his notions of the relationship of word and tone in song were differently constituted than theirs. When he was twenty-nine years old, he responded to a questionnaire in which he wrote that apathy about composition could vanish instantly whenever he browsed through volumes of poetry. When a particular poem attracted his notice, usually because it reflected his mood at the moment, music would, so he wrote, spring to mind immediately. But when his chosen poem failed to produce inspiration, he would bend his musical mood to fit the words "as best I can," the song thus being made, not born.[6] Somewhat defensively, he would tell his good friend Max Marschalk years later, "By the way, work is also a matter of talent!" – thus asserting the labor that went into fashioning his beautiful melodies.[7] There is on occasion something of the dutiful Bavarian laborer about Strauss, evident in the determination to compose even when the mysterious creative wheels in the brain were failing to turn with their customary alacrity. That one can tell when he was churning out music regardless and when he was inspired is only to be expected.

But there are gems to discover for those who wander off the beaten path and more grounds for admiration than the doubters might suspect. Consequently, I plan to dwell in this chapter on a few of the less well-known songs in which nothing is routine, songs devoid of the arch sentimentality that mars the likes of "Heimliche Aufforderung" ("Secret Invitation"); the composer, I believe, misread John Henry Mackay's poetic scenario and made of hidden love a splashy, exhibitionistic display. Given inevitable word limits on these occasions, I have also committed sacrilege and omitted the *Vier letzte Lieder* from my slate; they are among the most studied of all Strauss's songs[8] and will assuredly continue to draw notice, given their place as the crowning glory of Strauss's oeuvre, his *opus ultimum*. I believe that other lieder by this composer deserve that honor too.

Of contemporary poets, early mastery, and an aesthetic of song

At age twenty-one, Strauss began offering his songs in the public market-place of print. For the ten years from 1885 to 1895, the Biedermeier poets prominent in his youthful songs gave way to two later groups of poets: (1) those belonging to the generation or two before Strauss's own day, such as Hermann von Gilm zu Rosenegg (1812–64), Adolf Friedrich von Schack (1815–94, whose poetry Brahms also liked), and Felix Dahn (1834–1912); and (2) the composer's own contemporaries, includ-ing Detlev von Liliencron (1844–1909), Richard Dehmel (1863–1920), Otto Julius Bierbaum (the masterful translator of Albert Giraud's *Pierrot lunaire*, 1865–1910), Emanuel von Bodmann (1874–1946), Carl Busse (1872–1918), and Karl Henckell (1864–1929), the latter a Socialist who waged a war of words on behalf of the proletariat in poems such as "Die kranke Proletarierin" ("The Ill Worker-Woman"), "Der Polizeikommissar" ("The Police Commissioner"), and "Kaiser und Arbeiter" ("Emperor and Worker"), before ceding to sweeter, simpler nature and love poems late in his life. Felix Dahn (whose photograph in old age displays a splendid forked beard, neatly divided into two "V"-shaped bundles) was a virulent anti-Semite whose scholarship would later help shore up Nazi ideology during its brief span, but Strauss was only interested in his lyric poems, which provided the texts for the *Schlichte Weisen* (*Simple Melodies*) of Op. 21 and the *Mädchenblumen* (*Maiden-Flowers*) of Op. 22.[9] None of these writers were of the first rank, and their names might not have endured without the musical settings by the likes of Brahms, Strauss, and Schoenberg. Several of Strauss's contemporaries were properly grateful to the composer for his services on their behalf; Henckell, to whom Strauss sent a dedicatory copy of "Ruhe, meine Seele!" ("Rest, my soul!"), was able to recognize the qual-ity of this "music that shivers so lightly, with hardly a wave breaking … it seems to me that you have transcribed the verse, or absorbed it, or what-ever the correct expression is, quite magnificently."[10] It is amusing to see a poet thus admit to being flummoxed about the proper terminology for the transfer of poetry into music. The astute recognition that "something hap-pens" to poetry in the process is present and accounted for.

The first lied in Strauss's first song opus, "Zueignung," Op. 10, No. 1, is a setting of a feeble effusion by Gilm (his poetry was composed in secret and only published posthumously), and it establishes certain patterns consistent with many of Strauss's works thereafter.[11] On the positive side, the consummate writing for the voice is a hallmark of Straussian song, manifested in sweeping melodic phrases designed for maximum sensuous delight on both the performer's and listener's part. It is no wonder that singers love this repertory. On the negative side, Strauss at times makes use of standard figuration in the piano in a fashion that extends the harmonies but cannot be understood as an outgrowth of the poetry after the manner of Schubert or (differently) Schumann. Where Schubert resorts to conventional figuration, he shapes it to poetic purposes in inventive ways; for example, the repeated chords in the right-hand part throughout "Der Einsame" ("The Solitary Man") are integral to this vivid portrait of a nameless, slightly priggish and self-important but nevertheless dear man immersed in quiet happiness by the hearth. In the ticking chords, we hear time pass in utter contentment, and we are told of the muted vitality that pervades this bliss devoid of drama. The left-hand chords that fill Strauss's "Mein Auge" ("My Eye"), Op. 37, No. 4, on the other hand, seem merely a way to stretch out harmonies by means other than orchestral; they are a somewhat mechanical way of redressing the decaying sound of harmonies even on the biggest, loudest modern pianos. There are, to be sure, cases where routine patterns such as broken-chordal figures are marvelously appropriate, as in the hypnotic, lulling, harp-like waves throughout the "Wiegenlied," Op. 41a, No. 1, on a poem by Dehmel (the song is nevertheless at its best in orchestral guise), but elsewhere, conventional figuration can seem like Strauss soldiering away at his writing desk no matter what.

From a potpourri of comments, letters, and statements, one can piece together at least a partial Straussian aesthetic of song, beginning with Strauss's belief that poetry at its most superlative had no need of music.[12] He was speaking in particular of one of his household gods, Goethe, whose witty definition of vocal music (*Vokalmusik*) as singing in which one only hears the vowels (*Vokale*) Strauss quotes in a letter of March 4, 1943 to Karl Böhm; the conductor is enjoined to copy out the pun in large letters and hang it in the director's room as a *mene tekel* for those singers who fail to pay proper attention to consonants.[13] The encomiums to Goethe are sprinkled throughout the Straussian record: accused of this, that, and the other influence on the libretto of *Guntram*, Strauss replied that "for the last four months I've studied only Wagner, Goethe, and Schopenhauer," and, while sightseeing in Egypt, he wrote of "luxuriating" in *Wilhelm Meisters Wanderjahre* – "dear God, there's so much in that book," he said. He read Goethe on the boat to South America in 1920; in 1928, he quoted Goethe's advice that everybody should write memoirs; and in the terrible year of 1944, he reread the entire Propyläen edition, minus the *Farbenlehre*.[14] But if immersion in Goethe is a constant in his life, Goethe songs are not, with occasional exceptions.[15] For lieder, he was more wont to gravitate to the likes of Henckell, whose verse may not be stellar but who provided the impetus for some stellar songs from Strauss's pen.

The first of Strauss's ten Henckell songs, "Ruhe, meine Seele!," Op. 27, No. 1, is an exceptional work by anyone's reckoning. I wonder whether Strauss remembered the beginning of Schubert's great Heine song "Am Meer" when he set this poem invoking rest and peace for the soul in Nature's quiet midst, whatever history's storms raging outside? It is the repetition of slurred half-note harmonies in the piano at the start that brings the earlier work to mind. Despite very different subject matter, both poets, one a genius, one not, establish a contrast between zones of joy and beauty on the one hand, of horror on the other; it is an inspired reminiscence, whether or not Strauss was aware of it. Certainly he engineers the contrasting regions differently. His introductory chords are different varieties of seventh chords in inversion, one after another, with tonal certitude as clouded as the possibility of peace in the soul. Common-tone linkage and chromatic sideslipping from the previous chord tones glue the harmonies together in a progression but fail to give firm tonal ground; the key signature is C major, but in the harmonic murk of the song's first half, we wonder at first whether we might be headed for B major – but no. It is a very Straussian maneuver to begin a song in or around a key other than the principal tonality, sometimes treated as ultimate goal rather than point of origin. "Ruhe, meine Seele!" does not achieve quiescence on an unclouded C major chord until the final two bars of the song, although the intimation of C is there from the beginning.[16] Up to that point, we are slowly, solemnly awash in seventh chords that cannot resolve as long as there is any remaining consciousness of the storms raging in the poet's soul (Example 9.1). Only once before the end do we hear a triadic point of arrival for "Diese Zeiten" ("these times"), their F minor horror a certainty, but because this is far from peace, the F minor promptly engenders another succession of seventh chords … until the directive "und vergiß, und vergiß, was dich bedroht!" ("and forget, and forget, what threatens you!"). The oracular sound of this injunction stems from the novelty of pure root-position triads in succession, including the typically Straussian elements of third relationships and the cross-relation between A♮ and A♭ pitches in chords of D-minor-going-to-F-minor. In a last wonderful detail, the singer "ends" with the 5–1 scale pitches of perfect authentic cadence but because his or her last word is "bedroht" ("threatens"), a C major chord of arrival would hardly be appropriate. Instead, we have a revoicing, this time over C in the bass, of the menacing chords from the start of it all before the piano can finally clear away all of the chromatic storminess and allow C major to have the last word. From the mere fact of chromatic complication right up to the final harmony, we apprehend how fragile this peace is, how threatened by the resumption of history's storms lurking beyond the last measure line.

Example 9.1 "Ruhe, meine Seele!," mm. 1–7

Desire, mystical rapture, and death: three turn-of-century masterpieces

In the late 1890s, as the turn of the century neared, Strauss continued to gravitate mostly to the poetry of his contemporaries, with one detour in Op. 36 for poems of a bygone age (Friedrich Klopstock, poems from *Des Knaben Wunderhorn*, and the Orientalist poet Friedrich Rückert). One of the most exquisite songs of this period is "Leises Lied" ("Gentle Song"), Op. 39, No. 1 of 1898, on a poem by Richard Dehmel, whose works were set to music by a glittering panoply of composers.[17] Dehmel was notorious for the eroticism of his verse; the poem "Venus consolatrix" was eliminated from the second edition of his anthology *Weib und Welt* by order of the censors. Here, he creates his own variation on medieval *hortus conclusus* imagery. "A garden enclosed is my sister, my spouse; a spring shut up, a fountain sealed," we read in the Song of Solomon 4:12, and from its passionate imagery derives a long tradition both of Marian iconography and secular erotic poetry.

Leises Lied

In einem stillen Garten
An eines Brunnens Schacht,
Wie wollt' ich gerne warten
Die lange graue Nacht!

Viel helle Lilien blühen
Um des Brunnens Schlund; –
Drin schwimmen golden die Sterne,
Drin badet sich der Mond.

Und wie in den Brunnen schimmern
Die lieben Sterne hinein,
Glänzt mir im Herzen immer
Deiner lieben Augen Schein.

Die Sterne doch am Himmel,
Die stehen all' [stehen uns all] so fern;
In deinem stillen Garten
Stünd' ich jetzt so gern.[18]

Gentle Song

In a silent garden
by a well shaft,
how I would love to wait there
through the whole long gray night!

Many bright lilies bloom
around the well's abyss;
the golden stars are floating there,
the moon bathes there.

And as the dear stars gleam
In the well,
so your dear eyes' light
ever glows in my heart.

But the stars in the sky
are all so far away;
I would linger now
in your silent garden.

Brahms's setting of Franz Kugler's "Ständchen" gives us the "clean" version of the same script, with its Germanic folkloric scenario of a lover waiting patiently in a garden for his beloved to appear, but only the very innocent could fail to recognize the erotic symbolism on display in Dehmel's poem. The quiet garden and the well that sinks deep into the earth are not difficult to decode as composite symbols for female sexual organs; when the persona announces that he would gladly spend the night there, any reader post-Freud will get the point. Because Dehmel sought to extol erotic experience as a way to break free of middle-class convention, he converts the lilies of the second stanza from medieval emblems of virginal purity (they surround the Virgin Mary in Sandro Botticelli's *Madonna of the Lilies*) into blossoms that flourish all around the cavity of the well. Sexuality is quasi-mystical rapture, he declares. This second verse gives us a poetic convention as old as the hills – stars reflected in the water are as the beloved's eyes reflected in a lover's heart – while the third verse sweeps away the celestial analogies to proclaim the persona's preference for physical experience. Throughout, Dehmel calls on poetic tradition to buttress a tender, rapt celebration of sex.

Strauss understood what Dehmel was doing and compounds several different musical symbols for the ecstasy of love into a beautifully economical lied. The loveliest and also the slyest is his recourse throughout the song to whole-tone figures within the span of a tritone. Tritones, of course, were *diabolus in musica* according to medieval music theory, and to churchmen and society's arbiters, sex could be the very devil as well. But whole-tone progressions are also open, mystical, either rootless or at least calling rootedness into question; Liszt's "liberation" of the augmented triad, his innovative uses of it in the *Dante* Symphony – mysticism and rapture of a different sort – are predicated on a similar openness. What had once been dissonant is no longer treated as such. The vagueness of tonal location and the banishment of hierarchical distinctions in scale formation are ways to suggest the effect of love-making on consciousness of the world's borders and strictures. Strauss begins the song with an initial measure of pulsation in the treble on the interval of a third, harmonically indeterminate. Are we in B♭ major? G minor? Some other tonal realm? Impossible to say as yet. The pulsation continues while the left hand doubles the vocal line exactly (if a female singer) or at the octave (if a male singer). The D and F♯ pitches hint at a G minor orientation, but what is G♯ doing here in that instance? The pitch certainly changes the way we hear F♯, such that the first half of m. 5 sounds much stranger than the second half of m. 2. This way of suggesting both the dark and the light sides of relative major and minor modes while throwing both of them open is wonderfully fitted to Dehmel's poetic scenario (Example 9.2). And the translucency of the texture, the delicacy of the voicing, is almost Debussyan; it is rare indeed that one can make analogies between Strauss and Debussy, but they are apropos here.

One of the most beautiful aspects of Strauss's late-Romantic tonal language is the ease with which he shifts between distant tonal planes and his propensity to alternate passages of complication/dissonance/tonal uncertainty with purest diatonicism in unusual relationships. At the beginning, we "wait" – like the lover – in suspended rapture for a tonality to be revealed, and when an authentic cadence finally happens in mm. 9–10, it is not what

Example 9.2 "Leises Lied," mm. 1–6

we might think from the opening bars. A root-position G minor harmony, followed by its leading tone, sounds at the start of m. 7 (the start of the second phrase), but not as a "tonic" harmony; rather, it is a passing tone/chord (on the downbeat!) as part of a desire-laden slide downwards by semitones in the doubled vocal line and left-hand part. The "long gray night" is not the enemy of love (one wonders whether "graue" was picked for its dark diphthong leading to the "ah" sound of "Nacht"), but its rich, profound climate, the first certainty of the poem: B♭ minor. The ultimate goal of the song is B♭ major, but how we arrive there is quite distinctive. Rather like physical rapture itself, we move in and out of focus, with passages that hover in whole-tone mid-air and then touch down to earth, if never for long. For example, following the momentary arrival on B♭ minor, Strauss quietly drops the root tone of that harmony and repeats the major-third interval (D♭–F) that is left after the fashion of m. 1 before reinterpreting those pitches as constituents of a D♭ major harmony. Here, the "many bright lilies" are accompanied by seraphic harp-chords in the high treble, the left hand no longer doubling the singer but wafting into the empyrean and hovering on D♭ for a moment. Returning to whole-tone openness for the "Brunnens Schlund" (this hardly seems coincidental or unrelated to the words), we hear tritones both in simultaneity and outlined horizontally before touching down again, this time on E major: a tritone away from the first such cadence (Example 9.3). In like manner, we rise another minor third/augmented second for the returning figure from m. 2 – D at first, then F, then G♯ – to repeat the cycle, leading this time to a cadence on D major.

Example 9.3 "Leises Lied," mm. 11–21

The third stanza is the goal of the poem: the statement that the physical is infinitely preferable to the metaphysical. In a tenderly witty maneuver, Strauss retraces his footsteps in the final stanza, returning to the "garden" in B♭, now radiant on major mode, by the end. At the hinge-word "doch" ("Die Sterne doch am Himmel"), the whole-tone figure heads downwards, not upwards, and we are en route back to the plane of the beginning. When Strauss reiterates the sensuous chromatic semitone slide downwards from mm. 7–8 in rhythmic augmentation at the crucial words "stünd' ich, stünd' ich" ("I would linger, I would linger") near the end, he conveys his exquisite understanding of Dehmel's purposes. The whole-tone aggregate (A–C♯–E♭–F) preceding the resolution to the first B♭ major chord at the end of the texted body of the song, at the word "gern" (gladly), is the gently dissonant aggregate of desire's tension before melting into release and calm.

This entire song is a study in economy: every note, every texture, every rhythmic pattern derived in logical fashion from the compound of gestures at the beginning and from the alteration between tonal hovering and tonal landing.

And there is another Dehmel setting from this same period of great productivity in song that deserves to be better known than it is (the great pianist Roger Vignoles is championing its cause these days): "Am Ufer" ("At the Shore"), Op. 41, No. 3. The poem comes from Dehmel's best-known anthology, *Weib und Welt* (*Woman and World*) of 1896:

Am Ufer
Die Welt verstummt, dein Blut erklingt;
in seinen hellen Abgrund sinkt
der ferne Tag,

er schaudert nicht, die Glut umschlingt
das höchste Land, im Meere ringt
die ferne Nacht,

sie zaudert nicht; der Flut entspringt
ein Sternchen, deine Seele trinkt
das ewige Licht.[19]

At the Shore
The world falls silent, your blood sings;
in its bright abyss sinks
the distant day,

it does not shiver, the glow embraces
the highest land, the distant night
grapples with the sea,

it does not hesitate; from the waters arises
a little star, your soul drinks
the eternal light.

Reading this poem, one can understand both why Stefan George hated Dehmel's poetry and why Strauss would have been attracted to it at this particular time in his life. The woolly mysticism; the ultra-late-Romantic acclamation of night; the unnamed beloved or perhaps the poet himself (to whom "dein Blut" or "your blood" belongs is not clarified, but the poem seems sunk so far inward that self-reference is at least likely); the persona's location on the threshold between the world and the otherworldly, his very being bent on things eternal: only the turn of the century could have produced such a work. The poem is a clever formal construction, with its repeated -gt and -kt word endings (erklingt/sinkt, umschlingt/ringt, entspringt/trinkt), its insistent parallelisms (der ferne Tag/die ferne Nacht, er schaudert nicht/sie zaudert nicht, dein Blut erklingt/die Glut umsch-lingt/der Flut entspringt), and its multiple enjambments winding their way to the end, but Strauss sweeps all of that aside. Not only does he turn Dehmel's words into prose but he elongates them in such exaggerated fash-ion as to induce the desired state of mystical rapture in his listeners by that means alone. In fact, every category of compositional choice – harmony, tonality, melody, form, texture, meter, tempo, chord-voicing, register, and more – is bent to that end. This song is an utmost distillation of Straussian thumbprints, of the most profound hallmarks of his musical language stripped of any glitter. (His virtuosity *can* be both necessary for his vision of a particular text and thoroughly enjoyable, I hasten to add.) No one else could have composed "Am Ufer."

Strauss marks this song *Sehr langsam und feierlich* (*Very slow and cere-monially*) and sets it in an F♯ major tonality with a long history in Romantic song; this is Schubert's key for "Die Mondnacht" ("The Moonlit Night"), D. 238 to a text by Ludwig Kosegarten, whose persona expresses moon-lit, rapturous harmony with the beloved. "Die Schwestergruss" ("Sister's Greeting"), D. 762 and "Totengräberweise" ("Gravedigger's Melody"), D. 869 are other Schubert songs in F♯ minor/major, in which he evokes spirit worlds and the afterlife.[20] Solemn chords, one per measure of very slow 3/4 meter, prevail, but three times Strauss bids the pianist waft upwards via a sextuplet sixteenth-note figure comprising open-fifth intervals spanning a ninth – a dry description of Strauss's inspired means of transport from the depths into the empyrean, but those conjoined perfect intervals are essential to the cosmic aura of this music. This seamless passage extend-ing from mm. 1–16 – although Strauss knew that his singer would need to draw breath at least three times in this span, there is not a single rest indi-cated either in the vocal line or in the piano until the "gap" in the singer's part at mm. 16–17 – is the first instance of one of Strauss's principal means throughout this song to tell of the attempted sacralization of the phenom-enal world: the metamorphosis of harmony, as if it were the soul, one tone at a time in order to touch lightly on distant redemptive places.[21] If F♯ major is the "tonic," it is so by fact of repetition at the beginning, middle, and ending sections of the body of the song and in the postlude, not because Strauss establishes it in more conventional fashion. The same is true of the harmonic places we visit in the song; we do not dwell there or even linger long. The first section is the tamest (but still amazing) specimen of the pro-cedure: we go from an initial state of profound contemplation sunk deep within the tonic chord at the start of it all to its beautifully blurry-disso-nant combination with the dominant seventh in mm. 5–6 (this reduction

Example 9.4 "Am Ufer," mm. 1–12

to bare essentials is what passes for "establishment" of a key in this song) to another pure triad (the submediant): a progression elongated in time. The submediant chord is then slowly transformed by chromatic alteration one or two pitches at a time (here, we are reminded of Strauss's Wagnerian obsessions), bringing us to its flatted version, or the "bright abyss" of D major chords – our effortless agent of transport downwards, back to the instrument's deepest depths (Example 9.4). From the half-cadence on A, it is mere sleight-of-hand to use C♯ as a common tone and return to F♯ major at mid-song. For such a weighty lied, every shift is handled with similar lightness, as if a god of harmony merely flicked a finger and rearranged the cosmos.

Strauss initiates the song's astonishing mid-section by recalling and condensing the move from tonic to the submediant harmony with which

Example 9.5 "Am Ufer," mm. 22–33

the first section began. But where the first stanza clings to the pitch F♯ until day sinks to its rest in m. 15, the second stanza is built upon a descending chromatic line spanning a fifth, from D♯ through the C𝄪 in the inner voice at "Glut," and on to C♯, C♮, B♮, B♭, an inverted order of A♭ first, then A♮ sinking to G♯ (V⁷ of C♯ major), and landing finally on the C♯ major triad. Only D♯ major, a $^6_4$ chord of E major, and C♯ major are triads here, Strauss perhaps impelled by the verb "ringen" ("ringt / die ferne Nacht") to create this slow-moving barrage of seventh chords. Their dissonances are the emblems of the battle between mystic lightness and darkness within the soul in a progression whose Straussian enharmonic transformations (A♯ to B♭, G♯ to A♭), common-tone shifts, and semitone side-slipping motion are rich and strange indeed (Example 9.5). (Here one remembers the very young Strauss in December, 1877 telling Ludwig Thuille that "… it is quite irrelevant how you mark the key into which you are moving, for between C♭ major and B minor is no difference at all, for here you have only an *enharmonic exchange*."[22] He would always be addicted to enharmony and all its possibilities.) It is here too that one notes the economy of this song, its middle section filled with gestures inherited from the initial section and wonderfully warped to fit the not-exactly-new organizing principle unifying mm. 21–36 (after all, the chromatic bass is an extension of the semitone shifts from before). The octave leap at "umschlingt" recalls the "Abgrund," the leaps of a sixth that fill the vocal line in the mid-section are already familiar, and the scalewise ascent near the end of the section is a chromatic variant of m. 11 ("in seinen hellen [Abgrund]"). The stringency and sophistication with which Strauss derives everything that comes after from the tightly compacted compositional choices at the beginning are cause for marvel.

Another feature of this song's unique power has to do with the nature of the vocal writing. One does not hear this song often because its virtuosity is not the flashy sort but depends instead on mammoth lung capacity and breath control, as well as the ability to traverse phrases filled with an extraordinary number of large intervallic leaps, all while singing very softly (always more difficult than bellowing). The brief scalar bits in mm. 11 and 31–2 are a rarity in this climate, where an enlarged soul expresses itself by means of an enlarged melodic wing-span. If the total range of the singer's part is not at all outré, extending from A♯ below middle C to the F♯ a thirteenth above, the athleticism of what transpires within those limits is far from ordinary. That these leaps are not filled in with melismas, that they conform to syllabic text-setting, only heightens their effect. Language and music are literally enlarged. In the song's final section, as Strauss rings the last changes on the *Stoff* of a musical cosmos paradoxically both small and immense, the vocal part becomes breathtaking in its wide embrace; the little star ascends from the waters to span the entire tessitura of the singer's part in a single four-measure phrase, richly entangled with the sextuplet figures that precede the passage and waft the singer up to the heights. "The eternal light," refulgent at the close, reworks the singer's very first elemental pitches (C♯, G♯, F♯) in a new order and in octave displacement: now we realize that the rapture was there all along. If it strikes deeper and rises higher at the end, that is but the completion of a process already enjoined in m. 1.[23] Dehmel told his first wife in a letter that he liked "Lied an meinen Sohn" and "Notturno" best of all Strauss's settings of his poetry, but "Am Ufer," so he told Strauss, "is one of my favorites."[24] I will second the motion.

An even greater work followed shortly after. At the turn of the century, Strauss turned to the late poetry of Conrad Ferdinand Meyer (1825–98), a Swiss writer best known for his novellas and ballads, and drew from his oeuvre a single superb song. "Im Spätboot" ("On the Late Ferry"), Op. 56, No. 3, is for bass voice and was composed between 1903 and 1906; one can only wonder at the proximity to *Salome*, completed in 1905.

Im Spätboot

Aus der Schiffsbank mach' ich meinen Pfühl.
Endlich wird die heiße Stirne kühl!
O wie süß erkaltet mir das Herz!
O wie weich verstummen Lust und Schmerz!
Über mir des Rohres schwarzer Rauch
wiegt und biegt sich in des Windes Hauch.
Hüben hier und drüben wieder dort
hält das Boot an manchem kleinen Port:
Bei der Schiffslaterne kargem Schein
steigt ein Schatten aus und niemand ein.
Nur der Steurer noch, der wacht und steht!
Nur der Wind, der mir im Haare weht!
Schmerz und Lust erleiden sanften Tod.
Einen Schlummrer trägt das dunkle Boot.[25]

On the Late Ferry

From the boat's bench I make my pillow.
Finally my fevered brow will be cool!
O how sweetly my heart grows chill!
O how softly joy and pain are hushed!
Above me the funnel's black smoke
goes to and fro in the wind's breath.
Over here and again over there,
the boat calls at many little ports.
In the scant light of the ship's lantern,
a shadow disembarks, and none takes its place.
Only the helmsman's awake and stands watch!
Only the wind that blows in my hair!
Pain and joy are gently put to death.
The dark boat bears one who slumbers.

This fourteen-line poem in rhyming couplets and trochaic pentameters is a "sonnet" or "sonnetto" in the same sense as Shakespeare's twelve-line Sonnet 126, also in rhyming couplets. Here, Meyer intermingles symbol and physical imagery until they all but fuse. The poet does not name Charon as the helmsman or the River Styx as the waters on which this ferry travels; such overt reference would displace this intimate presentiment of death onto the antique classical world and take away our necessary awareness of the present moment, of death here and now. The persona who speaks so ecstatically here narrates his own voyage into death from the moment he lays his head down for the last time until his final transmutation into "one who slumbers." This is an envisioning of death as anyone would wish it to be, given the iron law of mortality, and hence the same voice tells both of consciousness and, in the final couplet, of the last unconsciousness. There, the one who was dying and is now dead sees "the sleeper" as if from outside, a final farewell from the Self to its shell. En route, the boat stops at this, that, and the other small port; at each, a shadow disembarks, "and none takes its place." The solipsism of death, the fact that we each die alone, that no one's soul re-enters the ferry for the dying once death is completed, is suggested in the singularity of each shadow. Finally, only the persona is left. His last conscious awareness is of the wind blowing in his hair, the breath of life and of elemental Nature.

Strauss resists any temptation to turn Meyer's multiple exclamation points into rhapsodic ecstasies. Instead, the song floats gently on broken-chordal figuration that we hear, not as routine extensions of the harmonic progressions, but as gestures with poetic purpose from the beginning, where Strauss beautifully "blurs" the D♭ major tonic chord with the addition of the second scale degree.[26] The Straussian hallmark of first enriching harmonies either by added tones or passing tones, or as dissonant seventh, ninth, and eleventh chords, and then shortly thereafter clearing out all the accumulated dissonance with the flick of a compositional wand in order to arrive at a purely triadic resting point is here put to symbolic use. The rich, warm dissonances are followed by "small ports" of triadic repose, one diatonic harbor at a time, until all is at rest. Even Strauss's life-long love affair with enharmony is put to symbolic service here; in the singer's first two phrases, we rise an octave-and-a-half, from the depths to the word "endlich" ("at last"). At the invocation of the "fevered brow," the D♭s and A♭s are transformed into sharps, and the music cools into cadence on E major (Example 9.6). The motion to the enharmonic flatted mediant in major mode makes the relief of falling temperatures audible.

The points of arrival at the ends of phrases carry us from that cadence on E major to other ports-of-call at E minor and then to a bigger articulation of the dominant, A♭ major. If this seems an unusually customary arrival-point, the means of getting there is a hallmark of this composer's unique repertory of harmonic devices. As "joy and pain" both grow mute ("O wie weich verstummen Lust und Schmerz"), Strauss sends a brief jolt of electricity through the passage in a last reminiscence of joy and pain; via common-tone and neighbor-note motion, Strauss shifts suddenly from an A minor chord to a diminished-seventh chord on A♯, with a rare leap upwards in the vocal line to "Lust." One of the options to which that harmony can, and does, turn is B minor, but Strauss, in a typical wave-of-the-wand,

Example 9.6 "Im Spätboot," mm. 1–7

bids that harmony slip downwards to the dominant seventh of A♭ and from there to arrival at the A♭ chord of resolution. This is not where we expect to go when we disembark from E minor, any more than we expected the E major that follows so soon after setting off in D♭ major. Late-Romantic death floats on a mediant-imbued Lethe.

From A♭, the next port-of-call is a Phrygian-inflected cadence to C major, a Picardy third as well, this after an unusually repetitive and prolonged "black smoke" of non-resolving seventh and ninth chords that begin each time with a permutation of the eloquent gesture we first hear at the words "O wie süß" and "O wie weich." This gesture is defined by the anacrusis on a descending semitone interval and the subsequent drift downwards on the downbeat to a pitch a fourth, a tritone, a fifth, and finally a sixth lower; as we near the end, the interval widens. When Strauss transposes this motif

Example 9.7a "Im Spätboot," mm. 15–17

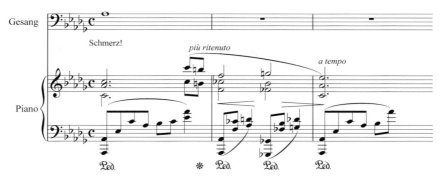

Example 9.7b "Im Spätboot," mm. 24–6

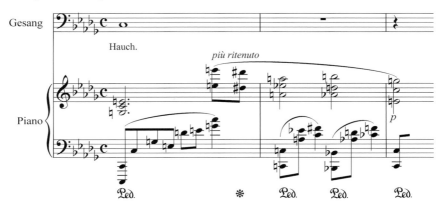

in two piano interludes, he ensures that we apprehend the sweetness and gentleness enveloping this passage into death's realm (Example 9.7). That there is a faint prick of life's lingering pain in the wonderful voice-leading by which the topmost voice sounds the leading tone (G♮ or B♮) against the flatted seventh in the bass demonstrates yet another way in which Strauss could bend dissonance–consonance pattern-making to symbolic purposes in this song.

The close linkage of music to words within a beautiful abstract overall design is particularly marked as we head towards song's end. Strauss, of all composers, could hardly be expected to resist the image of a "Steurer" who stands guard like a watchman, nor does he. Just before, he plunges briefly into the depths of G♭ major to tell of each solitary shadow disembarking. The singer's leap of a ninth downwards to the cadence at "niemand ein" is inexpressibly moving; in that one gesture, we *hear* that no one on the other shore can return to the ferry and that they would not wish to do so. For the watchman, the composer sounds a proclamatory fanfare, but in the treble, and what he announces is the final "Hauch" of life, set as the sort of sinking chromatic line that has a long, death-haunted tradition in western music. Each step along the descent is a small wavelet – the whole-tone anacrusis figure we have already heard so many times before – that rises before it falls. Nor does Strauss, prompted by the poet, shy away from the invocation of a last stab of pain at the close, rendered as a *sforzando* jangle of dissonance in the piano (a rhythmically augmented variant of the anacrusis motive) even as the singer wends his "very peaceful" (*sehr ruhig*) way to death. The exquisite deceptive motion to the submediant, or B♭ minor, for "sanften Tod" means that we return to D♭ only at the transmutation into "one who slumbers" at the end; even there, the chromatically altered tones remind us of rich melancholy before the song comes to rest on a wide-spanning last chord. Almost forty years before the *Vier letzte Lieder*, we have this premonition of its brooding, autumnal, darkly ecstatic welcome to Death.

"Her melodious lay": Ophelia's mad-songs

Strauss made a practice of organizing opuses by poet or poetic collection: not song cycles per se, but a coherent grouping, as in the *Acht Gedichte aus "Letzte Blätter"* on poems by Gilm, Op. 10; the *Sechs Lieder aus "Lotosblätter"* on poems by Schack, Op. 19; or the *Mädchenblumen* of Dahn, Op. 21. These sets are usually mined for individual numbers, although it is worth pointing out that familiar songs reveal themselves in new ways when one performs the entire opus (for example, the "Ständchen" in Op. 17 when one follows it with "Das Geheimnis" and the other Schack songs). The same is not true of the first half of Strauss's *Sechs Lieder*, Op. 67: the *Drei Lieder der Ophelia*, always performed as a mini-cycle. Confronted with these plangent works, one remembers Strauss's formative experiences with his mentally ill mother Josephine Schorr, who attempted, so we are told by his sister Johanna, to intervene as peace-maker when Strauss and his autocratic father Franz quarreled. She first went into a nursing home when she was forty-seven and her son not quite twenty-one; thereafter, Strauss defended his mother, who "never uttered a cross word" and "always had to be so careful of her nerves," and spoke of her in idealizing ways.[27] But his experience of mental illness at close quarters left its mark. One treads on dangerous ground with life-into-art guesswork, and yet the humanity one hears in these songs, the avoidance of any taint of kitsch, is an invitation to do just that. Whether he could allow himself to think of his mother in terms of sexualized madness I will not speculate, but his Salome and Elektra are women whose psychoses have much to do with sexuality warped beyond bearing, and Ophelia too is infected with Hamlet's sexual disgust, his displacement of fury at his mother onto his betrothed. Female psychosis was a subject Strauss would address over and over again, and thus it was perhaps inevitable that he would join forces with the many painters, poets, and musicians at the turn of the century who were also fascinated by Ophelia.

Strauss found his Ophelia in the Shakespeare translations of Karl Joseph Simrock (1802–76) and Ludwig Seeger (1810–64), with Seeger listed as the translator of *Hamlet*.[28] It is in Act 4, Scene v that the mad Ophelia appears, a scene that begins with Queen Gertrude, Horatio, and a gentleman in conversation with one another about the young woman's sad state. The unnamed court gentleman muses about the ways in which sane people attempt to understand the language of insanity:

> … her speech is nothing,
> Yet the unshaped use of it doth move
> The hearers to collection; they aim at it
> And botch the words up fit to their own thoughts;
> Which, as her winks, and nods, and gestures yield them,
> Indeed would make one think there might be thought,
> Though nothing sure, yet much unhappily.
>
> (*Hamlet* IV.v.7–13)

Something similar is at work in the musical syntax of these songs, which, like all mad music, must radiate lunacy and yet connect, however tenuously, to the laws and logic of music in its own day. Shakespeare's character uses language – she has no other recourse – to say what she would never have said before, and the listener tries to force sense onto whatever coherence presents itself. And coherence is in fact to be found here: Strauss tells us both that madness has its own inner logic and that it slips in and out of contact with more conventional discourse.

Shakespeare is, of course, famously difficult to translate because his incessant word-play resists transfer onto other linguistic maps. Simrock and Seeger clearly tried to be as literal as possible, except when stumped by such expressions as the white shroud "larded with sweet flowers" (this becomes "Viel liebe Blumen trauern": "Many sweet flowers mourn") or the sexualized language of the Saint Valentine's song. "By Cock they are to blame" becomes the much tamer "Führwahr, das ist nicht recht" ("Forsooth, that is not right"), but the translator cleverly manages to substitute a German sexual inference for an English one at the song's end, when "An thou hadst not come to my bed" becomes "Wärst du nicht kommen herein." "To come inside" has two meanings here, as obvious in their lewdness as the words that so shock Claudius in the play. Of course, what any extraction of the songs from the play sacrifices is the context – the surrounding interjections by the king, Gertrude, and Laertes – who break the madwoman's songs into fragments and seek to deny Ophelia's increasingly uninhibited perception of her own sexuality and of corruption at the court. "Pretty Ophelia," the king cries, while the grief-stricken Laertes declares that "Thought and affliction, passion, hell itself, / She turns to favour and to prettiness." But the disruptive power of Ophelia's torment cannot be wished away in such fashion, and too much beauty in poem, painting, or song runs the risk of negating the hell of lascivious fantasy that drives her to suicide. Does Strauss avoid that particular danger without depriving her of the pathos intrinsic to her attraction?

Everything about the beginning of the first song, "Wie erkenn' ich mein Treulieb?" ("How Should I Your True Love Know?"), tells of an inner world gone awry. If one takes the stance described by Shakespeare's gentleman and seeks to make sense of the song's beginning, to place it in an ordered harmonic world, one might describe mm. 1–8 as an obsessively repeated ninth chord of B♭ in fourth inversion … except that the harmony formed by the aggregate pitches B♭–D–F–A–C never resolves. Rather, we hear two strands at dissonant odds with one another and with conflicts of other kinds built into each strand. In the left hand, we hear a meter-defying chain of syncopations across the measure line – we hover in mid-air – and a pitch cluster that no one could hear as firm tonal ground. A harmonic whole-step at the base joins forces with a perfect fifth in the left hand to produce both dissonance and hollowness simultaneously, while the right-hand melodic gesture also harps on an open fifth. The terminal pitch D is surrounded by its chromatic neighbors on either side, C♯ and E♭, and the result is softly bone-crushing dissonance against the left hand. Where are we …? We have no idea (Example 9.8). There are remnants of tonal discourse, memories of a tonal world, but they are not used to affirm any location we can recognize or in which we can remain, and the recourse to repetition without progression to recognizable places heightens our sense of having strayed into an alien landscape. In m. 9, the interval of the perfect fifth is warped into another recurring pattern that bespeaks disorientation, that of bell-like, falling tritone intervals that strike above, through, and below a semitone-displaced variant of the initial left-hand simultaneity. It is as if the tritone-/whole-tone-scale sexual rapture of "Leises Lied" had become, by hideous metamorphosis, that which now expresses sexually fraught descent into madness.

Thereafter, Strauss moves these figures around as if on a chessboard, with tonal surety always out of reach. When he shifts the original figures to sit above E minor and C major $^6_3$ triads starting in m. 11, we are allowed the briefest instant of C major clarity for the pilgrim's sandals worn by the phantom lover (his asceticism is in tragic-ironic counterbalance to her sense of sinfulness), but this brief evocation of clarity and purity is surrounded by edgy dissonance. Here, parallel fifths are part and parcel of an

Example 9.8 "Wie erkenn' ich mein Treulieb?," mm. 1–8

alternate universe, where transgressions compositional and sexual flood the air. Only for the outburst at the singer's last word, "Liebesschauern," does the bell-chiming figure ascend from the depths into the treble rather than drop into a pit via a ladder of tritones; only here does a pure triad, with no dissonant accretions, hold sway for an entire two-and-a-half measures. But even this climax, both radiant and desperate, is preceded by the harmony a tritone away (B♭ to E), and it is followed by a long postlude that returns us by degrees and by repetition to the song's beginning. The soft strains die away in the middle of the last bar, leaving us in the same indeterminacy in which we began. There is method to this madness, rigorous method in fact: every note is derived from the figures at the beginning, but its logic is not that of a sane world, centered on tonic–dominant polarities or any other fulcrum of functional tonality.

With the second song, "Guten Morgen, 's ist Sankt Valentinstag" ("Good morning, 'tis Saint Valentine's Day"), we turn abruptly from the depressive to the manic side of Ophelia's madness, to misandry made exhibitionistic. Here again, known elements appear in insane configurations, in patterns that have their own logic but not of the sort one finds either in composition textbooks or etiquette manuals for proper princesses. Once again, we ask, "Where are we?" and are vouchsafed no comfortable answer. The key signature would seem to indicate either G major or E minor for a song that begins and ends with E minor chords, but nothing that follows that beginning or precedes that ending resembles conventional late-Romantic syntax. If the entire song stops on the same chord as the anacrusis to m. 1, the relationship seems more the result of obsessive returns throughout the song to its starting point than anything resembling a usual ending. Closure is a quantity severely compromised in madness because there is no escape from the twisted processes of a mind diseased, and Ophelia's cadences must therefore be different from the mini-closures that the sane enact every day, with their completion of thoughts and actions in rounded, comprehensible fashion. The closest thing to an authentic cadence in Ophelia's second song is in mm. 8–10 ("will Euer Valentin sein"), the mad girl's declaration that she will reverse the standard roles in seductions-by-night: *she* will come to *his* window and sue for admittance, if only in fantasy. But this is far from your usual authentic cadence, in part because the resolution on D major does not continue the voice-leading just prior to it but is rather an elision with the start of another jigging passage on contrasting major–minor chord colors, back in the treble register where the song began and in which it lives most of the time. And the diminuendo throughout the cadence bespeaks a draining away of vital energies (Example 9.9).

Reversals pervade this song. In the alternation between the left and right hands throughout the piano's near-incessant figuration, the left-hand part nearly always falls on the weak half of the beat, the opposite of what one would expect for this pattern whereby a harmony is divided between the hands. Only twice in the entire song do the two hands join forces for emphatic accents on the downbeat ("ver-*spracht*" and "beim *Son*-nenlicht"), the result paradoxically a wrong-footing of the reversed pattern surrounding these two short-lived instances. The incessant motion of mania, the piano part bobbing up and down, continues unchecked until the postlude, where we hear the energy swiftly dissipate; broken by measures of silence, it finally stutters to a halt on the second half of the third and weakest beat of the measure.

The jigging motion is not all that is "off" about the piano figuration. If parallel fifths were one element of the first song, they are far more prevalent here, filling the air from start to finish; Strauss's Ophelia has become even more brazen in the ways she flouts proscriptions. Root-position triads follow one after another in many passages of this song but in progressions that are far from usual, to put it mildly. A song that starts with E minor, C minor, A minor, B major, G major, and G minor triads in mm. 1–3 is not in the realm of tonal normalcy. But the virtuosity with which Strauss typically manipulates common-tone and side-slipping neighbor-note chord progressions is on display here; once again, there is logic at work, albeit logic with an elliptical relationship to the sane world. At times, the succession of root-position triads gives way to equally unorthodox seventh chords or to parallel first-inversion chords in the right hand, but always we come back to the root-position chords and parallel fifths en masse.

Example 9.9 "Guten Morgen, 's ist Sankt Valentinstag," mm. 1–10

In particular, the alternation between major and minor forms of the same chord is the most prevalent recurring feature of this song, a mirror of insanity's extreme instability. This is not, as in Mozart or Schubert, either the momentary darkening or lightening of the one mode by the other or the contrast of a plateau in major with a plateau in minor or vice versa (for example, G♭ major becoming F♯ minor in the exposition of the first movement of Schubert's 1828 opus posthumous, the B♭ Piano Sonata, D. 960). Rather, the two color possibilities alternate within the measure, and neither modal color continues onwards to define a key; since each bar has three beats, Strauss has the minor chord predominate in some bars, the major in others. The fact that there is usually a leap of a perfect fourth in the topmost voice such that the highest pitch is in the middle of the bar only adds to our sense of a mind in disarray. In those rare cases where the composer both returns to the alternating chord colors and *descends* at mid-measure rather than leaping up, he puts an accent on the second beat in the piano, lest we find even momentary surcease from the conflict between meter and melodic profile regnant throughout the song (for example, in m. 35 at the word "Geschlecht!" and repeated in mm. 36, 38, and 39).

But again, there is method in this madness because we keep coming back to the same illogical harmonies we have already heard. At the beginning, in mm. 2–5, we hear jigging back and forth on G major–minor and E minor–major, followed by the same device in mm. 10–11 on D minor–major and in mm. 14–15 on C major–minor. Thereafter, we return in mm. 27–9 to mm. 1–3, again in mm. 37–9, and finally in mm. 62–3, the stitching between the singer's "cadence" and the piano postlude. Not surprisingly, the "ending" of this song is as inconclusive as the "ending" of the first song. We sense that the manic mechanisms producing the jittery contrasts are running out of energy when the triads darken to become all minor towards the close of the piano postlude (the first three chords of the song are also all minor). These F minor and D minor triads surround E minor in a manner that once again denies us any means of hearing "closure" or any sense of secure tonal location. The song saddens and then simply stutters to a stop.

Because the rules of normal connection in a sane world are not the law here, Strauss just slips from the E minor harmony at the end of the second song to the bassless E♭ minor harmony at the start of the third song, "Sie trugen ihn auf der Bahre bloß" ("They bore him naked on the bier"). Anticipating the flowing water in which Ophelia will shortly die, Strauss hangs the "tonic" harmony between octave columns of the chord's fifth degree and warps it suggestively; again, we ask where we are, on what ultimate path to suicide. Slipping back up to the E minor strand of the second song in m. 4, Strauss resorts once again to the parallel descending motion endemic to the Ophelia songs, reiterated before one of the most heart-stopping moments of the cycle in mm. 11–15. "Fahr wohl, fahr wohl, meine Taube!" ("Farewell, farewell, my dove!"), she sings to typically Straussian third-related triads (E♭ major and G major), and we are reminded of the "Liebesschauern" climax in the first song. In these poignant-radiant moments of refulgence, we hear a recollection of her beauty of spirit in happier times (Example 9.10).

Because she is mad, such moments cannot last, and hectic gaiety overthrows the sad tenderness. What eroticized waltzes at the turn of the century mean for the likes of Ravel and Strauss, in their very different ways, is a fascinating subject, and here, the sprightly sensuality of a *Rosenkavalier* world invades her mind. That the bright A major – an intrusion, as we do not change key signature – is pervaded by octave plunges downwards is

Example 9.10 "Sie trugen ihn auf der Bahre bloß," mm. 11–15

enough to induce vertigo. The giddiness skids to a halt at the realization that "he will never come again" ("Er kommt dir nimmermehr"), set to yet another succession of root-position triads linked by *echt* Straussian side-slipping chromatic motion (G major, B♭ minor, E major, G minor) and culminating in seventh chords. "Er ist tot, o weh!" ("He is dead, oh woe!"), she sings, and then begins all over again: the warped water-music, the nausea-inducing waltz, the *wieder langsam* chords that signal realization all return, varied and transposed until, at last, she sings her farewell blessing, "Gott sei mit euch!" ("God be with you!"). The final harmonic gesture, echoed an octave lower, is the apotheosis of Straussian neighbor-note and common-tone motion leading to an unforgettable last point of repose: a diminished-seventh harmony on A♮–C–E♭–G♭ slides softly sideways to the final E♭ major chords. The traditional Picardy-third close for Baroque compositions in minor mode here has tragic meaning. Surcease is finally at hand, she now knows, but only at the cost of self-extinction.

Here at the close, indignant readers will, I know, carp about the omission of this, that, or the other special Strauss song, and I can only plead exigencies of length and my desire to draw attention to my own favorites. Who, once exposed to "Im Spätboot," could ever forget it? Other writers will surely follow suit to "talk up" other gems, just as singers and pianists are now beginning to perform songs other than the standard few. May both missions continue.

10 Last works

JÜRGEN MAY

TRANSLATED BY JÜRGEN THYM

As difficult as it may appear to define the beginning of a characteristic *Spätwerk* in the case of Strauss, the composer himself has made it easy for us to delineate the last phase of his creativity. The works in question are a group of compositions all finished, albeit not begun, after the completion of his opera *Capriccio*:

> Concerto for Horn and Orchestra No. 2 in E♭, TrV 283
> > Completion: Vienna, November 28, 1942
> Sonatina No. 1 in F for 16 Wind Instruments, "From the Workshop of an Invalid," TrV 288
> > Completion: Garmisch, July 22, 1943
> *Metamorphosen* for 23 Solo Strings, TrV 290
> > Completion: Garmisch, April 12, 1945
> Sonatina No. 2 in E♭ for 16 Wind Instruments, "Joyful Workhop," TrV 291
> > Completion: Garmisch, June 22, 1945
> Concerto in D for Oboe and Small Orchestra, TrV 292
> > Completion: Baden (Switzerland), October 25, 1945
> *Duett-Concertino* in F for Clarinet and Bassoon, String Orchestra, and Harp, TrV 293
> > Completion: Montreux, December 16, 1947
> *Vier letzte Lieder* after Poems by Hermann Hesse and Joseph von Eichendorff for Soprano and Orchestra, TrV 296:
> > I. "Frühling" ("Spring") (Hermann Hesse)
> > Completion: Pontresina, July 18, 1948
> > II. "September" (Hermann Hesse)
> > Completion: Montreux, September 20, 1948
> > III. "Beim Schlafengehen" ("On Going to Sleep") (Hermann Hesse)
> > Completion: Pontresina, August 4, 1948
> > IV, "Im Abendrot" ("At Sunset") (Joseph von Eichendorff)
> > Completion: Montreux, May 4, 1948

Two additional compositions, which in the context of the late phase of Strauss's creativity are not at all marginal, will not be considered here: the "memorial waltz," "Munich," TrV 274a (completed February 24, 1945), a new version of an "occasional waltz" (*Gelegenheitswalzer*) with the same title of 1939; and the nine-part chorus "An den Baum Daphne," TrV 272a, composed as an epilogue to the opera *Daphne*, Op. 82 (1937).

Furthermore, not considered in the present discussion will be several occasional compositions written during the last years: the songs "Sankt Michael" (TrV 280) and "Blick vom oberen Belvedere" (TrV 281), both after texts by Josef Weinheber (which Strauss wrote for the fiftieth birthday of the poet on March 9, 1942); and the *Festmusik der Stadt Wien* (TrV 286), composed around the turn of the year 1942–3, in gratitude for the city's honoring him with the Beethoven Prize shortly before. Also outside the scope of our study are two interesting compositional projects that remained incomplete, and that only came down to us in the form of sketches and drafts: the symphonic poem *Die Donau* (*The Danube*; Strauss worked on the project in 1941 and 1942),[1] and the school opera *Des Esels Schatten* (*The Donkey's Shadow*), composed for the Gymnasium of the Benedictine Abbey in Ettal, where Strauss's grandson Christian went to school.

With the opera *Capriccio* Strauss brought his creativity, in the most emphatic meaning of the word, to a conclusion. He presented everything composed later as meaningless. On April 8, 1943 he wrote to Willi Schuh:

> My life's work has been concluded with *Capriccio*. Whatever notes I scribble down now are wrist exercises for the *Nachlass* [estate] that have no bearing on music history – like the scores of all the other symphonists and variationists. Their only function is to pass the hours with a minimum of boredom, since one cannot read Wieland or play Skat the entire day.[2]

The term "estate" might have been understood by Strauss in several ways. First, it meant some kind of "musical memoirs" – a retrospective of his own creativity and of the origin of his own artistic existence in terms of cultural history. Second, the term "estate" held a very pragmatic meaning: the possible fruits of his works – i.e., success and, above all, royalties – would not benefit the composer, but would be harvested by his descendants. Such a purpose, which sounds strange only when we cling to a Romantic ideal of the artist, is supported by the fact that all his last works, with the exception of *Metamorphosen* and the Oboe Concerto, were published after the death of the composer (although Strauss carefully prepared their publication): when Strauss lived in Switzerland between October, 1945 and May, 1949, he connected (via Ernst Roth) with the English music publisher Boosey & Hawkes, with whom the works finally appeared.

Even though Strauss obviously intended a publication of his musical "estate" and also hoped for appropriate financial rewards, he always tried to play down the significance of those compositions. Not only did he call them, as mentioned, "wrist exercises" and "study material," he stopped assigning opus numbers to his works after *Capriccio*. He wrote to his grandson (in reference to *Till Eulenspiegel*) that he preferred to spend his time by copying scores of earlier compositions rather than "manufacture senile original works."[3]

To understand the rationale for these understatements we must turn to Strauss's view of music history and his own role in it. Strauss saw – and he emphasized this view again and again – in the music of Mozart, Beethoven, and, finally, Wagner "the completion and the high-point of humankind's cultural development" ("Abschluß und Gipfel der bisherigen Culturentwicklung der Menschheit").[4] He thought of himself as the last representative of this tradition, which had come to a conclusion with his work. The destructions of World War II and the attendant decline of Germany were for Strauss not the cause, but merely the manifestation of this historical closure. He was convinced "that the political Germany *had to be* destroyed, after it fulfilled its world mission, namely creating and perfecting German music."[5] Since Strauss did not stop composing – even though there was, musically, nothing more to say – the resultant utterances would be merely an epilogue, from his perspective.

At the same time, Strauss, by dint of his understatement, pre-empted any possible criticism of his last works. If the composer himself already emphasized the lack of significance of this music, no critic could start from such a point.

But exactly this is the reason for the special attraction of the late compositions. By declaring the closure of his own creativity and the end of cultural history, Strauss freed himself from all demands: from audience expectations as well as implications of the times, from "the state of musical material" as well as from his own claims of artistry. Detached from such demands, Strauss was able to give free reign to his artistic fantasy – but, in the end, he did not leave it at that.

If Strauss thus continued to produce music after his life's work was finished, we must ask why he decided in favor of this or that genre, in favor of this or that instrumentation. It is worth noting that, first of all, he avoided opera entirely and he turned again to purely instrumental music – a kind of music he thought had found closure in the works of Beethoven. Here we already have an indication of the retrospective character of Strauss's late works.

By thoroughly studying the sketches to any one of these works, we notice that the sketchbooks of the last years contain a wealth of motives, themes, and more or less elaborate passages, which can be attributed only in part to the completed last works (and we should admit that the materials have not been explored in their entirety). Strauss, it seems, jotted down the musical ideas that occurred to him during those years without initially knowing their specific compositional purpose; spurred on by a concrete occasion, some of them jelled into a work.

Horn Concerto No. 2 and Oboe Concerto

Such an external impetus – the visit of John de Lancie, oboist of the Pittsburgh Symphony Orchestra, to Strauss's home in Garmisch in May, 1945 – is known for the Oboe Concerto, TrV 292, but not for the Horn Concerto No. 2, TrV 283, composed shortly after the premiere of the opera *Capriccio*. Both solo concertos may be considered representative of the style of the last products from Strauss's workshop. Not only the choice of genre itself, but also the almost persistently conventional approach, especially to musical form and structure, is indicative of the retrospective nature of these works. Strauss follows the Classical three-movement structure with a rondo (Horn Concerto) or a rondo-like movement (Oboe Concerto) as finale. And the tonal disposition of the movements – E♭ major, A♭ major, E♭ major in the Horn Concerto; and D major, B♭ major, D major in the Oboe Concerto – does not reveal any surprises at first glance. It is obvious that Strauss takes as his point of departure here the Classical and early-Romantic models of his musical youth rather than his own concerto-like works of the 1920s (*Parergon, Panathenäenzug*). Still, there are typical "Straussian" melodic shapes, harmonic successions, and rhythmic characteristics that reveal the identity of their creator. The composer looks back to a past aesthetic from the perspective of someone who has lived through the paradigm changes of the nineteenth and twentieth centuries. In that respect, one might call the last works of Strauss postmodern.[6]

We do not know what made Strauss compose a second horn concerto as the first of his late works. However, its link to the past is very clear: the work is the counterpart of the Horn Concerto No. 1, Op. 11, which the young Strauss composed sixty years earlier. The first concerto was dedicated "To my dear father Franz Strauss" (in its autograph arrangement for piano and horn); the autograph of the second concerto bears a notation by the seventy-eight-year-old composer "To the memory of my father" – a posthumous dedication that, however, did not make it into the printed score. The parallels between both works in the succession of movements are obvious: tempo, meter, and tonal disposition are very similar.

While the two virtuoso outer movements of the Horn Concerto No. 2 place high demands on the soloist (without abandoning musical substance), the Andante con moto evokes times past in several ways. The highly expansive cantilena of the theme appears like a return to the Romantic era, and it also alludes to the melancholy of the "moonlight music" of *Capriccio* – which happens also to be in A♭ major! But as if the composer wanted to remove any budding traces of sentimentality, the concerto concludes with a rondo full of spirit and wit, a movement that comes across like a scherzo: the motion of the 6/8 meter is interrupted by frequent syncopations and hemiolas.

Example 10.1 Oboe Concerto, first principal motive

Example 10.2 Oboe Concerto, second principal motive

Worth noting (and characteristic for Strauss's last works in general) is the compositional procedure in the Horn Concerto: a few elements are the point of departure for the development of the entire composition. Motives and thematic fragments can mutate into accompanimental figures, and vice versa: what initially appears to be accompaniment can turn into motivic substance.

What can already be seen in the Horn Concerto is shown by Strauss in truly exemplary fashion in the Oboe Concerto. In a manner reminiscent of Haydn rather than his revered model Mozart, Strauss succeeds in turning almost nothing into something.

Three principal elements are at the foundation of the Oboe Concerto. The figure introduced by the cello right at the outset appears, initially, to be merely an accompanimental figure, but soon enters into the thematic discourse (Example 10.1). By dint of the nearly continuous presence of this figure – it is actually nothing but a short, written-out trill – especially in the first and second movements, even the chains of trills in the solo cadenza leading to the final Vivace appear to be integrated into the motivic discourse.

The second element can be found in different variants in almost all of the late instrumental works: a sustained tone tied to a playful figure in shorter durational values (Example 10.2). It is introduced initially by the solo oboe and then given for some time to soloistically used orchestral instruments such as viola and clarinet, before it pervades also the string tutti textures.

Strauss introduces the third building-block relatively late in the first movement (at rehearsal no. 8 in the printed score); it is no less significant: a fourfold repetition of a tone followed by different variants of continuations (Example 10.3). The motive clearly refers to *Metamorphosen*, completed just before the Oboe Concerto – a remarkable example for the thematic

Example 10.3 Oboe Concerto, third principal motive

links between the last instrumental works. The incipit of this motive especially – the threefold repetition of a tone – evolves finally into a similarly energetic character as the trill of the beginning.

Only the Vivace-finale seems to free itself from dependence on the three building-blocks described here. A new musical element is introduced by the characteristic downward leap of a fourth with which the theme begins. The unity of the work, however, is re-established at last with the entry of the tone-repetitions that occupy an entire section of the movement. The second solo cadenza is followed by a surprise: instead of returning to the thematic material of the Vivace, Strauss concludes the work with a dance-like Allegro in 3/8 meter. Even though the conclusion picks up the familiar motives once again, partly in transformations, it comes across, because of meter and thematic substance, as if it were an additional, fourth movement with a character of its own.

Sonatinas for Winds

If the Second Horn Concerto may be considered to hearken back to Strauss's early compositions, the same may be said, and for several reasons, of the Sonatinas for Wind Ensemble composed between 1943 and 1945. The two youthful contributions to the genre – the Serenade, Op. 7, written when Strauss was just seventeen, and the Suite, Op. 4, of 1884 – were indeed keystones in the career of the budding composer and conductor. Not only was the premiere of the Serenade conducted by Franz Wüllner, who later rendered a great service by performing Strauss's tone poems; the work also made a deep impression on Hans von Bülow, who, subsequently, encouraged the composer to write the Suite for the same ensemble. His reading of Bülow's writings early in 1943[7] may have spurred Strauss on to try his hand, once again, at a genre that was so closely linked with such an important supporter.

Strauss's return to Classical models is particularly obvious in the Sonatinas for Wind Ensemble. On the last page of the autograph score of the Second Sonatina, the composer notated: "To the *Manes* of the divine

Mozart at the end of a life full of thanksgiving." Mozart's Serenade No. 10 in B♭ ("Gran Partita") has been pointed out many times as the model of Strauss's works for wind ensemble.

When Strauss began work on the First Sonatina, he obviously did not yet have a clear idea of the formal design of the composition. Initially he may have had thoughts of writing, in analogy to the Horn Concerto No. 2, a second suite for winds.[8] The *Romanze und Menuett*, already completed by February, 1943 finally became the second movement of a three-movement "Sonatina" – again one of those understatements typical of Strauss, considering that the entire work has a duration of more than half-an-hour. On May 31 Strauss reported to Willi Schuh: "The composition of a so-called workshop scene – a three-movement sonatina for sixteen winds – has helped me get through many gloomy hours."[9] Here Strauss refers to the illness of his wife Pauline – "a heavy burden for all of us, which also affected me badly."[10] Alluding to this situation, Strauss gave the First Sonatina the subtitle "From the Workshop of the Invalid," which later, in the printed version of the work, was changed by the publisher to "From the Workshop of an Invalid."

The First Sonatina was initially to have the same number of instruments, namely thirteen, as the youthful compositions for winds, albeit in a slightly modified combination. The ensemble was amplified in the final version – in comparison with Opp. 4 and 7 – by the addition of clarinet in C, basset-horn, and bass clarinet.

In the First Sonatina for Winds, Strauss continues the compositional procedure, observed already in the Horn Concerto No. 2 and the Oboe Concerto, of working with small elements that, considered by themselves, appear insignificant. It seems here as if Strauss helped himself to the entire repertory of figures and formulas of the Classical symphonic style – perhaps this is the reason for the impression, conveyed in numerous passages, of reminiscences of something familiar without the listener being able to pinpoint exactly to which work Strauss is alluding. It is, however, also remarkable how Strauss uses this material. He renders it not only in all the colorful facets characteristic of his harmonic idiom, presents it not only with the richness of timbres and nuances available in the ensemble, but also transforms it through a multitude of rhythmic variants such as triplets, hemiolas, ligatures, and syncopations. As a result, in the course of each movement, sections that are in part musically related and in part strongly contrasting are combined in ever more complex overlaps and interactions.

In contrast to the First Sonatina, which seems to have originated initially without a concrete plan of disposition and movement order, the Second Sonatina was planned, from the start, as a multi-movement work. A few months after completing the First Sonatina, Strauss told Willi Schuh on December 22, 1943 about "another one: introduction and finale, as a wrist exercise – all for the 'estate', i.e., superfluous music from a historical perspective – at best useful for eager instrumentalists as an ensemble étude, without any interest whatsoever for the general public, like a thousand other things."[11] Once again Strauss tried to downplay the significance of these compositions – an assertion, however, that sounds increasingly curious in view of the fact that after the first "superfluous" sonatina he considered adding a second.

Starting with the broadly conceived final movement – it alone already has a duration of around fifteen minutes – Strauss worked on the remaining three movements in the order of their position in the sonatina. The first movement was completed two months after the finale on March 6, 1944. It seems, however, that he encountered major problems with the Andantino, which was conceived as a variation movement. On March 21, 1944 he wrote to his friend, the conductor Clemens Krauss – perhaps only half-jokingly – that the variation form "seems to be miffed at me, since in *Don Quixote* I have reduced it to absurdity, once and forever. One should not poke fun at music history."[12] Eventually, work on the Sonatina was temporarily abandoned – obligations in Vienna and Salzburg as well as the escalation of war events may have been the reason. Instead Strauss devoted himself to the composition of *Metamorphosen* as well as, simultaneously, to the revision of the "Munich" waltz, now called a *Gedächtniswalzer* ("memorial waltz"). He finished the waltz on February 24, 1945, and *Metamorphosen* on April 12 of the same year.

Not until after the war did Strauss pick up again the work on the Second Sonatina. Within a few weeks – in fact, by June 22 – the two missing movements were completed. Even though it exceeded the First Sonatina in scope, and its movement disposition corresponded with that of a Classical-Romantic symphony, Strauss decisively rejected the proposal of Clemens Krauss to call the work a "Symphony."[13] He kept the title "Sonatina" and added, as he did for the first, a subtitle: "Joyful Workshop." Nevertheless, when the work first appeared in 1952, it carried the title "Symphony for Winds."

Even though the Second Sonatina resembles the First, in compositional style and in character, Strauss strikes an audibly more joyful tone here. The thematic elements appear more concise, the formal design seems more compelling. In particular, the two shorter middle movements, characterized by memorable principal themes, establish a counterweight to the more broadly conceived and weighty corner movements. Even the composer preferred the E♭ Sonatina over "the seemingly very arduous [*schwer*] one in F major." On November 27, 1944 he confided to Clemens Krauss: "*Entre nous*, I think the Second Sonatina in E♭ major is the better one."[14]

Metamorphosen and *Duett-Concertino*

How deeply Strauss delved backwards into music history in his last instrumental works is shown also in his abandonment of any programmatic pretext, at least in a large portion of these compositions. In the context of his tone poem *Macbeth* the composer, twenty-four years of age, had postulated a poetic model as a paradigm for continuing to write purely instrumental music. Now, in old age and in his last works, such considerations did not need to bother him any longer. Still, he could not quite emancipate himself from programmatic composition in his *Metamorphosen* for 23 Solo Strings and the *Duett-Concertino* for Clarinet and Bassoon – two works that have far more in common than meets the eye in view of their very different characters. The sketchbooks of those years even suggest a common genesis for both pieces.

While the *Duett-Concertino* indeed has a programmatic basis comparable to the programs of the tone poems, the programmatic nature of *Metamorphosen* is established solely by the title, which however points to cultural and literary history in multiple ways and generates an arch of reference reaching from classical antiquity (Ovid) to German literary classicism (Goethe). It remains unclear to what extent Strauss's music for strings was inspired by one or the other of these poets; the composer himself remained silent on the issue.

The genesis of *Metamorphosen*, however, has meanwhile been established with far-reaching certainty.[15] After all, the work was composed – and the dedication confirms it – for the Collegium Musicum Zürich and the philanthropist and conductor Paul Sacher, who also premiered the piece. But when Strauss received the commission, parts of the composition were already drafted. The earliest sketches go back at least to 1943, perhaps even to 1942.[16]

Because of his shaky health Strauss planned in the last years of the war to go to the Swiss spa Baden near Zurich, but he was unable to get permission to travel abroad. In this situation, Willi Schuh, Paul Sacher, and Karl Böhm jointly conceived the plan to commission Strauss to write a piece for the Collegium Musicum Zürich. The commission, as well as an invitation to the premiere, were to help the composer get the desired permit. In a letter of August 28, 1944, Karl Böhm formally commissioned the composition of a "Suite for Strings."

The work on the composition, however, proceeded only slowly. Supply bottlenecks during the war affected Strauss not only physically; he also suffered from severe mood changes. Willi Schuh had to urge Strauss, repeatedly, to continue the work.

When Strauss reported the completion of the work to Willi Schuh on May 10, 1945, the war was over, but the situation had not become easier.

Example 10.4 *Metamorphosen*, mm. 1–3

He did not get a travel permit until the beginning of October. On October 11 Strauss entered Switzerland, and on January 25, 1946 the piece was premiered in Zurich with Paul Sacher conducting.

The *Metamorphosen* were not conceived from the start for a large ensemble of twenty-three strings. In his response to Böhm's letter of August 28, Strauss mentions that he had been working "for some time" on an "Adagio for circa 11 solo strings."[17] When writing the particell of the work, Strauss initially even planned an ensemble for only seven strings that, in the course of the compositional process, was however expanded.[18]

By giving an impression of funeral music, the *Metamorphosen* correspond to the composer's state of mind during the last years of the war. The beginning of the decline of western culture – that is at least how Strauss perceived it – a culture of which he considered himself a part, always sent him into a state of depression. As if to reassure himself, the aging composer steeped himself again and again in the works of Goethe and writings on cultural history. As much as one needs to be cautious in pointing out relations between an artist's biography and the creative process, they are obvious in this case. Strauss provided not only a date of conclusion in the score, but also – the only time he did this – a date when he started writing it down: "Begun on March 13, 1945" – one day after the destruction of the Vienna opera house.

The introductory measures, intoned by violoncellos and double basses only – a characteristic double upward leap of a fourth with unusual harmonies – immediately establish a peculiar atmosphere of rapture (Example 10.4). Right from the outset, the composition evolves out of emotionally charged material: the *passus duriusculus* (a chromatic descent – see Example 10.5) and *saltus duriusculus* (a "hard" leap outlining a diminished or augmented interval – see Example 10.6), semitone suspension, syncopated descent, and descent in triplets – Strauss applies here all the rhetorical means that developed over centuries musically to express pain.

Example 10.5 *Metamorphosen*, mm. 1–2, *passus duriusculus*

Example 10.6 *Metamorphosen*, mm. 1–2, *saltus duriusculus*

But it is especially the ever-present allusion to the Funeral March from Beethoven's *Eroica* Symphony – at the end of the composition even appearing in form of a direct quotation and highlighted through the remark "In memoriam!" – that intensifies the impression that Strauss composed here a musical monument, if not a tombstone, for "more than three thousand years of humankind's cultural development" (a phrase that Strauss invoked over and over again in old age).[19]

In contrast, the *Duett-Concertino* for clarinet and bassoon, finished two-and-a-half years later, appears at first glance to be serenity-turned-music, without any traces of the personal problems and the repercussions of the times. A fairy tale, as can be read in many publications, provided the program for the piece. A glance into Strauss's sketchbooks seems to confirm this: a love story between a beggar and a princess may have provided the point of departure for the music.

Strauss was still alive when the guessing began about exactly which fairy tale might have served as a model. Two different stories appear alternately as candidates in concert guides and program notes. In a program booklet of 1954 Roland Tenschert, citing Clemens Krauss as a key witness, names Hans Christian Andersen's "The Princess and the Swineherd."[20] Heinrich Kralik's version of 1963 goes back to Hugo Burghauser, former bassoonist of the Vienna Philharmonic Orchestra; here the *Concertino* is said to be based on the story of a princess and a bear, who, at the end, turns into a prince – a variant of the fairy-tale motive of the beast-bridegroom.[21] Both Burghauser and Krauss base their respective versions on the composer himself, a claim that however raises doubts in view of the discrepancies between the alleged models. These doubts are intensified when one compares Strauss's programmatic hints in the sketches with the two fairy tales. It turns out that they square with neither of the stories.[22]

All programmatic remarks, however, fit with a mythological subject from Greek antiquity that had already occupied Strauss for a long time: the shipwreck of Odysseus at the Phaeacian island of Scheria and his subsequent encounter with the king's daughter Nausicaa. Strauss had not only pondered turning the subject into an opera or ballet;[23] he had also steeped himself in the last years of the war by reading Homer's *Odyssey*. The parallels between the fate of Odysseus – saved in an emergency in a country of affluence and yet dependent on support and always hoping for the possibility to return home – with Strauss's own situation during his stay in Switzerland after October, 1945 are obvious.

An autobiographical component in the program of the *Duett-Concertino* is suggested also by the first sketch of the work dating back perhaps to 1943. There, the bassoon part ends in a motive that strikingly resembles the beginning of *Metamorphosen*. The motive has a text underlay "Ich häng mich auf!" ("I'll hang myself!"). Only a few pages later in the same sketchbook there is an early variant of the beginning of the *Metamorphosen* with a heading "Last metamorphosis."

Whether the program as outlined here applies indeed to the *Duett-Concertino* has to remain open at the moment. Strauss himself consistently refused to give any kind of explanation when asked about a program. In any case, it seems to have played only a subordinate role in the final version of the work. Only in the first and in the very brief second movement – little more than a slow transition – has the sketched material with programmatic indications been used. The dance-like third movement – having a longer duration than the first two movements taken together – is dominated by the playful character of the Oboe Concerto. But then a theme in 4/4 meter is introduced, allowing the solo instruments to abandon the continuing 6/8 meter of the accompaniment: a peculiar melody in A♭ major/C minor presented by both instruments in octave unison; without any mediation, it puts a brake on the unconcerned playfulness (Example 10.7).

This melody comes across as a reminder of a long bygone time – and that is indeed what it is. Strauss uses here a type of melody characteristic of Beethoven's early chamber music.[24] The echoes of something familiar yet bygone on the one hand, and the parallel voice-leading of clarinet and bassoon on the other, imbue the melody with a quality of wistfulness. In this context it may be appropriate to cite an addendum made by Strauss in Berlioz's *Treatise on Instrumentation*, which Strauss had edited. Commenting on "the bassoon joining the descant melody one or two octaves apart," he wrote: "One can't help hearing the voice

Example 10.7 *Duett-Concertino*, third movement, rehearsal no. 22

of an old man humming the melodies dearest to him when he was a youth."[25]

Vier letzte Lieder

On May 22, 1950, eight months after the composer's death, Kirsten Flagstad premiered in London four orchestral songs that Strauss had composed in Switzerland in 1948. Wilhlelm Furtwängler conducted the orchestra. Disregarding a few smaller occasional works, among them the song "Malven" based on a text by the Swiss poet Betty Knobel, these orchestral songs constitute the conclusion of Strauss's oeuvre.

The title *Vier letzte Lieder*, under which the songs were published and became famous, is, however, not by Strauss, but by the publisher Boosey and Hawkes. And still there is a debate about the order in which the songs ought to be performed, since in this respect the process of composition, the premiere, and the printed edition all differ.

The first indication of the songs' genesis can be found in a sketchbook of that time. Inside the cover of the book, Strauss jotted down on April 3, 1946 the Eichendorff poem "Im Abendrot" – the text of the song he completed first. Soon Strauss copied the text into his so-called "Swiss diary," which he kept during his stay in Switzerland.

A year later, in the summer of 1947, Strauss encountered the poems of Hermann Hesse, from which the texts of the three other *Last Songs* are taken. A Swiss friend, perhaps Willi Schuh, gave Strauss an edition of the poems of Hesse, which appeared in June of that year, as a present. Strauss met the poet a little later in Lugano.

That there was no earlier encounter between the two artists has to do with the political situation of the post-war period. At the end of 1945, Strauss and Hesse were both guests of the Verenahof in Baden near Zurich, and the owner Franz Markwalder tried, in vain, to facilitate a meeting. The attempt failed because of Hesse's refusal. "While I was in Baden," he wrote to a friend on February 1, 1946,

> Strauss was there as well. I carefully tried to avoid meeting him … That Strauss has Jewish relatives is, of course, not a recommendation and excuse for him. Precisely because of those relatives Strauss, already well situated and affluent for a long time, should have refused to accept privileges and honors from the Nazis … We have no right to place great blame on him. But I believe we have the right to distance ourselves from him.[26]

After encountering Hesse and his poems in the summer of 1947, Strauss was occupied at first with the completion of the *Duett-Concertino* and the concert tour to London. On May 6, 1948 he concluded the score of the Eichendorff song "Im Abendrot"; Hesse's "Frühling" is dated July 18, then follow "Beim Schlafengehen" (August 4) and "September" (September 20). Whether Strauss ever had a definite order for performance and publication in mind is not known (see Table 10.1). It is not even quite clear whether, and to what extent, Strauss wanted the songs to be understood as a cycle, although their common origin, as well as genre characteristics and musical language, make such a presumption plausible. The sole hint is given on an autograph title page, which, however, was intended only for the Hesse songs. It bears the inscription: "Songs by Hermann Hesse for high voice and orchestra by Richard Strauss."[27]

Table 10.1 *Order of the* Vier letzte Lieder.

	Composition	Premiere	Publication
1.	"Im Abendrot"	"Beim Schlafengehen"	"Frühling"
2.	"Frühling"	"September"	"September"
3.	"Beim Schlafengehen"	"Frühling"	"Beim Schlafengehen"
4.	"September"	"Im Abendrot"	"Im Abendrot"

The *Vier letzte Lieder* were conceived from the outset as orchestral songs – and not only because of the subtle orchestration and the richness of timbres. The soprano is so strongly integrated with the orchestral sound – indeed she is almost treated as an additional orchestral instrument – that one is tempted to speak of an orchestral work with an obbligato vocal part. For that reason, a performance of the songs with piano accompaniment must always remain unsatisfactory.

The *Vier letzte Lieder* were and are considered Strauss's swansong. Indeed three of the texts he composed treat the subject of death and life's transitoriness through a multitude of metaphors, and in particular Eichendorff's "Im Abendrot" suggests a connection to Strauss's own situation. In the setting of this poem, Strauss creates – not for the first time – a musical link to his own life and work: at the poem's last line, "Ist das etwa der Tod?" (Is this perhaps death?), there emerges out of the orchestral texture the theme of transfiguration from his early tone poem *Tod und Verklärung*.[28]

PART III

Perspectives

11 Strauss's place in the twentieth century

ALEX ROSS

Not long ago, the idea of devoting an essay to Richard Strauss's influence on twentieth-century composition might have seemed absurd. From around 1918 onwards, the erstwhile "leader of the moderns" and "chief of the avant-garde" was widely ridiculed as a Romantic relic, whose undoubted native talent had been tainted by poor taste or unprincipled commercialism.[1] Charles Ives identified Strauss with "the comfort of a woman who takes more pleasure in the fit of fashionable clothes than in a healthy body."[2] Aaron Copland described Strauss's tone poems as "the offspring of an exhausted parentage … the final manifestation of a dying world."[3] Igor Stravinsky, in conversation with Robert Craft in the late 1950s, issued an incomparably withering putdown: "I would like to admit all Strauss operas to whichever purgatory punishes triumphant banality. Their musical substance is cheap and poor; it cannot interest a musician today." Stravinsky went on: "I am glad that young musicians today have come to appreciate the lyric gift in the songs of the composer Strauss despised, and who is more significant in our music than he is: Gustav Mahler."[4] Strauss in no way despised Mahler, but the point holds. Composers at various points on the stylistic spectrum, from Copland and Britten to Boulez and Berio, hailed Mahler, not Strauss, as the *fin-de-siècle* prophet of modernity.

It was different in Strauss's intellectual heyday, in the years of *Salome* and *Elektra*. Mahler called *Salome* "one of the greatest masterworks of our time."[5] In early 1913, a few months before the premiere of *The Rite of Spring*, Stravinsky heard *Elektra* "with total delight" at Covent Garden, announcing in an interview that among operas written after *Parsifal* there were only "two that count": *Elektra* and *Pelléas et Mélisande*, in that order.[6] Debussy, writing as Monsieur Croche, identified Strauss as "practically the only original composer in modern Germany" and admitted that "it is not possible to withstand his irresistible domination."[7] The young Béla Bartók threw himself into composing after hearing a performance of *Also sprach Zarathustra* in 1902, and got to know Strauss's scores well enough that he could play several of them from memory at the piano.[8] Few of Strauss's colleagues neglected to criticize one aspect or another of his output, but they saw him fundamentally as a force to be reckoned with, one from whom much could be learned. The tone poems and operas from 1894 to

1909 – *Till Eulenspiegel* to *Elektra* – constituted a kind of mother lode of modernist gestures.

How did Strauss become the great unmentionable in twentieth-century music history? The obvious culprit is his seeming retreat from modernist tendencies in the period after *Elektra* – at least according to conventional definitions of modernism in music. That picture of Strauss has come under skeptical scrutiny in recent years, with scholars such as Walter Werbeck, Bryan Gilliam, and Charles Youmans tracing essential continuities in Strauss's idiosyncratic approach to tonality, form, and aesthetics, from *Guntram* to *Elektra* to *Daphne* to *Metamorphosen*.[9] Gilliam proposes that Strauss's music from *Rosenkavalier* onward should be considered *more* progressive: "Strauss realized that the musical language for the new century should be one that intentionally lacks stylistic uniformity … one that arguably foreshadows the dissolution of the ideology of style in the late twentieth century."[10] Yet the fact remains that Strauss's tonal language became less overtly radical just as modernism moved to the forefront. Another obstacle was the uneven quality of his work in the twenties and thirties. Latter-day listeners may have learned to savor operas such as *Intermezzo* and *Die ägyptische Helena*, but one can understand how the man who wrote *Schlagobers* and *Friedenstag* cut a less impressive figure than the one who wrote *Don Quixote* and *Salome*. Finally, Strauss's official activities in Nazi Germany and ties to the Party leadership cast a pall that not even the most apologetic biographers were able to dispel. Reactionary, creatively exhausted, sympathetic to fascism – such was the profile that Strauss presented in later years.

It is striking, then, that Arnold Schoenberg, who had withstood insults from Strauss and had good reason to join the censorious stampede, generally refrained from doing so. One comment, from 1923, stands out: "I was never *revolutionary. The only revolutionary* in our time was Strauss!"[11] Plainly this remark was something other than a fulsome compliment; revolutions, Schoenberg observed, "simply bring reaction out into the open," implying that in Strauss the revolutionary and the reactionary went hand in hand. Yet, with his sense of fair play, Schoenberg was acknowledging the older man's looming presence in the world of his youth. In a 1946 memorandum, he went further, defending Strauss against accusations of Nazi leanings and reasserting his significance unambiguously: "I believe that he will remain one of the characteristic and outstanding figures in musical history. Works like *Salome, Elektra, Intermezzo*, and others will not perish." (Schoenberg's liking for *Intermezzo* is surprising, since the opera lies well outside the canon of the "acceptable" Strauss. In a 1926 letter to Webern, Schoenberg said that although he found the music "very poor in invention and primitive in technique" he nonetheless emerged with a sympathetic impression of Strauss's personality.)[12] The final sentence of the 1946 note is most telling: "I speak from the standpoint of honesty."[13]

Honesty requires a more rigorous accounting of the legacy of a composer who has always been better appreciated in concert halls and opera houses than in intellectual circles. Indeed, in recent decades, as the definition of "modernism" has been expanded to include not merely a progression towards increased harmonic and rhythmic complexity but also a more complex, pluralistic approach to the question of style, Strauss has undergone a rehabilitation. Once more he serves as a model for contemporary composers of various stylistic orientations. Yet the task of describing Strauss's historical position remains difficult. Because this composer cannot be identified with a clearly demarcated body of techniques, his influence seems amorphous. The glue that holds his works together – the best ones, at least – is not a coherent system or a language but a musical personality that agglomerates disparate materials. One might see him everywhere or nowhere, depending on how one chooses to look. In this chapter I will give particular attention to Strauss's effect on Schoenberg, Webern, and Berg, with briefer observations following on his connections to Stravinsky, Messiaen, and various late-twentieth-century composers in both Europe and America.

Strauss and the Second Viennese School

Schoenberg's relationship with Strauss has drawn considerably less attention than his relationship with Mahler, although Strauss had no less an impact on the younger composer's musical development. Biographical evidence suggests that Schoenberg felt a certain awe in Strauss's vicinity. This is from a typically obsequious letter of 1903: "I would like to take this opportunity to thank you, honored master, once again for all the help you have given me at a sacrifice to yourself in the most sincere manner. I will not forget this for the whole of my life and will always be thankful to you for it."[14] The meekness persisted as late as 1912, as Schoenberg's Berlin diary records: "He was very friendly. But I was very awkward. Bashful, as a fifteen-year-old boy isn't with me (Zweig!), I stammered and must have come across as an off-putting devotee."[15] Often, the young Schoenberg seemed to be following Strauss's lead or moving in tandem with him. In 1898 he made sketches for a symphonic poem entitled *Frühlingstod*, based, like *Don Juan*, on a poem by Nikolaus Lenau. In the year 1899, both composers were immersed in the poetry of Richard Dehmel – Strauss in the extraordinary song-scene *Notturno*, Schoenberg in *Verklärte Nacht*. In 1901 Schoenberg worked on a libretto for a prospective opera entitled *Die*

Example 11.1 *Salome*, beginning, clarinet

p

Schildbürger; back in 1894 Strauss had plotted an opera with the title *Till Eulenspiegel among the Schildburgers*. Schoenberg's *Pelleas und Melisande* came about when Strauss suggested the Maeterlinck play as a subject.[16] Walter Frisch has suggested that the formal design of Schoenberg's First Chamber Symphony owes something to Strauss's *Don Juan*.[17]

Schoenberg's "Strauss phase" reached its height in 1905 and 1906, the years of *Salome*. The opera made an enormous impression on Schoenberg; Mahler gave him a copy of the vocal score sometime in 1905, and, when Egon Wellesz went to study with Schoenberg that fall, he saw the score resting on his teacher's piano, open to the first page. "Perhaps in twenty years' time someone will be able to explain these harmonic progressions theoretically," Schoenberg said to Wellesz.[18] When *Salome* had its Austrian premiere, in Graz, in 1906, Schoenberg made sure to attend, bringing with him no fewer than his six of his pupils: Berg, Heinrich Jalowetz, Karl Horwitz, Erwin Stein, Viktor Krüger, and Zdzisław Jachimecki.[19] The expedition had the appearance of a class field trip for the nascent Second Viennese School.

What on the first page of *Salome* did Schoenberg find so interesting? The first notes on the clarinet provide a possible clue (Example 11.1). The first four notes belong to the scale of C♯ major, but the second set of four seem to refer to the scale of G major. With the ninth note, the second G♯, the music returns to the realm of C♯, but those G major notes indicate, in an almost subliminal way, traditional harmony splitting at the seams. The C♯–G polarity is confirmed by the arrival of a G dominant seventh in the seventh measure.

From his earliest years Strauss felt an urge to stage harmonic collisions across the interval of the tritone. He took his lead from the later Wagner operas, especially *Tristan* and *Götterdämmerung*, where the chord on the lowered fifth becomes almost an alternative dominant. (In a youthful letter to Ludwig Thuille, Strauss mocks a passage in *Die Walküre* where chords of G and C♯ appear close together; perhaps his interest was aroused all the same.)[20] The "tritone complex," as it might be called, surfaces, among other places, in the opening chords of "Ruhe, meine Seele!" (where C dominant sevenths alternate with F♯ minor sevenths); at the end of the introduction to *Don Quixote* (where the pitches E♭ and B♭ sound against an incomplete

Example 11.2 *Elektra*, four mm. before rehearsal no. 178

Example 11.3 *Salome*, "kiss" chord, quoted in Maurice Ravel, "An Interview with Ravel," in Arbie Orenstein, ed., *A Ravel Reader* (New York: Columbia University Press, 1990)

A dominant seventh); in the battle sequences of *Heldenleben* (where, at rehearsal no. 59, trumpets alternate chords of E major and B♭ minor); and in *Symphonia domestica* (where an abrupt juxtaposition of F major and B major characterizes the marital tension of Richard and Pauline Strauss). In *Elektra*, he takes the step of letting tritonally opposed triads sound simultaneously – usually B minor and F minor. A prominent example occurs alongside Hofmannsthal's line "Ich habe keine guten Nächte" ("I have no good nights"; Example 11.2).

Another instance of Straussian polytonality is the famous chord that accompanies Salome's kiss of the severed head of John the Baptist. Maurice Ravel once singled out that harmony by way of observing that Strauss's effect on Viennese modernism had been underestimated. In a 1931 interview, Ravel stated that Schoenberg and his followers "detest Strauss (who hates them as well), but they owe a great deal if not to Strauss the composer, at least to Strauss the musician." Ravel continued: "… Strauss was the first to superimpose lines which were harmonically incompatible. Look at this chord in *Salome* [Example 11.3], which stubbornly resists any cadential analysis – it is at best understood as a simultaneous use of different tonal areas. That is surely one of the sources of Strauss's so-called atonal style."[21] Richard Taruskin, in the fourth volume of his *Oxford History of Western Music*, casts doubt on the "kiss" chord's radical reputation, noting that it does in fact easily allow for cadential analysis; Strauss has simply superimposed two conventional progressions within the key of C♯ major: I–IV–I

Example 11.4   Arnold Schoenberg, sketches for Chamber Symphony No. 2

Example 11.5   Schoenberg, Op. 15, No. 14, vocal line, m. 2

Example 11.6   Schoenberg, Op. 11, No.1, end

and I–♭VI–I. The result, Taruskin states, is an "intensification" of cadence, not a nullification.[22] Yet the sheer density of the chord – there are eight notes sounding together, the vocal score having omitted B♯ in the flutes – surely destabilizes the feeling of cadence on the practical acoustical level. Indeed, the C♯ tonality immediately gives way to a brutal postlude in and around the key of C minor – as if Strauss were resolving, after a 100-minute delay, the G dominant seventh that was left hanging in the seventh measure of the opera.

Yet it was probably not Strauss's superimposition of disparate triads that most interested Schoenberg. In the most frenzied moments of *Salome* and *Elektra*, the syntax of tonal harmony seems on the verge of breaking down into an interplay of constituent intervals. One need only remove the middle note from those two superimposed triads to arrive at what Hans Heinz Stuckenschmidt called the "primal cell" of Schoenberg's music: a harmony made up of two fourths separated by a tritone.[23] The same configuration of notes can be obtained by extracting the notes G♯, C♯, D, and G from the initial clarinet scale of *Salome*. Sketches for the Second Chamber Symphony,[24] which was begun in April, 1906, show Schoenberg playing around with the elements of that primal cell while remaining barely within the bounds of tonality (Example 11.4). A similar pattern appears in the fourteenth song of *Das Buch der hängenden Gärten* (Example 11.5). In the final measure of the first of the *Drei Klavierstücke*, among other places, the fourths are telescoped into a single harmony (Example 11.6). As Stuckenschmidt shows, Schoenberg

Example 11.7 (a) *Salome* at rehearsal no. 355; (b) Anton von Webern, Op. 6, No. 4 (original version), m. 12

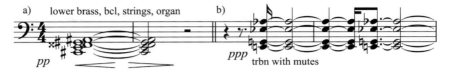

Example 11.8 Alban Berg, *Altenberg Lieder*, "Hier ist Friede," end

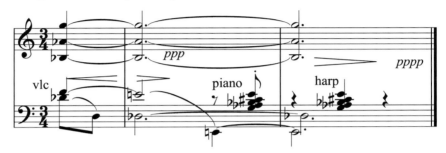

had long relished the sound of a fourth with a tritone above it – the notes A, D, and G♯ can be heard grinding together in both *Gurre-Lieder* and *Pelleas und Melisande* – but the pungent new dissonances in Strauss's scores, particularly the emphasis on semitone clashes, may have spurred him on.

Webern and Berg, too, had their youthful Straussian adventures, which left a mark on their mature works. In the fourth of Webern's *Orchestral Pieces*, Op. 6, one finds low, groaning sonorities that are not dissimilar to the famously chilling chord that appears at the beginning of Salome's final monologue (Example 11.7).

In the long run, Strauss's low-lying chord may have mattered more to Second Viennese School practice than the "kiss" chord cited by Ravel – particularly since it is generated by a verticalization (with one semitone alteration) of the short melody from the first full measure of the opera. In "Hier ist Friede," from the *Altenberg Lieder*, Berg makes what seems to be a direct homage to Strauss's deathly harmony (Example 11.8), and a transposition of this chord appears in *Wozzeck*, just before Marie's murder (Example 11.9). Georg Büchner's text – "How the moon rises red! Like a bloody iron!" – anticipates Oscar Wilde's *Salomé* as translated by Hedwig Lachmann.

Schoenberg and his pupils also helped themselves to typical Straussian gestures – the washes and smears of orchestral color, the phrases that leap about and are cut off abruptly, the tendrils of sound scattered across the page. In a curious way, Strauss scores and Second Viennese School scores *look* alike even when they sound different. For example, Strauss had a habit

Example 11.9 Berg, *Wozzeck*, Act III, mm. 100–1

Example 11.10 *Salome*, four mm. after rehearsal no. 300, horns

Example 11.11 Schoenberg, *Die glückliche Hand*, beginning, bass clarinet and bassoons

of appending a held note or a trill to a spasmodic run of sixteenth or thirty-second notes. A famous instance is the whooping of the horns in *Salome* when Herod discovers that he has lost his ring of power (Example 11.10); compare what the bass clarinet and bassoons play at the very beginning of Schoenberg's *Die glückliche Hand* (Example 11.11).

Erwartung and *Pierrot lunaire* are especially rife with this nervous scurry-and-trill gesture, which, like so much in Strauss, seems to come from Wagner (compare the music for Klingsor and Kundry in Act II of *Parsifal*), and which can also be found in Mahler. It would become a favorite device of Boulez, Berio, and many other post-World War II composers, and remains commonplace in the work of even the youngest composers today. A certain lineage can be seen in Examples 11.12a–c.

Some other Straussian gestures that apparently interested the Second Viennese School: the chilling sound of muted brass playing *fortissimo*; piercing high harmonics in the double basses (compare the cistern sequence of *Salome* with the sleeping soldiers in *Wozzeck*); flutter-tonguing in the brass (compare the bleating of the sheep of *Don Quixote* with various passages in Schoenberg's *Five Pieces for Orchestra* and *Erwartung*);[25] rapid diminutions of durations (compare *Tod und Verklärung*, mm. 5–6 after X, with the final measure of *Erwartung*); chromatic or whole-tone ostinatos on the timpani (compare *Salome*, rehearsal no. 362, with *Wozzeck*, Act I, m. 295); and obsessive repetitions of intervals such as the minor third (compare *Salome*

Example 11.12a *Salome*, three mm. before rehearsal no. 228, flute

Example 11.12b Schoenberg, *Pierrot lunaire*, I, m. 6, flute

Example 11.12c Pierre Boulez, *Le Marteau sans maître*, V, m. 31, flute

at rehearsal nos. 306 or 350 with the second of the *Drei Klavierstücke*). Certainly, not all of these gestures and devices germinated in Strauss or were unique to him. But their rapid proliferation in Strauss's tone poems and operas from 1894 to 1914 helped to propel them into twentieth-century discourse.

Perhaps the most fascinating line of descent from Strauss to Schoenberg involves twelve-tone writing. Strauss's twelve-note subject for the "science" fugue in *Also sprach Zarathustra* is often cited alongside the opening of Liszt's *Faust Symphony* as a precursor to dodecaphony, and it is not an isolated event: surprisingly often, Strauss approaches total chromaticism by arranging triads in mutually complementary sets. The pianist Glenn Gould was among the first to notice Strauss's propensity to capitalize on "the harmonic consequences of triads that divide between them the twelve-tone capacity of the chromatic scale," although Gould went on to make the important point that Strauss was mainly concerned with contrasting his saturated harmonic field with straightforward diatonic formulae.[26] Tethys Carpenter, in a study of *Elektra*, demonstrated that the opera can profitably be analyzed with the pitch–class–set vocabulary one would apply to a twelve-tone score.[27] Returning to *Salome*, the work that Schoenberg knew so well, one notes with interest the sequence of chords that sounds in the orchestra when Herod calls for Salome's death, immediately after the "kiss" chord has sounded (Example. 11.13). D minor is the tonality associated

Example 11.13 *Salome*, five mm. after rehearsal no. 361

Example 11.14 *Salome*, three mm. before rehearsal no. 255

with *Salome*'s Five Jews – a chord of righteous indignation. The second chord is a whole-tone collection. Then a C minor triad is set against an appregiated Gb major triad, echoing the tritone complex with which the work began. And the lower brass play arpeggios in Ab minor (hardly audible in performance). These chords together – D minor, C minor, Gb major, and Ab minor – cover eleven of the twelve tones of the chromatic scale. Another tremor of twelve-tone writing occurs immediately after Salome demands Jochanaan's head, the complementary triads being Db major, Eb minor, G major, and A minor (Example 11.14). Such episodes are the presumably accidental by-product of Strauss's urge to leap across the tritone while holding on to conventional tonal relationships within opposed spheres (D minor as the supertonic of C major, Ab minor as the supertonic of Gb major).

We are now within hailing distance of the tonally biased twelve-tone works of Alban Berg – particularly *Lulu*. Berg, too, knew his *Salome*; after seeing the opera in Graz in 1906, he subsequently went to see *Salome* no fewer than six times when the Breslau Opera gave a run of performances in Vienna. As it happens, the Basic Series of *Lulu*, so designated by George Perle in his study of the opera,[28] can be broken down into almost the same complex of four triads that sounds when Herod calls for Salome's death (Example 11.15). A similar array duly appears in Lulu's Entrance Music (Example 11.16). This is a passage that the Strauss of *Elektra* might have composed.

Example 11.15 Berg, *Lulu*, Basic Series

Example 11.16 Berg, *Lulu*, Prologue, m. 44

Relations between Strauss and the Second Viennese School came to a bad end. Strauss had supported Schoenberg in the early phase of his career, but the advent of atonality caused a break between the two. In 1909, Schoenberg sent Strauss his *Five Pieces for Orchestra*, having written them more or less at Strauss's request. "You are … the person who could best risk taking somebody like myself under his protection," Schoenberg wrote plaintively in a letter.[29] "People in Europe believe in you …" Strauss answered with a carefully worded statement to the effect that these "daring experiments in content and sound" were unsuitable for his conservative Berlin public. He also suggested that Schoenberg hire an orchestra to try out the pieces – the implication being that Schoenberg might be surprised to find what they actually sounded like. Despite that veiled insult, the two composers remained on friendly terms for several more years. Then, in 1913 or early 1914, Strauss wrote Alma Mahler a letter in which he suggested that Schoenberg would be better off shoveling snow than scribbling on music paper. Alma Mahler showed the letter to Erwin Stein, who decided that Schoenberg should know about it.[30] Schoenberg subsequently wrote to an associate of Strauss: "He is no longer of the slightest artistic interest to me, and whatever I may once have learnt from him, I am thankful to say I misunderstood."[31] As we have seen, Schoenberg later arrived at a more balanced assessment of Strauss's place in musical history.

Games of style

Let's go back to the slithering little clarinet scale that begins *Salome*. Schoenberg, studying the vocal score on his piano, may have seen it as a crack in the façade of tonality – the beginning of the disintegration of the tonal system into a non- or pan-tonal play of intervals. But this bifurcation does not necessarily point in the direction of atonality – that is, a conscious avoidance of the basic chords of the tonal system. Alternatively, it might suggest a new, kaleidoscopic kind of tonal harmony in which familiar chords are combined in unfamiliar ways. This ambiguity exhibits in microcosm the larger ambiguity of Strauss's legacy to twentieth-century music – to Schoenberg and his school on the one hand, and to Stravinsky, Bartók, and Messiaen on the other.

Strauss never renounced diatonic tonality, but from *Till Eulenspiegel* onwards he treated the tonal system with a certain detachment, as if he no longer believed in it wholeheartedly. Think of the textbook dominant–tonic progressions that pop up at the very end of *Der Rosenkavalier* – a surreally, almost insolently simple conclusion to an opera that is heavily freighted with harmonic complexity. Such sequences are more like images of tonality than the real thing. Leon Botstein has written: "… one might suggest that *Rosenkavalier* is itself a radical work, a harbinger of neoclassicism and an ironic deconstruction of notions of history and progress."[32] In *Ariadne auf Naxos*, Strauss deliberately toyed with past styles, reducing his orchestra to Mozartian proportions and confronting his second soprano with outrageously anachronistic coloratura writing.[33] There was always a side of Strauss that wished to escape, even to undermine, the grandiose architecture of Germanic tradition. While his quest for Nietzschean lightness may be deemed a failure – in no way did he become "the Offenbach of the twentieth century," as he once claimed – he did his part to dismantle the Wagnerian apparatus and to nudge music in a fresh direction.

That one 1913 comment about *Elektra* aside, there is little evidence that Stravinsky made positive contact with Strauss's music. But musical influence is a mysterious process, proceeding sometimes through direct contact and sometimes along indirect, even unconscious lines. The Stravinsky who wrote *Petrushka* might have absorbed certain ideas that Strauss had put into the air. The flexibility of Strauss's language in the tone poems and the early operas – the abruptness of the transitions, the habit of abbreviating and truncating themes, the entire quicksilver manner that Debussy, in a review of *Ein Heldenleben*, prophetically labeled "cinematographic" – comes enticingly close at times to Stravinsky's *Petrushka* manner. Notice, for example, Strauss's savagely curt way of announcing the death of the protagonist in *Till Eulenspiegel*, with a sudden snare-drum roll that slices into the middle of a boisterous D major progression. Petrushka's demise is signaled much the same way; indeed, the snare-drum roll becomes an organizing principle of the composition. Compare also the motive of Herod's command in *Salome* with one of Petrushka's principal motifs (Example 11.17). The resemblance becomes even more marked when, in

Example 11.17 (a) *Salome*, six mm. after rehearsal no. 361, first trumpet; (b) Igor Stravinsky, *Petrushka*, six mm. after rehearsal no. 125, first trumpet

Example 11.18 Stravinsky, *Petrushka*, six mm. before end, trumpets

the final measures of the ballet, four trumpets are split between the keys of C major and F♯ major, echoing both the instrumentation and the harmonic ambiguity of the "command" figure (Example 11.18). The likeness might, of course, be entirely accidental. As Richard Taruskin demonstrates in *Stravinsky and the Russian Traditions*, Stravinsky's tendency to combine chords across the tritone is derived from Rimsky-Korsakov, who made a habit of the device well before Strauss wrote *Salome*.[34] Still, one can understand why Strauss himself thought that Stravinsky was borrowing a trick or two from him. "It is always interesting to hear one's imitators," he said on hearing *The Firebird* in 1912.[35] There, perhaps, is the source of Stravinsky's later venom on the subject of Strauss.

The putative "neoclassicism" of *Ariadne* surely did not affect Stravinsky directly. There is no reason to doubt him when he says, in conversation with Craft, "*Ariadne* makes me want to scream."[36] All the same, in a curious historical twist, *Ariadne* exerted an oblique gravitational pull on Stravinsky's career. In 1912, the Princesse de Polignac attended the premiere of the original version of *Ariadne* in Stuttgart, and, in the words of her biographer, Sylvia Kahan, "experienced something of an epiphany." Strauss's economical employment of an orchestra of thirty-six instruments gave her the idea that "the days of big orchestras were over and that it would be delightful to return to a small orchestra of well chosen players and instruments."[37] She proceeded to commission from Stravinsky a score requiring thirty-to-thirty-six instruments, even specifying the instrumentation. She did not mention the Strauss connection, which would surely have rubbed Stravinsky the wrong way. In response, Stravinsky made plans for a piano concerto, although it would be twelve years before the Concerto for Piano and Winds emerged. In roundabout fashion, Strauss helped guide Stravinsky towards his neo-Baroque and neoclassical writing of the 1920s and after.

Paul Hindemith was one of a number of early-twentieth-century composers who divested themselves of an adolescent Strauss infatuation. He conspicuously mocked Strauss's middle-period, grand-operetta style in the "Duett Kitsch" of *Neues vom Tage*. Even so, aspects of the hard-edged, biting style favored by Hindemith and other young central European composers of the 1920s have pre-echoes in obscure corners of Strauss's turn-of-the-century music. In the years when Strauss was engaging with leftist, socialist, anarchist, and/or anticlerical poets such as John Henry Mackay, Karl Henckell, and Oskar Panizza, he occasionally adopted something like a "protest" voice in his songs, although efforts in this line proved to be little more than experimental dabbling. The 1901 song "Das Lied des Steinklopfers," on a text by Henckell, might easily be mistaken for the work of a radical young Berliner of the pre-Nazi years: its restless, driving rhythms, percussive piano sonorities, and angrily thrusting vocal line dramatize Henckell's statement of solidarity with the poor, hungry worker who seethes at having to "break stones / For the Fatherland."[38]

Among more conservative-minded composers of the World War I and interwar period, Strauss remained a potent force. The old guard of German music – the likes of Franz Schmidt, Max von Schillings, Hans Pfitzner, and Joseph Marx – struggled, with mixed success, to emerge from Strauss's shadow; Pfitzner fulminated against Strauss to the end of his life, believing himself to have been unjustly overlooked. Ottorino Respighi, in *Fountains of Rome*, unabashedly borrowed from the mountain-climbing motives in Strauss's *Alpine Symphony* – a work that was admittedly fair game, given its own brazen theft from Max Bruch. Karol Szymanowski openly imitated early Strauss in works such as *Hagith*, then worked his way to a much more individual style in the Third Symphony and *King Roger*, although the ecstatic, ear-saturating climaxes of these pieces show lessons learned from *Salome*, particularly in the art of puncturing an essentially tonal surface with eruptions of dissonance.

Of particular interest is Strauss's effect on a group of partly or fully Jewish composers who thrived in the interwar years but went into eclipse with the advent of the Third Reich. This group includes Alexander Zemlinsky, Franz Schreker, Bernhard Sekles, Walter Braunfels, and Erich Wolfgang Korngold. None of these composers can be described as a follower of Strauss, but partial fingerprints can be detected in more than a few measures of their work – perhaps most obviously in Korngold's athletically leaping melodic figures and impressionistically hazy harmonies. They are all rooted in late Romanticism, but they generally avoid the inborn conservatism of Pfitzner and company, not least in their choice of subject matter.

Example 11.19 *Der Rosenkavalier*, Act II, one m. after rehearsal no. 25, celesta and harp

Strauss's scandalous success in setting Wilde's *Salomé* apparently inspired a slew of Wildean ventures: Sekles's 1913 ballet on the tale "The Birthday of the Infanta," Schreker's 1908 pantomime of the same title, and, most notably, Zemlinsky's operas *A Florentine Tragedy* and *Der Zwerg*. Now that such eclectic, energetically middle-of-the-road music is escaping decades of neglect and finding a new audience, Strauss, by extension, comes to seem a less marginal figure.

Perhaps the most improbable "Straussian" of the mid twentieth century was Olivier Messiaen. There is little direct evidence that Messiaen had any high regard for – or knowledge of – Strauss, although it is arresting to find this statement from him in Joan Peyser's biography of Pierre Boulez: "There are people who go unperturbed through change. Like Bach. Like Richard Strauss."[39] And, coincidentally or not, the opening scale of *Salome* reappears as Mode 6 in Messiaen's textbook *Technique de mon langage musical*. Messiaen probably heard much about Strauss from his teacher Paul Dukas, who admired the German composer and was admired by him in turn. (Strauss even attempted to arrange performances of Dukas's *Ariane et Barbe-bleue* during the Nazi period.)[40] Dukas and Strauss had in common a freewheeling approach to harmony that featured tonal chords in mercurial, shimmering sequences – a habit that both composers shared with Debussy and Rimsky-Korsakov. While it is difficult to isolate unambiguously Straussian elements amid the welter of turn-of-the-century mannerisms that fed Messiaen's omnivorous language, a comparison of Examples 11.19 and 11.20 suggests that the young Frenchman may have harbored a secret love for *Rosenkavalier*. The harmonies are considerably more dense in the Messiaen example, but the constructive principle – stringing together major and minor triads – is much the same. Notice also the tritone complex that underpins the sequence. A faint *Rosenkavalier* atmosphere returns several times in Messiaen's later music, notably in *Des Canyons aux étoiles*. When I hear the brilliant climax of "Bryce Canyon et les rochers rouge-orange," or the lush, glittering music of "Les Ressuscités et le chant de l'étoile Aldébaran," I always picture, for a moment or two, the Presentation of the Silver Rose.

Example 11.20   Olivier Messiaen, "Cloches d'angoisse et larmes d'adieu," m. 5

Strauss in recent decades

After 1945, Strauss's influence effectively went underground for several decades. The composer seemed entirely eclipsed as a force in contemporary music, his reputation doubly damaged by his associations with Nazi Germany and by the seeming victory of a teleological, progress-oriented vision of music history. Stravinsky's slashing judgments in his conversations with Craft were hardly controversial; they confirmed the prejudices of most young composers and music intellectuals of the 1950s and 1960s. The maverick opinion was Glenn Gould's, in his remarkable essay "Strauss and the Electronic Future": "It is entirely likely that Strauss, a man who seemed remote from the time in which he lived and totally unconcerned about the future, will, because of the new orientation of that future, gather a greater admiration than he ever knew."[41]

The new orientation that Gould had in mind was a less regimented and linear conception of the unfolding of musical history. Electronic media, the pianist predicted, would mean that new generations of composers, musicians, and listeners would be "exposed to the most astonishing variety of idiom without necessarily having to encounter it in any specific social situation." Indeed, in the later 1960s, composers began to avail themselves of a wider array of stylistic sources. Tendencies variously named "pluralism," "polystylistics," "New Simplicity," and "New Romanticism" came to the fore. Tonality enjoyed something of a resurgence, to the extent that it had ever faded. And Strauss's playful, unpredictable, often sardonic manipulation of tonality again received respectful attention. The sound-world of a work such as *Salome* – its polymodality, its intermittent polytonality, its abrupt juxtapositions of common chords and more or less unheard-of dissonances, even its seeming lapses into vulgarity – might be seen not merely as a historically transitional phenomenon but as a vital response to an enduringly multiplicitous stylistic condition.

One important difference was that composers born in, say, 1935 or 1945 no longer displayed the aversion towards Strauss's sumptuous orchestration that seemed automatic among their elders. Copland, in *Our New Music*, spoke for most members of his Stravinsky-besotted generation when he wrote, "To us the general sound of Strauss's orchestra is over-rich ... [His scores] have little relationship to the more sober and precise orchestration of the present day."[42] Latter-day American composers such as John Corigliano, David Del Tredici, John Adams, and Aaron Jay Kernis display a quite different mindset; they often take the attitude that the capabilities of the late-Romantic orchestra are, in a sense, to be enjoyed to the max, and with them Strauss's orchestration once again becomes a plausible if not dominant model. An ironic yet potent quotation from *Salome* – the threatening theme of Jochanaan – appears in Act II of Adams's *Nixon in China*, where it is associated with the totalitarian aesthetic of Mao Zedong's China. David Del Tredici, in his sequence of works on the subject of Alice in Wonderland, revels in fatty, protein-rich, quasi-Straussian textures and timbres; his fellow composer Robin Holloway cited Del Tredici's "super-Strauss/Respighi orchestration of a common chord" as an instance of musical surrealism, of a composer becoming "original-*through*-clichés."[43] Holloway himself is unafraid to take inspiration from Strauss in his music. The late Nicholas Maw felt much the same. Certain delicately ravishing effects in recent works of Osvaldo Golijov – in particular, the opera *Ainadamar* and the cello concerto *Azul* – reflect a study of the twilight tonality of *Daphne*.

The latter-day cult of Strauss is not limited to sybaritic Anglo-American neo-Romantics. German composers, too, have been lending him new ears. Even at the height of the post-war avant-garde, Hans Werner Henze showed an inclination to taste, on occasion, forbidden Straussian fruit – as at the opulently orchestrated, *Elektra*-like climaxes of *The Bassarids*. In his autobiography, Henze identified himself as a Mahlerian and denied taking direction from Strauss, yet he accepted one colleague's description of his music as "Strauss turned sour."[44] Members of younger generations generally remain circumspect about their progenitor, but the orchestral music of Wolfgang Rihm, among others, exhibits an awareness of how the Second Viennese School language emerged from the primordial Straussian ooze. For example, Rihm's violin concerto *Lichtzwang* (1975–6), written in memory of Paul Celan, contains a smattering of Straussian and/or Mahlerian gestures that would have been more or less unthinkable in preceding decades: flamboyantly leaping and plunging figures for unison horns or trombones, self-consciously tragic utterances that descend in consecutive octaves, stagey dissonances that betray their tonal components. Logically enough, when the conductor Kent Nagano became the music director of the Bavarian State Opera, he commissioned Rihm to write *Das Gehege* (2006), a one-act companion to *Salome*.

Even so committed an avant-gardist as Helmut Lachenmann – a composer whose works exhibit no surface similarity to Strauss's – has concluded that the "leader of the moderns" is due for a reconsideration. In 2002, Lachenmann made some notes about Strauss's *Alpine Symphony*, in anticipation of a concert by the Ensemble Modern in which the *Alpine* would follow Lachenmann's nearly hour-long 1984–5 piece *Ausklang*. The idea for the pairing came from the composer himself, who, it seems, had long been fascinated by Strauss's largest orchestral work. He proposed that the piece be heard as a psychologically risky adventure in which tonality functions as a "railing," a provisional path through a sonic wilderness:

> The important thing is not to stigmatize aesthetic regression with contempt as being a vice of the subscribing audience, but to recognize and see through it with the highest degree of attentiveness, intelligence, and enthusiasm. By intelligent listening, the "effort of perception" that goes far beyond observing variations of sound, we can decide whether the *Alpine Symphony* with its "nature-like" liveliness and demonic, theatrical thunder is only a romantic work or – perhaps in contrast to its creator's intention – also a tragic, instructive, enlightening piece …

Lachenmann also offers the provocative suggestion that post-war avant-garde works have more in common with Strauss's nature-painting than one might expect. He cites Stockhausen's *Gruppen* as "a kind of *Alpine Symphony* with calls from the various pinnacles in the middle" – presumably alluding to the famous sequence in which six-note brass chords ricochet among three spatially distinct orchestral groups. Lachenmann leaves us with the intriguing suggestion that Strauss's works, far from offering a dead end, may present a half-unexplored landscape for those seeking new paths:

> … [T]he dialectics of today's aesthetic situation seem to create a new false sense of security in seemingly inhospitable environments – the escape from the familiar has become the escape from oneself into falsely heroic zones. The adventure consists of recognizing the regressively colored aesthetic landscape as a "wasteland" or perhaps as a "glacier" which one can slide down or climb up in order to find oneself in unknown zones.[45]

12 Musical quotations and allusions in the works of Richard Strauss

GÜNTER BROSCHE

TRANSLATED BY JÜRGEN THYM

I have no taste for philologists' reminiscence-hunts. RICHARD STRAUSS (1944)[1]

Introduction and overview

Appropriation of pre-existing music and melodies, whether from one's own compositions or those of other composers, is as old as polyphonic music itself. We may think, for instance, of the cantus-firmus masses of the sixteenth century, in which composers built a polyphonic web above a borrowed melody; or of variation works from the eighteenth, nineteenth, and twentieth centuries, in which melodic and harmonic transformations of a theme produce an independent work. In recent history, musical borrowing has occurred most often in the form of quotations or reminiscences – a practice in which, as Roland Tenschert has observed, the musical quotation has the same function as a quotation in language.

> It does not matter, in principle, whether the materials come from the works of other masters or from one's own compositions. The mere fact that something is "quoted" establishes the particular appeal and, occasionally, also results in a humorous punch line. Since this appeal is lacking when the context is not recognized, knowing the quotation is a condition for the intended effect.[2]

If the effect is thus limited to the small number of listeners who possess a comprehensive musical knowledge, it nonetheless holds a special appeal, even for Richard Strauss, in spite of the dim view he expressed in the motto cited above. (The negative tone stemmed from the displeasure he felt when Willi Schuh called his attention to an inadvertent quotation in one of his works.)

Musicologists agree that few composers have contributed more numerous and original examples of quotation than Richard Strauss. A comprehensive list is of course out of the question; rather we must limit ourselves to a few essential examples. Moreover, further quotations surely remain to be discovered in Strauss's works.

As with all musical quotations, Strauss's have different meanings. Roughly, one can distinguish a handful of different functions. There is, first of all, the quotation as a means to underscore and portray a text, often in a humorous way, or as a means to represent the local color and the historical background. Quotations can also characterize the milieu or the *dramatis personae* in a stage work, and they can allude to emotional states such as joy or sadness. (Musical allusions to one's own works can refer to these states with special clarity.) Quotations have their deepest meaning, however, when they evoke ideological and philosophical issues.

We can assume that many a quotation "slipped" unintentionally into the score during the act of composition. The appearance of the tempest motive from *Die Walküre* in the *Burleske for Piano and Orchestra*, Op. 85 (beginning eight measures before Kk) seems such a case; certainly its meaning is unclear. Somewhere between an inadvertent quotation and a conscious reference to the source's meaning is perhaps the use of the Swiss popular song "Freut euch des Lebens" in the opera *Die schweigsame Frau* – an example to which we shall return later.

Quotations elicited by a text

Witty quotations often interpret and underscore the sung text. The lavish dinner at Monsieur Jourdain's in *Der Bürger als Edelmann*, Op. 60, movt. 9, for instance, is illustrated several times: the "Rhine Salmon à la Count Palatine" appears to the swaying textures of Wagner's Rhinemaidens; the second course, "A Leg of Mutton in the Italian Style," arrives with the bleating-sheep motive from *Don Quixote*; and, lastly, "a little meal of thrushes and larks with sage and thyme" calls forth bird-song such as awakens Octavian and the Marschallin from their morning rapture in the first act of *Der Rosenkavalier*.[3] The many borrowings from, and allusions to, the compositions of Jean-Baptiste Lully suggested themselves as a matter of course, since Lully had already written incidental music to Molière's play in 1670. Quotations from this work can be found in the prelude to the second act, in the sarabande-like entrance of Cléonte, in the Turkish scene, and in the madrigal of the three Sylphes at the end of the third act.[4]

A quotation probably meant humorously by Strauss, but perhaps inadvertent and certainly puzzling in its implications, can be found in *Intermezzo*, a "bourgeois comedy with symphonic interludes." For this work he wrote the libretto himself, since both Hofmannsthal and Hermann Bahr had declined, pointing out to him that only he could write such a text. After the turbulent farewell scene in the first act between Christine (Pauline) and her husband, the court conductor Robert Storch (Strauss),

Christine makes an ugly and mocking remark about her husband's frequent travels: "I believe he has Jewish blood in his veins!" The text here expressly carries the comment: "Quotation."[5] William Mann has speculated that with the motive sounded by the first horn, the principal theme of the first movement of Schumann's "Spring" Symphony, Strauss in fact meant to cite Mendelssohn Bartholdy.[6] To date we have no other compelling explanation for this obvious "quotation."

Intermezzo contains several other playfully ironic quotations. The critics' motive from *Ein Heldenleben* chimes in with the wife's remark, "The critic who cannot stand him has called me the better half." In the card-playing scene (Act II, Scene i) the quotations become more frequent. The sarcastic comments of the chamber singer ("At the beginning of each season your eagerness to rehearse is colossal; once we get to March you calm down") feature the beginning of the overture to Mozart's *Le nozze di Figaro* in the orchestra – a work that Strauss always rehearsed most intensely.[7] The unsuitable operatic quotations of the chamber singer ("Have you said your prayers, Desdemona?" from Verdi's *Otello*[8] and "Weak even he, all of them weak!" from *Parsifal*,[9] as well as "An error – is it worth such penitence?" from *Der Freischütz*[10]) might be understood as allusions to the limited intellectual horizon of a tenor. When Storch mentions that "a little card game is a pleasure, the best recuperation after music," the orchestra's quotation from *Tristan und Isolde* reveals what he understands by "music."[11]

Another cluster of humorous quotations can be found in *Krämerspiegel*, Op. 66, twelve songs by Alfred Kerr for voice and piano. Since differences of opinion with publishers inspired the work, Kerr juxtaposes the names of German music publishers (for example, Bote and Bock) with titles of compositions by Strauss. Musical citation from these works was thus an obvious choice. At the words "Once the ram [*Bock*] came as messenger [*Bote*] to the cavalier of the roses [*Rosenkavalier*]," two motives sound from *Der Rosenkavalier*: the waltz, and the oboe motive from the Presentation of the Rose. When the text describes merchants bringing death to music, but transfiguration to themselves, it is clear that the respective motive from *Tod und Verklärung* is quoted (see below for further discussion of this motive). The hero and his adversaries are characterized in song 11 through the hero's and critics' themes from *Ein Heldenleben*. As Günter von Noé observes, "the continuation of 'Der lässt ein Wort erklingen / Wie Götz von Berlichingen' is underscored with the opening motive from Beethoven's Symphony No. 5, whose rhythm matches the words" – the words being, of course, Götz's infamous "Leck mich im Arsch."[12] And when the text reins in the merchants with a mention of Till Eulenspiegel's new *Schelmenweis'* ("fool's tune"), there is naturally a musical reference to the tone poem.

Humorous allusions to his own works can still be found in Strauss's last stage work, *Capriccio*. When La Roche utters a diatribe against the farce in his justification speech, the orchestra cites, in rich self-irony, the beginning of the *buffo* quartet "Die Dame gibt mit trübem Sinn / Sich allzu sehr der Trauer hin" ("This lady is too much inclined / to yield to misery of mind"[13]) from *Ariadne auf Naxos*. And a little later, appropriate self-quotations from *Ariadne* and *Daphne* spice up several scathing remarks about shelf-worn mythological subjects.[14]

With many a tiny humorous citation, one cannot help thinking that Strauss wanted to test the knowledge of his audience. A few examples must stand for many such cases. In the first scene of *Arabella*, Zdenka tells Matteo concerning her sister, "And yesterday she was at the opera," while the orchestra indicates, through a measure from *Lohengrin*, which work she has seen. Likewise, the words "The falcon has her" in *Die ägyptische Helena* are accompanied by the falcon motive from *Die Frau ohne Schatten*.

Local color and historical background

A famous quotation capturing local color (and an early example of Strauss's spiritual and musical occupation with folk songs) can be found in *Aus Italien* (1886). In the fourth movement, the finale entitled "Neapolitanisches Volksleben," Strauss cites the Neapolitan "folk song" "Funiculì, funiculà" – a melody that remains extremely popular even today and not only in Naples. The piece in question, however, is no folk song but the most celebrated work of the Italian song composer Luigi Denza (1846–1922), who wrote more than 500 popular Neapolitan tunes. Strauss encountered "Funiculì" (1880) during his first journey to Italy in April and May of 1886, and incorporated it in September of the same year into the finale of his work.[15]

Strauss introduced local color referring to Munich in the early *Singgedicht*, *Feuersnot*, through quotations of folk songs from his home town. Noé sets the stage:

> In the crowd scene at the beginning of the opera, the Old-Munich folksong "Der alte Peter" provides a commentary on the pompous provinciality of the tavern owner. A little later the ballad of the giant Onuphrius is sung to the melody of
>
> Mir san net von Pasing, mir san net von Loam,
> Mir san von dem lustigen Menzing dahoam.
> (We are not from Pasing, we are not from Loam,
> We are at home in cheerful Menzing.)

whereby the old folksong is adjusted to allude to the giants' motive in *Rheingold*. A third folksong, the drinking song "Guten Morgen, Herr Fischer" animates the waltz scene. All three quotations are footnoted in the score.[16]

Even the narrow-mindedness of Munich's citizens and critics is characterized through quotations. The fact that Wagner, pressured by public opinion, had to leave Munich in 1865 is denounced by way of the Valhalla motive. It sounds shortly after the text (thus clarifying who Master Reichhart was):

> Im Hause, das ich heut zerhaun,
> Haust' Reichhart einst, der Meister.
> Der war kein windiger Gaukler, traun,
> Der hehre Beherrscher der Geister.

> The house that I demolished today
> Was once the home of Master Reichhart;
> He certainly was not a windy charlatan,
> But the noble sovereign of the spirits.

The libretto continues:

> Sein Wagen kam allzu gewagt euch vor,
> Da triebt ihr den Wagner aus dem Tor!
> Den bösen Feind, den triebt ihr nit aus,
> Der stellt sich euch immer wieder aufs neue zum Strauß.

> When his carriage appeared too daring to you,
> you expelled the wheelwright [*Wagner*] from the city.
> But you could not dislodge the evil enemy:
> He comes back again and again as an ostrich [*Strauß*].

The first line is set to the Dutchman motive from *Der fliegende Holländer*, the last to the battle motive from *Guntram*.

Another quotation underscoring the local color of a plot is the famous waltz in *Rosenkavalier*. It pervades the entire opera, assuming particular prominence in the second and third acts. The generating idea may have come from Hofmannsthal, for in a letter of April 24, 1909 from Rodaun he remarks to Strauss: "Make sure in the last act to come up with an old-fashioned Viennese waltz, partly sweet, partly frivolous, to weave through the entire act."[17] Whether this letter was the initial stimulus for the *Rosenkavalier* waltz we do not know, but the theme already has a major role in the second act, providing the setting for Ochs's salacious words:

> Ohne mich, ohne mich, jeder Tag dir so bang,
> Mit mir, mit mir, keine Nacht dir zu lang.

> Without me, every day will be worrisome for you,
> With me, no night will be too long for you.

Strauss took the incipit for the waltz from *Dynamiden*, Op. 173, by Josef Strauß (1827–70), the brother of Johann Strauß, Jr., the "Vienna Waltz-King." But after only four measures the piece takes a completely different path and character, leaving us with a mere echo or faint allusion. Of course, this is not the only waltz in *Rosenkavalier*; over and over again the opera is pervaded by waltz rhythms pointing to Vienna as the locale of the action. For that reason, *Der Rosenkavalier* has been called the "opera of waltzes."

There is evidence that Strauss consulted a folk song collection as a source for two quotations in *Arabella* – a procedure that otherwise is rare with him. The quotations here have two functions: on the one hand, they provide the local color of Mandryka's home country; on the other, by way of their nature-loving, innocent ambiance they provide a contrast to the dubious characters of Viennese society represented by Count Waldner, whose gambling habits have driven Arabella's family into debt. On July 13, 1928 Hofmannsthal had impressed upon Strauss the importance of local color to the dramaturgy of the work:

> The tone of *Arabella* is quite different from that of *Rosenkavalier*. Granted, the locale in both cases is Vienna, but what a difference lies between them – a full century! The Vienna of Maria Theresia – and the Vienna of 1866! …The atmosphere of *Arabella* – already very close to our own time – is plainer, more conventional, and more ordinary. The three counts who frivolously chase girls, the whole questionable milieu of Rittmeister Waldner has something unsavory, a somewhat boorish and dangerous Vienna surrounds these characters – the self-reliant and courageous Arabella and the movingly disoriented Zdenka stand out from this background – but, above all, the frivolous Vienna steeped in entertainment and gambling, is the foil for Mandryka: he is surrounded by the purity of his villages, of the oak forests that never have been touched by an axe, of his folk songs. Here the spaciousness of great semi-Slavic Austria enters a Viennese comedy.[18]

Strauss took these words to heart in Act I, when Arabella asks Zdenka whether the beautiful roses were delivered by a hussar from a foreign traveler. Of course, she hopes that the flowers come from Mandryka. But when Zdenka says that they came from Matteo, Arabella talks very indifferently about him. Zdenka's reaction is so vehement that Arabella correctly assumes her sister is in love with him. Arabella states: "Er ist der Richtige nicht für mich!" ("He is not the right one for me!"). When Zdenka insinuates that Arabella had been in love with Matteo, she responds: "A man quickly means a lot to me, but as quickly he turns out to be nothing for me!" Immediately she sings her principal "hit":

> Aber der Richtige – wenn's einen gibt für mich auf dieser Welt –
> Der wird einmal dastehn, da vor mir
> Und wird mich anschaun und ich ihn,
> Und keine Zweifel werden sein und keine Fragen,
> Und selig werd' ich sein und gehorsam wie ein Kind.

> But the right man – if he indeed exists for me in this world –
> Will one day stand there, in front of me
> And he will look at me and I at him,
> And there won't be any doubts or questions,
> And I will be in bliss, and obedient like a child.[19]

For this text Strauss used, as he did later for the love duet between Arabella and Mandryka in Act II, a Croatian folk melody from a three-volume collection that he borrowed from the Court Library (today's Austrian National Library), as he wrote to Hofmannsthal on December 21, 1927: Franjo S. Kuhač, *Južno-slovjenske narodne popievke* (*South-Slavic Folksongs, Collected, Arranged and Edited with Piano Accompaniment*; Agram: K. Albrecht, 1878–82). Today these volumes are located, as are the copies Strauss made, in the Music Department, but, except for faint pencil markings, they show no comments from Strauss.

At the second quotation, in the love duet of Arabella and Mandryka in Act I:

> *Arabella*: Und du wirst mein Gebieter sein, und ich dir untertan.
> …
> *Mandryka*: Meine Allerschönste, in dieser Stunde erhöhe ich dich,
> Und wähle ich dich zu meiner Frau.

> *Arabella*: And you will be my master, and I will serve you.
> …
> *Mandryka*: My most beautiful woman, in this hour I elevate you
> And choose you to be my wife.

a footnote in the score indicates that the music is derived "from a south Slavic folk melody."[20]

Brief quotations with historical allusions serve to represent local color and historical background in *Capriccio*, Strauss's last work for the theater – "not an opera, but intellectual theatre, food for the brain, dry witticism," as Strauss characterized its purpose to his collaborator Clemens Krauss during the genesis of the libretto in a letter of September 14, 1939.[21] The libretto's indication of the place and time of the opera – "A castle near Paris at the time when Gluck began his operatic reform, *c.* 1775" – is illustrated with a quotation of the beginning of Gluck's overture to *Iphigénie en Aulide*. When theater director La Roche introduces the artists of his company – an Italian female singer, an Italian tenor, and a young female dancer – they perform an Italian duet based on a text by Metastasio (from his *Adriano in Siria*) as well as historical dances such as the passepied, gigue, and gavotte. These belong, of course, to the "ironic allusions" to Italian opera in general, which Strauss, quite a number of times, slipped into his comedies for the stage.[22]

Strauss's librettists – Hofmannsthal, Stefan Zweig, and Clemens Krauss – provided him with the occasions for these ironic allusions. The best-known "Italian" number in all of his operas is the aria of the Italian singer in the first act of *Der Rosenkavalier*, "Di rigori armato il seno." The text could also have been by Metastasio, but in fact comes from the "quatrième entrée" of *Ballet des nations*, which concludes Molière's *Bourgeois Gentilhomme*.[23] Irony is achieved here by exaggeration. Strauss intensifies the melodic line and the expressive sonorities by using parallel thirds and sixths as embellishments. The vocal part contains all the mannerisms of *bel canto*, amplified by Strauss: brilliant peak tones emphasized through long-held fermatas; exaggerating portamenti; melismas inserted on "Ah" to conclude a phrase.[24] *Commedia dell'arte*, *opera seria*, and *opera buffa* likewise introduce Italian elements in *Ariadne auf Naxos*, and in *Die schweigsame Frau* the role of Henry, tenor of an Italian opera company, prompts many allusions to Italian opera and quotations from real works.

In this context the "Song of the Piedmontese" in *Friedenstag* occupies a special position. Here Joseph Gregor, the librettist, used an original Italian song text that he had heard during World War I in the Alto Adige province of the South Tyrol and later reconstructed with the help of an Italian writer. Strauss, however, set the text to a melody of his own, whose luscious *italianità* shows his affinity to and fondness of Italy – a country where he often traveled.[25] Of course, he spoke of Italian operatic music with disdain: "I will probably never convert to Italian music, it is simply trash. Even the *Barber of Seville* is only palatable in an excellent staging."[26]

To characterize the local and period flavor of London in his opera *Die schweigsame Frau*, Strauss used quotations from the Fitzwilliam Virginal Book, which was put together a century before the action of Zweig's libretto. The keyboard compositions originated in the seventeenth century, whereas the opera takes place in "approximately 1760" – although Strauss was not very particular in such matters. For the fake wedding of Morosus and Aminta he uses two quotations, one by an anonymous composer and another by Martin Peerson, identifying the former in his score as "From the English by Anon" because he mistakenly took the abbreviation of "anonymous" for the composer's name (a funny error indeed!). For the fake divorce of the couple he quotes a piece by John Bull. Aminta's voice lesson in Act II is announced by two quotations: the first identified in the text with the words "Here is your part, the aria from Monteverdi's *L'incoronazione di Poppea*!," the other through a footnote in the score: "From the opera *Eteocle e Polinice* by Legrenzi, Venice 1675." Significantly, Strauss used the original old texts but his own melodies; he was not unduly concerned with authenticity when he quoted.

Strauss's carefree delight in quotation is let loose in a veritable conglomerate of quotations, now from more recent operas, at Sir Morosus's outburst of desperation: "Alas, how inventive is this species of jackasses when it comes to speculation!" The following text is set to appropriate musical quotations:

> Das fiedelt und flötet,
> Das pfeift und trompetet,
> Das brummt und das schrummt,
> Das rauft und besauft sich,
> Das klimpert und stümpert
> Und setzt niemals aus.

Noé observes of this passage (translating as he goes),

> There are fiddles (ostinato figure in the violin) and flutes (waltz from Gounod's *Faust* in the piccolo), there are whistles (hunting motive from *Tannhäuser* in the oboe) and trumpets ("Behüt dich Gott" from Viktor Nessler's *Der Trompeter von Säckingen*), there is muttering and strumming (snare drum, with head-motive of *Die Meistersinger* in the timpani), there is scuffling and drinking, there is tinkling ("Der Vogelfänger bin ich ja" from *Die Zauberflöte* in glockenspiel and harp) and bungling, and there is no end to it.[27]

A little later Wagner's Rheingold motive sounds ironically at the words: "As long as folks have money in the pocket, they want to booze." But we also find quotations that wittily allude to emotional states: the social song "Freut euch des Lebens" by the Swiss composer Martin Usteris becomes a sound-symbol for finding comfort and pleasure in enjoying the evening of one's life far away from worldly activities.[28] That this quotation slipped into Strauss's composition inadvertently – as occurred quite frequently with him – is evident from his rather acerbic reaction in a letter to Willi Schuh on January 23, 1944 after reading an article by Schuh in the *Neue Zürcher Zeitung* of January 1, 1944:

> Frankly, I did not particularly enjoy "Freut euch des Lebens" – I have no taste for philologists' reminiscence-hunts. Besides, I do not know the folk

song, and can hardly remember whether I heard the melody somewhere. In any case, it is not a conscious quotation! If you begin with [here Strauss inserts the first four measures of the *Eroica* Symphony, in G major] where do you end up?!²⁹

Emotional states and philosophical meaning

Quotations that express emotional states appear in quite a number of works by Strauss, for example in *Eine Alpensinfonie*, with the Alpine wanderer's expression of amazement at the scenic miracle of the *Erscheinung* (appearance) against the background of a cascading waterfall. Here the horn brings, in the words of Specht, "an intimately animated vocal motive (indeed, the second subject of the symphonic movement), which later, soaring broadly, reaches its most expressive intensity."³⁰ The theme, a self-quotation with development, comes from the song "Anbetung," Op. 36, No. 4, to a poem by Rückert. The words "wie schön, wie schön … o wie schön" ("how beautiful, how beautiful …oh how beautiful") must have come to Strauss's mind along with the melody, which appears in the oboe and the first violin.³¹

A telling example of self-quotation as textual interpretation, alluding to the emotional state of the poem – specifically, expectancy of death and subsequent transfiguration – can be found at the end of "Im Abendrot," the last of the *Vier letzte Lieder*, composed in 1948 after a text by Eichendorff. At the last stanza:

> O weiter stiller Friede!
> So tief im Abendrot,
> Wie sind wir wandermüde –
> Ist dies vielleicht der Tod?

> O spacious, tranquil peace!
> So profound in the evening's glow.
> How tired we are of traveling –
> Is this perhaps death?

we hear a quotation, intoned *pianissimo* by four horns, of the transfiguration motive from the tone poem *Tod und Verklärung*, composed fifty-nine years earlier (Example 12.1). The theme evidently had special symbolic significance for Strauss, for on his deathbed, twenty-four hours before he passed away, he remarked to his daughter-in-law and caregiver, Alice: "It is peculiar, Alice – dying is exactly as I composed it in *Tod und Verklärung*. It is peculiar …"³²

Table 12.1 *Instances of self-quotation in* Ein Heldenleben

Work	Number of quotations
Don Juan	4
Macbeth	3
Tod und Verklärung	4
Guntram	8
Till Eulenspiegels lustige Streiche	1
"Traum durch die Dämmerung," Op. 29, No. 1	1 (the line "Ich gehe nicht schnell, ich eile nicht")
Also sprach Zarathustra	3
Don Quixote	5
"Befreit," Op. 39, No. 1 (one m. from an interlude)	1

Source: Friedrich Haider, "Der Held und die Gefährtin: Anmerkungen zum *Heldenleben*," liner notes for Richard Strauss, *Ein Heldenleben*, Tokyo Philharmonic Orchestra, cond. Haider (Nightingale Classics, 1995), NC 11618642, pp. 13ff.

Example 12.1 "Im Abendrot," mm. 77–8, quotation of *Tod und Verklärung*

Strauss reaches the ultimate in self-quotation with *Ein Heldenleben*, in which borrowings underscore the work's autobiographical content. In the section "Des Helden Friedenswerke" ("The Hero's Works of Peace"), we find at least thirty such citations, from tone poems, songs, and the only opera written so far, *Guntram*. Considering that Noé found eighteen motives in 1985, while ten years later Friedrich Haider identified thirty, it would appear that other quotations remain to be located (which, in the case of a monumental score such as *Heldenleben*, is not always easy). Haider's list appears in Table 12.1.

Whether the relatively large number of quotations from the "problem child" *Guntram* indicates this work's special significance for the composer, one can only speculate, but it seems not unlikely.

In *Also sprach Zarathustra* we find quotations of a philosophical nature, giving evidence of Strauss the avowed "Antichrist," who would write to Stefan Zweig in May, 1935, "Perhaps you do not know how passionately anti-Christian I am."[33] In the tradition of Friedrich Nietzsche he contrasts the Christian idea of redemption with the belief in self-liberation through creative work. In the section *Von den Hinterweltlern* ("Of the afterworldsmen") – the term refers to people who assume the existence of another (better) world behind the real one, such as Christians, who believe in transcendence – he intones the liturgical formula *Credo in unum Deum*,[34] and in the following section *Von der großen Sehnsucht* ("Of the great longing") he cites the *Magnificat*.[35]

Several quotations from Beethoven's works have a double significance: on one hand, they clarify Strauss's own emotional states; on the other, they hold philosophical-ideological significance. Next to Mozart, Beethoven was Strauss's most important model of creativity throughout his long life. Despite the awe he felt for this idol, he viewed himself to some degree as a successor and thus borrowed from Beethoven quite frequently. Such quotations were called for in the melodrama he wrote for the festival play *Die Ruinen von Athen*, of which the title-page refers to "music composed by partial use of Beethoven's ballet *Die Geschöpfe des Prometheus*." A pointed motive from the finale of Beethoven's Fifth Symphony is particularly characteristic, since it is repeated nine times. As Jürgen May has observed, "This motive apparently occupied Strauss for a long time – its similarity to the ascending theme in the *Alpensinfonie* appears not to be coincidental … Strauss seems to have seen in the character of the artist (in the melodrama) certain elements that reminded him of the wanderer of his *Alpensinfonie*."[36] The provisional title of *Eine Alpensinfonie*, *Der Antichrist*, alluded to Nietzsche's view of human development as a continuation of the Prometheus character.

Along these lines is a quotation of singular significance, yet still within the category of quotations that portray emotional states: the allusion to the "Funeral March" from Beethoven's *Eroica* in the principal theme of the *Metamorphosen*. Noé rightly locates the substance of the quotation in "the Lombard rhythm of its third measure," a gesture that "pervades in many metamorphoses the rich harmonic and contrapuntal textures of the entire work."[37] A verbal note on the last page of the score provides the final clarification: Strauss wrote below "Garmisch, 12 April 1945" the words: "IN MEMORIAM!" Here the composer-conductor expressed his grief over the loss of all the opera houses important to him in the German-speaking world – Berlin, Dresden, Munich, and Vienna – and of other cultural icons, such as the recently destroyed "holy house of Goethe in Weimar." Moreover, as a new study has shown, the quotation has in addition to this plausible interpretation another, more profound meaning, relating to the sphere of cultural politics.

The facts surrounding the work's commission and origin are clear, but not Strauss's reasons for choosing this unusual ensemble, nor especially the kind of spiritual content he wanted to communicate. Laurenz Lütteken raises pointed questions in this regard: "Why should Strauss feel compelled to write a luxuriant piece for strings for an occasion that was truly incommensurate with opulence and voluptuousness, and what role did Beethoven occupy in this context[?]"[38] When one takes into consideration the significance that Beethoven had for Strauss throughout his life, a reading of the work as a musical elegy, with a quotation meant to express grief, seems far too simple. Lütteken's new approach to *Metamorphosen* attempts to expand the horizon, arguing that "the many referential layers of the composition itself" provide a commentary "encompass[ing] Strauss's entire oeuvre" and indeed "the highly controversial history of music during the first half of the twentieth century."[39]

The history of western music was thought by the aging Strauss to be finished, its end marked by the arrival of atonality. Positioning himself, consciously and emphatically, at the end of the history of world culture and civilization, he offered the *Metamorphosen* as a résumé following the end. It is a meditation on "the end of a 3,000-year cultural development," with his own biography and creative oeuvre – replete with references to Mozart, Beethoven, Wagner, and Goethe – symptomatically woven into the history of humanity. While for Ovid the idea of continuity in transitoriness was already at the center of the concept of metamorphosis, Goethe reinterpreted it by defining life as metamorphosis – a view Strauss accepted as the essence of his composition.[40]

Accordingly, the words of Countess Madeleine in his last work for the stage, *Capriccio*, stand like a credo at the end of Strauss's life and work:

Fühlt es mit mir, dass allen Künsten
Nur *eine* Heimat eigen ist:
Unser nach Schönheit dürstendes Herz!

Feel it with me: all the arts
Have only one source –
Our heart, thirsting for beauty!

13 Strauss in the Third Reich

MICHAEL WALTER

TRANSLATED BY JÜRGEN THYM

I ... would like ... to declare simply under oath that I have never been a member of the National Socialist Party, and that I never sympathized with it nor engaged in propaganda for it. My only relations to Mr. Goebbels's Department of Propaganda are the result of the following: having been a leading German musician for forty years, and having worked, as founder and long-time president of the *Genossenschaft deutscher Tonsetzer* [Guild of German Composers], on a reorganization of *STAGMA* [*Staatlich genehmigte Gesellschaft zur Verwertung musikalischer Aufführungsrechte* (Corporation for the Utilization of Musical Performance Rights)], I was in 1933 appointed by Dr. Goebbels in Berlin, without being asked for my agreement, to the post of President of the new *Reichsmusikkammer*; I did not reject this honorific post immediately, since I did not know the new men in power and believed that I could, perhaps, do some good for music and musicians. When I realized after a year that my position was only a front and that I had no influence whatsoever on the workings of the *Reichsmusikkammer*, I was relieved from my post by Dr. Goebbels on the basis of a letter to my friend and collaborator Stefan Zweig, intercepted and used against me by the Gestapo; in the letter I had spoken critically about the *Reichsmusikkammer*. For ten years, I have not had any dealings with the Department and the Party, except for plenty of harassments and hostilities.[1]

Read from a historical and source-critical perspective, hardly any of the statements in this letter of January 1, 1947 by Strauss are correct. Yet the misrepresentation, although made in connection with Strauss's denazification process, was not entirely tactical but corresponded in substance to Strauss's private assessment of his own biography. Subjective "truth" and selective memory come together here to form idiosyncratic autobiography. If the result withstands historical scrutiny only here and there, that is nonetheless the very reason why posterity, when judging Strauss's activities during the Third Reich, has been more interested in a "moral verdict"[2] than a historical inquiry.

The long-standing conflict between adherents and opponents of Strauss boils down to the issue of judging his moral behavior during the Third Reich. Moral judgments, however, require a choice between black and white, good and evil, and when these polar opposites are made a precondition of historical study, they cover up the gray areas and contradictions that matter so much if one wants to understand what really happened. Precisely because scholars have sought a "moral verdict," Strauss's role in the Third Reich has long been controversial,[3] and to some extent remains so today, although the frontiers between competing interpretations have lately become more flexible. Moral denunciation of the fact that he made himself available to the National Socialist regime pre-empted discussion of whether this was, at the same time, a declaration of sympathy with the politics of the National Socialists, and, if so, to what degree. But it would also be wrong, on the other hand, to view Strauss only as a "case study" for the "problem of rationalizing material advantages with distasteful ideological extremes."[4] Such an approach would conceal the individual motivations of Strauss – a cultural icon whose prominence distinguished him enormously from the average German, and who through his actions not only pursued material advantages but also non-material cultural goals. Depending on one's perspective, these goals can be viewed as an ideological restoration of past times or an attempt at permanent realization of an ideal German cultural achievement.

In any case, Strauss in 1947 "constructed" a world for himself, much as he had done in the Third Reich. And in both cases his construction collided with the reality in which he lived, a reality he did not want to acknowledge but one that, since he was part of it, he could not ignore completely. The world of Strauss was a world as he wanted it and as he tried to realize it. Reality, conversely, was a world that Strauss, at least after 1933, perceived only in fragments and thus could no longer sufficiently assess. When he judged reality, he did so with the yardsticks of the successful Wilhelminian bourgeois, who ranked, until well into the 1920s, as the only German composer of international standing, and who saw himself as the legitimate heir of Wagner, responsible for the consummation of German musical life.

It seems fair to say that Strauss no longer understood the German world after 1933. Certainly, when judged from the distance of history he bears responsibility for collaborating with the powerful in a world he did not understand. But he had his reasons. Strauss was attempting to reverse the wheel of history in order to make the new world square with his own illustrious past. Until the end of World War I, he ranked as a global figure whose operas were performed even outside Europe. In German opera houses he was long the most-performed native composer. The modern German system of composers' rights came into being through his influence. His financial success extended far beyond conventional prosperity. Young composers such as Arnold Schoenberg admired him and sought his counsel. The political rulers in Berlin – above all, the emperor – may not have understood his music, but they were aware that Strauss, like no one else, represented German musical life and the significance of German music.

When World War I came to an end, Strauss continued initially to embrace this prominent role in musical life; indeed he wished to remain active not only as a composer but also as the shaper of an ideal German musical culture (one that included Austria). In 1919 he became opera director in Vienna, and it seemed that this wish – a vain hope during the

Wilhelminian era – had become reality.[5] But there were clear indications that his tenure would be brief. Berlin had rejected Strauss as opera director during the Weimar Republic, and in Vienna he got such a position only by teaming with Franz Schalk as co-director. Soon, thanks to his administrative incompetence and his disregard for the new political and social conditions of art, he was forced to resign after a clever gambit by the government.[6] His financial well-being was no longer guaranteed, since the money he had invested in London, a substantial part of his wealth, had been confiscated. His operas premiered after the war were far less successful than the pre-war works (which in turn also resulted in lower royalties). Increasingly, his active participation in musical life was no longer desired.

In the time between the wars Strauss thus became a relic whose works, though historical in stature, had little innovative significance for contemporary music. For his part, Strauss did not take notice of musical life by the end of the 1920s – current musical production no longer interested him. It was not the fault of the Weimar Republic that medals of distinction no longer existed at the time of Strauss's sixtieth birthday (1924), leaving him without an honor that in former times would have been a foregone conclusion. But from his perspective, the episode confirmed the cultural decline to which he, and German music, had fallen victim. The enormously prominent position that Strauss occupied during the emperor's era thus shrank during the time of the Republics (both Weimar and Austrian) to a position of past (i.e., historical) greatness. Strauss resisted this development, because it turned him into a monument of himself, at a time of his life when he had no doubts about his creative power and, especially, about his energy to restore German musical life and turn it into the primary manifestation of German culture. Strauss wanted to be the ruler of German music, a position "which neither Emperor Wilhelm nor Herr Rathenau" offered him.[7] When the National Socialists presented him with such an opportunity, it was only natural that he grabbed it.

Strauss did not tumble into a trap. He moved into the lion's den, and he knew it. Moreover, he did so for his own advantage as much as for the benefit of German musical life. Yet Strauss had never drawn a distinction between the two; one can say with little exaggeration that what was good for Strauss was, from his perspective, also good for German musical life. We can assume, for example, that he considered the post of president of the *Reichsmusikkammer* (*RMK*) an opportunity to increase the number of performances of his own works. He believed that these works were the most important of the contemporary German repertory, and so there was no contradiction between the pragmatic goal of increasing royalties for himself and the idealistic purpose of enriching German musical life. Indeed, this discrepancy probably never occurred to him.

His own statements notwithstanding, no one forced Strauss to become president of the *RMK*. On November 10, 1933, he received a telegram from the Ministerial Council of the Department of Propaganda asking him whether "he would accept the appointment [as president of the *RMK*]" intended by Goebbels and "whether he would participate in its ceremonial opening session."[8] Strauss's response is not known, but he would hardly have contemplated refusal. While overestimating his own position in the Third Reich, he failed to appreciate that any higher office in this Reich would in principle be political, however sincerely its holder regarded it as non-political. What Strauss understood as a non-political dimension was really his own egotism: the promotion of his own works and his own musico-political goals, an agenda characterized by a complete absence of political savvy and realism. In its essence, Strauss's thinking was still guided, as for many of his generation, by the maxims of the bourgeoisie during the Wilhelminian empire – in particular, a nearly religious reverence for "serious" music, which, in Strauss's perspective, had reached its teleological zenith in his own works (or at least in some of them).

Strauss was not a democrat and had no political instincts. Already in 1901, he had denounced as *Kuhhandel* (horse-trading)[9] any political compromise during negotiations over new authors' rights legislation, and he called the representatives of the Reichstag "morons and barbarians" (*Böotier und Kaffern*). He understood politics as merely a special kind of intrigue, in which cause and effect could always be traced to individuals.[10] It concerned him only when it affected him or his family personally, or when it had an impact on German musical life – which for Strauss was ultimately also a personal matter. In particular, Strauss did not understand political mechanisms, especially those of a totalitarian regime like that of the National Socialists. What Michael Kater calls one of the "most persuasive proofs that Strauss never understood the workings of totalitariansm"[11] is a letter by the composer to Leo Ritter, the director of *STAGMA*. Strauss reacted in this letter to the abolishment of the *STAGMA* schedule for distributing royalties in 1941; up to then composers of "serious" music had gotten a better deal than composers of entertainment music. Strauss wrote to Ritter: "Dear Mr. Ritter! According to the approved by-laws of the *GEMA* [*Genossenschaft zur Verwertung musikalischer Aufführungsrechte,* or Cooperative for Musical Performance Rights, a forerunner of *STAGMA*] we ourselves decide on issues of distribution. Dr. Goebbels has no say here."[12] His lack of political instincts and the personalization of political issues were for Strauss proof of his own non-political attitude. Along with them we find a certain unscrupulousness, which was not always self-serving but likewise betrayed political naïveté, and opportunism, a habit cultivated already in his youth.

The anti-Semitic statements of Strauss, which can be found again and again from the end of the 1870s to the years after World War II, are a mixture of opportunism and social convention.[13] Strauss was most definitely not a racist anti-Semite along the lines of National Socialism; he was perhaps not even a convinced anti-Judaist in a nineteenth-century sense. When in conversation he had reason to assume that his partner expected an anti-Semitic statement, Strauss provided it without much thought, and also without taking it too seriously. What Strauss considered a mere social convention during the Wilhelminian empire, however, took on a different content in the years between the two World Wars, culminating in the murderous anti-Semitism of the National Socialists. But Strauss's anti-Semitism in those years still did not extend beyond social resentments. He did not adopt, or indeed perceive, the historical change in the nature of German anti-Semitism. This was not a conscious decision but simply intellectual inertia – the continued reliance on a Wilhelmian mode of thinking, maintained by careless habit. The possibility that other people, especially after 1945, could judge such utterances differently was apparently of so little concern for him that in 1948 he could still make an anti-Semitic remark about the critic Paul Bekker to the conductor Joseph Keilberth.[14] When Strauss wanted to insult someone, any means was acceptable, as when in 1935 he called Bruno Walter a "slimy brat" (*schleimiger Lauselumpen*).[15] Whether this remark, made in a moment of agitation, had anti-Semitic implications is not clear; Strauss's other statements about Walter leave the question open. In 1932 the composer remarked to Clemens Krauss, "I have nothing against Walter and am not an anti-Semite ...," but a few lines later we find an anti-Semitic allusion: "Granted, a German composer must consider himself lucky today when he is performed before his death at German festivals, but it irks me that I am allowed to figure [in a performance of *Die Frau ohne Schatten*] only as an upbeat at Sukkot [*Laubhüttenfest*, the Jewish holiday of the spring harvest]."[16] (Strauss had been annoyed at how often Bruno Walter conducted at the Salzburg Festival and how little consideration, in his estimation, his own works received.) Especially in the correspondence with Clemens Krauss, whom Strauss probably considered receptive to such allusions, the composer refers, over and over, to Walter's Jewish origin, for instance by calling him "Schlesinger"[17] – thereby using the conductor's original name in a denunciatory form that was fashionable in the anti-Semitic press, particularly in the *Völkischer Beobachter*.

On the other hand, it cannot be overlooked that for Strauss Judaism was not a racial issue but a matter of religion, to which he attributed little importance when it came to art. In contrast to a true anti-Semite, Strauss insisted during his time as co-director of the Vienna State Opera on a good production of *Le prophète*, Meyerbeer's "Jewish opera of splendor" (*jüdische Prunkoper*), as Schalk, his partner in the directorship, called it.[18] Strauss also encouraged Schalk to engage Fritz Zweig – "even though Jewish" – as a conductor.[19] And when difficulties arose in hiring Georg Szell as Kapellmeister, he advised, "Sz[ell] should let himself be baptized, immediately."[20] In 1907 Romain Rolland expressed surprise that Strauss would befriend a Jew whom Rolland characterized as "boot-licking and a little overbearing" (*kriecherisch und ein wenig aufdringlich*).[21] In this case, the writer had anti-Semitic prejudices that Strauss apparently did not share. Mahler's Jewish origin was certainly no impediment to a friendship with Strauss, nor did Stefan Zweig's Jewishness hinder a collaboration.

A conversation with Otto Klemperer in 1932 demonstrates that Strauss was well aware of the National Socialist brand of anti-Semitism, but that he did not take it seriously enough. Indeed, at this early date he seems to have believed that anti-Semitism could be held in check by the mere fact that German musical life could not do without Jews. As he remarked to Klemperer: "But, tell me, what is going to happen to German theaters and opera houses when all Jews leave?"[22]

When Strauss was president of the *RMK*, he made light of the concrete preparations then underway to Aryanize German musical life. The implementation of the *Reichskulturkammergesetz* of November 1, 1933 resulted in questionnaires sent to all members of the *Reichskulturkammer*. These surveys were meant to examine the "loyalty and suitability" of individual members, but they also contained questions about religious affiliation and racial background. Roderich von Mojsisovics, a composer living in Graz (that is, in Austria!) was justifiably concerned. An inquiry to Strauss regarding the issue was answered by Strauss's son Franz:

> Garmisch, 16 December 1933 –
> Herrn Dr. Roderich v. Mojsisovics
> GRAZ
> Plüddemanngasse 27
>
> Sehr verehrter Herr Doctor!
> My father, Herr Dr. Richard Strauss, has asked me to respond to your kind letter of 14 December. He thanks you for writing and wants to assure you that there is no reason for concern. As to the questionnaire – that is a generally applicable bureaucratic formality, which he had to undergo as well as president of the *Reichsmusikkammer*. All other outstanding issues will be settled soon by Papa, such as the membership of Austrian composers, etc. With expressions of sincerest respect
> I remain your
> Dr. Franz Strauss"[23]

The letter is symptomatic in a twofold sense: (1) because Strauss did not bother to reply personally to an administrative question, but let his son respond; and (2) because there is no reason to doubt that Strauss considered the questionnaire irrelevant. Presumably he considered it part of the revolutionary exaggerations of the new regime. In March, 1933 Strauss told the publisher Anton Kippenberg, "I brought back powerful impressions from Berlin and good hope for the future of German art – once the initial revolutionary storms have run their course."[24]

What Strauss probably expected in March, 1933 was an autocratic regime with national conservative character: a government that would restore many cultural values, especially musical ones, which he believed had been lost during the Weimar Republic. From his perspective, this meant automatically that he would resume his position as the leading German composer and legitimate heir to Wagner, a role he had lost during the Weimar Republic. And this, in turn, would lead to an increase in performances of his operas – a goal for whose realization Strauss used all available means. But the composer misjudged two essential characteristics of the National Socialist regime: first, the racist and biologistic anti-Semitism that, clearly distinguished from Wilhelminian anti-Semitism, was alien to him; and second, the desire of the National Socialist regime to be modern, rather than returning, culturally, to the days of the emperor. Especially in music, this claim of modernity was difficult to realize. But for Goebbels serious music played only a minor role compared to entertainment music, which could be used to reach the "masses." Strauss was put down by Goebbels in 1941, impolitely and with unmistakable clarity: "Lehár has the masses, you don't! Stop babbling about the significance of serious music! That is not a way to raise its value! Tomorrow's culture is different from yesterday's culture! And you, Herr Strauss, are from yesterday!"[25] With some justification, Goebbels considered Strauss's musico-political ideas incompatible with the goals of National Socialism. As Pamela Potter has observed of Goebbels's diaries, "many of the passages in which he mentions Strauss express his contempt for Strauss's persistence on certain pet issues regarding music policy."[26] That the diaries also contain passages in which Goebbels seems to make positive statements about Strauss can be explained by the fact that Strauss fulfilled an important function as a cultural figurehead of the Third Reich, and by the special nature of Goebbels's diaries, which were not a private document but intended ultimately to be made public. Goebbels had to be mindful of the historical significance of Strauss, even though the composer, personally, got on his nerves.

Three events that strongly damaged Strauss's international reputation preceded his ascendance to the presidency of the *RMK*. First, Strauss had conducted the Berlin Philharmonic Orchestra on March 20, 1933 in place of Bruno Walter, following the latter's removal from the concert by the Department of Propaganda. The symbolic power of substituting for Walter cannot be underestimated, because Strauss's appearance proved that Jewish musicians, even when they were prominent, could easily be replaced by German ones. Strauss recognized this implication, because initially he refused to substitute for Walter. But on the insistence of the concert's promoter Louise Wolff, and possibly others[27] – who told him that both the Wolff and Sachs concert agency and the Berlin Philharmonic Orchestra desperately needed the income – Strauss consented to conduct, turning over his honorarium to the Philharmonic Orchestra. The refusal of pay was clearly a sign of his bad conscience, because when it came to honoraria, Strauss, as the public knew, accepted no excuses. The event was reported immediately in the *Völkischer Beobachter*, giving it a National Socialist "spin": "Dr. Strauss has not been contractually obligated but, on the contrary, has agreed to conduct the concert as a salute to the new Germany under the condition that the honorarium set aside for Herr Bruno Walter go in its entirety to the orchestra."[28]

Second, Strauss signed the *Protest der Richard-Wagner-Stadt München* (*Protest of Richard Wagner's City of Munich*), a denunciation of Thomas Mann formulated in response to his lecture "Sufferings and Greatness of Richard Wagner" at the University of Munich on February 10, 1933. The National Socialists interpreted Mann's lecture as an appropriation of Wagner for "tedious liberalism," and by signing the *Protest* Strauss lent his name to this complaint.[29] The episode was more than just a "stupid incident,"[30] as he described it after the War: it resulted in condemnations, especially from abroad. Here again Strauss misjudged the results. We may speculate what made him consent to sign the document: to please Hans Knappertsbusch, who probably wrote the *Protest* and who Strauss hoped would conduct his works more frequently in Munich; to deny Pfitzner, who had also signed the manifesto, the role as leading German composer; or to make an opportunistic concession to the new regime. Certainly it could not have escaped Strauss that the text addressed a primarily National Socialist concern.[31]

Third, Strauss replaced Toscanini in the summer of 1933 in Bayreuth. Toscanini had already canceled his 1933 Bayreuth engagement in 1931, partly because of Winifred Wagner's political convictions, but in the summer of 1932 he was persuaded to rescind his decision. Once Hitler was appointed Reichskanzler in January, 1933, Toscanini again considered canceling and, in March, 1933, leaked the rumor that he would do so in protest at the persecution of the Jews in Germany. Asked to reconsider by Hitler personally in early April, Toscanini hesitated again, but then finally canceled his participation at the end of May – a decision that was announced in the press early in June. Toscanini's political stance was, until May, 1933, not particularly clear, although on April 1 he had telegrammed Hitler to criticize Strauss's take-over of the Bruno Walter concert. Strauss had probably already been asked in March by Heinz Tietjen (or at the latest in April, 1933 by Winifred Wagner herself) to conduct *Parsifal* (but only in the event of a Toscanini cancellation, it seems). Whether Strauss knew the political background of Toscanini's vacillation is not clear. When he was contacted by the Bayreuth directorate, Strauss had no evidence that Toscanini had canceled because of political motives; he took over *Parsifal* for "Bayreuth's sake," as he wrote to Stefan Zweig. Meeting an obligation to Wagner's work rather than to the Wagner clan, he offered what he called "my modest support for Bayreuth," adding, "This has nothing to do with politics. Whatever scribbling journalists [*Schmierantenpresse*] say does not matter to me."[32]

In these three episodes, Strauss amply demonstrated that he would not publicly challenge the regime and that his opportunism could accommodate moral corruption. Goebbels was sufficiently impressed to install Strauss as cultural-musical figurehead of the Third Reich. On November 15, 1933, the *Reichskulturkammer* with all its subdivisions was inaugurated in the presence of Hitler and the entire government in Berlin – an event during which Strauss himself conducted his *Festliches Präludium*, Op. 61.

Placed now by the Third Reich in the position he so painfully missed during the Weimar Republic – openly recognized as Germany's greatest living composer and musical leader – Strauss nonetheless offered a vision that constrasted markedly with Goebbels's. As his speech at the first meeting of the *RMK* shows, Strauss saw the future of German musical life in a return to the conditions of the end of the nineteenth century:

> It is true that German music, especially in the nineteenth century, experienced the greatest triumphs throughout the entire world; it has secured the reputation of German art and the German artist to a degree that has hardly been reached by another artistic medium. But the general cultural, economic, and technical development of the last forty or fifty years has demonstrated that, however great the individual achievements, the German people as a whole became more and more alienated from the higher, art music. An attendant problem was the decline in the economic situation of the German musician, as well as, viewed from the other side, a degeneration of musical taste, which inevitably had a most lasting influence on the shape of our overall culture.[33]

Casually, but with sufficient clarity, Strauss had shown that he wanted to turn the wheel of history backwards to the time when he was the celebrated star of musical modernity. But he had nothing to say on one of the key elements in the cultural politics of the National Socialists: the elimination of Jews from the *RMK*.[34]

The reality of Strauss's new position fell short of his expectations, as we read in a private note that he jotted down in September, 1935. "My position as president of the *Reichsmusikkammer* was just a front that earned me only animosity and insults from abroad without my having the satisfaction of enacting decisive measures for the German theatre and musical culture."[35] In June of that year Strauss had written to Zweig that he only "play-acted" the role of president of the *RMK* "to do some good and to prevent larger mishaps."[36] Both documents are problematic from a historical perspective. Strauss was completely on the mark with his insight that he had been without real power as president of the *RMK*. But when he started his job he did not know this, as is also shown by the statement that he wanted "to prevent larger mishaps." Clearly he believed at the outset that he could turn back the music-historical clock (in a few narrow ways, and to an idealized past) and that he could shape National Socialist policy on music, notwithstanding his uncertainty as to the duties of his office.

As president of the *RMK*, Strauss did attempt some "decisive measures" in his sense. Not surprisingly, he was active only in areas for which he had lobbied for decades. First and foremost was the protection and expansion of authors' rights for German composers of serious music (which meant especially an increase in royalties). Strauss discussed this topic with Goebbels as early as the summer of 1933 in Bayreuth, since the Department of Justice was then working on a proposal that Strauss found unsatisfactory in every way. A year later he again broached the topic, and again in Bayreuth – this time with Hitler himself. In addition to an extension of the protection time to fifty years, Strauss wanted to build "an effective wall against the corruption of valuable artworks by irresponsible arrangers and exploiters."[37] Aside from the question of authors' rights, he wanted to increase performances of German music by spa orchestras, to exclude "Viennese operetta trash"[38] (by which he meant especially the works of Lehár, whose *Die lustige Witwe* numbered among Hitler's favorite pieces), and to prevent arrangements of pieces such as the Funeral March from *Götterdämmerung*. But most importantly, Strauss wanted to return German operatic life to its pre-1914 state. He planned an enlargement of orchestras and choruses, an increased budget for operatic productions (which, of course, would have benefited the performances of his own works), and "for the large theaters," a "restoration of their budgets to pre-war levels, or, if necessary, even an increase."[39] The necessary money was to be raised through subsidies from the Reich (*Reichskulturgroschen*). Operettas were to disappear from the opera houses and non-German repertory was to be reduced to one third of the total. The latter measure

would have affected especially the works of Puccini and Verdi, automatically increasing the share of Strauss's own operas in the repertory. Strauss's
demand for "the promotion of contemporary literature"[40] would have
yielded the same result. Policy proposals so blatantly informed by personal interests brought a predictable outcome; in October, 1934 Strauss
wrote to Julius Kopsch, "My extensive and serious proposals have been
turned down by Goebbels."[41]

Goebbels thought of opera houses as antiquated and elitist bourgeois
institutions not to be subsidized more than necessary, especially since
they were not suited as propaganda channels to reach the masses. Strauss's
nostalgia for the Wilhelminian era must have struck Goebbels as absurd.
STAGMA did provide Strauss with a minor success in the improved distribution of royalties for composers of serious music, but that privilege was
rescinded by Goebbels in 1941.

Two factors particularly limited Strauss's effectiveness as president of
the *RMK*. First, Strauss continued to reside in Garmisch and only rarely
showed up in Berlin. This arrangement was already causing difficulties at
the end of 1933, and Strauss did not adjust.[42] By May, 1935 Heinz Ihlert,
the secretary of the *RMK*, complained that Strauss pursued only his own
agenda and a secondary agenda through his cronies in the *RMK*, that he
left the secretary (Ihlert) in the dark about his goals and activities, that
he did not provide any guidelines to his coworkers, and that he was practically out of reach in Garmisch. "Although he serves as chair of the profession of German composer, Strauss has not endorsed its statutes and
articles, because these regulations provided for the exclusion of Jews
from membership. Strauss knows no more about the structure and policies of the *RMK* than a complete outsider."[43] Strauss's recalcitrance had
manifested itself already in April, when, in connection with the establishment of a "department for German vocal culture," he demanded the "abo-
lition of singing in the Hitler Youth."[44] His refusal to sign the statutes, as
mentioned by Ihlert, was a demonstration of his personal disagreement
with the National Socialist policy towards the Jews. The *Richtlinien für die
Aufnahme von Nichtariern in die Fachverbände der Reichsmusikkammer*
(*Guidelines for Membership of Non-Aryans in the Professional Associations
of the Reichsmusikkammer*), which were published on April 15, 1934 in the
Amtliche Mitteilungen der Reichsmusikkammer (*Official Communications
of the Reichsmusikkammer*) and designed to exclude all Jews from membership, were indeed not signed by him but by Ihlert. To interpret his refusal
to sign as an overt act of resistance, however, is difficult: in no way was it
a publicly perceivable action, since Ihlert was authorized, in principle, to
sign official documents on Strauss's behalf. That may have been the reason
for Goebbels's tacit acceptance of Strauss's refusal.

Second, the leadership structure of the *RMK* was deliberately designed in such a way that Strauss's influence was minimal. The true center of power in the *RMK* was Ihlert, whom Goebbels had installed as a faithful comrade of the National Socialist Party. Strauss recognized Ihlert's function, and indeed he supported it through his own inactivity and by giving Ihlert full power of attorney so that he would not be bothered by the day-to-day operations. But from the perspective of National Socialism, these routine administrative operations, which included the handling of Jewish issues, were the ones that mattered politically. For day-to-day business Ihlert could rely on the *RMK*'s administrative council (in which Strauss had only a few confidants) to decide in Ihlert's and Goebbels's favor.

Strauss's weak position as president of the *RMK* may explain his submissive reaction to the Hindemith affair, in contrast to the outrage felt abroad at this episode. Hitler had banned the premiere of Hindemith's opera *Mathis der Maler* planned by Furtwängler. In turn, Furtwängler published an article in the *Deutsche Allgemeine Zeitung* on November 25, 1934, in which he spoke out in favor of Hindemith. In a performance of *Tristan und Isolde* on the same evening, with Goebbels and Göring in attendance, Furtwängler was celebrated by the audience with ovations that clearly related to his support of Hindemith. A few days later Furtwängler resigned from his official functions, including the vice-presidency of the *RMK*. Goebbels in turn used the occasion of a speech in the Berlin Sportpalast to rant and rave against Hindemith – without referring to him by name. Even though Strauss heard about the speech only from the newspaper, it must have been clear to him that the target of Goebbels's vendetta was Hindemith. Strauss asked his son Franz to formulate a telegram to Goebbels, which, after "being approved" by his father, was sent off. It read: "On the occasion of your superb address on culture I send my cordial congratulations and enthusiastic approval. In loyal admiration, Heil Hitler – Richard Strauss."[45]

This act of blatant political opportunism suggests that Strauss had already noticed the clouds gathering around him. As early as October, 1934 there had been discussions in the Department of Propaganda of replacing Strauss as president of the *RMK* with Peter Raabe, the Generalmusikdirektor in Aachen and a trustworthy party comrade.[46] Not least because of his untrustworthiness on the "Jewish issue," Strauss had become a pawn in the power struggle between Goebbels and Alfred Rosenberg, Goebbels's rival in matters of cultural politics. A decisive issue here was the fact that Stefan Zweig, the librettist of *Die schweigsame Frau*, the latest opera by Strauss, was Jewish.[47] Goebbels accepted this arrangement for the time being, although it weakened his position vis-à-vis Rosenberg. Hitler and Goebbels initially even planned to attend the opera's premiere in Dresden on June 24,

1934. But Strauss discovered just before the premiere that Zweig's name was missing on the poster advertising the performance and insisted that it be restored. In turn, Hitler canceled his attendance of the premiere, and Goebbels, who was already on a plane on his way to Dresden, was called back by radio signal.

The event that decided the forced resignation of Strauss as president of the *RMK*, however, was a letter by Strauss – intercepted by the Gestapo on the orders of Mutschmann, the district governor of Saxony – to Stefan Zweig on June 17, 1935. This letter contained, among other things, Strauss's claim (cited earlier) that he had only "play-acted" the role of *RMK* president. Mutschmann passed the letter on to Hitler who, in turn, instructed Goebbels to dismiss Strauss as president. Goebbels sent Otto von Keudell, a ministerial official, to Garmisch, who demanded that Strauss immediately resign for health reasons. Strauss complied, but drafted an embarrassing letter of justification to Hitler on July 13, asking for a personal meeting. Hitler never reacted to the letter.

Strauss did not immediately become a *persona non grata* of the regime, because he continued to be useful for Goebbels, especially for propaganda purposes abroad. Contrary to his claim (cited at the beginning of this essay) that in the period following his dismissal he had no contact with the Department of Propaganda and the Party and suffered "harassments and hostilities," he continued to communicate sporadically with Goebbels and the Department, especially since he wanted Goebbels to intervene in recognizing his Jewish daughter-in-law and his grandchildren as "Aryans." But Strauss's family was indeed subject to "harassments" as early as the end of the 1930s.

In June, 1934, the *Ständige Rat für international Zusammenarbeit der Komponisten* (*Conseil Permanent pour la Coopération Internationale des Compositeurs*; or Permanent Council for the International Collaboration of Composers) had been founded on the initiative of Strauss. Its three goals were: international protection of authors' rights, international collaboration to protect the professional interests of composers, and "artistic exchanges between nations on a major scale."[48] Strauss did not found the *Ständige Rat* for propagandistic purposes, but the organization fulfilled this function for Goebbels, because it was de facto the National Socialist counterpart of the International Society for New Music (ISNM). As president of the *Ständige Rat*, Strauss pursued a policy directed especially against "atonal" music and thereby automatically also against the ISNM. Even here, however, he handled the "Jewish issue" in a way that did not square with official directives. When he learned of the banning of a performance of Dukas's opera *Ariane et Barbe-bleue*, an event planned for the

Tonkünstlerfest in Hamburg in 1935 in collaboration with the *Ständige Rat*, Strauss reacted by withdrawing completely from any program-planning – partly to protest the grounds of the rejection (Dukas was a Jew), but also because he was personally insulted. As president of the *Ständige Rat*, Strauss served in a representative capacity, particularly from an international perspective. Thus he remained, with Goebbels's authorization, an official representative of the Third Reich. After he resigned as president of the *RMK*, neither were his travel activities curtailed (at least not initially) nor were there other public sanctions by the regime. On the contrary, Strauss was scheduled to conduct his own works during the World Exposition in Paris in 1937, but, to the regret of Goebbels, was unable to do so because of illness. At the *Reichsmusiktage* in Düsseldorf in 1938, Strauss conducted his opera *Arabella* and, as a prelude to a speech by Goebbels, his *Festliches Präludium*. His seventy-fifth birthday was pompously celebrated in 1939, in 1942 he received the Beethoven Prize of the City of Vienna, and in that same year the Department of Propaganda began preparations for a propagandistic exploitation of Strauss's eightieth birthday. (It was not to happen.) It is not without its irony that between 1935 and 1945 Goebbels made Strauss precisely what the composer did not want to be during the Weimar Republic: a monument of German music turned into a propaganda tool.

Behind the glittering façade of Strauss the monument, however, there were repeated harassments of Strauss the person in the form of infringements on his family by representatives of the National Socialist regime – infringements that made clear the precariousness of his position, especially since it was known that his daughter-in-law Alice was Jewish (and thereby his grandchildren of "mixed race"). The Strauss family was not popular with the local party officials in Garmisch, and it is likely that Goebbels consciously allowed these bureaucrats a free hand, so that Strauss realized again and again that the well-being of his daughter-in-law and grandchildren depended on the favors of Goebbels. There were ominous signs: the capture of one of his grandsons by the SA, the search of the Garmisch villa for his daughter-in-law Alice in 1938 by two SA men, and the confiscation of their Austrian passports. Against this background it becomes understandable why Strauss let himself be used for propagandistic purposes by the National Socialist regime. In December, 1941 the family finally relocated to Vienna, where Strauss owned another house and where Baldur von Schirach was governor. Schirach was fond of Strauss and, being an inner-party rival of Goebbels, tried to establish Vienna – against the wishes of Hitler and Goebbels – as a "cultural counterpart" to Berlin. Yet in spite of Schirach's protection, Strauss's son Franz and his wife Alice were briefly imprisoned in Vienna in 1943 by the Gestapo – a frightening episode, to be sure, albeit a local one not directly aimed at Strauss himself.

It was not until 1944 that Strauss himself fell out of favor with the regime, when he refused to accept in his Garmisch villa people who had been bombed out, remarking to the responsible county official that it did not matter to him when soldiers on the front constantly risked their lives: "for him, no soldier needed to fight."[49] The event caused public consternation and led, finally, to a personal decision by Hitler: the managing director of the *Reichskanzlei* Martin Bormann communicated in a circular to all leading party officials on January 24, 1944 that any personal contact with Strauss was undesirable (even though his operas continued to be performed). Strauss's eightieth birthday was publicly acknowledged, but very modestly and only to avoid international embarrassment for the regime. As of June, 1944, Strauss was no longer allowed to travel abroad.

By November 1944 Strauss had sunk into a deep depression:

> In my shattered life, family is the last and only ray of light … My life's
> work is destroyed, German opera ruined, German music consumed in the
> inferno of a machine, where its tortured soul ekes out a miserable exist-
> ence. My dear beautiful Viennese home, which was my great pride, has
> been turned into rubble and ash. I will never again hear or see my works in
> this world. I wish Mozart and Schubert had called me to Elysium after my
> eightieth …[50]

Even in the self-absorption of these lines Strauss shows that his "life's work" meant not just his own compositions but German musical life in general. And once again, Strauss did not differentiate between the material loss he suffered through the destruction of his house in Vienna and the devastation of his idealistic goals for German musical culture. Throughout his life, Strauss lacked the ability to distinguish between the personal and the public, between the political and the artistic. During the Third Reich, he overestimated his importance and position but was opportunistic enough to placate the regime – though not, however, on the "Jewish issue." He did not understand the dictatorial nature of the National Socialist regime, even though he was aware of its political goals. And he was not an active follower of the National Socialists, but he lent his services to National Socialist purposes, because by doing so he believed he could further his own goals.

Strauss failed to achieve these goals during the Third Reich, but he did not learn anything from the failure, because he was unable to recognize what lay outside his subjectively constructed biographical reality. By June, 1945 he was already forging plans for a reconstruction of musical life in Munich (in which his own works would play an essential role),[51] and he counted himself among the people who should be entrusted with the German reconstruction. "There have always been some decent people in Germany, and now after Churchill's brilliant speech, 'cultured France and Germany' have to wait, until *we are called to serve* [emphasis in original]. We can probably wait for that for a long time!"[52]

14 Strauss and the business of music

SCOTT WARFIELD

Many people have thought a love of money the cause of Strauss's decay ...   PAUL ROSENFELD,
THE DIAL (FEBRUARY, 1920)[1]

Strauss was the first composer to adopt the gesture of the idealized big industrialist.
THEODORE ADORNO[2]

With the words of a now forgotten journalist from the composer's own day
and the more lasting condemnation by perhaps the twentieth century's most
influential music and social critic, we are easily reminded of the image of
Richard Strauss as a "money grubber," which held for much of the last 100
years and only recently has begun to fade. Given a twentieth-century popular
culture obsessed with every facet of the lives of celebrities, especially professional athletes, actors, and musicians, it is not surprising that so many people
in Strauss's day were curious to know the details of his finances. For several
decades – from the mid 1890s to at least the 1920s – he was the undisputed
leading figure in serious music for Europe and America. With his audacious
tone poems and scandalous operas, he and his music commanded headlines
in ways that later composers of art music could only envy.

A longer view of history reveals, however, that Strauss is hardly the
first significant composer to be placed in a less-than-flattering light where
music and money were connected. In the late Middle Ages, there is evidence of priest-composers angling for multiple benefices, with little work
to support themselves.[3] In the Renaissance, Josquin des Prez was known for
both his high fees and his lack of deference to his employer's wishes.[4] Two
centuries later, Johann Sebastian Bach complained in a letter to a friend
that the people of Leipzig were not dying at a fast enough rate, and thus
his income from playing funerals was not what had been promised when
he had been hired by the Board of the *Thomaskirche*.[5] According to Neal
Zaslaw, virtually everything composed by Wolfgang Amadeus Mozart was
made for a specific business purpose,[6] and as one of the first full-time professional composers, Ludwig van Beethoven was notorious for his dealings with publishers. (At one time he had five different publishers believing
that they each had exclusive rights to the *Missa solemnis*.)[7] Even as modern
copyright laws were taking shape, Chopin knew how to exploit differences
in the laws of various countries in order to secure income from his publications that might otherwise be lost.[8] Closer to Strauss's own day, Puccini,
who left a quite sizeable estate at the time of his death, was well known as

[242]

"close fisted" with money, although he "spent freely on himself."[9] At the end of the twentieth century, Andrew Lloyd Webber, perhaps the most financially successful composer in history, has regularly been derided in some quarters precisely because of the widespread popularity of his music and his intense interest in the business of musical theater.[10]

Compared to the words and actions of those composers and others throughout history, Strauss's own concerns about earning a living as a musician were hardly unreasonable or unique. As the son of an ordinary court musician, he was heir to no fortune and raised in modest affluence, thanks chiefly to the largesse of his mother's family. When he became a successful composer, Strauss was not afraid to ask for the full value of his work, and his reasons for doing so were quite simple. First and foremost was to ensure that his family was taken care of, both in the present and the future; and second was to secure as much free time as possible for composition.[11] During his heyday in the decades on either side of 1900, Strauss also recognized that his works might soon wane in popularity, and thus it was only prudent that he make the most of his opportunities while he had them. It is also worth noting that his transactions with publishers and others were completely above board. Strauss did ask for and often received high fees, but he did so on a forthright "take it or leave it" basis, with no feelings of ill will, whatever the outcome. In fact, Ernst Roth, his last publisher, said that "Strauss had no business sense at all" and was perfectly willing to leave contracts, investments, and related matters in the hands of his lawyers and advisors.[12]

A careful examination of the published criticism of Strauss and his music shows that nothing condemning him as avaricious was written before he joined the fight for composers' rights in the late 1890s.[13] Such attacks from music critics and others reflect an outmoded notion of "art music" that was already dying in the late nineteenth century, and even though modern sensibilities no longer hold composers to such standards, Strauss's reputation still carries some undeserved taint from those critics. Rather than defend Strauss against such hollow charges, this chapter will delve into some of the reasons why Strauss acted the way he did where money and music were connected, especially in his earlier years. Through an examination of those events we may come to understand better how the business of music was changing at the beginning of the twentieth century and how Strauss navigated his way through those uncharted waters.

Starting a career and making a name

Strauss's education in the business of music-making undoubtedly began with his father, Franz Strauss, a man whose own worldview was colored by a difficult upbringing.[14] As a professional horn player in the Munich Court Opera Orchestra, Franz's income was so modest that he courted his future wife, Josephine Pschorr, daughter of the well-to-do owner of Munich's leading brewery, for nearly seven years before mustering the courage to ask for her hand in marriage.[15] Moreover, after their union in 1863, the couple lived in apartments above the Pschorr brewery, and their children were the not-infrequent beneficiaries of significant monetary gifts from their Pschorr in-laws and cousins. Such familial generosity surely reminded Franz of the limits to his ability to support his family, and there may be echoes of such feelings in Richard's concerns about his own family. While it is not easy to say how deeply the circumstances of Franz Strauss's life marked his son, the parallels cannot be ignored.

Up to 1881, music had been purely an avocation for Richard, centered on piano lessons, family musicales, and the composition of works for performance within a private circle of Pschorr cousins and friends. In March, 1881, however, four public concerts in Munich featured compositions by the young Strauss. These began with the String Quartet in A major, Op. 2, played by the Benno Walter Quartet on the 14th. Two days later, three songs on texts by Emanuel Geibel (TrV 75) were heard in a recital by Cornelia Meysenheim, and in the final week of March, two orchestral premieres – the Wilde Gung'l's performance of the *Festmarsch*, Op. 1, and the Munich Hofkapelle's performance of Strauss's (First) Symphony in D minor (TrV 94) – completed the sixteen-year-old composer's public debut.[16]

Such a convergence of concerts did not happen by chance, and the hand of Franz Strauss is evident in all these performances. Benno Walter was Franz's cousin, while Meysenheim was a colleague at the court opera. Doubtless both were glad to present Richard's music as a favor to Franz. The Wilde Gung'l was an amateur orchestra in Munich that Franz Strauss conducted, and, in fact, the Wilde Gung'l had already played a few of Richard's earliest scores, beginning in 1878.[17] Having a work premiered in a Musical Academy concert by Munich's leading professional orchestra was an entirely different matter, however. Franz had secured a reading of Richard's Symphony in rehearsal, after which the conductor Hermann Levi agreed to the public performance. As a quid pro quo, Franz consented to play the premiere of *Parsifal*, which Levi would conduct the following summer in Bayreuth. Such an action by Franz, who thoroughly detested Wagner, suggests the price he was willing to pay to open doors for his son.

Important as those performances were, to be taken seriously as a composer, Richard also needed to have his works appear in print. His simple gavotte for piano, *Aus alter Zeit* (TrV 72), became his first published work when it appeared in 1879 in a modest collection alongside the works of two other unknown composers.[18] Nothing is known of how or why that work found its way into print. More important, however, was the publication of Strauss's *Festmarsch*, Op. 1, in 1881 by Breitkopf and Härtel. Germany's leading music publisher accepted the work only because Richard's uncle agreed to underwrite the costs, and thus, at first glance, the march might be written off as simply a vanity publication. Richard's letter of February 8, 1881 to the publisher suggests, however, that he had a greater goal in mind. After acknowledging his own very modest standing as a composer, and brief mentions of his father, his composition teacher Friedrich Wilhelm Meyer, and his uncle, who would pay for the publication, Strauss came to the point: "I now turn to you with the request that you kindly publish the *Festmarsch*, because your name, renowned in every way and influential in the world of music, will make the name of a young aspiring musician known."[19] Strauss went on to note that his Quartet and Symphony were soon to be played in Munich, and if both were successful, he hoped that Breitkopf and Härtel might consider them for publication. Nothing ever came of that bold suggestion, however.

Instead, Strauss found a publisher closer to home who was willing to take the String Quartet. The Munich-based Aibl Verlag, owned by the Spitzweg family, would be Strauss's publisher from 1881 until 1898, during which time the firm issued thirty-one of his works.[20] Even with the successful premiere of the Quartet, it seems unlikely that the young Strauss would have approached any publisher on his own. Rather, Franz Strauss probably arranged for the printing of his son's Quartet, perhaps even easing the way by offering a few of his own compositions to Eduard Spitzweg.[21] Spitzweg's willingness to take Richard's early works was also undoubtedly influenced by the fact that Strauss's manuscripts cost nothing. Strauss himself made no mention of fees for any works prior to the mid-to-late 1880s, and in fact, an exchange of letters in 1884 between Strauss and Eugen Spitzweg (son and successor of Eduard as owner of Aibl Verlag) suggests that the Horn Concerto No. 1, Op. 11, was the first of his works to earn a fee.

The impetus for Strauss's request to be paid for his Horn Concerto came from his trip to Berlin in the winter of 1883–4. That journey had been undertaken so that Richard could meet some of Germany's leading musicians, critics, and publishers, and introduce his music to them.[22] Richard's letters to his parents describe many of his encounters both along the way and in the capital city, and his initial business dealings seem to have gone quite well. Strauss secured a number of performances for his works, and he also made many professional contacts. One letter in particular describes a meeting with the publisher Hugo Bock. Strauss's Concert Overture in C minor (TrV 125) had been played with some success only a few days earlier in Berlin, and so the composer asked about having it published by Bote and Bock. Although the publisher declined to take any of Strauss's scores at that time, Bock did promise to speak again with the composer in a few months. While nothing ever came of that slight interest, Strauss did note in that same letter that Otto Lessmann, critic of the *Allgemeine Musikzeitung*, had said that Strauss could now demand an honorarium for his music.[23]

When Strauss first raised the issue of a payment for his music, Eugen Spitzweg turned to the conductor Hans von Bülow for advice. Bülow, who had regularly been giving Spitzweg his opinions about the value of various composers' works, responded in a letter of July 16, 1884, with a detailed suggestion that Spitzweg offer Strauss an honorarium, but to make it clear that the token amount was only an act of professional friendship, for which Spitzweg was to expect some loyalty from Strauss, should other publishers show interest in his music within a few years. Most importantly, Spitzweg was not to indicate to Strauss the growing value of his music.[24] Less than a week later, Spitzweg wrote to Strauss, following Bülow's instructions to the letter, and thereby guaranteed that Strauss's music would continue to appear in the catalog of Aibl Verlag for the foreseeable future.[25]

Breaking through and maximizing the profits

The relationship between Strauss and Spitzweg continued to prosper, if only modestly, over the next few years, as Strauss began his professional career in earnest as the assistant conductor under Bülow in Meiningen during the 1885–6 season. Several more of Strauss's works were issued around that time by Aibl Verlag, but no honoraria were paid, because Spitzweg complained that Strauss's works did not sell very well. In fact, the cost of engraving the Symphony No. 2 in F minor, Op. 12 – 1,000 marks – was paid by Franz Strauss, who was, however, quickly reimbursed out of the proceeds from the sales of that work.[26] Strauss's emerging reputation between the late 1880s and early 1890s is evident from the increasing amounts that he began to receive for his works a few years later, starting with 200 marks for a set of songs sold to the Berlin publisher Dan Rahter, who issued them as Strauss's Op. 15, and the 500 marks paid by Spitzweg for the then controversial *Aus Italien*, Op. 16.[27] Nevertheless, the apparent lack of fees for Strauss's other works published around that time suggests two things. First, Strauss was probably more interested in the exposure that any publications gave his name than any money his works might earn. Second, the balance of power still rested with publishers, who could offer minimal fees or even refuse to take the works of a young composer with only a modest reputation.

That situation began to change almost overnight with the astonishing premiere of *Don Juan*, Op. 20, on November 11, 1889. Spitzweg had traveled to Weimar, where Strauss had only recently taken the position of second conductor, to hear the tone poem, and following its unquestionable success, which was widely reported in the national music press, he made Strauss an offer that began a series of negotiations that would last more than a year. Spitzweg initially offered to publish *Don Juan* and also to take *Tod und Verklärung*, Op. 24, a work that Strauss had just recently finished and not yet premiered. Spitzweg knew it only from a piano run-through by Strauss a few days earlier, but the success of *Don Juan* had raised the potential value of Strauss's other scores. Recognizing the strength of his new bargaining position, Strauss looked beyond just the money to the future. Rather than publish *Don Juan* and the still unheard *Tod und Verklärung* immediately, Strauss offered *Don Juan* and a set of five songs, *Schlichte Weisen*, Op. 21, while planning to hold back *Tod und Verklärung* for perhaps another year, during which time that score might be tested in performance.[28]

Strauss's counter-offer to Spitzweg also included a bit of news that was obviously intended to tip the negotiations in Strauss's favor. Another publisher, Max Abraham, owner of C. F. Peters, had secretly offered to publish any of Strauss's tone poems, but had refrained from making a direct offer to the composer, because he was not certain of the precise business arrangement between Strauss and Spitzweg. Strauss admitted his interest in publishing some works in the Peters Edition, but out of loyalty, Strauss would deal with Abraham only with Spitzweg's permission. Specifically, Strauss wanted to offer Abraham another set of songs, *Mädchenblümen*, Op. 22, which Strauss described as "complicated and singular experiments," as well as his first tone poem, *Macbeth*, Op. 23, neither of which he thought that Spitzweg would want. Five days later, Spitzweg agreed to take both *Don Juan* and *Schlichte Weisen* under the terms that Strauss had proposed. *Macbeth* was another matter, however, and Spitzweg reminded Strauss that he had already agreed with Bülow and Spitzweg that it be held back for some undetermined length of time.

From the publisher's standpoint, it is easy to understand why *Macbeth* should not have been issued at that time. In late 1889, Strauss already had two recent major orchestral works in print, and Spitzweg hoped to add the newly premiered *Don Juan* and perhaps even *Tod und Verklärung* to them in the immediate future. Although *Macbeth*, which fell between *Aus Italien* and *Don Juan* in its conception, was not without merit, it had not measured up to its successors in rehearsals and piano readings. Publishing a work of uncertain value like *Macbeth*, especially at a time when Strauss's reputation was poised to rise sharply, risked either damaging that reputation or diluting the market for his works. No doubt following Bülow's advice, as he had done for some years, Spitzweg would therefore neither take *Macbeth* nor release it to Peters, until Strauss resorted to an act of blackmail.

Strauss's reasons for wanting his first tone poem in print were not simply monetary. Instead, he stressed his desire to have his newest works appear in print, preferably in the order in which they were composed, so that audiences might understand the evolution of his style.[29] Tension continued to mount as two additional performances of *Don Juan* added to the work's reputation, and near the end of April, 1890 Strauss informed Spitzweg that he would offer *Macbeth* to Abraham, if Spitzweg still had no interest in that work. On May 13, 1890, Strauss wrote directly to Abraham, offering him *Macbeth* and a four-hand piano arrangement of it for the combined price of 1,500 marks. Two days later, Strauss received a letter from Abraham in which the publisher stated that although he had expressed some interest in Strauss's music through an intermediary, so long as Spitzweg refused to release *Macbeth*, Abraham would not make a formal offer for it.[30]

Strauss regained his leverage less than two months later when *Tod und Verklärung* premiered at the annual summer meeting of the *Allgemeiner Deutscher Musikverein*. Played by a hand-picked orchestra for an audience that consisted primarily of Germany's leading musicians and critics, Strauss's third tone poem scored a success that eclipsed even that of *Don Juan* only a few months earlier, and in the process, Strauss became the undisputed leader of the German avant-garde. *Tod und Verklärung* was praised in the press as Strauss's greatest work to date, and its success quickly drew interest from orchestras in Vienna and Munich. When Spitzweg tried to arrange for those performances, which would maintain interest in Strauss's music while *Don Juan* and *Tod und Verklärung* could be engraved for sale to the public, Strauss twice refused to release the score of *Tod und Verklärung* in manuscript to either city.[31] Between those two letters, Strauss premiered *Macbeth* (in its first orchestral setting) in Weimar on October 13, 1890. Although only a marginal success, the performance was good enough for Strauss to continue pressing his case, and on November 27, 1890, Spitzweg capitulated, taking all three of Strauss's tone poems, including *Macbeth*, rather than allow any of Strauss's works to go to other publishers.

Although Strauss was the victor in these negotiations, one should remember that this was not simply a financial success. While he soon began to earn ever-increasing fees from Aibl Verlag – although not as high as he demanded from other publishers[32] – the real lesson learned was how to maximize the synergy between well-received performances and the timely publication of scores, parts, and especially the various piano reductions that supplied a personal market interested in Strauss's music. In the days before recorded sound, such arrangements were important for playing and studying large-scale orchestral works in the home.[33] The popularity of such editions may be gauged from the various reductions issued of Strauss's *Don Juan* – for example, for piano two-hands, piano four-hands, two pianos four-hands, and two pianos eight-hands – some appearing in multiple editions as late as 1933.[34] These single editions could be produced and marketed more quickly to a larger market than could complete sets of parts, which only a handful of ensembles might want, and thus publishers' ads in the leading German music periodicals often advertised piano reductions even before parts and scores were available.[35]

In the case of *Don Juan*, however, its success was so swift and perhaps unexpected that no piano reductions were ready for some time. In fact, Ludwig Thuille, who prepared one of the *Don Juan* reductions, complained in April, 1890 about how difficult it was to translate Strauss's orchestral timbres into something suitable for the keyboard.[36] Adding this problem to the negotiations that had delayed the engraving of *Don Juan* for over a year, one might wonder how much potential revenue was lost before any printed materials for these works were available for sale. As late as April, 1891, ads for Aibl Verlag indicated only that the score to *Macbeth* was "in preparation," while the score and parts for *Tod und Verklärung* were "soon to appear" and its piano reduction would be ready "in the near future."[37]

Four years later, the premiere of *Till Eulenspiegel*, Op. 28, showed what this composer and his publisher had learned. Strauss finished the score on May 6, 1895, and only four months later, before his fourth tone poem had even been heard in public, an ad for Aibl Verlag stated that the score and parts of *Till Eulenspiegel* would appear "in the near future" and that Hermann Levi's piano arrangement for four hands was already available. Additionally, the ad noted that performances for the 1895–6 season were already set, and that the performing rights could be obtained only directly from the publisher.[38] On November 5, 1895, just six months after Strauss had finished the score, Franz Wüllner conducted Cologne's Gürzenich Orchestra in the premiere of *Till Eulenspiegel*. Moreover, within a year, there were at least twenty-five additional performances of *Till Eulenspiegel*, far more than any of Strauss's previous orchestral works had received early on.[39] In short, the debut of *Till Eulenspiegel* was a marketing coup unlike anything Strauss and Spitzweg had previously experienced. Each of Strauss's following tone poems would appear in a similar fashion, issued only months after its completion in a carefully co-ordinated promotional campaign that included a series of performances with leading orchestras and readily available printed materials, all of which guaranteed both publisher and composer the maximum financial return and the widest exposure of Strauss's name and music.

On the podium and in the concert hall

By the late 1890s Strauss's position as one of the leading composers of his generation ensured that his income from his published works would rise significantly, a point noted by Strauss in his reminiscences and thus echoed by most who have written about his business dealings.[40] Ignored in virtually every discussion of Strauss's finances, however, are his earnings from performances as a conductor and occasionally as an accompanist, and especially the income generated as royalties from performances of his music. To be sure, Strauss's annual contracts from his early years as a Kapellmeister are noted in the literature and, as with the honoraria for published scores, the numbers show a consistent rise, from only 1,500 marks in Meiningen (1885–6) to 18,000 marks in Berlin (per year for ten years, 1898–1908).[41] Still, almost nothing has been written about the fees that Strauss earned as a conductor outside his regular contracted duties.[42]

A glance into Strauss's *Schreibkalender* does provide some revelatory information.[43] In 1903, for example, Strauss made a twenty-four-day concert tour through southern Europe that began in Teplitz on March 1 and then went through other cities before swinging through Italy, southern France, Switzerland, and Germany, ending in Basel on March 24. Strauss noted the individual fees for all twenty-five concerts, which ranged from 500 to 1,000 marks. Most were billed at 650 marks. In just over three weeks, Strauss grossed an amount that exceeded two-thirds of his annual salary in Berlin. That same year also included two major Strauss festivals and other appearances, which suggests that in some years the majority of his income may have been generated primarily from guest-conducting and the like. Such extended tours and brief "run-outs" to single events were fairly common in Strauss's career, especially in the two decades leading up to World War I, even to the point that his family expressed concerns about his health.

A letter from Strauss to his parents, written near the end of that 1903 tour, reported on his recent concerts, his ambitious plans for the next season, and also a sore throat that had kept him confined to his room in Paris. Both of his parents responded the next day with earnest concerns. Franz Strauss worried that Richard was gambling with his health and especially that he would "destroy his splendid God-given talent in such an ugly money-craving manner," while his mother added, "What good then is hard-earned money, if your health is ruined?" Strauss eased his parents' fears two days later with the following lines:

> Your anxious letter was completely unnecessary: no one has ever gotten
> sick from lots of work, if he otherwise lived a moderate and reasonable life,

and that I do … There are many people, lawyers, businessmen, etc., who work much more than I and consider themselves in good health for it. For me it is neither avarice nor Jewish greed – but why should I not work as long as I can and feel no complaints from it? Thus you may set your minds completely at ease.[44]

The reasons for such an attitude are also not hard to find. Prior to his wedding in 1894, Strauss said nothing in public and very little in private about money. Beginning in the late 1890s, however, his correspondence reveals a man concerned primarily with providing for his young family in an era that had nothing of the welfare state erected by western Europe in the second half of the twentieth century.

His move from Munich to Berlin in 1898 is particularly instructive. After four years in his native city, Strauss's relationship with the Court Opera Intendant, Karl Freiherr von Perfall, had deteriorated to the point that Perfall wanted to cut Strauss's salary, and so Strauss was casting about for a new position in Hamburg, Berlin, or New York. The position in America (to replace Anton Seidl at the Metropolitan Opera) would have paid more than double (40,000 marks) what Strauss eventually received in Berlin, but as Strauss wrote to his mother at the time, it was more important that he build his reputation in Europe before exploring opportunities in America.[45] Even before looking to leave Munich, Strauss had been attempting to negotiate a permanent appointment there for only 12,000 marks annually, in contrast to the 15,000 marks that he had been offered by Hamburg's Intendant, Bernhard Pollini. Moreover, Strauss had tied his interest in Hamburg to Pollini's willingness to engage Pauline at the opera, something that Perfall had flatly refused to do in Munich. Strauss and his wife discussed nearly every aspect of these competing offers in an exchange of letters, and in the end Pauline advised her husband to forget about her career. Whether they moved to Hamburg or stayed in Munich should be based solely on what was best for his career and the support of their young family. As for Strauss, he was much more inclined to accept the long-term security of a permanent appointment in Munich, "something that will take care of us for the rest of our lives," he said, and which would allow them to "spend the rest of our days without a care and devote ourselves to our little boy."[46] In this light, Strauss's bitterness at leaving Munich for the second time is entirely understandable, especially when he might gladly have stayed for only 80 percent of what his Berlin appointment paid.

Whatever Strauss's financial goals were around 1900, they were motivated by entirely normal and reasonable personal needs. As a freelance musician, he was dependent upon his ability to negotiate relatively short-term employment contracts of only a few years' duration and to market his services as a guest conductor. Likewise, his ability to sell music to publishers rested on his standing with his audiences. Under those conditions, it is not surprising that he favored a permanent appointment in Munich over better-paying, but less secure positions elsewhere. Even when the Munich situation deteriorated, Strauss was still able to negotiate a relatively lengthy ten-year contract in Berlin, complete with pension benefits for himself and his widow. Moreover, he also was guaranteed significant free time in the summer for composition and liberal leave during the concert season for guest-conducting, both of which would add to his income. Such a decision reflects Strauss's industrious nature, which was born out of his father's own belief in the value and necessity of hard work. Still, Strauss could not guarantee how long he might hold his audience, and thus for the sake of his family he had to make the most of his opportunities while he had them. To his way of thinking, this was not greed, but rather prudence.

The fight for composers' rights

Given Strauss's concerns about supporting his family, his involvement in the fight for composers' rights – an act that in the eyes of many defined Strauss as a musical robber baron from the moment it became public knowledge – would seem an obvious way for him to increase his income. By the late 1890s, however, Strauss's reputation was such that he could virtually name his price when selling new works to publishers, and even before the debate over concert royalties took center stage, Strauss was already being offered a portion of the income that publishers were sometimes collecting from performers.[47] In short, Strauss had little to gain in this battle, and thus many assume that he simply lent the prestige of his name and position to help colleagues who were less well off. In fact, Strauss's concerns for and work on behalf of copyright reform would occupy him well into his seventies.

Far too many authors misstate Strauss's role in the initial phases of this crusade by making him the instigator, when in fact Hans Sommer was the intellectual father of the cause.[48] It was only after Sommer had published an article on the issue in early 1898 and then sent a copy to Strauss, that Strauss actively joined the movement.[49] There was some urgency to the matter, as the Reichstag was scheduled to vote later that year on reforms of the copyright law of 1870, which had at least two serious problems. The first, which was the focus of Sommer's article, was the relatively short term of only thirty years' protection for intellectual property after the death of a work's author. The second concerned serious problems with the assertion of an author's rights and the manner in which a composer could collect performance royalties. Both issues had significant consequences for the income that a successful composer might earn, especially in the future for his heirs, and thus it is not surprising that Strauss responded to Sommer to express his full agreement. Strauss then circulated an open letter among German composers, in which he urged their support for a memorandum, drafted by Sommer and Friedrich Rösch (a boyhood friend of Strauss who became a lawyer and also was a composer), that would be forwarded to the government.[50]

The extension of copyright protection for one's heirs was easily understood, but the issue of royalties was much more complex. According to the 1870 law, a printed notice of "Author's rights reserved" had to appear at the top of a score, and any public performance then had to be sanctioned by the composer. Most composers did not exercise that right, however, because such notices discouraged the performance of new works. Publishers, who routinely purchased the performing rights with the score, were also loath to include the notice on a published score, since the inhibition of performances naturally reduced the sale of parts and scores. Once a piece had been issued without the notice, however, there was no way to reclaim the abandoned right. Thus, as a practical matter, a composer had to give up the right to royalties in order to secure performances of his music, but then earned nothing beyond the original fee for the manuscript, no matter how popular the work became. From the standpoint of concert organizers, it was cheaper and safer to program older, well-known works, which in turn exacerbated the predicament of new composers. As Strauss wrote to Sommer, "our great masters of the past are taking away those places that should be occupied by the living." The publishers responded to this argument with a proposed one percent royalty on all new concert music to be split fifty–fifty with the composer. No formal notice would be required, but the right would extend to the heirs for only thirty years after a composer's death. Strauss countered by noting that unless the law was extended to cover older works that were already "free," the situation would not change. He further proposed that the royalties on the works of deceased composers be paid to any surviving heirs and, if there were none, that the money be used to support and encourage "young, impecunious talent" or to establish a similar program "furthering artistic progress."[51]

Thus, while financial considerations were admittedly an important part of the discussions about copyright reform, for Strauss at least, the money was secondary to an underlying belief in the value of the artwork itself. For him, the fundamental issue was to ensure that all composers – especially those without reputations and thus easy access to performance venues – had the opportunity for their works to be heard and judged on their aesthetic merits. No doubt, Strauss expected that success in the concert hall would lead to financial gains and long-term security for deserving composers, but it was the way in which those fiscal rewards might be earned that eluded Strauss's critics in the popular press. The selling of scores or seats in a concert hall was not an end in itself, but rather the means by which music could be disseminated to the widest possible audience, after which aesthetic judgment might begin to be rendered. The distinction may at first seem to be irrelevant, but as a matter of principle, the difference is quite significant.

The founding of the *Genossenschaft Deutscher Tonsetzer* (GDT) in 1903, after several intermediary steps over the preceding five years, thus represents a victory for Strauss the idealist, who wanted the marketplace to determine the value of a composer's work. As evidence of Strauss's principles on this point, one need only remember that he frequently supported composers for whose music he had little sympathy: for example, Arnold Schoenberg.[52] At the same time, the ever-practical Strauss, who was almost always alert to the commercial potential of his own music, personally benefited greatly from the establishment of a formal organization that protected the rights of individual composers in the marketplace. No other composer at the time could count on so many performances of his own music, and thus Strauss became the easiest target for critics of the GDT. Strauss also did not help his reputation with two performances in Wanamaker's New York department store on his first American tour.[53]

Final years and preserving his legacy

Worse still, historically, was Strauss's infamous letter of June 17, 1935 to Stefan Zweig, in which his statement that "the people exist for me only at the moment they become [an] audience" is read by some as Strauss at his most cynical and venal.[54] Compounding the damage is the vague association of that letter with his "Nazi problem." In fact, Strauss's own memorandum less than a month after having written the letter to Zweig notes, however, that the statement in question concerned the financial support of theaters in general if they were "to fulfill truly higher cultural goals" and never his own income.[55] Indeed, Strauss's problems with the Nazis go back to his willingness to assume the presidency of the *Reichsmusikkammer* primarily so that he could influence copyright reforms in favor of serious art music.[56] Still, while Strauss's finances might have benefited from those proposed reforms, there were too many instances where he refused easy fees for anyone to claim that he joined with the Reich simply for his own avaricious interests.[57]

At the same time, one must not forget that throughout the twentieth century, Strauss's personal fortune was almost constantly in flux, and several times he had to begin over accumulating the wealth that he hoped would ensure his family's future. His letter of June 22, 1921 to Franz Schalk is quite direct on that point and reveals Strauss's most naked fears:

> [Y]ou ask me why I go to America? Not for my pleasure! After England confiscated the majority of my wealth, I have no pension to look forward to from anyone – I am entirely dependent upon the royalties from my works in case anything were to happen to me today that prevented me from conducting anymore. Even [my] operatic successes are unreliable – if the royalties of my works ceased today, which for the present I hope not, I am a beggar and leave my family in "poverty and shame." I must rid myself of this worry in order to be able to work again in peace – if I go a second time to America, I can make up somewhat for the damage that the war brought me, and [I] can look forward with some reassurance to an old age in sickness and the inability to work …[58]

Indeed, Strauss probably reached the nadir of his finances in the years immediately after World War II. Living in exile in a Swiss hotel, he resorted to copying out his early orchestral masterworks by hand, so that those autograph manuscripts could guarantee payment of his bills. His letters to his post-war publisher Ernst Roth are filled with questions about embargoed royalty payments to German nationals, possible commissions and concerts, and even the sale of his remaining unpublished manuscripts, all to provide only basic sustenance for his family during his last years and perhaps a bit beyond.[59]

Although the Strausses were the recipients of numerous acts of kindness from many individuals during those dark days, Strauss himself did continue to provide for his family to the end of his life. Among the most memorable events of those years was Strauss's 1947 concert trip to England, which was arranged by Roth. There is no mention of the fees, but they must have been significant to have goaded the eighty-three-year-old Strauss into his first-ever airplane flight. Interestingly, several other major projects in the post-war years, which might have generated significant income for the impoverished Strauss, went nowhere. A request from a British film producer to use a few minutes of the *Salome* and *Rosenkavalier* scores for £20,000 was rejected by Strauss when he learned that his works might be cut or otherwise debased.[60] In contrast, when Strauss was approached in 1948 by the American publisher Edward B. Marks for a "short choral work," Strauss offered *Die Göttin im Putzzimmer* (TrV 267) – a score he had finished in 1935 – but the deal never went through, because Marks could not afford Strauss's requested honorarium of $10,000.[61]

What is perhaps most remarkable about these two failed deals is the matter-of-fact tone in which each was bargained and then almost forgotten.

Either sum would have been more than sufficient to ease Strauss's financial woes for some time in the late 1940s, yet there is no hint that he was ready in the first case to prostitute his art or in the second to reduce his price.[62] Such a willingness to forgo easy solutions during extraordinarily difficult times does suggest how strong Strauss's life-long principles were. One might also remember the *Krämerspiegel* affair of 1918, in which Strauss reluctantly fulfilled a disputed contract for some lieder with songs based on texts that mocked a nettlesome publisher who had insisted on his due, regardless of Strauss's creative mood at the time. By providing virtually unsellable songs, Strauss reminded all involved of the distinction between art and commerce. For Strauss music was always music, and business was simply business, no matter what others might imagine he thought.

15 Kapellmeister Strauss

RAYMOND HOLDEN

The opera house and the concert hall

Richard Strauss bestrode the nineteenth and twentieth centuries like a musical colossus. As the last great composer-conductor, he was professionally active for more than seven decades and produced a seemingly endless string of important works. He was approached constantly by impresarios and orchestras to perform these pieces at their concerts, but those invitations often had little appeal for Strauss, who preferred instead to conduct the music of his heroes, Mozart, Beethoven, and Wagner, and to promote works by his contemporaries. Although often misrepresented as a mercenary musician interested solely in the promotion of his own compositions, Strauss was an artist of catholic taste, who invariably placed art before ambition.

Strauss was the son of Germany's most celebrated horn player, Franz Strauss.[1] Described by Hans von Bülow as "the Joachim of the *Waldhorn*," Franz was a member of the Munich Hofkapelle for forty-two years. A notoriously conservative musician who abhorred the works of Wagner and his followers, he regarded the great Classical composers as iconic figures to be admired above all others. As the Hofkapelle's principal horn, he played under Wagner and his "*alter ego* ...the master-conductor Hans von Bülow"[2] on a regular basis in the 1860s and was constantly at loggerheads with them. Nevertheless, Franz was happy to allow leading Wagnerians to champion Richard's early compositions and to let them support his son's career as a performer. Consequently, one of the first major conductors to recognize Strauss's talent publicly was Hermann Levi, who gave the first professional performances of the composer's Symphony in D minor and the Concert Overture in C minor at Munich in 1881 and 1883 respectively.[3] Bülow also took an early interest in the young composer and performed his Serenade for Winds, Op. 7 with the Meininger Hofkapelle in 1883. Impressed by Strauss's potential, Bülow then "commissioned [him] to write a similar piece for the Meiningen orchestra": the Suite for Winds, Op. 4, which the orchestra premiered at Munich's Odeonssaal on November 18, 1884 with the composer conducting.[4] Having never conducted before, Strauss was understandably nervous about his debut and later recalled that he "conducted [his] piece in a state of slight coma."[5] After the concert, his father attempted to thank Bülow but was set upon by his old enemy who shouted "You have nothing to thank me for … I have not forgotten what you have done to me in this damned city of Munich. What I did today I did because your son has talent and not for you."[6] Despite spoiling Strauss's moment of glory, Bülow more than compensated for this vitriolic outburst by arranging for Strauss to be appointed Hofmusikdirektor at the Grand Duchy of Meiningen in 1885.

Confident of his new assistant's abilities, Bülow introduced him to the Grand Duchy by having him perform the solo part in Mozart's Piano Concerto No. 20[7] and conduct the local premiere of his own Symphony in F minor on October 18, 1885. As Bülow's protégé, Strauss observed his mentor's conducting style at first hand. Each morning, he attended the Hofkapelle's rehearsals, which Bülow directed solely, and was particularly impressed by his approach to the works of Beethoven. In later life, Strauss recalled that Bülow's interpretations were compelling in their intensity, were without any trace of arbitrariness, and were the direct result of the work's form and its poetic content. As a teacher, Bülow insisted that Strauss should learn to read Beethoven's scores accurately and to use that accuracy as the basis for his interpretation. Strauss also absorbed Bülow's painstaking method in rehearsal, his eye for detail, and (as a finished conductor) his graceful baton technique. The profound influence that Bülow exerted during Strauss's short stay at Meiningen was life-long, and in maturity he wrote that "The touching interest he took in me and his influence on the development of my artistic talent were … the most decisive factors in my career."[8]

Strauss's first opportunity to stamp his authority on the Meiningen orchestra came on December 6, 1885, when he directed his first concert with the Hofkapelle as Bülow's successor. The program included Gluck's overture to *Iphigenie en Aulide*, Mozart's Requiem and Brahms's *Schicksalslied*. Typically, Strauss concluded the Gluck overture with Wagner's concert ending and revised Süßmayr's orchestration in the Requiem.[9] But with Bülow gone and with the imminent reduction of the orchestra to thirty-nine players, Strauss soon began to lose interest in Meiningen. Despite being offered an increased salary of 2,000 marks[10] to stay in the Duchy, he left the Hofkapelle in April, 1886 to become Musikdirektor (third conductor) at the Munich Hofoper from the beginning of the 1886–7 season.

After an extended holiday in Italy, Strauss began work at Munich on October 1, 1886. Apart from the pleasure of directing a first-rate orchestra that included his father, the job proved disappointing. For much of the time, and in keeping with the rank of Musikdirektor, he was obliged to conduct operas from the standard repertoire. Along with a performance of Mendelssohn's incidental music to *Ein Sommernachtstraum*

(*A Midsummer Night's Dream*) on January 25, 1887, Strauss took charge of twenty performances of nine operas by eight composers during his first season: eleven French, eight Austro-German and one Italian. With the exception of Mozart's *Così fan tutte*,[11] an opera that he championed throughout his life and with which he would later be associated closely, all the operas that he performed were popular and in keeping with his junior rank. Strauss's second season at Munich bore a striking resemblance to his first, with four of the eight operas being carried over from the previous year. His third season as Musikdirektor was again dominated by repeat performances, with only Donizetti's *La favorite* and Verdi's *Un ballo in maschera* new to his repertoire.

During his stay at Meiningen, Strauss met and befriended the violinist and composer Alexander Ritter,[12] who bombarded the young musician with the writings of Schopenhauer and Wagner and who converted him quickly into a fervent Wagnerian. It was with some excitement, then, that as third conductor in Munich Strauss took responsibility for the first ever production of Wagner's early opera, *Die Feen* (1833–4), in June, 1888. Preparations for the staging began in the spring of that year and the young conductor continued to superintend the production until the final rehearsals. But at the eleventh hour, the Intendant, Baron Karl von Perfall, informed Strauss that his immediate superior, Franz Fischer,[13] was to take charge of both the dress rehearsal and the first performance. Strauss was devastated. Although granted an early and valuable insight into the machinations of operatic life, he felt nothing but contempt for his superiors at Munich, later describing Perfall as "a disgusting cad" and Fischer as "one of the most untalented musicians I have ever met and a real criminal at the rostrum."[14] It was with some relief, therefore, that he accepted the post of Second Kapellmeister at the Weimar Hoftheater from the beginning of the 1889–90 season with a salary of 2,100 marks.

Although Strauss later argued that he had not been a particularly effective third conductor at Munich, Bülow continued to take an interest in his career and brokered his appointment as Kapellmeister at the Grand Duchy of Saxe-Weimar-Eisenach.[15] For a German musician of Strauss's generation, Weimar was of particular significance. With its links to Bach, Goethe, Schiller, and Liszt, its rich artistic heritage was the basis for a lively cultural environment that allowed Strauss to explore new musical avenues while discovering masterworks from the past. Working with a well-disposed Intendant, Hans Bronsart von Schellendorf, and an amiable Hofkapellmeister, Eduard Lassen, Strauss developed musically within a secure environment that valued his abilities, both as a creative and as a performing musician.[16] His interest in *Zukunftsmusik* was nurtured at Weimar and, with the help of Bronsart and Lassen, he explored some important works by Mozart and Beethoven. As Strauss had to balance responsibilities in the opera theater with duties in the concert hall for the first time, his exploration of those works included not only the operatic but also the symphonic repertoires.

Between 1889 and 1893, Strauss conducted sixteen subscription concerts with the Weimar Hofkapelle. Of those, eleven contained music by Beethoven, the composer that he conducted most frequently at that series.[17] Less frequently performed by Strauss were the orchestral works of Mozart, Wagner, and Liszt, which were heard at three, five, and seven concerts respectively.[18] Keen to promote his own works and eager to be seen as a successor to Liszt and Wagner, Strauss also included his own compositions in the subscription series from the beginning of his tenure, and after accompanying the tenor Hans Zeller in a performance of his *Ständchen* at his first Weimar concert on October 28, 1889, he conducted the world premiere of his tone poem *Don Juan* at his second.[19] As the darling of the avant-garde and as a passionate advocate of new music, Strauss naturally also included works by some of his contemporaries; along with compositions by Lassen, Stavenhagen, and Halir, his Weimar programs included music by Ritter, Thuille, Humperdinck, Bülow, Bruch, Saint-Saëns, Weiss, Brahms, and Draeseke.

Although Strauss's concerts with the Hofkapelle did much to increase his public profile, his principal duty at Weimar was to conduct operas at the Hoftheater. There, he gave 199 operatic performances between September 22, 1889 and June 1, 1894.[20] The red threads that ran through that fabric of performances were the operas of Mozart and Wagner. Of the former, he gave thirty-three performances and, of the latter, fifty-two. Unsurprisingly, and in keeping with contemporary trends, his Mozart repertoire centred on *Don Giovanni*, *Le nozze di Figaro*, and *Die Zauberflöte*, the work with which he made his local debut on September 22, 1889. An exception, however, was *Bastien und Bastienne*, which he performed as part of a double-bill with *Hänsel und Gretel* in the 1893–4 season.[21] Strauss's Wagner repertoire at Weimar included *Tannhäuser*, *Lohengrin*, *Rienzi*, *Die Meistersinger von Nürnberg*, and *Tristan und Isolde*. As a young and relatively inexperienced conductor, he must have found these works demanding. But as a fervent Wagnerian, he leapt at the chance of performing them and decided to challenge contemporary trends by conducting *Tristan und Isolde* without cuts. While this proved particularly controversial, it did much to secure Strauss's reputation as one of the leading Wagner interpreters of his generation. His commitment to new music was also reflected in his operatic programming at Weimar; along with Ritter's two one-act operas *Wem die Krone?* and *Der faule Hans* in a double-bill in June, 1890, he conducted the world premieres of Metzdorff's *Hagbart und*

Signe, Humperdinck's *Hänsel und Gretel*, Mottl's *Fürst und Sänger*, and his own *Guntram* at the Hoftheater.[22]

In the spring of 1893, Strauss was head-hunted by the Munich Hofoper. With Levi's health failing, the theater needed a dynamic young musician who could work side-by-side with him and who could absorb some of his duties. As a native of Munich and as a former member of the Hofoper's music staff, Strauss seemed the logical choice. As in Weimar, Strauss made his debut as Kapellmeister with *Die Zauberflöte*. That reading was the first of 272 performances of thirty-five works by twenty-four composers that he conducted at the Hofoper between October 7, 1894 and October 18, 1898. Unafraid of new challenges, Strauss continued to add works to his repertoire throughout his second Munich period and, of the operas performed, eighteen were new to him. He also continued to champion the works of his contemporaries when possible, giving the world premieres of Thuille's *Theuerdank* and Hausegger's *Zinnober* on March 12, 1897 and June 19, 1898 respectively. Eager to introduce his *Guntram* to his fellow Müncheners, Strauss conducted the work at the Hofoper on November 16, 1895. In contrast to its reception at Weimar, where the work was a reasonable success, *Guntram* provoked hostility from the start at Munich, causing the singers to rebel, the orchestra to demand to be freed of "this scourge of God [*Gottesgeißel*]," the critics to take a hostile stance, and Wagner's family to consider the opera a betrayal of the Master's principles.[23] *Guntram* never recovered fully from its failure at Munich and it has remained on the periphery of the operatic repertoire since that time.

Strauss consolidated his reputation as a Mozart and Wagner interpreter during his second Munich period by directing ninety-eight operatic performances of the former and eighty-five of the latter. Although he had always been a passionate advocate of those works, his senior position at Munich meant that he was able to explore them more fully. With the producer Ernst von Possart,[24] Strauss established an annual series of Mozart and Wagner performances in 1895 that began each August and continued until either the following fall or winter. At the first of those discrete seasons, Possart and Strauss mounted thirteen performances of *Rienzi*, *Tannhäuser*, *Tristan und Isolde*, and *Die Meistersinger von Nürnberg*. Those operas then formed the basis for the following three summer seasons, during which twenty-nine further performances of operas by Wagner were heard.

When Strauss accepted the post of Hofkapellmeister on the retirement of Levi in 1896, the summer repertoire was extended to include operas by Mozart. That year, Strauss and Possart staged a highly acclaimed new production of *Don Giovanni*, followed by new productions of *Die Entführung aus dem Serail*, *Così fan tutte*, and *Die Zauberflöte* in 1897 and 1898.[25] Those readings stimulated new interest in the operas of Mozart, thanks to a series of theatrical and musical innovations that have since been called the "Munich Reforms."[26] At the Residenztheater, Munich's ornate rococo theater, Strauss and Possart used an orchestra of twenty-six players, sets and costumes characteristic of the eighteenth century, Hermann Levi's revised translations of the libretti, orchestral and vocal material based on Mozart's autographs, a revolving stage (for the first time), the Prague version of *Don Giovanni*,[27] and a fortepiano for the recitatives, played by Strauss, who acted both as conductor and as continuo player. In later years, Strauss looked back on those performances with affection; in 1928 he wrote that the "Mozart Festivals, which I inaugurated together with Possart ... stand out among the truly wonderful memories of my life."[28]

During his second Munich period, Strauss continued to work as an orchestral conductor and accepted the direction of the subscription concerts of both the Berlin Philharmonic and the Munich Hofkapelle in 1894. With the death of Hans von Bülow earlier that year, Hermann Wolff needed a conductor to lead the prestigious Philharmonic Concerts in Berlin. By reputation and pedigree, Strauss seemed the obvious choice for the job. With programs that were catholic and pan-European, he offered Berlin audiences a well-balanced series of concerts that regularly juxtaposed the new with the familiar. Beethoven figured centrally in his Berlin repertoire, with works in seven of the ten concerts. Modern music was also a regular feature, with compositions by Saint-Saëns, Schillings, Rubinstein, d'Albert, Ritter, Gernsheim, Stenhammar, Sauret, and Mahler. Curiously, Strauss's orchestral works were not included in his Berlin programs, with only extracts from *Guntram* being heard at his last Philharmonic Concert on March 18, 1895. Despite interesting and colorful programs, his season with the Berlin Philharmonic was far from successful. Unable to fill Bülow's shoes, Strauss was replaced the following year by the charismatic Hungarian, Arthur Nikisch.

Commuting between Prussia and Bavaria for much of the 1894–5 season, Strauss conducted eight subscription concerts that year with the Munich Hofkapelle. For practical reasons, some of the works that he performed in Berlin were also heard in Munich. In general, however, the content and character of Strauss's concerts with the Hofkapelle were different from those that he directed with the Berlin Philharmonic. That said, he was no less demanding of his Munich public than he was of his Berlin audience, with six of his eight concerts containing a work by a less-familiar contemporary composer. During the 1895–6 season, the symphonies of Beethoven pushed new music somewhat to the background, as Strauss gave his first cycle of those works, which he conducted in numerical order. Yet in Munich, as in Berlin, he failed to convince fully as an orchestral conductor and, after his second season as director of the Hofkapelle's subscription series, he restricted his conducting activities in Munich to the opera pit.

Although Strauss's success in the concert hall was conditional, he continued to excel as an opera conductor and, in 1898, he was appointed Hofkapellmeister at the Berlin Hofoper. Understandably, Strauss wanted to incorporate the new theatrical techniques that he had pioneered in Munich into the Berlin theater's productions, but his reforms were slow to be accepted. Nevertheless, the Prussian capital was soon alive with talk of Strauss's interpretations of Mozart and, in particular, his playing of the harpsichord for the accompaniment of the recitatives. Having made an immediate impact with his readings of Mozart and Wagner,[29] Strauss was able to pursue his interest in their operas and, of the 959 operatic perform-ances that he directed at the Hofoper either as a tenured or a guest con-ductor between November 1, 1898 and July 1, 1939, 131 were of Mozart and 253 were of Wagner.[30]

As Hofkapellmeister, Strauss was able to perform his own operas on a regular basis. Previously, he had given a mere five performances of his opera *Guntram*.[31] While the opposition that the work met at Munich was an irritant that never fully left Strauss,[32] the extraordinary success of *Salome*, *Elektra*, and *Der Rosenkavalier* made him Germany's leading opera composer. Even Kaiser Wilhelm II, to whom the Hofoper's music staff and administrators were answerable directly, could not deny these works a permanent place in the theater's repertoire. It was with some satisfaction, therefore, that Strauss gave 200 performances of his operas at that house between 1902 and 1939.

After his promotion to Generalmusikdirektor in 1908, Strauss took charge of the Berlin Hofkapelle's subscription concerts.[33] Between 1908 and 1935, a period that incorporates his activities both as a staff and a guest conductor, Strauss directed 130 concerts with the orchestra.[34] Although thirty-three concerts contained a work, or works, by him, it was the music of Beethoven and Mozart that dominated his Hofkapelle programs, with 116 of his concerts containing a work by the former and twenty-nine by the latter. As always, Strauss championed the cause of contemporary compos-ers, performing Mahler's Symphonies Nos. 1 ("Titan") to 4, that composer's *Das Lied von der Erde*, and the world premieres of at least seventeen works by fourteen composers. Some modern commentators have understated Strauss's interest in the music of his contemporaries and have accused him of being concerned solely with the promotion of his own compositions, but when his activities at Berlin are considered fully,[35] that notion can be dismissed easily.

Between 1919 and 1924, Strauss served as *Leiter* (director) of the Vienna Staatsoper alongside the infamous Brucknerian Franz Schalk, who held the same title. Vienna had a special place in Strauss's affections and when the opportunity arose for him to occupy a titular post at Europe's most prestigious opera house, the temptation to accept was overwhelming. Yet Hugo von Hofmannsthal initially opposed the appointment, advising Strauss that he was not the right man for the job, even though he "would add outward luster to the Opera."[36] Specifically, the librettist was concerned "that … [Strauss] would put [his] own personal convenience, and above all the egoism of the creative musician, before the uphill struggle for the ultimate higher welfare of [the Staatsoper]."[37] In response, Strauss accepted Hofmannsthal's objections and recognized "that [he] neither could, nor would want to, accept this post today in the way Mahler filled it."[38] Even so, he "could well imagine [himself]" participating in "the necessary new engagements of singers and young conductors" and "the reorganization and rejuvenation of the magnificent orchestra."[39] Further, he argued that, "[s]ince I am generally regarded as a very good Mozartian and Wagnerian conductor, the works of these masters (in addition to Gluck and Weber) would be the first to be chosen for revival."[40]

In the end, Hofmannsthal's concerns were realized partially. Of the 187 operatic performances given by Strauss in Vienna between 1919 and 1924, six were of Weber, twelve were of Beethoven, thirty-five were of Mozart, forty-three were of Wagner, and seventy-one were of Strauss. Not surprisingly, he was attacked from all sides. The press, who considered Strauss a foreigner, complained that he was often absent from Vienna and that, when in attendance, he was only interested in performing his own compositions. Austria's fragmented political situation also worked against him, and when the new republic replaced the Austrian emperor as the driving force behind the Staatsoper, the directors encountered trouble with both the unions and the workers' councils. For some, it seemed that Schalk shouldered the heavy burden of administrative responsibility while Strauss basked in the glory. The acrimony between the two directors increased and, by 1924, after unsuccessfully demanding Schalk's dismissal, Strauss resigned. Despite this unhappy ending, Strauss returned regularly to Vienna in later years, enjoyed the sumptuous comfort of his newly built villa in the Jacquingasse and continued to participate actively in the city's cultural life.

The recording studio

Strauss was one of the first major composer-conductors to exploit the new medium of sound-recording. Like many of his contemporaries, he was unconvinced by the crude sound that early recordings produced. Even so,

that technology provided a means by which to document and to disseminate his methods, both as a creative and as an executant musician. While
recording offered financial rewards, it would be wrong to suggest that
money alone was his motivating force. In the early twentieth century, companies such as Deutsche Grammophon were keen to document music that
was both popular and profitable. As Strauss's tone poems were heard regularly in the concert hall and could be marketed easily, they were an attractive prospect for the fast-growing record industry. Moreover, as Strauss was
a well-known interpreter of music by Mozart, Beethoven, and Wagner, he
seemed the obvious choice to document works by those composers.

Performing on the popular medium of the piano-roll, Strauss made his
recording debut in 1905 with selections from *Salome* and *Feuersnot*, the
love scene from *Ein Heldenleben*, and four of his lieder specially arranged
for solo piano. The rolls were designed to be played on a reproducing
piano and were recorded by Welte at the company's Freiburg studios. A
publicity photo released by the firm at the time of the recording shows
Strauss at the piano with the score of *Salome* in front of him and surrounded by members of the recording company. As the opera received
its first performance the same year,[41] the roll probably acted as a form
of advance publicity. Nine years later, in 1914, Strauss recorded rolls of
excerpts from the 1912 version of *Ariadne auf Naxos*, the love scene from
Ein Heldenleben, and an extract from his moribund ballet, *Josephslegende*
for Hupfeld. Unlike the Welte rolls, those for Hupfeld were made for the
mass market and were designed to be played on ordinary player pianos.[42]
Although Strauss's pianism was far from virtuosic at the time of these
recordings, and although the devices on which he recorded were often
flawed technically, these sound-documents do reflect his approach to
tempo, articulation, and balance in general. They are, therefore, not only
a valuable insight into a now largely undervalued historical resource but,
also, a useful guide to Strauss's approach as a performing artist in the first
two decades of the twentieth century.

Strauss's first orchestral recordings were made for Deutsche
Grammophon in 1916 with the Berlin Hofkapelle.[43] The works that he documented at those early sessions included *Don Juan*,[44] *Till Eulenspiegel*, and
the suite from *Der Bürger als Edelmann*. Some five years later, Strauss was
asked to record the dance from *Salome* and the Menuett and Intermezzo
from *Der Bürger als Edelmann* during his third tour of America.[45] Those
sessions took place in New York on December 30 and 31, 1921 and directly preceded the last of thirty lieder, chamber music, and orchestral
concerts that he gave in the United States between October 26, 1921 and
January 3, 1922.[46]

En route from America to Germany, Strauss visited London, where he conducted concerts on January 17 and 23, 1922 with the London Symphony Orchestra at the Royal Albert Hall. At the first of those engagements, the program included *Don Juan*, which he recorded the following day for Columbia. Then, in 1926, he returned to London, where he recorded the music for the silent-film version of *Der Rosenkavalier* with the Augmented Tivoli Orchestra on April 13–14, for HMV.

His next series of recordings were made with the Berlin Staatskapelle and the Berlin Philharmonic. As one of the leading composers of the day, Strauss devoted the bulk of his studio time to his own music. Fortunately, however, Deutsche Grammophon also recognized the importance of securing some of Strauss's interpretations of Mozart, Beethoven, and Wagner. Of particular significance are his commercial recordings of Mozart's last three symphonies and the overture to *Die Zauberflöte*, which he made with the Berlin Staatskapelle between 1926 and 1928. Strauss was the first conductor to document Mozart's last three symphonies as a unit, and those recordings, along with his discs of Beethoven's Symphonies Nos. 5 and 7, were the only major symphonic recordings that he made of a composer other than himself.[47]

In 1929 and 1930, Strauss returned to the studio to record *Don Juan*, *Till Eulenspiegel*, and *Der Bürger als Edelmann* with the Berlin Staatskapelle. By this date, he had long since completed his major tone poems but had recorded only *Don Juan*, *Till Eulenspiegel*, *Ein Heldenleben*, and *Tod und Verklärung*.[48] Why such works as *Don Quixote*, *Symphonia domestica*, and *Eine Alpensinfonie* were not recorded during the 1920s, nor indeed during the 1930s and 1940s, is a conundrum. It is possible that the record companies felt that these works were not viable commercially because of their length and complexity, but in neither respect did they exceed *Ein Heldenleben*. Their absence from Strauss's early discography must remain a mystery.

Vienna celebrated Strauss's eightieth birthday in June, 1944 by mounting his important operas at the Staatsoper and by organizing a series of concerts and radio recordings with the Philharmonic.[49] The composer-conductor's lengthy association with the city had begun with the premiere of his Violin Concerto on December 5, 1882,[50] although his debut with the Vienna Philharmonic was delayed until August, 17, 1906, when he substituted at short notice for an indisposed Karl Muck at Salzburg. On the strength of that performance, the orchestra invited him to conduct four of their subscription concerts at the Musikvereinsaal over the next two years.[51] He continued to work with the Philharmonic for a further forty years, and between February and June, 1944 he recorded many of his major tone poems with the orchestra on magnetic tape for broadcast by Reichssenders Wien.[52]

The podium

No discussion of Strauss's activities as a conductor would be complete without mentioning his controversial podium manner. His critics have suggested that his economical method was a sign of boredom with the music that he was performing, a notion that can be dismissed as naïve. At Meiningen and during the first term in Munich, his gestures lacked sophistication, prompting his father to write that "it is unattractive when conductors make such snake-like movements."[53] Franz suggested further that a conductor's left hand had no other function but to turn pages and that it should be motionless when conducting from memory. Richard quickly adopted his father's ideas and modified his technique accordingly. His restrained approach then became a feature of his podium style and, in later life, he argued that "The left hand has nothing to do with conducting. Its proper place is the waistcoat pocket from which it should only emerge to restrain or to make some minor gesture for which in any case a scarcely perceptible glance would suffice. It is better to conduct with the ear instead of with the arm: the rest follows automatically."[54] Strauss regularly used a long, thin, tapered baton and believed that shorter movements of the arm ensured the players' complete attention.[55] He also emphasized the need for the conductor to prepare the music with a decisive upbeat from the wrist, followed by an "extremely precise" downbeat. Furthermore, "the second half of the bar [was] immaterial" because he "frequently conduct[ed] it like an *alla breve*."[56] Along with a judicious use of the eye, these techniques, wittily caricatured in his tongue-in-cheek *Ten Golden Rules for the Album of a Young Conductor*, then became the fundamental elements of Strauss's podium style.[57]

Ten Golden Rules for the Album of a Young Conductor
1. Remember that you are making music not to amuse yourself but to delight your audience.
2. You should not perspire when conducting: only the audience should get warm.
3. Conduct *Salome* and *Elektra* as if they were by Mendelssohn: fairy music.
4. Never look encouragingly at the brass, except with a short glance to give an important cue.
5. But never let the horns and woodwind out of your sight: if you can hear them at all they are still too strong.
6. If you think that the brass is not blowing hard enough, tone it down another shade or two.
7. It is not enough that you yourself should hear every word the soloist sings – you know it off by heart anyway: the audience must be able to follow without effort. If they do not understand the words they will go to sleep.

8. Always accompany a singer in such a way that he can sing without effort.

9. When you think you have reached the limits of *prestissimo*, double the pace.*

10. If you follow these rules carefully you will, with your fine gifts and your great accomplishments, always be the darling of your listeners.

(*c.* 1922)

* Today (1948) I should like to amend this as follows: go twice as slowly (addressed to the conductors of Mozart!).

Strauss's death on September 8, 1949 ignited a debate that quickly proved divisive. While some commentators lamented his passing as the end of the great Austro-German Romantic school of composition, others considered him no more than an artistic dinosaur whose contribution to music effectively ceased with the premiere of *Elektra*. Few, however, discussed his achievements as a conductor and the profound effect that his practices and principles had on subsequent generations of performers. His reforms at Munich during the 1890s influenced the Mozart styles of Fritz Busch, George Szell, Herbert von Karajan, Sir John Pritchard, and Wolfgang Sawallisch; his restrained podium style was adopted famously by the Hungarian-born conductor, Fritz Reiner; and his advocacy of new music helped secure a place in the repertoire for works that might otherwise have been overlooked. It is clear, then, that Strauss's achievements as a conductor were legion. One must ask, therefore, why his activities as a performer have failed to inspire serious research until relatively recently.[58] The answer of course lies in his phenomenal success as a composer. But to ignore his work as a performing artist is a mistake, because Strauss was proud of his achievements as a conductor and used his rich and varied experiences on the podium to inform his work as a creative musician.

16 Strauss and the sexual body: the erotics of humor, philosophy, and ego-assertion

BRYAN GILLIAM

Affirmation of the will must properly be called affirmation of the body.   RICHARD STRAUSS (1893)[1]

[In Strauss's work,] the main lines reveal themselves: a philosophical one, a humorous one, and an erotic one.   PAUL BEKKER (1909)[2]

What Paul Bekker observed in his *Musikdrama der Gegenwart* had been evolving in Strauss's artistic personality for nearly two decades. In his "breakaway" tone poem *Don Juan* (1888), the erotic and the humorous are inseparable, while the philosophical, latent but unreflective, had not yet become a symmetrical part of this equilateral triangle. Within a few years, however, Strauss would go through a period of intensive reading, discussion, and introspection that bore fruit in a series of philosophically informed creative products: the composer's operatic debut, *Guntram* (1893), the second cycle of tone poems (*Till Eulenspiegel, Also sprach Zarathustra, Don Quixote*, and *Ein Heldenleben*), the two symphonies of the early twentieth century (*Symphonia domestica* and *Eine Alpensinfonie*), and finally the operas *Feuersnot* and *Salome*.

Without doubt, Bekker's three elements endure in Strauss's later works: the playful erotics of *Der Rosenkavalier, Arabella*, and *Die Liebe der Danae*; the humor of *Intermezzo* and *Die schweigsame Frau*; or the philosophical in such pieces as the *Deutsche Motette* and the *Metamorphosen*. But it was only in the music of the 1890s and the beginning of the twentieth century that they were so profoundly intermingled, each one feeding off the other to produce the creative spark of these often misunderstood musical works. This triangular entanglement had a singular motivation, one central to the young Strauss's developing artistic personality: the desire to reject Arthur Schopenhauer's concept of the denial of the Will. It is only in relation to this philosophical concern that Strauss's treatment of the erotic and the ironic becomes comprehensible.

In praising "affirmation," the composer echoed Schopenhauer's own words from Book IV of *The World as Will and Representation*: "The body of man is already the objectivity of the will ... instead of affirmation of the will, we can also say affirmation of the body."[3] Strauss knew, however, that Schopenhauer considered the sexual act a grave danger; it was the purest expression of the will to life, the "strongest affirmation of life," while that very life (the direct product of carnal assertion) was one of suffering and inevitable death. Thus it was that Strauss, who had by the mid 1890s rejected the notion of redemption through music, now embraced Nietzsche, who transformed Schopenhauer's fatalistic "will to life" into a celebratory "will to power," affirming the life-generating force that the latter sought to deny. Nietzsche's Zarathustra, who decried the "despisers of the body" as being unable to create beyond themselves, ignited an anti-philistine, anti-bourgeois flame within Strauss.[4] If the Individual were the measure of *all* things, that being – that human body – should be able to laugh, think, create, and, indeed, procreate. During his second conducting term in Munich (beginning in 1894) and especially after his move to Berlin (in 1898), the composer was determined to shock his audience with the graphic, the outrageous, and, particularly, the sexual.

Redemption through sex: *Feuersnot*

Those in Strauss's small circle of friends at this time were not only aware of Strauss's deep immersion in nineteenth-century German philosophy but also active participants in an ongoing discussion of music and metaphysics during that critical decade of the 1890s, when the composer's worldview began to grow and flourish. The earliest record we have was written by one of his most influential intellectual friends, Arthur Seidl, who was born in Munich a year before Strauss, was his schoolmate, attended philosophy lectures at the University of Munich with him during the winter semester 1882–3, and was in Weimar during Strauss's tenure there. Seidl was among the first to note Strauss's Socratic method of appearing as a blank slate, as an unreflective Bavarian so that "in this disguise" he could ultimately show his opponents even deeper wisdoms.[5] In practice the disguise worked too well; Strauss managed to fool many well into the twentieth century and beyond.[6] In *Feuersnot*, the first opera to follow *Guntram*, the central point of the work, according to Strauss, was the protagonist Kunrad's final narrative attacking the self-satisfied Wagner-philistines of Munich. Contemporary reception shows that humor and eroticism obscured this vital message.

Strauss's 1894 apppointment as Kapellmeister of the Munich Court Opera had been poisoned early on. After *Guntram*'s November, 1895 failure, an event intended to crown Strauss's new position, promises for future performances were broken. Beneath the surface, he was seething against what he believed to be a narrow, indolent, self-satisfied Bavarian bourgeoisie, and he was determined to compose his second opera as a vehicle with which to pour scorn on "beer-and-wurst"-consuming dilettantes who had failed to appreciate his first work for the stage. He would achieve his aim with humor, but by no means a kind or innocent type – rather a Nietzschean one, a laughter dismissing all current social, religious, and artistic institutions, the brash, iconoclastic laughter (*lachender Tod*) of Siegfried on Brünnhilde's mountaintop at the end of Act III of Wagner's opera.

Such joviality was, no doubt, informed by Zarathustra's mountainous laughter in "Of Reading and Writing":

> You look up when you feel the need for elevation. And I look down because I am elevated. Who among you can laugh and be elevated at the same time? Whoever climbs the highest mountains laughs at all tragic plays and tragic seriousness. Brave, unconcerned, mocking, violent – thus wisdom wants us … I believe only in a god who could dance … Not by wrath does one kill but by laughter. Come, let us kill the spirit of gravity![7]

The dance, especially the waltz – drunken, brash, and overwrought – became a major topos for Strauss beginning with his *Also sprach Zarathustra*, first appearing on the stage in *Feuersnot* in unabashed vulgarity, then with self-destructive maenadic movements in *Elektra*, and, of course, with costumed irony in *Der Rosenkavalier*. Indeed, it is hard to think of a Strauss opera without a reference to dance (*Ariadne*'s *commedia dell'arte*, *Intermezzo*'s waltzes, *Arabella*'s ball, the Dionysian dances of *Daphne*, and so forth). Thus, it was without a trace of sentimentality that Strauss called Johann Strauss, Jr. the "laughing Genius of Vienna."[8] In *Nietzsche contra Wagner* the philosopher reminds us that Wagner swims and floats, but does not dance; Strauss, however, used the bodily gesture of dance throughout his life as a response to Wagner, as the signifier for an artist free of metaphysics.

Even before *Guntram*'s failure in Munich, Strauss, now converted to Nietzsche and Stirner, sought to make manifest his rejection of Schopenhauer, something he had not yet done in a musical work. His first instinct was to compose another opera, one that pitted a "laughing philosopher" against a narrow-minded, backward village. The idealist was named Till Eulenspiegel and the backwater village (a thinly disguised Munich) was the town of Schilda. In the opera scenario, the hapless, empty-headed townspeople at first sentence Till to death, then ultimately make him their mayor.[9] Strauss abandoned the idea, opting for a tone poem version instead. To understand fully the philosophical basis of *Feuersnot* we must first consider *Till Eulenspiegel*, his first modern artistic manifesto, presented in the symphonic genre.

If this tone poem "acted as a kind of artistic manifesto," according to Charles Youmans, "it did so partly because Strauss for the first time used a method of ironic disguise that he would retain even after he moved on to opera."[10] As James Hepokoski and Walter Werbeck have shown, the "central conflict" of *Till Eulenspiegel* was, from its very conception, the protagonist's encounter with the narrow, pedantic, self-satisfied philistines.[11] *Till Eulenspiegel* began a series of post-*Guntram* tone poems, each one becoming increasingly graphic in the presentation of its program, whether a literary source or the invention of its composer. But the pattern became clear; a humorous iconoclast would precede a serious one: thus Till was followed by his alter-ego, Zarathustra, and the anti-heroic Don Quixote gave way to the hero of *Ein Heldenleben*. *Till* initiated the pattern, but what Strauss still wanted, above all, was a major statement for the operatic stage, for he saw opera, above all other genres, as his ultimate artistic goal. He searched for various options until he came across an outlandish Flemish saga entitled *The Extinguished Flames of Audenaerde* in a collection of Flemish sagas published in German translation in 1843.

The story takes place in a narrow-minded town, where the mayor's daughter humiliates a young man who is avenged by a wise old hermit-magician who extinguishes all fire in the village: no light, fuel, energy, or warmth. The sorcerer explains that fire can only be restored if the offending woman stands in the town square and removes her clothes. Each citizen is given a candle, which is ignited from a flame emanating from her backside.

Strauss suggested the story to his friend, the poet Ernst von Wolzogen, who, completely at one with Strauss's worldview at this time, knew precisely what the composer was trying to articulate with this obscure saga. He, too, embraced Wagner, but distanced himself from the conservative Wahnfried circle, which included Wolzogen's estranged half-brother, Hans. Soon, Wolzogen saw a way to transform the bawdy Flemish saga into an opera libretto:

> I have the following idea: *Feuersnot* – one act – setting old Munich in legendary Renaissance period. The young love hero [Kunrad] is *himself* the magician, the *great old man*, his mentor, whom the good Münchner had once driven out of town, [and] does not appear [on the stage]. At the urging of the town officials and citizens, the naughty girl [Diemut] offers her virginity to the young magician in order to restore light [i.e. fire] to the city. When love unites itself with the magic of genius even the most annoying philistine sees the light![12]

He recognized from the beginning that the central element of this project was the intimate relationship between creative power and sexual desire, a power that comes not from above but from within, as Wolzogen explains:

> Art, at least for cultured people, offers life primarily light, color, warmth, deeper meaning. Every true artist is a Prometheus who creates humans in the image of God. But he does not need to steal the distant heavenly light for his creatures; he can take the fire from earth, because:
>
> All warmth springs from woman,
> All light stems from love ...
>
> For that is the very moral of this little [libretto].[13]

Thus, *Feuersnot* is not an opera about artistic inspiration derived from lofty notions of some quasi-metaphysical "eternal-feminine" or the like: rather from sensual urges, which include libido, genitalia, erotic secretion, and sexual fire.

It is hard to fathom a scenario more difficult to stage even by today's standards, but that is precisely the challenge Strauss set for himself and Wolzogen. *Till Eulenspiegel* admittedly lacked the blatantly erotic, and this new scenario provided ample material in its recasting of the basic elements of the Eulenspiegel story. No longer was the credo a Wagnerian "redemption through love," but an unabashed "redemption through sex," a potent symbol for the affirmation of the Will. Thus love and sexual passion are consciously, even conspicuously, separated from any context of idealism – a separation reinforced through humor and graphic orchestration, often working together. As early as 1893, Strauss described the post-coital bliss on a woman's face: "That smile – I have never seen such [an] expression of the true sensation of happiness! Is not the way to redemption of the Will to be sought here (in the condition of the receiving woman)! ... Affirmation of the will must properly be called the affirmation of the body."[14] With *Till Eulenspiegel* and *Feuersnot*, Strauss had created a two-pronged artistic manifesto: one symphonic, one operatic, and both carefully manipulated beneath a bright, energetic, sonic surface of ironic wit. Perhaps for this reason, Adorno believed *Feuersnot* to be the most characteristically Straussian in all its controlled spontaneity. If anyone beyond Strauss's inner circle recognized what the composer was up to, it was certainly Adorno, who easily recognized Strauss's newly formulated idea of "redemption through sex": "[Strauss's] ego-ideal is now fully identified with the Freudian genital-character, who is uninhibitedly out for his own pleasure and is kindly disposed to pleasure as such, tolerant towards extravagance and occasionally toward perversion as well. In *Feuersnot*, the deflowering of the [mayor's daughter] is officially celebrated by the town."[15] *Feuersnot* failed to become a mainstay in the operatic repertoire, and one wonders whether Strauss truly intended this "non-opera" (as he called it)[16] to attain such status in the first place with its blatant obscurity: the cabaret-like in-jokes, the over-the-top sexual innuendoes, and the precious textual puns lampooning Wagner and others. This early Berlin period was a time when Strauss was hunting around for various sexual comedies for the operatic stage or even the ballet. Frank Wedekind, whose *Erdgeist* (*Earth Spirit*) Strauss attended in 1906, earlier tried to lure Strauss to the musical stage with a racy satirical ballet scenario entitled *Die Flöhe* (*The Fleas*). In this "dance" a little insect gets beneath the skirt of a young woman, offering ample opportunity for light-hearted, even slapstick, choreography. Strauss also tried his hand at writing another, less ambitious satirical-flimflam Eulenspiegel-like opera libretto of his own (*Ekke und Schnittlein*), but stopped after two drafts. He turned it over to Wolzogen, who made a complete libretto now known as *Coabbradibosimpur; or, The Bad Boys of Seville*, but while the libretto contains some musical marginalia by Strauss, he dropped the project in favor of *Salome*.

Salome contra *Parsifal*

The most overtly sexual opera that Strauss ever wrote was *Salome*, which he viewed as a pendant work to *Feuersnot*. Though *Salome* was clearly the more successful opera, neither work has been fully understood: humor, irony, and satire obscured the bizarre sexuality of *Feuersnot*, and it is safe to say that *Salome*'s surface eroticism (and the fact that the title role is female) overshadowed its own share of irony, humor, and satire. Until recently, few have commented on the critical implications of *Salome*'s subtitle ("Music Drama"). *Salome* can be seen as part of a new century's sea change towards the *femme nouvelle*, and Strauss was hardly oblivious to the huge marketing potential in composing operas with such strong, central female characters as Salome and Elektra. But there were also important psychological implications, rich literary allusions, and another opportunity for an open artistic response to Wagner, whose worldview focussed more on male heroes with the woman serving as a redeeming force.

Composing a work such as *Salome* and labeling it as a "music drama," thereby inverting Wagner – the *ewig weiblich* seduces the redeemer (John the Baptist), then has him executed – was a calculated affront by Strauss. The House of Wahnfried was aghast, particularly as Strauss exploited their outrage for all it was worth, even to the point of personal insult. On Good Friday, 1905, Strauss played (and sang) the final scene of the not yet orchestrated *Salome* on the piano for Cosima Wagner, who was visiting Berlin at the Hotel Bellevue. She was horrified. "This is madness!" she exclaimed.[17] Thereafter, they never spoke to one another.

The split between Strauss and Wahnfried had now reached the point of no return, though the process of separation had been gradual, beginning fifteen years earlier when Strauss, as Kapellmeister in Weimar, shared with Cosima his recently composed erotic masterpiece, *Don Juan*. Then Strauss was on friendly terms with Wagner's widow, and he performed the tone poem on the piano from start to finish. Cosima, despite her maternal sympathies towards this young talent, could not hide her feelings. She was appalled, not only by its flagrant eroticism but also by the cinematic concreteness of his sonic narrative and musical materials. In short, she found the work devoid of any transcending qualities, and she strongly urged him to follow his heart and not his brain.[18]

Strauss paid no heed, and by the time of the Hotel Bellevue incident Cosima had reached the breaking-point. The friction also extended to Cosima's son, Siegfried, whose friendship with Strauss came to an end shortly after *Salome*. Siegfried wrote an open letter bemoaning Strauss's modernist direction, declaring that, thanks to *Salome*, his father "has already turned in his grave." He accused Strauss of playing the role of musical speculator: of "tailoring" his operas for money, for momentary "sensationalism and success," playing to the lowest appetites of the modern audience.[19]

If *Feuersnot*, in its medieval Munich setting, was a satirical response to ossified Wagnerism via *Die Meistersinger von Nürnberg*, then *Salome* was an even greater sacrilege, an ironic response to *Parsifal*, where the redeemer is not redeemed, rather beheaded. Scholars of twentieth-century German opera have, over the past decades, observed the creative crisis, the hiatus of important German opera between *Parsifal* and *Salome*. What has not been emphasized, however, is that the solution to the crisis was *Salome*'s specific rejection of the very "cause" of that crisis, the religious *Parsifal*. If few people understood the connection, it was not lost on Siegfried Wagner, who dreaded the day when, after copyright, *Parsifal* might literally share the same "stage floor boards" upon which the "disgusting" (*ekelhafte*) Salome had walked.[20]

Strauss cannot realistically have believed that he could win Cosima and her son over to the "left-wing" Wagner cause. Certain aspects of *Salome* were, frankly, disgusting: Salome's pathological narcissism, Herod's incestuous glances, the bloody execution culminating in a final monologue blurring the boundaries between lust, violence, necrophilia, and the like. No less provocative were the unrequited homosexual desire of the Page (set for mezzo) for Narraboth, the bisexual ambiguities in Herod's character, and, of course, the Dance of the Seven Veils itself.

Strauss knew Huysmans's *A rebours*, which had partially inspired Wilde's play, especially when that novel describes Gustave Moreau's *Salome Dancing before Herod*:

> [Her] nipples hardening under the friction of her whirling necklaces; the diamonds adhering to the moist skin glitter; her bracelets, her belts, her rings, flash and sparkle … [She was] that superhuman, strange Salome of whom [the protagonist] dreamt. No longer was she just the dancer who by a shameless gyration of her hips wrests a lustful, ruttish cry from an old man, who destroys the resoluteness and breaks the will of the king with thrusts of her breasts, undulations of her belly, and quiverings of her thighs.[21]

In Wilde's play there is surely a nervous fascination with various forms of decay and the confusion between art and life, even a "profound surface" that recalls Bloch's pejorative against Strauss. Yet, ultimately, Strauss was not at one with Wilde's worldview, a fact that continues to cloud the opera's reception even today. Despite all his internal antagonisms between Irish Anglicanism and the Roman Catholic Church, despite the inner inconsistencies with regard to Christianity itself, Wilde was, in the end, a believer. From Oscar Wilde's *De profundis*, we know that the playwright ultimately found solace in Christ the "Artist" who performed the great miracles, as reported by Jochanaan in Wilde's play. Accordingly, Christ

> could bring peace to souls in anguish, [so] that those who touched his garments or his hands forgot their pain; or that as he passed by on the highway of life people who had seen nothing of life's mystery, saw it clearly, and others who had been deaf to every voice but that of pleasure heard for the first time the voice of love and found it as "musical as Apollo's lute."[22]

In *Salome*, in this cauldron of mixed pre-Christian elements (Judaism, paganism, and the like), Wilde believed that Christ would, in some form, finally show the way. Strauss, however, was deaf to the Apollonian lyre and had no interest in religious miracles; he cut almost all references to Christ's miracles from his play. The image of Christ the redeemer held no inherent attraction for him; indeed, he found it abhorrent.

The general public failed to understand Strauss's lack of sympathy for John the Baptist and, as late as the 1930s, the composer believed he still needed to explain that he had composed Jochanaan "as a clown," because "a preacher in the desert, especially one who feeds on locusts, seems infinitely ridiculous to me. Only because I had already caricatured the five Jews and also poked fun at Father Herod did I feel that I had to follow the law of contrast and write a pedantic-Philistine motif for four horns to characterize Jochanaan."[23] Deaf to Strauss's cruel humor, contemporary critics disparaged the "Philistine motif" for being precisely what it was supposed to be. Paul Bekker characterized Jochanaan's music as that of a soap-box orator, as overwrought Mendelssohn.[24] Alfred Heuss criticized, likewise, that same music's sentimentality: "Who would believe that the sentimental chords of the horns, which are unimaginatively repeated, actually characterize the crude prophet."[25]

Parsifal and Jochanaan both reject physical pleasure, yet the outcomes could hardly be more different. Parsifal redeems the collective in a manner reminiscent of Diemut, who however achieves it by the opposite means: she offers her virginity for the sake of the philistine community, and light is restored. Salome retains her virginity, sublimated by ordering the execution of her love object, and is, in turn, murdered beneath the dark shields of Herod's guards; light is extinguished ("Put out the torches," Herod exclaims, "Hide the moon, hide the stars!"). Herod's court may be purged of two dangerous, narcissistic elements – sexual pathology and extreme asceticism (an inverted hedonism) – but this collective is in no way redeemed.

"Affirmation of the body" thus succeeded in *Feuersnot*, while the denial of the body, through perverse chastity, proved to be quite dangerous in *Salome*, a work Strauss called a "scherzo with a fatal denouement."[26] Strauss had exhausted his preoccupation with bodily affirmation, redemption (Wagnerian and non-Wagnerian), and its inversion. His artistic engagement with Hofmannsthal, another artist who believed that Wagner's oeuvre had become a dead end in a modern world, could not have come at a better time. Hofmannsthal, who had rejected decadence around the time Wilde's play had been translated into German, would take Strauss toward a new type of modern direction, one away from the solipsism of symbolist poetry towards the social gesture of drama.

Elektra as Dionysian tragedy

While Hofmannsthal was writing his play *Elektra*, he was still operating under the aura of Nietzsche, for although Salome and Elektra – and Kunrad and Elektra, for that matter – are sexually exact opposites (that offer some compelling negative binaries), they are still ego-assertive individuals on the periphery of an indolent society. In the recognition scene – when she sees her brother for the first time since their father, Agamemnon, was murdered – Elektra explains how she was once beautiful, that she had her share of sexual desire, but now that has all been sacrificed; her hair is as unkempt, matted, and unwashed as the ascetic John the Baptist. Elektra says to her brother, Orestes: "Do you imagine, when I took pleasure in my body, that [Agamemnon's] sighs, his groans did not penetrate to my bed? The dead are jealous: and [Agamemnon] sent hatred to my side, hollow-eyed hatred to be my bridegroom." Hofmannsthal goes on to liken hatred to a monstrous viper that slithers into Elektra's sleepless bed forcing her "to know all that goes on between a man and a woman." Elektra confesses that she was not without her wedding night, sacrificing her virginity to "hollow-eyed hatred," and feeling the "agony of childbirth [bringing] nothing into the world."

In the polarities of Salome and Elektra – virgin–non-virgin, innocent-ruined, beautiful–defaced, sexual–asexual – we find some fundamental similarities: two strong, ego-assertive women with the power to kill, both with distorted views of sexual relationships, and both, in the end, undone by their own neurotic fixations. It is no coincidence that Max Reinhardt, who directed both plays in Berlin, chose the same actress to play both roles: Gertrude Eysoldt. Her performances mesmerized Strauss, who later suggested that her riveting presentation of Elektra partly inspired his decision to transform the play into an opera.[27]

But the dialectical combined with the philosophical, namely Nietzsche. As suggested above (see Chapter 7, pp. 120–1), Hofmannsthal approached Greek myth from the standpoint of Nietzsche's *The Birth of Tragedy*, wielding the tragic Dionysian as an ego-assertive, modernizing social force. A further catalyst for Hofmannsthal's turn towards Greek myth were the lectures of Alfred von Berger, Privatdozent and later professor in aesthetics and philosophy at the University of Vienna (1887–96) as well as dramaturg at the city's Burgtheater.[28] What Berger consolidated for Hofmannsthal was a deep understanding of the work of both Freud and Breuer, as well as Nietzsche. In an article entitled "Surgery of the Soul," Berger lauded the Breuer–Freud studies in hysteria as "the herald of a new psychology."[29] His lectures on "Beauty in Art" (which focussed on Nietzsche) and "The Dramaturgy of Ancient Tragedy" in the 1890s inspired Hofmannsthal to reread Nietzsche's *Birth of Tragedy* and devote himself to a modern approach to Greek drama, transfusing "the Greek ghosts and steering clear of German 'Classicism.'"[30]

According to Nietzsche, Socrates had drained tragedy of its life's blood, and it was not until Wagner (or so he thought at the time) that tragedy had been replenished. Hofmannsthal made no secret that his *Elektra*, which notably excludes any element of her sister, Iphigenia, was a modern response to the neoclassical Goethe. Strauss, too, heeded Nietzsche's call to challenge earlier idealized notions of neo-Socratic, "white-marble" Greek culture, and he later remarked that a central catalyst in his decision to compose *Elektra* was his desire to counter Johann Joachim Winkelmann with Hofmannsthal's "demonical, ecstatic Hellenism."[31]

Instead of the erotic "Dance of the Seven Veils" that Salome executes for the voyeuristic pleasure of Herod and his court, Elektra undertakes a nameless "Dance of Death" (*Totentanz*), and with that death, it is safe to say, went also Strauss's Nietzschean impulse. Humor and eroticism continued to be essential elements throughout Strauss's life, but his intense preoccupation with Schopenhauer and Nietzsche had, for the time being, come to an end. He would revisit it during his period of crisis in the years following the death of Hofmannsthal in 1929, but not in the context of an interdependence among sexuality, irony, and philosophy: a complex that had operated so powerfully in his process of maturation.

17 Strauss and the nature of music

CHARLES YOUMANS

Introduction: music about music

Though he occupies a modest corner of the pantheon, Richard Strauss produced what is arguably the most familiar ninety seconds of European music: the dazzling, radiant sunrise of *Also sprach Zarathustra* (1896), an iconic sound-tableau as deeply embedded in today's popular consciousness as the main theme of Beethoven's Fifth Symphony. Endlessly appropriated by artists high and low, this music sears itself instantly into the memory, with a thrilling brand of high-definition tone-painting calculated for maximum emotional and visual effect. Strauss would create a multitude of compelling musical illustrations during his seven-decade career, from the exquisite moonlight of "Die Nacht," Op. 10, No. 3 (1885) to the melancholy lark-song of "Im Abendrot" (1948). But in *Zarathustra* he spoke with a transcendent power not easily duplicated, by himself or anyone else.

Sensitive listeners will remark that this passage is not just a representation of nature *in* music, but a commentary on the nature *of* music. Beneath its masterful cinematography Strauss's *exordium* surveys all the technical elements of the art: the range of audible sound, the overtone series, the major and minor modes, the basic principles of functional harmony, and the western instrumentarium. Moreover, it pays homage to earlier musical creation-scenes, with clear echoes of Beethoven's Ninth, Wagner's *Das Rheingold*, Haydn's *Die Schöpfung* (*The Creation*), and any number of Bruckner symphonies. In a few eloquent moments, then, the work establishes three distinct layers of musical expression – a natural scene, a primer of the musical elements, a network of intertextual associations – and challenges the listener to sort out the relationships among them.

Strauss's interweaving of musical meanings in *Zarathustra* lived up to a claim he had articulated six years earlier in an exchange with Cosima Wagner, who chafed at the graphic qualities of *Don Juan* (1888). Walking the line between subservience and self-determination, Strauss explained that all his music had multiple levels of meaning, which existed independently and operated in tension. The "intelligence" (*Intelligenz*) of his tone-painting, he maintained, was balanced on a non-narrative level by "feeling" (*Gefühl*), as would always be the case for composers with a "deep artistic nature."[1] Cosima remained unconvinced, warning that flamboyant superficiality might cloud or conceal a work's underlying substance. Her young protégé would not be swayed, however, and they agreed to change the subject.

One hundred and twenty years later, it seems that Cosima had a point. Strauss scholarship has occupied itself for several decades now with a kind of excavation, by which a deceptively familiar exterior is dusted away to reveal unexpected, subtle, lost meanings. Sardonic parody beneath revolutionary sonorities in *Salome* (1905), modernist historicism folded into sumptuous tonality in *Der Rosenkavalier* (1910), incipient postmodernism hidden by musico-technical regression in the late operas, formal deformations outshone by narrative detail in the tone poems – the most interesting levels of signification in Strauss often require unearthing.[2]

The most important of these, I would suggest, has only begun to be explored. One of the few constants in Strauss's jarringly heterogeneous career is his lifelong interest in music "about" music.[3] However peculiar his individual compositions may seem, however different from what preceded or followed them, they almost always engage in some way with external musical material: a specific work, a composer, a style, a genre (other than the one in which he is composing), an issue of form, and so on. This predilection manifests itself from his earliest student efforts, scribbled on the sly during Gymnasium lectures, to the valedictory effusions of a cultural monument who seemed to have outlived himself. Critics noticed it long before Strauss's death; Ernst Otto Nodnagel predicted in 1902 that Strauss's "playing with art" would lead to the "end of music," while Adorno remarked (in his lesser-known 1924 essay) that *Ariadne auf Naxos* (1912; revised 1916) crowned a tendency in which "the work of art itself becomes the theme of the work of art."[4] Today, however, it remains largely uncommented upon, especially as a potential hallmark of his oeuvre as a whole.

In this essay I consider the importance of *Musik über Musik* in Strauss by discussing four types that are both distinct and wide-ranging. This set is by no means exhaustive, and the list of works considered in each case could easily be expanded. But with a preliminary treatment I hope to indicate something of the breadth and variety to be discovered when we tune our ear to Strauss's musical ruminations on the nature of music. Such an awareness seems increasingly useful for an understanding of the composer and his reception.

The "Indian summer"

Nowhere is Strauss's tendency towards musical self-reflection more evident than in the last period of his creative life, the so-called "Indian summer," when a final blossoming of inspiration yielded a long list of works and two universally acknowledged masterpieces: *Metamorphosen*, TrV 290 (1945) and the orchestral lieder that came to be known as the *Vier letzte Lieder*, TrV 296.[5] Here, as so often with Strauss, his own life served as subject matter and artistic catalyst. The music surveys the three main genres of the composer's early maturity – "absolute" instrumental music, programmatic music for orchestra, and the Wagnerian vocal–orchestral medium – with references to particular works in each case. Thus we have a kind of musical autobiography, with late music that recalls and rethinks specific early compositions or compositional approaches. And most strikingly, each of the referents was itself a self-conscious artistic evaluation of a pre-existing style; the octogenarian was revisiting a series of youthful experiments in which he had sampled identities in search of his own.[6]

The late music is therefore not just about music, but about music that is about music. The Sonatinas for Winds, for example, No. 1 in F major, TrV 288 (1943) and No. 2 in E♭ major, TrV 291 (1945), hark back to the Serenade in E♭ major, Op. 7 (1881) and the Suite in B♭ major, Op. 4 (1884), with which Strauss attracted the attention of Hans von Bülow and set his professional career on a fast track. With these essays in Classicism, the young man considered whether the music loved by his father (and by Brahms) could remain a living art in the twentieth century. The answer was a qualified "no," the qualification being that, for a musician, this dead art was great fun. Hence the absurd spectacle in 1945 of a "Sonatina" that lasted over a thousand bars, with an endless, playful spinning-out of the same motives; we hear the same approach in the Oboe Concerto, TrV 292 (1945; revised 1948) and the *Duett-Concertino*, TrV 293 (1947). Strauss's harsh characterization of these latter pieces – "workshop doodlings without an iota of music-historical significance" – explains obliquely why in the 1880s he had looked elsewhere for his compositional future, in spite of the promising reception of his music in this vein.[7] The elderly Strauss did not regret that choice, but nor did he forget the pleasure to be found in this particular cul-de-sac.

Metamorphosen, a programmatic work for orchestra but not explicitly a "tone poem," reopens the central questions of Strauss's maturation. As we have learned from recent studies of Strauss's private documents, the triumphant emergence of a finished musical genius in *Don Juan* and *Till Eulenspiegels lustige Streiche* (1895) proceeded from no small degree of private trauma.[8] Three mentors had been cast aside, conclusively, unrepentantly, but nonetheless painfully: Franz Strauss, ardent defender of the formal and stylistic legacy of the Classics; Hans von Bülow, who by the 1880s advocated the Brahmsian modernization of that legacy; and Alexander Ritter, arch-Wagnerian and Strauss's tutor in Schopenhauerian musical idealism. In their place Strauss adopted the spiritual guidance of Nietzsche, whose optimism, so strongly felt in *Till*, relied on a counterweight of nihilistic perspectivism, or indeed existential terror, which is what motivates Zarathustra's collapse (mm. 329–36 of the tone poem). This opposition remains for all to hear, unsolved and unsolvable, in the alternation of B and C at the music's end.

When Strauss returned to this genre in *Metamorphosen*, disguising it as a "study for strings," he relived his leap into the gravity-free world of decentered subjectivity. But now Goethe rather than Nietzsche provided the intellectual stimulus, with a poem used as inspiration, if not a kind of hidden program: *Niemand wird sich selber kennen* (*No One Can Know Himself*).⁹ A flurry of musical intertextuality – including the obvious quotation of the *Eroica* but also stylistic or contextual interactions with Beethoven's Fifth Symphony, *Tod und Verklärung*, *Tristan und Isolde*, and *Ein Heldenleben* (1898) – dramatizes the psychological struggle of a hero who, unlike his models, has no hope of a final triumph, because he can fully comprehend neither his world nor himself.¹⁰ The work's pessimism obviously comments on the German cultural and political catastrophe, yet it also reflects Strauss's own crisis of subjectivity – the frightful predicament of a self-reliant artist without a reliable self in which to ground his artistic expression.

The celebrated *Vier letzte Lieder* (the label did not originate with Strauss) contrast sharply with the despair of *Metamorphosen*, not by anything resembling optimism but with an acceptance that exudes wisdom. The richness is all Wagner; no composer wielded the intoxicating power of Wagner's harmonic and orchestrational medium more easily than Strauss, and no composer loved it more. Yet paradoxically these songs also distance themselves from Wagner, vocally, in ways none too subtle: astonishing lyricism; soaring melismas at once elegant and exquisitely overextended; vivid madrigalisms; a stunning range of vocal color, gently and sensitively supported by the orchestra. Here as in *Guntram* (1893), his superficially epigonic first opera long since buried in the back yard (literally), Strauss proved himself a Wagnerian anti-Wagnerian, a disciple who through betrayal found a deeper fidelity. As in *Metamorphosen*, we hear reminiscences of compositions produced as the young Strauss fought to free himself from Wagner: experienced listeners will easily discern not just *Guntram* but *Tod und Verklärung*; "Morgen," Op. 27, No. 4; and *Der Rosenkavalier*, the Straussian *Meistersinger*. Now the memories speak contented resignation, however, in tribute to Pauline, whose voice we hear as a memory in Strauss's sweeping soprano melodies, and whose companionship fills the crowning song of the set, "Im Abendrot" ("Through sorrow and joy we have walked hand in hand"). Nature, family, and artistic creation, the creed of the *Symphonia domestica* (1903), return here with an unexpected sublimity.[11]

Music and dance

Strauss's habit of alluding to his own music earned him a fair degree of notoriety, especially with the naked self-absorption of *Ein Heldenleben*, *Symphonia domestica*, and their operatic descendant *Intermezzo* (1923). This tendency had its source, however, in a broader inclination to infuse his works with other people's music, a practice that tended to complicate, perhaps wittingly, the immediacy traditionally associated with musical expression. Günter Brosche's chapter in this volume offers an abundance of examples: the French Baroque in *Der Bürger als Edelmann* (1912; revised 1917), Croatian folk song in *Arabella* (1932), the *Querelle des bouffons* in *Capriccio* (1941), seventeenth- and eighteenth-century Italian opera along-side quotations from the Fitzwilliam Virginal Book in *Die schweigsame Frau* (1934), and of course Wagnerian and Mozartian moments scattered liberally throughout the works. For those with ears to hear, Strauss's music is not unlike a collage built from discrete fragments of compositional reception.

The profusion of references extends even to general musical categories, and especially to dance, which Strauss brought into his musical discourse at crucial moments, though not always with the clearest of motivations.[12] The superficiality and formalist nature of dance imposed an objectivity, or an appearance of objectivity, that in turn allowed Strauss to build climaxes that do not rely on subjective expression for their power. Thus *Also sprach Zarathustra*, *Salome*, and *Der Rosenkavalier*, works at the heart of the Straussian canon, all reach their culmination through dance, even though, as the composer would explain in 1940, dance represented the antipode of the Hauseggerian musical "expression" to which he had ostensibly pledged himself under Ritter's guidance.[13] Reflecting on "musical inspiration," a Strauss wise with age assessed the Hanslick–Hausegger conflict in surprisingly even-handed terms; these two nineteenth-century figures had advocated different but equally valuable kinds of music: one originating in "the desire to give artistic form to religious adoration," the other in the dance, the ultimate source (Strauss claimed) of Hanslick's "forms moved in sounding."[14] From this vantage-point he freely admitted that his music owed as much to one side as to the other.

Salome, the work that made Strauss a superstar, ends not just with a dance but with a deliberately bad one. We have long known that he put little effort into composing it; Mahler was appalled to learn, when treated to a performance of the entire work by the composer in a Strasbourg piano shop, that the Dance of the Seven Veils, the musical and dramatic cap-stone, had yet to be composed. How, Mahler wondered, could the musical substance of a Salome opera not be derived from the dance? What he did not grasp, and what Strauss refused to explain to him, was that this would be "the music that Herod likes" (in the words of Alex Ross): kitsch, drivel, vulgarity, suited to the taste of a royal buffoon.[15] Such a choice required a self-confidence, or a recklessness, that may well have been unique to Strauss *c.* 1900. But nonetheless, it, as much as any other feature, created the delicious horror that audiences found so appealing; ostentatious tast-lessness served as a complementary extremism to nauseating dissonance, radical tone-painting, and overblown seriousness (John the Baptist). Its very weakness, then, plays no small role in transferring the listener to the diegesis, an alternate reality come to life. And in the process, the music abandons all pretense of revealing the composer's inner realm of experience.

The waltz in *Zarathustra* aims at something similar. According to Strauss, the work's overall form traced an evolutionary path towards the "superhuman" (*Übermensch*), Zarathustra's central prophecy.[16] Our expect-ation, then, carefully cultivated for over twenty minutes, is that we will hear a musical rendering of this gravity-free higher state of existence. In Nietzsche's text, however – which Strauss consulted in detail – Zarathustra recognizes that his vision is flawed by his own humanity, the very weak-nesses that produce the comical dysfunctionality of Herod's palace.[17] Any hope of permanently transcending human limitations is in vain, Nietzsche tells us, doomed by the "little man" and his need for redemption. The mean-ing of eternal recurrence is an endless cycle of joy and disgust (*Ekel*); even the greatest among us always "all too human."[18]

Zarathustra's recognition of this truth comes in the shattering catas-trophe of "Der Genesende" ("The convalescent"), mm. 329–36, a musical peripeteia based on the cold, grim Nature motive. In its aftermath we await its opposite, and discover that it is … a waltz. This is an odd choice, to say the least, but on the crucial points it proves curiously efficient: light-ness vs. intensity, physicality vs. spirituality, joy vs. fear, the present vs. the eternal, the collective vs. the isolated, the social vs. the private. Perhaps most importantly, it retreats from the preoccupations of an individual with his personal fate, and offers a glimpse, optimistically but with eyes wide open, of a happiness transcending subjectivity. For this step Strauss needed music that would place him outside himself. True to the implications of his comments some forty-five years later – in which a subjectively marked, Hauseggerian "expression" contrasted with an implicitly objective for-malism – he chose the dance. As in *Salome*, then, the qualities that struck some critics as irremediably wrong were precisely the ones that Strauss found right.

If the waltz is a goal in *Zarathustra*, it is the very substance of *Der Rosenkavalier*, even in the most sublime moments. The concluding trio for the Marschallin, Octavian, and Sophie, a monument of western musical culture for its soaring beauty and depth of feeling, grows out of the blasé and ordinary waltz that accompanies Mariandel's (the disguised Octavian's) rejection of Ochs ("Nein, nein! I trink' kein Wein").[19] This process of transformation captures musically the spiritual progress of the opera's central character, the Marschallin, even though the waltz is more directly associated with other characters. In Act I she takes the stage fresh from a romp in the sack with a seventeen-year-old man-boy, but then slips into melancholy as she considers the mystery of time. Like Zarathustra, the Marschallin must come to terms with her weaknesses, including the transience of her very existence; she must find a consolation that will not delude. A beautiful, enlightened, high-born woman, she stands on the threshold of middle age, contemplates a horrifying truth, and becomes, finally, a philosopher – to the sounds of music that has traveled a similar path to its own dignified enlightenment.[20]

When Hofmannsthal asked for "some old-fashioned Viennese waltz, half sweet, half cheeky," he must have recognized, at least intuitively, the potential for profound expression in the joyous superficiality of this dance.[21] We do not know whether he had heard *Zarathustra*, or what he thought of its waltz climax. He knew all too well, however, that Strauss the artist was defined by a pedestrian exterior hiding unimagined depth. Hofmannsthal saw that here the composer and his material became one. During the opera's genesis, as the Marschallin increased in importance, so too did the waltz, and in the final product both of them serve independently to push the farcical elements gradually to the background, or rather to bring about their transfiguration, which we witness, reverently, at the end. The Marschallin, Octavian, and Sophie are finally as much allegories as characters; they are states of human experience, to which the individuals abandon themselves while marveling at the mystery of it all. And somehow, this new consciousness and the music that embodies it have emerged through the mediation of a waltz. The roots of Hanslick's formalism detach expression from the subjective; the personal becomes universal by means of the dance.

The composer as theme

In several important cases, Strauss used music to consider the ultimate source of music: the composer. These works, which count among his best if not best known – *Ariadne auf Naxos* (the 1916 revision), *Intermezzo*, and *Capriccio* – thematize the question of music's meaning by making it the explicit concern of a dramatic character. In subject matter so deeply personal to Strauss, it is more important than ever to calibrate one's ear to his sense of irony, or risk colossal misunderstandings of an artist not inclined to suffer fools. The brilliance of his musical technique, or more precisely the power of his musical rhetoric, sets up illusions that are all too easy to believe, especially where seriousness and sincerity are the targets of his satire.

The myth of Ariadne, the daughter of Minos rescued by Dionysus (Bacchus) after Theseus abandoned her on the island of Naxos, had understandable resonance for Strauss, who saw himself as a twentieth-century, Nietzschean answer to the predicament in which music had been left by Wagnerian–Schopenhauerian metaphysical ideology. From the beginning of the project Strauss wanted to juxtapose Ariadne's tale with formulaic character-types drawn from *commedia dell'arte* and from *opera seria* in its eighteenth-century heyday: a Greek character animated by Wagner's high seriousness would be analyzed and brought down to earth by overtly artificial dramatic styles. The clash exposes Ariadne as stereotypical prima donna and her overblown solemnity as kitsch, while the *commedia* types emerge as something more than buffoons, with elements of truth easily recognized in their wisecracks. But in the end Ariadne is partially rehabilitated, for we see, through the comedians' eyes, that her suffering has something genuine in it. That is why the second version can conclude with an apotheosis of sorts, a sentimental reduction of what Nietzsche called Wagner's "high style." With her highfalutin $^6_4$ chords cut down to size by mockery and sheer contrast (the Bavarian beer-garden music of her antagonists), Ariadne's authentic profundity can unfold without self-caricature.[22]

Strauss's Composer, who became a significant character only with the opera's revision, would be the main critical target. We know that his art, *opera seria*, will be the one most damaged by the Master's decision to have the comedy and the tragedy performed at the same time. His very suffering, with all its melodrama, explains sufficiently why he must be made to suffer. The portrayal of this character is not without sympathy; we hear both genuine passion and deep technical competence in his utterances. And yet he is obsolete; when he declares that "music is a holy art," he is the voice of Strauss's past, a past that had been overcome. Music's dangerous seductive power is the real topic of the *Tristan*-esque G♭-to-B♭ mystery with which the Composer introduces Ariadne's paean to death, and that power is what created the need for a counterweight in the equally massive scene for Zerbinetta, and the more explicit conquest represented by Zerbinetta's seduction of the Composer. This relationship replays the story of Strauss's creative life. At the moment when music is recognized as a "holy art," the comedians arrive, and they are not to be suppressed. A typically Straussian battle among styles ensues (compare, for example, *Feuersnot* [1901]), ensuring that neither side will be able to forget the other.[23] As distinct and persuasive as the competing visions of Zerbinetta and Ariadne may be, in the end the piece works because of their interaction – especially in the final moments, where we view Ariadne's hyper-dramatic climax through the cool eyes and ears of Zerbinetta.

The light "conversation-piece" *Capriccio* follows Strauss's last tragedy *Die Liebe der Danae* in a manner not unlike the Ariadne–Zerbinetta succession. Notwithstanding the modest title, the opera has an underlying seriousness – Strauss called it a "theoretical comedy," a philosophical reflection without the typical pretentiousness – proving again that he did his most profound thinking in the most superficial settings. This time the composer is pitted against the poet, a worthwhile debate for someone whose creative career divided into periods of "absolute" music (during his apprenticeship), program music, and opera. Strauss freely admitted that for most of his life he did not know how to begin composing without a poetic stimulus; when kept waiting too long by a librettist he could become desperate. Yet in his operas as in his tone poems he was not one to let a text or poetic idea get in the way of a musical impulse, and so the debate between poetry and music, much on his mind as he wrote his first libretto since *Guntram*, had never really ended.[24]

Strauss's agnosticism, which usually manifested itself as indifference to religion but did have important moments of conscious reflection, occasionally found its way into his aesthetics, and nowhere more strongly than in *Capriccio*. Asked to decide whether pride of place belonged to music or words, the Countess cannot choose (although the opera ends before her deadline), and she leaves us by declining to answer: "Is there any ending that isn't trivial?" The course of the conversation has likewise refused to accept the terms of the debate; the famous "theatrical fugue" widens the discussion to three elements – rhythm, speech, and ordering of tones – and La Roche, the theater director modeled on Max Reinhardt, argues persuasively for a third way required by the inescapable shortcomings of composers and librettists. It seems, then, that we are meant to see the conversation as an end in itself, an encouragement to exchange simplistic commitment for wise uncertainty. Such a conclusion would explain the naïve, cheerful, archaic, detached musical style, rich in citations that are not the slightest bit rhetorically assertive. The asking of important unanswerable questions becomes its own end, the highest joy a human can hope to find. (The style and its motivation are similar in works such as the Oboe Concerto and the *Duett-Concertino*.)

And yet, Strauss does hint at his own answer, the answer expected of a composer, and even if he leaves it unarticulated, we all witness it, at the very beginning of the opera. The Sextet that opens *Capriccio* has always been considered one of its musical high-points; if it had fallen short, the work would have been a colossal flop, for the Countess's rapture is believable only if we too feel an instinctive attraction to the music.[25] We do, as it happens, and thus the conversation between poet and composer, as they wonder about the emotional/spiritual/psychological substance of her listening experience, might just as well be about us. In fact the characters push us strongly towards reflection on our own experience, through the striking presence of music that is not only heard in the story world but discussed there, and "consumed" in the most important sense. The distinction between an audience outside the drama and the characters within it is relatively unimportant at the beginning, for we are all outside the music, and we are all listening in on something wonderful and mysterious, something the very inexplicability of which is what prevents it from being named the winner of the debate. Its effect is disrupted only by the words of the conversers.

That disruption was forecast crudely by *Intermezzo*, a cinematic opera in which orchestral transitions shuttle us among numerous short scenes, approximating montage.[26] The result is to pull us again and again from absolute music into the real world; the transitions focus our attention on the dramatic way-stations that frame them. A prototype had been tried on the first page of the *Symphonia domestica*, where we hear a reverie bordered on both sides by the everyday, down-to-earth, physically suggestive music that was Strauss's first love.[27] Within this cocoon the music becomes Music, a moment of inspiration that we, having been placed on the outside, recognize as nothing more than a brief interruption of normal life. (One wonders whether the music was composed from his wife's perspective.) Strauss deflates his own ego even more assertively in *Intermezzo*, naming Robert Storch a conductor rather than a composer in the list of characters, and avoiding, throughout the plot, any indication that Storch's creative gift makes him different from other people (aside from the musical reminiscences that float into his head during the card game; but even this is shared by the tenor). The treatment of autobiography and of artisthood here is radically different from what we find in any other Austro-German "serious" musician at the time, for example in his friend and rival Mahler, for whom the image of the artist-prophet survived undisturbed in the era of electricity and airplanes. But that is not to say that Strauss took his music any less seriously, for he enacted a thoroughgoing rejection of the heroic, mystical, spiritual associations of musical composition. When the composer about whom he wrote was himself, he gave his most honest assessment of the activity, seeking meaning in a critique of Romanticism, and profundity in a new, ordinary realism. Even Schoenberg appreciated the novelty, counting *Intermezzo* among the works of Strauss that "will not perish."[28]

Sonata form and musical idealism

There is in Strauss's portraits of composers, as in his self-portraits, a preference for criticism above personal revelation. In their cheerful superficiality they tell us openly what he was not, but leave us guessing as to what he was. This privileging of the critical can be recognized as well in the evolving practice of his tone poems, works that had much to say, in musical terms, about what music could not or should not do. Writing music that analyzed a false self was for Strauss a natural extension of writing music about false music.

The most prominent of Strauss's nineteenth-century targets was sonata form, which in the world of his youth remained the richest symbol of the purely musical. In the late 1880s Ritter taught the apprentice New German a crude reading of the "purely musical," reducing Hanslick's beliefs to the simplistic and baldly un-Hanslickian notion that music had no relationship to anything outside itself.[29] A bit of private philosophical study sufficed to reveal the idealism lying just beneath the surface of Hanslick's putative formalism, and to show Strauss that the debate over programmatic and absolute music was a struggle over a valuable piece of turf: the metaphysical claims that had lent music its high status among the arts over the previous century or so. Thus, whereas Strauss could tell Bülow in 1888 that sonata form had become "a formula … to accommodate and enclose a 'purely musical' (in the strictest and narrowest meaning of the word) content," by the time he had completed *Guntram* he recognized that the stakes were considerably higher.[30] Brahms's symphonies as heard by Hanslick aspired to the same idealistic sphere as the elevated programmaticism celebrated by Wagner in Liszt's symphonic poems; indeed, autonomy continued to hold the upper hand over program music in the twentieth century largely because it preserved this philosophical credibility despite changing social, intellectual, and historical contexts.

None of the first three tone poems (*Macbeth* [1888; revised 1891], *Don Juan*, and *Tod und Verklärung*) challenged the authority of sonata form as the structural foundation of large-scale composition, in spite of the conspicuous anomalies or "deformations" in these self-consciously notorious works. But with *Till Eulenspiegels lustige Streiche*, the first work of the second cycle, Strauss produced what James Hepokoski has called a "manifesto" of anti-idealism.[31] As this intensified critique played out in the second cycle of tone poems, Strauss would confront both idealistic camps, attacking the foundations of autonomy with a radical critique of sonata form even as he used aggressively explicit tone-painting to undermine the metaphysical aspirations of program music.

The dismantling of sonata form plays out systematically across these four works, with tactical moves that suggest conscious calculation and thus a wider agenda than we would infer from isolated cases of "sonata deformation."[32] *Till* takes aim at the defining tonal polarity of the sonata principle, offering up secondary material that is gesturally orthodox (with clear contrasts in mood, texture, orchestration, melodic character, etc.) but presented in the subdominant (*Gemächlich*, m. 179ff.). Forgoing both the traditional dominant–tonic relationship and the more up-to-date third relation, Strauss deprives the form of the structural dissonance that generates large-scale coherence and momentum. The fragmentary recapitulation described by Hepokoski, with a clear return of the main Till theme followed by bits of previous material zipping by as though in fast-forward, acquires its urgency from the search for a tonal conflict that does not exist; on the structural level there is nothing to resolve.[33] In contrast, *Zarathustra* presents a clear dichotomy between keys (B and C), but these remain antagonists all the way through the famous ending, in which C spoils the atmosphere of a *Tristan*-esque B major. The lack of resolution is prefigured by the set-up, which in its arrangement of events has nothing to do with sonata form: *Zarathustra* is in fact Strauss's first large-scale work that lacks a sonata exposition. The remaining pieces of the form – principally an apparent primary theme (mm. 115ff., "Of joys and passions"), a premature secondary theme (mm. 35ff., thirteen measures into "Of the backworldsmen"), and a clear moment of recapitulation (mm. 329ff., forty-two measures into "The convelescent") – are so reduced and bizarrely distributed that sonata form seems to have been shattered.[34]

That disintegration allowed Strauss to abandon the form altogether in *Don Quixote*, which in name ("Fantastic Variations on a Theme of Knightly Character") and deed presents itself entirely as a collection of fragments, devoid of a cohesive, organically developing large-scale structure. It is not surprising that at this decisive moment Strauss felt a pang of sentimentality, perhaps even guilt; however good-natured the work as a whole, and however affectionately Strauss rendered the Don's final moments, this tone poem consigns Ritter and Brahms to the same dungheap. The ironic distance between Strauss and his spectacular displays of symphonic grandeur is now spelled out by a framing device explicitly marked as a descent into insanity. But it is the audacious and utter dismissal of sonata structure that enacts the break with the work's parodied idealism, finalizing what had been approached step-by-step in the previous tone poems. From this moment, sonata form would be nothing more to Strauss than a historical relic – which explains, by another ironic twist, why in *Ein Heldenleben* the form can be placed so prominently and innocently in the foreground. The unambiguous correspondence of sonata-form sections with program-matic episodes renders the form strictly and overtly superficial, as does the contrast between the simple-minded transparency of the structure and the immensity of the single forty-minute movement. (Compare this piece's formal clarity, indeed crudity, with the rich ambiguity of Mahler's large first movements, such as those of the Second and Third Symphonies.) Sonata form finds a posthumous life here as a heuristic device, a handy plot-sequence for tongue-in-cheek autobiography. But as Adorno would say, the life that celebrates itself here is death; by 1899 heroism and the musical representation of heroism were no more than façades.

At the end of an apparently purposeful critical process, Strauss had effectively forced himself into a change of genre, from the symphonic to the operatic. After the debacle of *Guntram*, the tone poem had provided him with a refuge, a comfort zone where success – public and artistic – could be relied upon. For his second opera, he would leave himself no such option. Not only had sonata form, the basis of large-scale orchestral music in the nineteenth century, played itself out, but the critical questions that had motivated Strauss to become a composer of program music in the first place had now been answered to his satisfaction. His future, whatever it held, lay in the opera house.

Conclusion

The rejection of sonata form and its philosophical baggage was as cru-cial a prerequisite for *Salome* as the rejection of Wagner's metaphysics. Jochanaan's tonal grandiloquence, the high-flown bombast of a "clown [*Hanswursten*] … who feeds on locusts," is no less groundbreaking than Salome's cacophonous remix of Isolde's *Liebestod*.[35] We only have to look beyond musical techique to recognize that these critiques collaborate in undermining an idealism shared by Wagner and Brahms. The crucial mod-ernist feature of *Salome* is thus not technical innovation but irony – a qual-ity that would become both a source of Strauss's avant-garde authenticity and a defining trait of his artistic output.

Strauss learned and sustained this ironic distance largely through writ-ing music about music. The model compositions of his youth, at first mere pedagogically driven imitation, gradually developed into something more; if the reminiscences and stylistic juxtapositions of his music *c.* 1880 are plausibly unwitting (and plausibly not), by the second half of that decade we are confronted in pieces like the *Burleske*, TrV 145 (1886) and the Violin Sonata, Op. 18 (1887) with out-and-out caricatures and staged skirmishes among the forces competing for his allegiance. From there it is easy to see the style disengage from the creator; for Strauss every stylistic choice would be an experiment, a pose. In this light the wild changes of direction in his career begin to make sense. It is no use looking for authenticity on one side or the other of such pairs as *Symphonia domestica* and *Salome*, *Elektra* and *Der Rosenkavalier*, *Die Frau ohne Schatten* (1917) and *Schlagobers* (1922), or *Metamorphosen* and the Second Sonatina ("Happy Workplace"). The only stable artistic voice to be found in them is one equally removed from them all.

But that implies only that Strauss's music lacked a confessional intent in any nineteenth-century sense. Removal does not indicate an absence of intellectual or emotional involvement, but a reluctance to make unsustainable claims. Indeed, we might view Strauss's entire career as an extension of his youthful inquiries into the nature of the art – an oeuvre built from a productive, skeptical curiosity about what music could do. This was at the same time a curiosity about his own nature, for in contemplating music, this prodigiously talented musician, as gifted as anyone he ever knew, contemplated the peculiar manner in which his mind had been wired by Providence. In the end he did not claim to comprehend himself any better than his art. And in that respect he seems strangely sincere, as a person and as an artist.

Notes

1 The musical world of Strauss's youth
For their assistance in the preparation of
this article, I am indebted to William Weber
(California State University at Long Beach),
Thomas Grey (Stanford University), Wolfgang
Rathert (Ludwig Maximilian University of
Munich), Jürgen May (Richard-Strauss-
Institut), and Charles Youmans (Pennsylvania
State University).
1 Peter Gay, *Pleasure Wars: The Bourgeois
Experience, Victoria to Freud* (New York:
Norton, 1998), pp. 89–103.
2 *Ibid.*, p. 95.
3 Carl Theodor Heigel, *Ludwig I: König von
Bayern* (Leipzig: Duncker and Humblot, 1872),
p. 244.
4 Theodor von der Ammer [= Karl von
Perfall], *Münchener Bilderbogen: Humor und
Satire aus Isar-Athen* (Munich: Ph. Höpfner,
1878), p. 77.
5 Edward Wilberforce, *Social Life in Munich*
(London: W. H. Allen, 1863), pp. 247–8.
6 *Ibid.*, p. 256.
7 Theodore Child, *Summer Holidays:
Travelling Notes in Europe* (New York: Harper
and Brothers, 1889), p. 217.
8 Anon., *Maga Excursion Papers* (New York:
G. P. Putnam, 1867), p. 207.
9 Friedrich Kaiser, *Theater-Director Carl: Sein
Leben und Wirken* (Vienna: Sallmayer, 1854),
p. 20.
10 Adolf Ackermann, *München und
Umgebungen: Illustrirter Wegweiser mit
besonderer Berücksichtigung der Kunstschätze*,
Grieben's Reise-Bibliothek 19, new edn.
(Berlin: Albert Goldschmidt, 1867), p. 5.
11 W. H. K. Godfrey, *Three Months on
the Continent* (Waterbury, CN: American
Publishing Company, 1874); P. B. Cogswell,
Glints from over the Water (Concord, NH: P. B.
Cogswell, 1880); Curtis Guild, *Over the Ocean;
or, Sights and Scenes in Foreign Lands* (Boston:
Lee and Shepard, 1882); and Child, *Summer
Holidays*.
12 By the late nineteenth century, German
culture had well established itself in the United
States, so that an American traveler to Europe
may have already experienced a German beer
garden or *Gesangverein* at home.
13 Gay, *Pleasure Wars*, p. 97, from Theodor
Goering, "Das musikalische München zur Zeit
Ludwigs II. Münchener Musikzustände und

ihre Ursachen: Das Konzertwesen," in *Dreissig
Jahre München* (Munich: C. H. Beck, 1904),
pp. 145, 149.
14 Regarding the relationship between music
and social status, see (among others) Derek B.
Scott, "Music and Social Class," in Jim Samson,
ed., *The Cambridge History of Nineteenth-
Century Music* (Cambridge: Cambridge
University Press, 2002), pp. 544–67; and
William Weber, *Music and the Middle Class:
The Social Structure of Concert Life in London,
Paris, and Vienna* (London: Croom Helm,
1975).
15 Ackermann, *München und Umgebungen*,
p. 10.
16 Karl Baedeker, *Southern Germany and
Austria*, 2nd edn. (Coblenz: Karl Baedeker,
1871), p. 49.
17 Regarding musical institutions in Munich
of the nineteenth century before Ludwig II,
see, above all, Anton Würz, "Münchner Opern-
und Konzertleben im 19. Jahrhundert vor
Ludwig II," *Musik in Bayern* 2 (1972): 273–84.
18 See *Chronicle*.
19 Richard Strauss, "Reminiscences of My
Father," in *Recollections*, pp. 127–33 (p. 132).
20 The literature about the Munich Hofoper
is sparse, in comparison with that about
opera in Vienna and Bayreuth. See, above
all, Franz Grandaur, *Chronik des Königlichen
Hof- und National-Theaters in München*
(Munich: Theodor Ackermann, 1878); Otto
Julius Bierbaum, *Fünfundzwanzig Jahre
Münchener Hoftheater-Geschichte* (Munich: E.
Albert, 1892); Karl von Perfall, *Ein Beitrag zur
Geschichte der königlichen Theater in München:
25. November 1867–25. November 1892*
(Munich: Piloty and Löhle, 1894); Max Zenger,
Geschichte der Münchener Oper, ed. Theodor
Kroyer (Munich: F. X. Weizinger, 1923); Hans
Wagner, *200 Jahre Münchner Theaterchronik,
1750–1950* (Munich: Lerche, 1958); and
Hans Zehetmair and Jürgen Schläder,
Nationaltheater: Die Bayerische Staatsoper
(Munich: Bruckmann, 1992).
21 Franz Lachner has been the subject
of German dissertations throughout
the twentieth century, but on the 200th
anniversary of his birth in 2003, a
musicological symposium was held in Munich
that resulted in the important essay collection
edited by Stephan Hörner and Hartmut

Schick, *Franz Lachner und seine Brüder: Hofkapellmeister zwischen Schubert und Wagner* (Tutzing: Hans Schneider, 2006).
22 The figures derive from a table of all Hofoper performances between late 1867 and late 1892, compiled by Perfall in *Ein Beitrag zur Geschichte*, pp. 127–34.
23 Titles here follow the German of Perfall's table – the operas would have been presented in German translation.
24 Perfall's statistics base themselves on calendar years rather than seasons, and include performances of both *große Oper* and *Spieloper*, as well as incidental music that filled whole evenings of drama.
25 Perfall, *Ein Beitrag zur Geschichte*, pp. 136–8, provides statistics for composers as arranged into national categories. He counted Meyerbeer, Gluck, and Liszt among the German composers.
26 On the program were his *Die Stumme von Portici* (3), *Maurer und Schlosser* (3), *Fra Diavolo* (3), *Des Teufels Anteil* (2), and *Der schwarze Domino* (1).
27 For Meyerbeer: *Die Hugenotten* (19), *Robert der Teufel* (9), *Der Prophet* (5), *Die Afrikanerin* (1); for Lortzing: *Der Waffenschmied* (21), *Zar und Zimmermann* (18), *Die beiden Schützen* (7), *Undine* (7), *Der Wildschütz* (5).
28 *Chronicle*, p. 211.
29 Strauss's lifelong friendship with the composer and theorist Ludwig Thuille (1861–1907) began in 1872.
30 See the letters respectively dated early summer of 1878; June 6, 1878; and mid June of 1879 in Alfons Ott, ed., *Richard Strauss und Ludwig Thuille: Briefe der Freundschaft, 1877–1907* (Munich: Walter Ricke, 1969), pp. 166 (Auber), 169 (Boïeldieu), 183 (Lortzing).
31 About the Musikalische Akademie, see Heinrich Bihrle, *Die Musikalische Akademie Münchens, 1811–1911: Festschrift zur Feier des hundertjährigen Bestehens* (Munich: E. Mühlthaler, 1911); Roswitha Schlötterer-Traimer, *Richard Strauss und die Musikalische Akademie in München* (Munich: HypoVereinsbank, 1999); and Karl Malisch, *500 Jahre im Dienst der Musik: Hofkapelle –Musikalische Akademie– Bayerisches Staatsorchester München* (Munich: Prestel-Verlag, 2001).
32 Frithjof Haas, *Zwischen Brahms und Wagner: Der Dirigent Hermann Levi* (Zurich: Atlantis, 1995).
33 Ott, *Richard Strauss und Ludwig Thuille*, pp. 160–1.
34 The scholarly literature about this ensemble (which still exists) is rather sparse: Franz

Trenner, "Richard Strauss und die 'Wilde Gung'l,'" *Schweizerische Musikzeitung* 90 (1950): 403–5; Franz Trenner, *Orchesterverein Wilde Gung'l, 1864–1964: Festschrift* (Munich: Münchner Orchesterverein Wilde Gung'l, 1964); Hans Raff, *110 Jahre Münchner Orchesterverein Wilde Gung'l* (Munich: Münchner Orchesterverein Wilde Gung'l, 1975); and Nina Fischer, *Die "Wilde Gung'l": Geschichte eines Amateurorchesters* (Munich: Bayerischer Rundfunk, 1999).
35 Bryan Gilliam, *The Life of Richard Strauss* (Cambridge: Cambridge University Press, 1999), p. 18.
36 Thomas Lange and Rudolf Rieser, "Geschichte," in *Münchener Orchesterverein Wilde Gungl e.V.*, www.wilde-gungl.de/47/Gungl.html (accessed December 20, 2009).
37 This list derives from Trenner, "Richard Strauss und die 'Wilde Gung'l,'" reprinted in Raff, *110 Jahre Münchner Orchesterverein Wilde Gung'l*, pp. 15–16.
38 Oft-cited reviews of the young Strauss's compositional efforts as performed by the Wilde Gung'l appeared in the *Münchner Neueste Nachrichten* and the *Süddeutsche Presse* (only the local daily press – and not the musical press – covered the ensemble's concerts).
39 Trenner, "Richard Strauss und die 'Wilde Gung'l,'" p. 16, goes so far as to speculate that Strauss's love for the waltz dates back to his Wilde Gung'l experiences.
40 Anonymous observer C. F. commented in 1841 how "recitals, where quartets, quintets are performed and presented by dilettantes, are much rarer than in other German cities." C. F., *Münchener Hundert und Eins*, 2 vols., Vol. II (Munich: Georg Franz, 1841), p. 24.
41 "Wahrmund," "Tagebuchblätter aus dem Münchner Concertleben des Jahres 1881/82," *Allgemeine Musikalische Zeitung* 9 (March 1, 1882): 140.
42 *Chronicle*, p. 40.
43 Violinist Walter (1847–1901) was the first cousin of Franz Strauss, the concertmaster of the Court Orchestra, and Richard Strauss's first violin teacher. Pianist Bussmeyer (1853–1930) was a pupil of Liszt and a composition student of Rheinberger at the Königliche Musikschule, where he taught and (after 1904) served as director.
44 See the comments by "Wahrmund" in the "Tagebuchblätter …," *Allgemeine Musikalische Zeitung* 17 (March 8, 1882): 156–7.
45 *Chronicle*, p. 30.
46 Large quantities of "easy" (*leicht*) chamber music were being produced at the time for the lucrative salon market. See, above all, Thomas

Christensen, "Four-hand Piano Transcription and Geographies of Nineteenth-Century Musical Reception," *Journal of the American Musicological Society* 52 (1999): 255–98.

47 The most authoritative publication about the institution is Stephan Schnitt, ed., *Geschichte der Hochschule für Musik und Theater: Von den Anfängen bis 1945* (Tutzing: Hans Schneider, 2005).

48 William Weber, "Concerts at Four Conservatories in the 1880s," in Michael Fend and Michel Noiray, eds., *Musical Education in Europe (1770–1914): Compositional, Institutional, and Political Challenges*, 2 vols., Vol. II (Berlin: Berliner Wissenschafts-Verlag, 2005), pp. 331–49.

49 Strauss to Thuille, April 4, 1878. Ott, *Richard Strauss und Ludwig Thuille*, p. 162

50 For a review, see Berthold Kellermann, "Berichte: München," *Musikalisches Centralblatt* 2 (May 11, 1882): 194.

51 Strauss to Thuille, March 8, 1884. Ott, *Richard Strauss und Ludwig Thuille*, p. 191.

52 The most authoritative study of the many-faceted musical activities of Wüllner – primarily remembered today as the first conductor of *Das Rheingold* and *Die Walküre* – is Dietrich Kämpe's monograph *Franz Wüllner: Leben, Wirken und kompositorisches Schaffen* (Cologne: Arno Volk, 1963).

53 See for example the anonymous correspondence report "München, Ende Dezember 1877," *Musikalisches Wochenblatt* 9 (January 25, 1878): 59.

54 Ernst von Destouches, "Geschichte der Sangespflege und Sängervereine in der Stadt München," *Allgemeine Musikalische Zeitung* 9 (November 11, 1874): 710.

55 For Rheinberger's full program, see Harald Wagner and Hans-Josef Irmen, eds., *Joseph Gabriel Rheinberger: Briefe und Dokumente seines Lebens*, 9 vols., Vol. V (Vaduz: Prisca Verlag, 1984), pp. 92–3.

56 Joseph Gung'l remains little known, despite his significance for nineteenth-century musical culture. See Robert Rohr, "Musikgeschichtliche Beiträge ungarndeutscher Persönlichkeiten am Beispiel Joseph Gungls," *Studia musicologica Academiae Scientiarum Hungaricae* 36 (1995): 47–51.

57 Guild, *Over the Ocean*, p. 465.

58 "Münchener Musikleben," *Allgemeine Musikalische Zeitung* 1/7 (February 14, 1866): 57.

59 Whereas "Träume" is one of the *Wesendonck Lieder* (1857–8) and thus a relatively recent composition by Wagner, the other two lieder are unusual choices for Gung'l, since they are Hugo settings from

1839 and, while "Attente" was republished several times during the composer's lifetime, "La Tombe dit à la rose" remained a fragment. The question arises, then, how did Gung'l gain access to the work? I thank Thomas Grey for his insights into the source situation.

60 "b.," "Kürzere Berichte: München," *Musikalisches Wochenblatt* 3/4 (January 19, 1872): 58.

61 This reference is unclear, since Heinrich Marschner (1795–1861) was not a conductor of salon fare like either Strauss or Gung'l were, yet there was no conductor in Europe with the name "Marchner."

62 Henry Bedford, "A Vacation Ramble in Germany," *The Month and Catholic Review* 4 (1875): 28.

63 *Chronicle*, p. 30.

64 Richard Strauss, "Reminiscences of my Father," p. 132.

65 Georg Pschorr underwrote the printing costs, which convinced the publisher to take on the work. *Chronicle*, p. 48.

66 *Bayerische Gewerbe-Statistik (Aufnahme vom 1. Dezember 1875)*, Part I: *Die persönlichen Verhältnisse der Gewerbebetrieber* (Munich: Adolf Ackermann, 1879), p. xxxii.

67 See, above all, Hans Lenneberg's pioneering document collection *Breitkopf und Härtel in Paris: The Letters of Their Agent Heinrich Probst between 1833 and 1840* (Stuyvesant, NY: Pendragon, 1990), for valuable insights into how important these networks were for the dissemination of music in Europe.

68 Stephen Powers, "German Newspapers," *Harper's* 36 (January, 1868): 232–41 (p. 240).

69 Henry A. Powell, "Newspaper," in *Chambers's Encyclopaedia*, rev. edn., 8 vols., Vol. V (New York: Collier, 1887), p. 587.

2 Strauss's compositional process

1 See, for instance, the reports about the work on *Ein Heldenleben* in the *Allgemeine Musik-Zeitung* (Berlin) 25 (June 24/July 1, 1898): 380, as well as a few weeks later (July 29/August 5, 1898): 442. "As we have heard, Richard Strauss is working at the moment on a four-movement symphony with an heroic character, which will be named *Ein Heldenleben* and premiered next season in one of the museum concerts in Frankfurt am Main."

2 First published in its entirety in Walter Werbeck, *Die Tondichtungen von Richard Strauss* (Tutzing: Hans Schneider, 1996), pp. 534–9.

3 Richard Strauss, *Betrachtungen und Erinnerungen*, 3rd edn., ed. Willi Schuh (Zurich: Atlantis, 1981), 161–7; translated as "On Inspiration in Music" in Richard Strauss,

Recollections and Reflections, ed. Willi Schuh, trans. L. J. Lawrence (London: Boosey & Hawkes, 1953), pp. 112–17.

4 Carl Dahlhaus, *Zwischen Romantik und Moderne: Vier Studien zur Musikgeschichte des späteren 19. Jahrhunderts* (Munich: Katzbichler, 1974), p. 40.

5 Otto Zoff, *Die großen Komponisten gesehen von ihren Zeitgenossen* (Bern: A. Scherz, 1952), p. 319.

6 Strauss, *Betrachtungen*, p. 190.

7 Max Marschalk, "Gespräche mit Richard Strauss," *Vossische Zeitung* (October 15, 1918, evening edn.).

8 The initial version of this song can be found at the end of Sketchbook 6 in the numbering after Franz Trenner, *Die Skizzenbücher von Richard Strauss aus dem Richard-Strauss-Archiv in Garmisch* (Tutzing: Hans Schneider, 1977), p. 14. It is different from the final version of the song, however, in quite a number of details, including a much longer piano postlude.

9 Richard Strauss, "Zum 50. Geburtstag des Tondichters (11. Juni)," *Neues Wiener Journal* (June 6, 1914).

10 Theodor W. Adorno, "Richard Strauss. Zum Hundertsten Geburtstag: 11. Juni 1964," in Adorno, *Musikalische Schriften*, 6 vols., Vol. III (Frankfurt am Main: Suhrkamp, 1978), p. 569.

11 Stefan Zweig to Romain Rolland, December 18, 1932, in Waltraud Schwarze, ed., *Romain Rolland, Stefan Zweig: Briefwechsel 1924–1940* (Berlin: Rütten and Loenig, 1987), p. 484.

12 Charlotte E. Erwin, "Richard Strauss's Presketch Planning for *Ariadne auf Naxos*," *Musical Quarterly* 47 (1981): 348–65.

13 The conclusion of the *Zarathustra* particell, for instance, on July 17, 1896 (Sketchbook 3, p. 48) was confirmed in his calendar with the remark "Zarathustra sketch completed."

14 See the remarks by Werner Breig in Ulrich Müller and Peter Wapnewski, eds., *Richard-Wagner-Handbuch* (Stuttgart: A. Kröner, 1986), pp. 393–8.

15 Trenner, *Skizzenbücher*, p. vi.

16 In addition to Erwin, "Richard Strauss's Presketch Planning"; and Werbeck, *Tondichtungen*; see Bryan Gilliam, "Strauss's Preliminary Opera Sketches: Thematic Fragments and Symphonic Continuity," *19th-Century Music* 9 (1985–6): 176–88.

17 Page 6 is featured in *Richard Strauss: Autographen, Porträts, Bühnenbilder. Ausstellung zum 50. Todestag* (Munich: Bayerische Staatsbibliothek, 1999), p. 223.

18 Alfons Ott, ed., *Richard Strauss and Ludwig Thuille: Briefe der Freundschaft, 1877–1907* (Munich: Walter Ricke, 1969), pp. 15–150.

19 *Richard Strauss: Autographen*, pp. 222, 231.

20 Willi Schuh, *Richard Strauss: Jugend und frühe Meisterjahre. Lebenschronik 1864–1898* (Zurich: Atlantis, 1976), p. 59.

21 Pictured in Kurt Pfister, *Richard Strauss: Weg, Gestalt, Denkmal* (Vaduz: Liechtenstein Verlag, 1950), Illustration 29. The caption is misleading; when he composed the Violin Concerto, Strauss was not 14, but 17 years of age.

22 Schuh emphasizes as well that Strauss liberated himself from the piano early in his compositional career. See Schuh, *Jugend und frühe Meisterjahre*, p. 61 n. 18.

23 Trenner, *Skizzenbücher*, 7ff. The Sketchbooks 5–7 in Trenner's numbering correspond to Books II–IV in Strauss's count. Then follow Trenner 10 (= VI), 12 (= VIII), 16 and 18 (= IX). After IX Strauss seems to have abandoned the count in roman numerals. Sketchbook V is missing in the Garmisch collection. In the following the Garmisch sketchbooks will always be cited with Trenner's arabic numerals.

24 Strauss picked up the idea of beginning a piece in this way again in *Don Quixote*. The rhythm of the first measure is even the same as in the first draft of *Till Eulenspiegel*.

25 Reprinted in Werbeck, *Tondichtungen*, pp. 531ff.

26 In a letter to his wife of September 20, 1901 he writes: "I leafed through my sketchbook without receiving a significant inspiration … and I played a few fugues by Bach." Willi Schuh, "Das Szenarium und die musikalischen Skizzen zum Ballett *Kythere*" in *Richard Strauss Jahrbuch 1959–60* (Bonn: Boosey & Hawkes, 1960), pp. 84–98, esp. p. 86.

27 Gilliam, "Strauss's Preliminary Opera Sketches," p. 181.

28 Possibly meant for *Don Quixote*.

29 Sketchbook 1, p. 60.

30 Sketchbook 1, p. 32. See the transcription in Trenner, *Skizzenbücher*, p. 1. Strauss's text is an excellent basis for an analysis – reason enough always to consult the sketches when studying Strauss's music.

31 Sketchbook 1, p. 47. See also the transcription in Trenner, *Skizzenbücher*, p. 2.

32 The stormy conclusion, for instance, was replaced by a quiet coda.

33 Trenner classified them without differentiation as sketchbooks. Sketchbook 3 unifies the particells of *Zarathustra*, *Till Eulenspiegel*, and *Don Quixote*, while

the particell of the *Alpensinfonie* takes up the entirety of Trenner's Sketchbook 31. The particell for *Ein Heldenleben* is in the Mengelberg Collection in the Gementemuseum in The Hague.

34 There is a not entirely error-free transcription of the beginning by Manfred Hermann Schmidt, "Der Schluss des *Rheingolds* im *Zarathustra* von Richard Strauss," in Bernd Edelmann, Birgit Lodes, and Reinhold Schlötterer, eds, *Richard Strauss und die Moderne* (Berlin: Henschel, 2001), pp. 173–84, esp. p. 180.

35 Scott Warfield, "Neatness Counts: Orchestration in Richard Strauss's Compositional Method," unpublished paper read at the 13th Biennial Conference on Nineteenth-Century Music, University of Durham, July 6–9, 2004.

36 Richard Strauss, *Tod und Verklärung, op. 24: Faksimile-Reproduktion der Handschrift* (Vienna: Universal Edition, 1923). One can also see that Strauss proceeded somewhat cavalierly here, because he used paper with twenty-four staves, even though it must have been clear that twenty-five staves would be needed for the complete orchestra (with second harp and tam-tam). Because it lacked its own staff, the tam-tam part was notated separately at the bottom of pp. 68–73.

37 Such an instrumentation list is pictured for *Friedenstag* in the catalogue of the *Richard-Strauss-Ausstellung zum 100. Geburtstag*, ed. Franz Grasberger and Franz Hadamowsky (Vienna: Österreichische Nationalbibliothek, 1964), p. 126. The illustration refers to the music two measures after rehearsal no. 126.

38 See Ulrich Konrad, "Die Deutsche Motette op. 62 von Richard Strauss: Entstehung, Form, Gehalt," in Edelmann, Lodes, and Schlötterer, *Strauss und die Moderne*, pp. 283–310, esp. p. 288. With Strauss, measure-counts thus can have several functions: as reference for use in other positions (mostly in the sketches), as symbols indicating the metric position (in sketches, rarely in particells), and as measure numbers per system on a page of the score (only in particells).

39 Ernst Krause, *Richard Strauss: Gestalt und Werk*, 4th edn. (Leipzig: Breitkopf and Härtel, 1970), p. 110.

40 See n. 16, especially the studies by Erwin and Gilliam.

41 Krause, *Richard Strauss*, 122.

42 See Strauss's letter to Hofmannsthal of June 26, 1909, a facsimile of which appears in *Richard Strauss: Autographen*, p. 182.

3 Maturity and indecision in the early works

1 Max Steinitzer, "Richard Strauss' Werke für Klavier," *Die Musik* 24/2 (November, 1931): 105–9, quote from pp. 106–7.

2 In relation to Steinitzer's vision for a radio program, it should be noted that the recordings of many non-canonic Strauss works, including early compositions, have been released as part of an identically named series on the Koch Schwann label – *Der unbekannte Richard Strauss* ("The Unknown Richard Strauss").

3 Richard Specht, *Richard Strauss und sein Werk*, 2 vols., Vol. I (Leipzig: E. P. Tal, 1921), pp. 106, 127–8. Specht was fond of equating mechanical sound reproduction technologies with a lack of authentic inspiration; see, for example, the discussion of his reception of Strauss's score for the ballet-pantomime *Josephslegende* (1914), in Wayne Heisler, Jr., *The Ballet Collaborations of Richard Strauss*, Eastman Studies in Music (Rochester, NY: University of Rochester Press, 2009), pp. 49–50, 93.

4 Richard Strauss, "Recollections of My Youth and Years of Apprenticeship," in Strauss, *Recollections and Reflections*, ed. Willi Schuh, trans. L. J. Lawrence (London: Boosey & Hawkes, 1953), pp. 134–45.

5 Glenn Gould, "An Argument for Richard Strauss," in Gould, *The Glenn Gould Reader*, ed. Tim Page (New York: Knopf, 1984), pp. 84–92, quote from p. 88. See also Leon Botstein, "The Enigmas of Richard Strauss: A Revisionist View," in *Strauss and His World*, pp. 3–32, esp. pp. 14–15.

6 Bryan Gilliam, *The Life of Richard Strauss* (Cambridge: Cambridge University Press, 1999), p. 13. On Meyer, see also Scott Warfield, "Friedrich Wilhelm Meyer (1818–1893): Some Biographical Notes on Richard Strauss's Composition Teacher," *Richard Strauss-Blätter*, new series 37 (June, 1997): 54–74.

7 Stephan Kohler, Preface to Richard Strauss, *Trio Nr. 1 A-Dur für Klavier, Violine und Violoncello*, 1st edn. (New York: Schott, 1996).

8 Translated in *ibid*. Kohler modified the error in Susan Gillespie's translation of this letter to Thuille, in which it was incorrectly stated that the novel modulation in the Adagio was from F major to E major. See Susan Gillespie, ed. and trans., "Selections from the Strauss–Thuille Correspondence: A Glimpse of Strauss during His Formative Years," in *Strauss and His World*, pp. 193–236 (p. 200). The complete correspondence can be found in Franz Trenner, ed., *Richard Strauss, Ludwig Thuille: Ein Briefwechsel* (Tutzing: Hans Schneider, 1980).

9 Specht, *Richard Strauss*, Vol. I, pp. 105, 107.

10 Jürgen Schaarwächter, *Richard Strauss und die Sinfonie* (Cologne: Verlag Christoph Dohr, 1994), pp. 12–23.
11 Quoted in *Chronicle*, p. 52.
12 Erich Urban, *Richard Strauss* (Berlin: Gose and Tetzlaff, 1901), p. 13.
13 Steinitzer, *Richard Strauss* (Berlin: Schuster and Loeffler, 1911), pp. 208–9.
14 Urban, *Richard Strauss*, p. 13.
15 Ernest Newman, *Richard Strauss* (Freeport, NY: Books for Libraries Press, 1969), pp. 30–1.
16 Steinitzer, "Richard Strauss' Werke für Klavier," p. 106.
17 Gilliam, *The Life of Richard Strauss*, p. 19.
18 Norman Del Mar, *Richard Strauss: A Critical Commentary on His Life and Works*, 3 vols., Vol. I (Ithaca, NY: Cornell University Press, 1986), p. 20.
19 Steinitzer, *Richard Strauss*, p. 210.
20 Del Mar, *Richard Strauss*, Vol. I, p. 20; see also Specht, *Richard Strauss*, Vol. I, pp. 110–11.
21 Strauss to Thuille, January 6, 1884, quoted in *Chronicle*, p. 67.
22 Strauss to Thuille, March 8, 1884, in *ibid.*, p. 68.
23 Strauss, "Recollections of My Youth," pp. 136–7.
24 R. Larry Todd, "Strauss before Liszt and Wagner: Some Observations," in *New Perspectives*, pp. 3–40, quote from pp. 25–6.
25 Steinitzer, *Richard Strauss*, p. 210.
26 Arthur Seidl, "Richard Strauß: Eine Charakterskizze" [1896], in Seidl, *Straußiana: Aufsätze zur Richard Strauß-Frage aus drei Jahrzehnten* (Regensburg: Gustav Bosse, 1913), pp. 11–66, quote from p. 17.
27 Quoted in *Chronicle*, p. 99; see also Strauss, "Recollections of My Youth."
28 Todd, "Strauss before Liszt and Wagner," pp. 15–16, 25. On the influence of Brahms's large choral works on Strauss and documentation of the reception of *Wandrers Sturmlied*, see also Heiner Wajemann, *Die Chorkompositionen von Richard Strauss* (Tutzing: Hans Schneider, 1986), pp. 179–89.
29 Newman, *Richard Strauss*, pp. 37, 35–6.
30 Gilliam, *The Life of Richard Strauss*, pp. 38–9.
31 Strauss, quoted in Alan Jefferson, *The Lieder of Richard Strauss* (London: Cassell, 1971), p. 24.
32 Del Mar discusses Strauss's Opp. 10, 15, and 17 in *Richard Strauss*, Vol. III, pp. 264–73, quote from p. 266.
33 Richard Specht, Preface to Richard Strauss, *Aus Italien, Sinfonische Fantasie für grosses Orchester, G dur, op. 16* (Vienna: Universal Edition, 1904).

34 Romain Rolland, "Richard Strauss" [1899], in Rollo Myers, ed. and trans., *Richard Strauss and Romain Rolland: Correspondence, together with Fragments from the Diary of Romain Rolland and Other Essays* (London: Calder and Boyars, 1968), pp. 175–95, quote from p. 177.

4 The first cycle of tone poems
1 Strauss to his father, January 17, 1889 in Willi Schuh, ed., *Richard Strauss: Briefe an die Eltern 1882–1906* (Zurich and Freiburg: Atlantis, 1954), p. 104. Translations are my own except where otherwise indicated.
2 Strauss to Carl Hörburger, June 11, 1888, in Franz Grasberger, ed., *"Der Strom der Töne trug mich fort": Die Welt um Richard Strauss in Briefen* (Tutzing: Hans Schneider, 1967), p. 41.
3 Richard Strauss, "Recollections of My Youth and Years of Apprenticeship," in *Recollections*, p. 138.
4 Monacensia-Abteilung und Handschriftensammlung, Städtische Bibliothek, Munich (D-Mmb), Sammelstück No. 151; also reproduced in Walter Werbeck, *Die Tondichtungen von Richard Strauss* (Tutzing: Hans Schneider, 1996), pp. 527–30 (p. 528). This early account probably dates from January, 1898, and was sent to Eugen Spitzweg, Strauss's publisher.
5 A sophisticated revisionist reading of Ritter's contribution to Strauss's intellectual development is given in Charles Youmans, *Richard Strauss's Orchestral Music and the German Intellectual Tradition: The Philosophical Roots of Musical Modernism* (Bloomington: Indiana University Press, 2005), pp. 35–48.
6 Strauss's original enquiry and the receipt of his membership fee are found in Weimar, Klassik Stiftung, Goethe-Schiller Archiv, 70/37. He would later become president of this organization (1901).
7 Strauss to Hans von Bülow, March 11, 1887, in Gabriele Strauss, ed., *Lieber Collega! Richard Strauss im Briefwechsel mit zeitgenössischen Komponisten und Dirigenten* (Berlin: Henschel, 1996), p. 58.
8 Extensive discussion of both the programmatic and formal aspects of this work is to be found in my article "*Aus Italien*: Retracing Strauss's Journeys," *The Musical Quarterly* 92 (2009): 70–117.
9 Letter from Strauss to Karl Wolff, January, 1889, quoted in Werbeck, *Tondichtungen*, pp. 25–6 n. 3.
10 Letter from Strauss to Carl Hörburger, March 4, 1887, quoted in Felix Hörburger, "Über einige Briefe von Richard Strauss an Franz Carl Hörburger," in Hermann Dechant

and Wolfgang Sieber, eds., *Gedenkschrift Hermann Beck* (Laaber: Laaber, 1982), pp. 201–8 (p. 203).

11 Strauss described the movement as having "the form of a large first movement of a symphony," and he even labelled its constituent themes according to sonata-form practice. Richard Strauss, "*Aus Italien*: Analyse vom Komponisten," *Allgemeine Musikzeitung* 16/26 (June 28, 1889): 263–6 (p. 265).

12 Strauss, "Recollections of My Youth," pp. 138–9 (translation modified).

13 Strauss to Hans von Bülow, August 24, 1888, in Willi Schuh and Franz Trenner, eds., *Correspondence of Hans von Bülow and Richard Strauss*, trans. Anthony Gishford (London: Boosey & Hawkes, 1955), pp. 80–3.

14 Strauss to Ján Levoslav Bella, December 2, 1888, in Dobroslav Orel, *Ján Levoslav Bella: k. 80. narozeninám seniora slovenské hudby* (Bratislava: Philosophy Faculty of the Comenius University of Bratislava, 1924), p. 567.

15 Strauss to Bella, March 3, 1890, in *ibid.*, p. 570.

16 Strauss to Carl Hörburger, June 11, 1888, in Grasberger, *Der Strom der Töne*, p. 41.

17 Strauss to Hans Bronsart von Schellendorff, February 9, 1889, in G. Strauss, *Lieber Collega!*, p. 125.

18 In one letter from Strauss to Eugen Spitzweg (December 7, 1889) he actually uses both terms without making any distinction between them. Musik Abteilung, Bayerische Staatsbibliothek, Munich (D-Mmb), Sammelstück No. 30.

19 Letter from Strauss to Carl Hörburger, January 11, 1888, quoted in Max Steinitzer, *Richard Strauss* (Berlin: Schuster and Loeffler, 1911), p. 60. The letter itself has not survived.

20 The lack of counterpoint in Liszt's music was something on which Strauss explicitly commented: "So little artistry and so much poetry, so little counterpoint and so much music." Strauss to Alexander Ritter, probably May 1, 1890, quoted in *ibid.*

21 John Williamson, *Strauss*: Also sprach Zarathustra (Cambridge: Cambridge University Press, 1993), pp. 1, 16–17.

22 Strauss to Ludwig Thuille, November 19, 1890, in Franz Trenner, ed., *Richard Strauss, Ludwig Thuille: Ein Briefwechsel* (Tutzing: Hans Schneider, 1980), p. 115.

23 Rudolf Louis, *Die deutsche Musik der Gegenwart* (Munich and Leipzig: Georg Müller, 1909), p. 171; translated by Susan Gillespie in *Strauss and His World*, p. 309.

24 *Allgemeine Musikzeitung* 17/43 (October 24, 1890), quoted in Mark-Daniel Schmid,

"The Tone Poems of Richard Strauss and Their Reception History from 1887–1908" (Ph.D. diss., Northwestern University, 1997), p. 166. James Hepokoski cites a number of commentators down to the present day who adhere to this view. See "Structure and Program in *Macbeth*: A Proposed Reading of Strauss's First Symphonic Poem," in *Strauss and His World*, pp. 67–89 (pp. 68–70).

25 Carl Dahlhaus, "Wagner's Place in the History of Art," in Ulrich Müller and Peter Wapnewski, eds., *The Wagner Handbook*, trans. Alfred Clayton, ed. John Deathridge (Cambridge, MA: Harvard University Press, 1992), pp. 99–117 (p. 110).

26 In his sketchbooks, there is one additional, cryptic reference to a "grief melody" (*Schmerzensmelodie*; probably the cello figure in mm. 435–6, prefigured in m. 308), but still nothing comparable to the extensive programmatic indications found in sketches for later works; see Sketchbook 1, p. 27 and also Werbeck, *Tondichtungen*, p. 111.

27 James Hepokoski, "Fiery-Pulsed Libertine or Domestic Hero? Strauss's *Don Juan* Reinvestigated," *New Perspectives*, pp. 135–76 (pp. 136–7).

28 Strauss, "Recollections of My Youth," p. 139.

29 Scott Warfield, "The Genesis of Richard Strauss's *Macbeth*" (Ph.D. diss., University of North Carolina at Chapel Hill, 1995), pp. 412, 350–1.

30 Hepokoski, "Structure and Program," p. 74 tentatively suggests that mm. 20ff. illustrate "the witches' threefold prophecy to Macbeth (Act 1 scene 3)." Alternatively, one might associate these bars with Macbeth's dark ambition, the fatal flaw that drives the plot and leads eventually to his downfall.

31 *Ibid.*, pp. 75–6.

32 This has been interpreted as the arrival of the unwitting King Duncan to Macbeth's demesne, or (perhaps more plausibly) as Macbeth's own coronation.

33 Strauss to Hans von Bülow, August 24, 1888, in G. Strauss, *Lieber Collega!*, p. 81. In 1887, Bülow had reportedly ground his teeth in despair on hearing the subsidiary part of the "Macbeth" group (m. 20). "Tagebuch" Blau I, 18, Richard-Strauss-Archiv, Garmisch-Partenkirchen (RSA).

34 There are no fewer than three versions of *Macbeth*, but the first survives in only fragmentary form. As a result, it is difficult to determine with exactitude just how extensive was the initial revision process (which certainly included a reworking of the ending). For detailed discussion of the extant materials,

see Werbeck, *Tondichtungen*, pp. 107–13; and Warfield, "Genesis," pp. 293–367.

35 On hearing the work in 1890, he expressed himself satisfied with form and content, but determined to reorchestrate the whole. Strauss to Franz Wüllner, October 23, 1890, in G. Strauss, *Lieber Collega!*, p. 296.

36 "Sonata deformation" is a term coined by James Hepokoski to cover a number of standardized departures from a normative sonata structure. It has proved to be a particularly fruitful concept in analyzing music of the later nineteenth century (an early instance is Hepokoski's "Fiery-Pulsed Libertine"), but has also been challenged on a variety of historical and philosophical grounds. See *inter alia* James Hepokoski and Warren Darcy, *Elements of Sonata Theory: Norms, Types and Deformations in the Late-Eighteenth-Century Sonata* (Oxford: Oxford University Press, 2006), pp. 614–21; and (as a sample critical view) Julian Horton, *Bruckner's Symphonies: Analysis, Reception, and Cultural Politics* (Cambridge: Cambridge University Press, 2004), pp. 152–60.

37 Hepokoski, "Structure and Program," pp. 78–82.

38 One thinks of the important reprise of thematic matter in *Till Eulenspiegel* (m. 429), *Ein Heldenleben* (m. 631), and arguably also in *Also sprach Zarathustra* (m. 329).

39 See Schmid, "The Tone Poems of Richard Strauss," pp. 148–71.

40 Bülow to Eugen Spitzweg, March 8, 1891, in Marie von Bülow, ed., *Hans von Bülow: Briefe und Schriften*, 8 vols., Vol. VII: *Briefe VI 1880–1886* (Leipzig: Breitkopf and Härtel, 1908), p. 332.

41 Theodor W. Adorno, "Richard Strauss: Born June 11, 1864," trans. Samuel and Shierry Weber, *Perspectives of New Music* 3 (1964): 14–32; 4 (1965): 113–29 (p. 120).

42 Carl Dahlhaus, *Nineteenth-Century Music*, trans. J. Bradford Robinson (Berkeley: University of California Press, 1989), p. 334.

43 Nikolaus Lenau, *Don Juan*, in *Sämtliche Werke und Briefe*, 2 vols., Vol. I (Leipzig: Insel, 1970), pp. 893–940 (p. 939).

44 Sketchbook 1, 47, RSA and Werbeck, *Tondichtungen*, p. 116.

45 Strauss to Karl Wolff, January, 1889, quoted in full in Werbeck, *Tondichtungen*, pp. 25–6 n. 3; translation based on *Chronicle*, p. 136 (which uses a corrupt version of the text).

46 Strauss, "Recollections of My Youth," p. 139 (translation modified).

47 Strauss acknowledged as much in a letter to Hugo von Hofmannsthal, February 20, 1908; see *Strauss/Hofmannsthal*, p. 14.

48 Wilhelm Mauke, "*Don Juan*," reprinted in Herwarth Walden, ed., *Richard Strauss: Symphonien und Tondichtungen*, Meisterführer 6 (Berlin: Schlesinger, n.d. [*c.* 1908]), pp. 46–60. Mauke was the author of a composer-sanctioned guide to *Till Eulenspiegel*, so it is highly likely that his interpretation derives from Strauss. A useful summary of the main events in the poem is found in Norman Del Mar, *Richard Strauss: A Critical Commentary on His Life and Works*, 3 vols., Vol. I (London: Barrie and Rockliff, 1962), pp. 65–9.

49 Richard Wagner, *Sämtliche Schriften und Dichtungen*, 16 vols., Vol. V (Leipzig: Breitkopf and Härtel, 1912–14), p. 194.

50 See the correspondence between the two from February 25 to March 22, 1890, in Franz Trenner, ed., *Cosima Wagner, Richard Strauss: Ein Briefwechsel*, ed. with the assistance of Gabriele Strauss (Tutzing: Hans Schneider, 1978), pp. 26–37. See also Youmans's discussion of these issues in *Strauss's Orchestral Music*, pp. 54–6, 170–4.

51 Letter from Engelbert Humperdinck to Ludwig Strecker, June 26, 1890, in Eva Humperdinck, ed., *Der unbekannte Engelbert Humperdinck: Im Spiegel des Briefwechsels mit seinen Zunftgenossen*, 1 vol. to date, Vol. I: *1884–1893* (Vienna: Verlag Dr. Richard Strauss, 2004), pp. 72–3.

52 Hepokoski, "Fiery-Pulsed Libertine," p. 150.

53 Support for this reading of the opening in terms of sonata form can be found in Strauss's description of this section as a "glowing middle-theme" (*glühende Mittelthema*), this being his preferred designation for second themes. Strauss to Franz Strauss, November 15, 1889, in Trenner, *Eltern*, p. 121.

54 Werbeck, *Tondichtungen*, pp. 323–86.

55 Dahlhaus, *Nineteenth-Century Music*, pp. 331, 334.

56 Letter from Strauss to Eugen Spitzweg, November 19, 1890, in Grasberger, *Der Strom der Töne*, p. 56. In this context, Strauss is using "absolute" music to signify instrumental music.

57 *Chronicle*, p. 272.

58 Eduard Hanslick, *The Collected Musical Criticism of Eduard Hanslick*, 9 vols., Vol. VII (Farnborough: Gregg, 1971) p. 221.

59 *Chicago Daily Tribune* (February 24, 1895), quoted in Schmid, "The Tone Poems of Richard Strauss," pp. 186–7.

60 Extract from letter from Strauss to Friedrich von Hausegger about his compositional process, *c.* 1895, first printed in its entirety in Werbeck, *Tondichtungen*, 534–9 (p. 538). (Translation modified from *Chronicle*, p. 180.)

61 The official poem has been rather neglected in discussions of the work. It is symptomatic that in the Eulenberg edition it has been replaced by an abbreviated version of Del Mar's commentary. Various writers (including Mathias Hansen, *Richard Strauss: Die Sinfonischen Dichtungen* [Kassel: Bärenreiter, 2003], p. 81) have erroneously maintained that Strauss did not take the poem seriously, whereas in fact Strauss told his publisher that Ritter's poem was an excellent guide to *Tod und Verklärung* ("Bitte ich dich, dich an Ritter zu wenden, von dem das Gedicht ist, ich weiß nichts besseres dafür!"). Strauss to Eugen Spitzweg, December 23, 1890, D-Mmb: Sammelstück, 48.

62 Werbeck, *Tondichtungen*, p. 124. In addition to those concepts listed above, Werbeck states that the retrospective look at childhood and the emergence of the ideals theme were probably also formative elements. Other ideas to emerge early on were the reminiscences of infancy, boyhood, and youthful ardour. However, he demonstrates that the ordering and content of events did *not* remain unchanged from the beginning.

63 An expanded discussion of temporality in this work is found in Daniel G. Harrison, "Imagining *Tod und Verklärung*," *Richard-Strauss-Blätter* (new series) 29 (June, 1993): 22–52.

64 Gustav Brecher, *Richard Strauss: Eine monographische Skizze* (Leipzig: Hermann Seemann Nachfolger, n.d. [1900]), p. 23.

65 For more on the concept of transfiguration, see Camilla Bork, "*Tod und Verklärung*: Isoldes Liebestod als Modell künstlerischer Schlußgestaltung," in Hermann Danuser and Herfried Münkler, eds., *Zukunftsbilder: Richard Wagners Revolution und ihre Folgen in Kunst und Politik* (Schliengen: Argus, 2002), pp. 161–78, esp. p. 163.

66 German original published in the score of *Tod und Verklärung* (London: Eulenberg, 1961).

67 Brecher, *Richard Strauss*, p. 22, trans. Schmid, "The Tone Poems of Richard Strauss," p. 198 (wrongly attributed to Romain Rolland in the text at this point).

68 Admittedly, *Tod und Verklärung* is in the minor mode, which of its nature tends to involve a greater incidence of chromaticism than does the major. Furthermore, *Don Juan* is hardly devoid of chromaticism (see mm. 1ff., 28ff., 38ff., 148ff., 482ff., and esp. 505ff.).

69 Roland Tenschert, *Straussiana aus vier Jahrzehnten*, ed. Jürgen Schaarwächter (Tutzing: Hans Schneider, 1994), p. 34 relates the trajectory of *Tod und Verklärung* to

Beethoven's Fifth and Ninth Symphonies and Brahms's Symphony No. 1, and acknowledges that it can be seen as a "companion piece" [*Pendant*] to Liszt's *Les Préludes*.

70 Letter from Strauss to Wilhelm Bopp, February 9, 1931, quoted in *Chronicle*, p. 181 (translation modified).

71 Strauss noted that "*Tod und Verklärung* bringt das Hauptthema erst als Culminationspunkt in der Mitte." "Tagebuch" Blau V, RSA, 8. See also Franz Grasberger and Franz Hadamowsky, eds., *Richard Strauss-Ausstellung zum 100. Geburtstag* (Vienna: Österreichische Nationalbibliothek, 1964), p. 127.

72 Dahlhaus, *Nineteenth-Century Music*, p. 363.

5 The second cycle of tone poems

1 Milan Kundera, *The Book of Laughter and Forgetting*, trans. Aaron Asher (New York: HarperCollins, 1996), p. 86.

2 Much of the following discussion is based on material chronicled in Charles Youmans, *Richard Strauss's Orchestral Music and the German Intellectual Tradition: The Philosophical Roots of Musical Modernism* (Bloomington: Indiana University Press, 2005). Cf. also Charles Youmans, "The Private Intellectual Context of Richard Strauss's *Also sprach Zarathustra*," *19th-Century Music* 22/2 (1998): 101–26; and "The Role of Nietzsche in Richard Strauss's Artistic Development," *Journal of Musicology* 21 (2004): 309–42.

3 Youmans, *Strauss's Orchestral Music*, p. 92.

4 His reading of Nietzsche, it seems, was preceded by an interest *c.* 1892 in the writings of Max Stirner, "anarchic individualist" and promoter of the "explicitly antimetaphysical view of sexual love" – such works as *Der Einzige und sein Eigentum* (*The Ego and His Own*). See *ibid.*, pp. 86, 91.

5 Nietzsche's first proclamations appeared in *The Gay Science*, Section 108 ("New Struggles"), Book 3: "God is dead; but given the way of men, there may still be caves for thousands of years in which his shadow will be shown. – And we – we still have to vanquish his shadow, too." More famously, the line is shouted out in the famous parable of the madman crying out the death of God in the marketplace (Section 125): "God is dead. God remains dead. And we have killed him." Friedrich Nietzsche, *The Gay Science*, trans. Walter Kaufmann (New York: Vintage, 1974), pp. 167, 181. Kaufmann also provided (p. 167 n. 1) several references to the "God is dead" line in *Zarathustra*.

6 The temple/god image is adapted and recrafted from a well-known passage in Martin Heidegger, "The Origin of the Work of Art" (1935–6, 1950), in *Poetry, Language, Thought*, trans. Albert Hofstadter (New York: HarperCollins, 2001), pp. 40–9. The passage dwells on art, being, and truth from a very different perspective.

7 An extreme but telling variant of this conservative, old-world charge may be found in the ever-indignant Adorno's diatribes against Strauss for morally defiling the truth–content features of music (as posited a priori by the Frankfurt School writers) in favor of commercial success and bourgeois compromise. Among the reiterative *j'accuse*-indictments hurled by Adorno (and cf. n. 6 above, the Heideggerian image of the abandoned temple): "His work has the atmosphere of the Grand Hotel of childhood, a palace accessible only to money, yet not really a palace any more." Or: "[Strauss's music] thumbs its nose at inwardness … [abandons itself to] unmitigated exteriority." Theodor W. Adorno, "Richard Strauss: Born June 11, 1864," trans. Samuel and Shierry Weber, *Perspectives of New Music* 3 (1964), 25–26, 16–17. Cf. n. 16 below.

8 Alexander Ritter to Strauss, January 17, 1893, in Youmans, *Strauss's Orchestral Music*, p. 68.

9 Walter Werbeck, *Die Tondichtungen von Richard Strauss* (Tutzing: Hans Schneider, 1996), pp. 248–9, 255–9, 260, 262, 264. Several of these were collected and republished in Herwarth Walden, ed., *Richard Strauss: Symphonien und Tondichtungen* (Berlin: Schlesinger, n.d. [*c*. 1908]).

10 Arthur Seidl, "Richard Strauß: Eine Charakterskizze" [1896], in Seidl, *Straußiana: Aufsätze zur Richard Strauß-Frage aus drei Jahrzehnten* (Regensburg: Gustav Bosse, 1913), pp. 11–66 (p. 58; my translation). See also the more extended discussion of the *Till* program and its "esoteric" metaphor in James Hepokoski, "Framing Till Eulenspiegel," *19th-Century Music* 30/1 (2006): 4–43; reprinted in Hepokoski, *Music, Structure, Thought: Selected Essays* (Aldershot: Ashgate, 2009), pp. 273–312.

11 Arthur Seidl remarked in 1896 ("Richard Strauß," p. 62) that although Strauss's forthcoming tone poem would bear the title *Also sprach Zarathustra*, its actual subject (*Gegenstand*) would be *Human, All Too Human* (Youmans, *Strauss's Orchestral Music*, p. 90). The larger point is that Strauss was informed more broadly by the emancipatory spirit of Nietzsche in general. Even as key images from Nietzsche's *Zarathustra* (1883–5) recur

prominently in the tone poem, the point-of-view and flavor of the earlier *Menschliches, allzumenschliches: Ein Buch für freie Geister* (1878) are also congruent with that of Strauss's composition. The musician reprocessed what he needed from the philosopher to serve his own ends.

12 Friedrich Nietzsche, "Of Reading and Writing," in *Thus Spoke Zarathustra*, trans. R. J. Hollingdale (New York: Penguin, 1961), p. 68.

13 Strauss to Gustav Kogel, quoted, for example, in Werbeck, *Tondichtungen*, p. 262 n. 684.

14 Youmans, *Strauss's Orchestral Music*, p. 204, where Ritter is described as a proponent of "unhappy [and 'outmoded'] idealism" who "lived in semiretirement, buried in his books."

15 In *Strauss's Orchestral Music*, p. 181, Youmans provides an overview of these "interior" doubts, of Strauss's "professional insecurity, reflecting persistent questions about the validity of his antimetaphysical views and the advisability of destroying a musical aesthetic so widely held by his peers" – a "multileveled insecurity" that was turning him into a "misanthrope."

16 The charges of cynicism would be leveled most vituperatively in Adorno's 1964 essay, "Richard Strauss": "noncommittal *peinture* [that] denounces … all absorption as boredom" (p. 22); "a bourgeois coolness, a lack of participation on the part of the aesthetic subject" (p. 31). See also n. 7 above. Adorno's observations about Strauss and his style are by no means incorrect, nor can they be shrugged off by any current commentator on the composer. On the contrary, Adorno repeatedly put his finger on the most telling points of the style and its implications, often in unforgettable phrases that invite quotation and reflection. It is only that the moralistic Adorno, upholding his own variant of a by-then-eclipsed view of one's absolute duty to the revelatory truth-bearing value of music (in this era, posited as resistance to capitalism and the desires of "the bourgeois subject," non-accommodation with the culture industry, and so forth), had a visceral aversion to what he found in Strauss, and cast his observations in the form of repeated denunciations that current readers are likely to find exaggerated and self-indicting. Adorno's remarks are brilliant, to be sure, but they are also strident and open to historicizing and deconstruction.

17 Seidl, "Richard Strauß," p. 61.

18 Hans Merian, *Richard Strauß' Tondichtung Also sprach Zarathustra: Eine Studie über die moderne Programmsymphonie* (Leipzig: Carl Meyer, 1899). Merian's reading of *Zarathustra*

is more persuasive, more detailed, than the authorized (and somewhat cautious) version by Arthur Hahn.

19 *Ibid.*, pp. 5, 9–11. In the Foreword, Merian noted that the two central questions still being debated among critics were "will and can program music express specific thoughts? and in what ways can this happen?" (p. 4). He devoted his monograph to laying out the case for the presence of philosophical, Nietzschean thought – "specific ideas" – in *Zarathustra*.

20 Morten Kristiansen, "Richard Strauss, *Die Moderne*, and the Concept of *Stilkunst*," *The Musical Quarterly* 86/4 (Winter, 2002): 689–749 ("juxtaposing," p. 702; "aesthetic," p. 700; "contemporary zeitgeist," p. 702; "culture of nerves," p. 693). A central model for this detached, objective aesthetic of styles, remarked Strauss in a 1909 letter to Paul Bekker, was Mozart, "the incarnation of the pure artist, in comparison with the artists who also want to be confessors and starry-eyed idealists in their art" (*ibid.*, pp. 700–1). Kristiansen noted that he adopted the term *Stilkunst* from the literary history by Richard Hamann and Jost Hermand, *Deutsche Kunst und Kultur von der Gründerzeit bis zum Expressionismus*, 5 vols., Vol. IV: *Stilkunst um 1900* (Berlin: Akademie-Verlag, 1967).

21 Leon Botstein, "The Enigmas of Richard Strauss: A Revisionist View," in *Strauss and His World*, pp. 3–32 ("fragmentation in the use of the past and … irony," p. 18; "stylistic extraction," p. 18; "disregard for consistency," p. 19; "prefigured the aesthetics of postmodernism," p. 17). "In the tone poems he perfected a language of musical illustration that played with the illusion of realism" (p. 24).

22 Herwarth Walden (based on Arthur Hahn), "Don Quixote," in Walden, *Richard Strauss: Symphonien und Tondichtungen*, p. 130.

23 Youmans, *Strauss's Orchestral Music*, p. 205. The D–A♭–D swerve was noted and analyzed in Graham Phipps, "The Logic of Tonality in Strauss's *Don Quixote*: A Schoenbergian Evaluation," *19th-Century Music* 9 (1986): 189–205 (pp. 192–4). As Phipps observed (p. 190), the initial slippage from D to A♭ in the antecedent had been attacked by Heinrich Schenker in his *Harmonielehre* (Vienna: Universal Edition, 1906), pp. 299–300 as "unnatural and therefore inadmissible … [a] digression … not artistically composed, but, on the contrary, with disregard for nature … placed without proper linear working-out [*unmotiviert*] purely at the whim of a man who does not know what he wants, what is appropriate."

24 Seidl, "Richard Strauß," pp. 28–9.

25 On the format of a sentence, see n. 27 below.

26 Arthur Hahn, "*Also sprach Zarathustra*," reprinted in Walden, *Richard Strauss: Symphonien und Tondichtungen*, pp. 113; Merian, *Richard Strauß' Tondichtung* Also sprach Zarathustra, p. 17.

27 A sentence is a forward-driving melodic shape based on the vectored principle of short–short→long (*aa′b*) in which the two short impulses may be perceived as either identical or closely related as variants. (How far-ranging the *a′*-variant can be and still be considered *a′* is a matter of individual judgment.) The two *a*'s are called the presentation (or presentation modules); *b* is the continuation. The continuation is often (but not always) based on material from the presentation, and it typically drives towards an eventual cadence. When the continuation begins with its own complementary presentation modules, as here at the opening of *Ein Heldenleben*, that continuation is itself sentential (a "sentential continuation"), beginning another *aa′b* pattern. In turn its succeeding *b* can once again be initiated sententially, and so on. The result is a sentence-chain (*Satzkette*). Its effect is to produce a succession of presentational modules, paired short impulses, until a cadence is finally driven towards and attained. In *Heldenleben*, then, m. 5, nominally a continuation, begins with complementary *aa′*-style modules: mm. 5–6, 7–8; m. 9, nominally a new continuation, again begins presentationally with new complementary modules: mm. 9–10, 11–12. A non-sentential continuation (with its characteristic fragmentation and compression) and drive to cadence is reached only at m. 13. An introduction to Classical sentence-formats is provided in William E. Caplin, *Classical Form: A Theory of Formal Functions for the Instrumental Music of Haydn, Mozart, and Beethoven* (New York: Oxford University Press, 1998), pp. 35–48. For a more flexible discussion extending further into the nineteenth century and including a consideration of *Satzketten*, see Matthew BaileyShea, "The Wagnerian *Satz*: The Rhetoric of the Sentence in Wagner's Post-*Lohengrin* Operas" (Ph.D. diss., Yale University, 2003).

28 A delicious detail: at the beginning of the recapitulation (m. 631, rehearsal no. 77), the moment celebrating triumph over adversaries, the chromatic deformation from m. 7 is now straightened out into a confident diatonicism (m. 637).

29 Adorno, "Richard Strauss," pp. 19, 30–1.

30 The most thorough guide through the evidence bearing on these programmatic questions in all of Strauss's tone poems remains Werbeck, *Tondichtungen*, pp. 103–300.

31 Wilhelm Mauke, "*Till Eulenspiegels lustige Streiche*," reprinted in Walden, *Richard Strauss: Symphonien und Tondichtungen*, pp. 92–108. English equivalents are adapted from *Chronicle*, p. 397. For a complete list of the Mauke labels see also Hepokoski, "Framing Till Eulenspiegel," p. 13.

32 As is well known, the initial pitch-contour of all versions shown in Example 5.4 may allude to a familiar motive (tranquility or repose) from the love duet of *Tristan und Isolde*, Act II, while the jeering, tongue-protruding "Till chord," *sforzando* at m. 47, is the "*Tristan* chord" differently spelled and resolved. See also the discussion of these and related matters in Matthew Bribitzer-Stull and Robert Gauldin, "Hearing Wagner in *Till Eulenspiegel*: Strauss's Merry Pranks Reconsidered," *Intégral* 21 (2007): 1–39.

33 Steven Vande Moortele, "Beyond Sonata Deformation: Liszt's Symphonic Poem *Tasso* and the Concept of Two-Dimensional Sonata Form," *Current Musicology* 86 (2008): 49. A more extensive treatment, including studies of *Don Juan* and *Ein Heldenleben*, may be found in Vande Moortele, *Two-Dimensional Sonata Form: Form and Cycle in Single-Movement Instrumental Works by Liszt, Strauss, Schoenberg, and Zemlinsky* (Leuven: University of Leuven Press, 2009).

34 Cf. Carl Dahlhaus, *Nineteenth-Century Music*, trans. J. Bradford Robinson (Berkeley: University of California Press, 1989), pp. 236–44, 360–8; and William S. Newman, *The Sonata since Beethoven* (New York: Norton, 1969), pp. 134–5, 373–7. The issue of potential multimovement-cycle implications (*Mehrsätzigkeit*) in the second cycle (particularly in *Zarathustra* and *Heldenleben*) has also been treated by David Larkin, "Reshaping the Liszt–Wagner Legacy: Intertextual Dynamics in Strauss's Tone Poems" (Ph.D. diss., University of Cambridge, 2006), pp. 289–90, 296–9. More generally, the dual-function possibility has long been a commonplace within the analysis of several nineteenth-century (and later) symphonic forms. See also, for example, Werbeck, *Tondichtungen*, pp. 257, 304–6, 444–5; James Hepokoski, review of Werbeck, *Tondichtungen*, *Journal of the American Musicological Society* 51 (1998): 603–25 (p. 613); and James Hepokoski, "Beethoven Reception: The Symphonic Tradition," in Jim Samson, ed., *The Cambridge History of Nineteenth-Century Music* (Cambridge: Cambridge University Press, 2002), pp. 453–4. The likely eighteenth-century origins of the format are suggested in James Hepokoski and Warren Darcy,

Elements of Sonata Theory: Norms, Types and Deformations in the Late-Eighteenth-Century Sonata (Oxford: Oxford University Press, 2006), pp. 220–1.

35 On rotations as a general concept, see James Hepokoski, "Structure, Implication, and the End of *Suor Angelica*," *Studi pucciniani* 3 (2004): 241–64, which contains (p. 242) a list of complementary articles on the topic; reprinted in Hepokoski, *Music, Structure, Thought*, pp. 143–66. Cf. Hepokoski and Darcy, *Elements of Sonata Theory*, e.g. pp. 611–14.

36 For a more detailed study of the structure of this work, including the role and implications of its introduction (mm. 1–5) and epilogue (mm. 632–57), see Hepokoski, "Framing Till Eulenspiegel."

37 Merian, *Richard Strauß' Tondichtung Also sprach Zarathustra*, p. 39: "We could designate this melody as the *Weise des Ideals*. It is played in B major, the key of the achieved ideal. All dark and heavy instruments [now] lie silent." In the Strauss-authorized commentary of Arthur Hahn, this B major theme suggested "an overflowing, anticipatory sense of the feeling of happiness[-to-come], with liberation from all doubts and spiritual needs. In its passionate flight the soul ascends higher and higher." See Walden, *Richard Strauss: Symphonien und Tondichtungen*, p. 119.

38 Cf. the famous moment at the onset of the recapitulation of the first movement of Beethoven's Symphony No. 9, m. 301.

39 See, for example, Nietzsche, *Thus Spoke Zarathustra*, pp. 233–4. Following remarks originally stated in the authorized guide by Arthur Hahn as well as evidence from Strauss's own marked copies of Nietzsche, Charles Youmans (*Strauss's Orchestral Music*, pp. 93, 101–8, 194–5) has discussed the significance of this important moment to Strauss himself and has also explicated its implicit intertextual link to Faust's staggering confrontation with the Earth Spirit.

40 Having begun in an unambiguous C major (Nature), the piece's final section is grounded in B major (humanity, the spirit of question and questioning). The key of B remains unreconciled to C. The "C" implication at the end involves an upper-neighbor, incomplete French-sixth chord with C in the bass (eight bars from the end), resolving back to B major. As the music evaporates, one is left only with the residue ("C") of the upper-neighbor, surely not to be heard at the end as a convincing tonic.

41 I borrow the concept of referential sonata stations – touched upon as location-markers or "orientation-points" but then

abandoned – from Werbeck, *Tondichtungen*, e.g. pp. 427, 447, 476.

42 The relevance of the sonata-form concept to the *Quixote* variations has been a matter of dispute. Arguments on behalf of three embedded sonata structures traversing the whole of *Don Quixote* have been made by Phipps, "The Logic of Tonality," pp. 189–205, esp. pp. 203–5. My own view is that these sonata interpretations are unconvincing. This is also the conclusion of Werbeck, *Tondichtungen*, pp. 383, 457. Similarly, Youmans, *Strauss's Orchestral Music*, p. 203, considers *Quixote* to be the composition in which "Strauss for the first time completely abandoned this dialogue [with sonata-form conceptions]." On the other hand, Larkin, "Reshaping the Liszt–Wagner Legacy," pp. 239–45, considers Phipps to have "established" the sonata-form basis of the introduction (with two secondary keys in the "exposition," F♯ minor and F major) but proceeds to offer an alternative, single-sonata (deformation) proposal for the whole, in which mm. 1–160 (through the "Tema") constitute the exposition, Variations 1–10 form a huge and sprawling "set of variations (taking the place of the Development)," and the finale is a reversed recapitulation. Notwithstanding Larkin's caveats, I find this interpretation, too, to be strained.

43 This conclusion is both similar to and different from that of Larkin, "Reshaping the Liszt–Wagner Legacy." Larkin does propose a sonata-framing of the interior variations (see the note directly above), but after noting the difficulties with this assertion remarks (p. 242): "My alternative reading might be best described as an imaginative reconstruction of an imaginary entity, the sonata structure which 'would' have existed but for Quixote's madness."

44 Werbeck (*Tondichtungen*, p. 448) and others have argued that the entire primary thematic zone (P, mm. 1–117) itself constitutes a miniature sonata form: (small-scale) P, m. 1; secondary theme (S), m. 21; development, m. 45; reversed recapitulation starting with S in the tonic, m. 84 (86), and P following, m. 94. From the sonata point of view, it might be preferable to begin the small-scale recapitulatory space with P starting on E♭:I⁶ at m. 76 (rehearsal no. 9), with P at m. 94 as coda (perhaps dissolving into a transition). A stronger reading would construe mm. 1–117 as rotationally based and perhaps only secondarily in dialogue with the sonata concept: Rotation 1, mm. 1–16; expanded Rotation 2, mm. 17–45; Rotation 3, mm. 45 (rehearsal no. 5)–75; Rotation 4, mm. 76 (rehearsal no. 9)–94; Rotation 5, mm. 94–117.

45 My own view is that the secondary theme proper does not begin until m. 205, six measures after rehearsal no. 23, with the onset of the Wooing motive in the bass instruments.

46 See the brief accounts, for example, in Werbeck, *Tondichtungen*, pp. 446–7; and Larkin, "Reshaping the Liszt–Wagner Legacy," p. 292.

6 Strauss's road to operatic success: *Guntram, Feuersnot*, and *Salome*

1 For an overview of the post-Wagnerian libretto see Morten Kristiansen, "Richard Strauss's *Feuersnot* in Its Aesthetic and Cultural Context: A Modernist Critique of Musical Idealism" (Ph.D. diss., Yale University, 2000), pp. 95–172.

2 Strauss later noted that he would never have written an opera had it not been for Ritter's encouragement; see Richard Strauss, "Reminiscences of the First Performance of My Operas," in *Recollections*, pp. 146–67 (p. 146). For a detailed discussion of Strauss's relationship to Ritter see Charles Youmans, *Richard Strauss's Orchestral Music and the German Intellectual Tradition: The Philosophical Roots of Musical Modernism* (Bloomington: Indiana University Press, 2005), pp. 35–48.

3 Willi Schuh documented the genesis of *Guntram* in *Chronicle*, pp. 269–97.

4 For an exhaustive discussion of Wagner's presence in *Guntram*, see Charles Youmans, "Richard Strauss's *Guntram* and the Dismantling of Wagnerian Musical Metaphysics" (Ph.D. diss., Duke University, 1996), pp. 242–342. For the Tristan remark, see Oskar Merz's review of November 18, 1895 in Franzpeter Messmer, ed., *Kritiken zu den Uraufführungen der Bühnenwerke von Richard Strauss*, (Pfaffenhofen: W. Ludwig, 1989), p. 15.

5 Anonymous review in the *Neue Musik-Zeitung* 15 (1894): 142; cited in Youmans, *Strauss's Orchestral Music*, p. 38.

6 Ernest Newman, "Richard Strauss and the Music of the Future," *Musical Studies* (London and New York: John Lane, 1905): 249–304 (p. 254).

7 For detailed discussions of the music of each of Strauss's operas see Normal Del Mar, *Richard Strauss: A Critical Commentary on His Life and Works*, 3 vols. (Ithaca, NY: Cornell University Press, 1986).

8 A short extract from Ritter's letter of January 17, 1893 along with Strauss's responses appears in *Chronicle*, pp. 282–6; the entire letter is reproduced in Youmans, "Richard Strauss's *Guntram*," pp. 383–97. It also appears (untranslated) in Charles Youmans, ed., "Ten Letters from Alexander Ritter to Richard

Strauss, 1887–1894," *Richard Strauss-Blätter* 35 (June, 1996): 10–16.

9 Max Stirner (1806–56) advocated egoism and anarchy in *The Ego and His Own* (1845), which Strauss had read.

10 See Youmans, *Strauss's Orchestral Music*, pp. 59–99, for a thorough discussion of Strauss's interest in Schopenhauer and Nietzsche and their relevance to *Guntram*.

11 Roy Pascal, *From Naturalism to Expressionism: German Literature and Society 1880–1918* (New York: Basic Books, 1973), p. 58.

12 Eugen Schmitz, *Richard Strauss als Musikdramatiker* (Munich: Dr. Henrich Löwe, 1907), p. 24.

13 Richard Strauss, "Recollections of My Youth and Years of Apprenticeship," in *Recollections*, pp. 134–45 (p. 140).

14 See Strauss's letter to Cosima Wagner of April 10, 1893 in Franz Trenner, ed., *Cosima Wagner, Richard Strauss: Ein Briefwechsel*, ed. with the assistance of Gabriele Strauss (Tutzing: Hans Schneider, 1978), p. 155.

15 *Chronicle*, pp. 312–13.

16 *Ibid.*, p. 297.

17 Richard Strauss, "Betrachtungen zu Joseph Gregors 'Weltgeschichte des Theaters,'" in Strauss, *Betrachtungen und Erinnerungen*, 2nd edn., ed. Willi Schuh (Zurich: Atlantis, 1957), pp. 173–81 (p. 179). (The essay does not appear in *Recollections*.)

18 See Gustav Mahler to Richard Strauss, March 24, 1894, in Herta Blaukopf, ed., *Gustav Mahler–Richard Strauss: Correspondence 1888–1911*, trans. Edmund Jephcott (Chicago: University of Chicago Press, 1984), p. 32.

19 For a more detailed discussion of *Feuersnot* see Morten Kristiansen, "Richard Strauss before *Salome*: The Early Operas and Unfinished Stage Works," in Mark-Daniel Schmid, ed., *The Richard Strauss Companion* (Westport, CT: Praeger, 2003), pp. 245–73.

20 Romain Rolland noted in his diary on March 1, 1900 that Strauss felt tragedy to have been exhausted by Wagner and was looking for comedy, even buffoonery; see Rollo Myers, ed., *Richard Strauss and Romain Rolland: Correspondence* (London: Calder and Boyars, 1968), p. 125.

21 See Strauss, "Betrachtungen zu Joseph Gregors 'Weltgeschichte des Theaters,'" pp. 179–80; letter of November 17, 1901 in Gabriella Hanke Knaus, ed., *Richard Strauss, Ernst von Schuch: Ein Briefwechsel* (Berlin: Henschel, 1999), p. 47; and letter of October 30, 1901 in Trenner, *Cosima Wagner, Richard Strauss*, p. 243.

22 For a full profile of Wolzogen see Morten Kristiansen, "Strauss's First Librettist: Ernst von Wolzogen beyond *Überbrettl*," *Richard Strauss-Blätter* (new series) 59 (June, 2008): 75–116.

23 For reviews of the premiere see Messmer, *Kritiken zu den Uraufführungen*, pp. 20–9.

24 Even when Strauss clearly intends parody, such as the *Mittsommernacht* love duet between Kunrad and Diemut for which he directs the performers to sing "with exaggerated pathos throughout," the music itself does not signal parody (and in this case performers usually ignore Strauss's directions).

25 See Ernst Otto Nodnagel, *Jenseits von Wagner und Liszt* (Königsberg: Druck und Verlag der Ostpreußischen Druckerei und Verlagsanstalt, 1902), pp. 126, 186; and Wilhelm Raupp, *Max von Schillings: Der Kampf eines deutschen Künstlers* (Hamburg: Hanseatische Verlagsanstalt, 1935), pp. 78–9.

26 Schmitz, *Richard Strauss als Musikdramatiker*, pp. 35–7, 56.

27 See Morten Kristiansen, "Richard Strauss, *Die Moderne*, and the Concept of *Stilkunst*," *The Musical Quarterly* 86/4 (Winter, 2002): 689–749.

28 Leon Botstein, "The Enigmas of Richard Strauss: A Revisionist View," in Bryan Gilliam, ed., *Richard Strauss and His World* (Princeton: Princeton University Press, 1992), pp. 3–32 (p. 6).

29 Letter of January 14, 1907, in Alma Mahler, *Gustav Mahler: Memories and Letters*, 3rd edn., ed. Donald Mitchell, trans. Basil Creighton (London: John Murray, 1973), p. 284.

30 Oscar Bie, *Die moderne Musik und Richard Strauss* (Berlin: Bard, Marquardt and Co., 1906), p. 66.

31 Oscar Wilde, Preface to *The Picture of Dorian Gray* (1891); and "The Soul of Man under Socialism" (1891), in Wilde, *Complete Works of Oscar Wilde*, ed. J. B. Foreman (London and Glasgow: Collins, 1966), pp. 17, 1091, 1093.

32 For details on Strauss's cuts and alterations see Roland Tenschert, "Strauss as Librettist," in Derrick Puffett, ed., *Richard Strauss: Salome* (Cambridge: Cambridge University Press, 1989), pp. 36–50. This volume is a fine introduction to the background, analysis, and reception of the opera. Although it has often been claimed that Debussy's *Pelléas et Melisande* (1902) and Strauss's *Salome* were the first to set a play directly, Russian composers Dargomizhsky and Mussorgsky had done this decades earlier in *The Stone Guest* (1872) and the original version of *Boris Godunov* (1869), respectively. Heinrich Zöllner's direct settings of Goethe's *Faust* (1887) and Gerhart

Hauptmann's *Die versunkene Glocke* (1899) provide a German precedent.

33 See Charles Bernheimer, "Visions of Salome," in T. Jefferson Kline and Naomi Schor, eds., *Decadent Subjects* (Baltimore and London: Johns Hopkins University Press, 2002), pp. 104–38.

34 Some of the changes did have precedents; in Massenet's opera *Hérodiade* (1881) Salome and John the Baptist are in love, and she kills herself after his execution.

35 Review of the premiere in Leopold Schmidt, *Aus dem Musikleben der Gegenwart* (Berlin: A. Hofmann, 1909), p. 116.

36 Letter of May 14, 1907, in Myers, *Richard Strauss and Romain Rolland*, p. 82; and Romain Rolland, *Jean-Christophe*, 10 vols., trans. Gilbert Cannan (New York: Modern Library, 1913), Vol. VII [1908], p. 407.

37 Thomas Beecham describes the episode in *A Mingled Chime* (London: Hutchinson, 1944), pp. 97–105.

38 Richard Batka, *Aus der Opernwelt* (Munich: Callwey, 1907), p. 202.

39 Strauss, "Reminiscences of the First Performance of My Operas," p. 150.

40 Lawrence Gilman, "Strauss's *Salome*: Its Art and Its Morals," in Gilman, *Aspects of Modern Opera* (New York: John Lane, 1909), pp. 65–106 (p. 73).

41 Otto Roese, *Richard Strauss: Salome* (Berlin: Bard, Marquardt and Co., 1906), p. vii.

42 Strauss, "Reminiscences of the First Performance of My Operas," p. 152.

43 Gilman, "Strauss's *Salome*," pp. 88–9; Mahler, *Memories and Letters*, p. 275.

44 Batka, *Aus der Opernwelt*, pp. 197–8. See also Bie, *Die moderne Musik*, p. 69.

45 Heinrich Chevalley in Messmer, *Kritiken zu den Uraufführungen*, p. 48; letter of May 14, 1907, in Myers, *Richard Strauss and Romain Rolland*, p. 84.

46 Diary entry of May 22, 1907, in Myers, *Romain Rolland and Richard Strauss*, p. 155; letter of May 5, 1935, in Willi Schuh, ed., *A Confidential Matter: The Letters of Richard Strauss and Stefan Zweig, 1931–1935*, trans. Max Knight (Berkeley and Los Angeles: University of California Press, 1977), p. 90.

47 Gilman, "Strauss's *Salome*," pp. 77–9, 90–1; Joseph Kerman, *Opera as Drama*, rev. edn. (Berkeley and Los Angeles: University of California Press, 1988), p. 209.

48 Willi Schuh, "Richard Strauss und seine Libretti" (1970), in Schuh, *Straussiana aus vier Jahrzehnten* (Tutzing: Hans Schneider, 1981), p. 141.

49 Roese, *Richard Strauss: Salome*, p. xi; Schmidt, *Aus dem Musikleben der Gegenwart*, p. 119.

50 Rudolf Louis, *Die deutsche Musik der Gegenwart* (Munich and Leipzig: Georg Müller, 1909), pp. 102–3.

51 Gilman, "Strauss's *Salome*," p. 82; Schmitz, *Richard Strauss als Musikdramatiker*, p. 46.

52 See Sander L. Gilman, "Strauss and the Pervert," in Arthur Groos and Roger Parker, eds., *Reading Opera* (Princeton: Princeton University Press, 1988), pp. 306–27; and Anne L. Seshadri, "The Taste of Love: Salome's Transfiguration," *Women and Music* 10 (2006): 24–44.

53 See Lawrence Kramer, "Modernity's Cutting Edge: The Salome Complex," in Kramer, *Opera and Modern Culture: Wagner and Strauss* (Berkeley: University of California Press, 2004), pp. 128–66; Linda Hutcheon and Michael Hutcheon, "Staging the Female Body: Richard Strauss's *Salome*," in Mary Ann Smart, ed., *Siren Songs* (Princeton: Princeton University Press, 2000), pp. 204–21; and Carolyn Abbate, "Opera; or, The Envoicing of Women," in Ruth A. Solie, ed., *Musicology and Difference* (Berkeley: University of California Press, 1993), pp. 225–58.

54 Abbate, "Opera," p. 247.

55 Friedrich Nietzsche, *The Birth of Tragedy*, trans. Douglas Smith (Oxford and New York: Oxford University Press, 2000), p. 11.

7 The Strauss–Hofmannsthal operas

1 See *Strauss/Hofmannsthal*. The photograph can also be found in Norman Del Mar, *Richard Strauss: A Critical Commentary on His Life and Works*, 3 vols., Vol. I (London: Barrie and Rockliff, 1962), plate facing p. 292.

2 *Strauss/Hofmannsthal*, p. 482 (translation modified, here and elsewhere in this essay).

3 *Ibid.*, p. 92.

4 Strauss and Hofmannsthal first met in 1898 at a gathering at Richard Dehmel's home in Berlin.

5 Though *Kythere* was never realized, he used sketches in three later works by Hofmannsthal: *Ariadne auf Naxos*, *Der Bürger als Edelmann*, and *Josephslegende*.

6 Richard Strauss, "Ten Golden Rules for the Album of a Young Conductor," in *Recollections*, p. 38.

7 Michael Hamburger, "Plays and Libretti," in Hamburger, *Hofmannsthal: Three Studies* (Princeton, NJ: Princeton University Press, 1972), p. 111.

8 Carl Schorske, "Operatic Modernism," *Journal of Interdisciplinary History* 36/4 (Spring, 2006): 675–81 (p. 680).

9 Hofmannsthal to Strauss, mid July 1911, in *Strauss/Hofmannsthal*, p. 94.

10 Hofmannsthal to Strauss, June 15, 1911, in *ibid.*, p. 90.

11 One of the earliest discussions of the "allomatic," or mutual, transformation in Hofmannsthal's work is Judith Ryan, "Die 'allomatische Lösung': Gespaltene Persönlichkeit und Konfiguration bei Hugo von Hofmannsthal," *Deutsche Vierteljahrschrift für Literaturwissenschaft und Geistesgeschichte* 44 (1970): 189–207.

12 Hofmannsthal to Strauss, February 12, 1919, in *Strauss/Hofmannsthal*, p. 324.

13 Hofmannsthal to Strauss, March 20, 1911, in *ibid.*, p. 76.

14 This quotation comes from Hofmannsthal's prose rewriting of the libretto, which has been published in English as *The Woman without a Shadow*, trans. Jean Hollander (Lewiston, NY: E. Mellen Press, 1993).

15 Strauss to Hofmannsthal, July 28, 1916, in *Strauss/Hofmannsthal*, p. 259.

16 Joseph Auner, *A Schoenberg Reader: Documents of a Life* (New Haven: Yale University Press, 2003), pp. 316–17; *ibid.*, p. 316.

17 Strauss to Hofmannsthal, June 5, 1916, in *Strauss/Hofmannsthal*, p. 250.

18 Strauss to Hofmannsthal, early September, 1916, in *ibid.*, p. 262.

19 Joseph Gregor's libretto for *Die Liebe der Danae* was based on a 1920 scenario by Hofmannsthal; see below.

20 This passage is drawn from Hofmannsthal's well-known *Ariadne-Brief*, which the poet sent to Strauss in July, 1911 and subsequently published in an expanded version in Leopold Schmidt's *Almanach für die musikalische Welt* (1912). The full text can be found in Hugo von Hofmannsthal, *Ariadne*, in Hofmannsthal, *Gesammelte Werke*, 10 vols., Vol. V: *Dramen V* (Frankfurt am Main: Fischer, 1979), pp. 297–300 (p. 297).

21 Strauss to Gerty von Hofmannsthal, July 16, 1929, in *Strauss/Hofmannsthal*, p. 537.

22 Friedrich Nietzsche, *Also sprach Zarathustra*, ed. Giorgio Colli and Mazzino Montinari (Munich: Deutscher Taschenbuch Verlag and de Gruyter, 1993), Part III, Chapter 56, No. 23, p. 264.

8 Opera after Hofmannsthal

1 Strauss to Hugo von Hofmannsthal, March 11, 1906; April 21, 1909, in *Strauss/Hofmannsthal*, pp. 3, 29.

2 Strauss to Gerty von Hofmannsthal, July 16, 1929, in *ibid.*, p. 537.

3 Bryan Gilliam, *The Life of Richard Strauss* (Cambridge: Cambridge University Press, 1999), p. 137.

4 See Wayne Heisler, Jr., "'To drive away all cloudy thoughts': Heinrich Kröller's and Richard Strauss's 1923 *Ballettsoirée* and

Interwar Viennese Cultural Politics," *The Musical Quarterly* 88/4 (Winter, 2005): 594–629; "Kitsch and the Ballet *Schlagobers*," *The Opera Quarterly* 22/1 (Winter, 2006): 38–64; and *The Ballet Collaborations of Richard Strauss* (Rochester, NY: University of Rochester, 2009).

5 Strauss to Hofmannsthal, May 25, 1916, in *Strauss/Hofmannsthal*, p. 248.

6 Strauss to Hofmannsthal, July 28, 1916, in *ibid.*, p. 258.

7 Gilliam, *The Life of Richard Strauss*, p. 119.

8 Bryan Gilliam, "Richard Strauss's *Intermezzo*: Innovation and Tradition," in *New Perspectives*, pp. 264–6.

9 Strauss to Hermann Bahr, January 1, 1917, quoted in Joseph Gregor, ed., *Meister und Meisterbriefe um Hermann Bahr* (Vienna: H. Bauer, 1947), pp. 99–100.

10 *Ibid.*, pp. 101–2.

11 See Richard Strauss, "Preface to *Intermezzo*," in *Recollections*, pp. 95–102. An earlier version of the *Intermezzo* "Preface" not originally appended to the score, and which appeared only in the first (German) edition of *Betrachtungen und Erinnerungen* (ed. Willi Schuh [Zurich: Atlantis, 1949]: 135–9), has been subsequently reprinted (with a translation by Stewart Spencer) in Richard Strauss, *Richard Strauss Edition*, 30 vols., Vol. XI: *Complete Stage Works*. Intermezzo: *Ein bürgerliche Komödie mit sinfonischen Zwischenspielen in zwei Aufzügen, op.72* (Vienna: Dr. Richard Strauss, 1996), pp. xiv–xviii.

12 *Ibid.*, p. xvi.

13 Gilliam, "Strauss's *Intermezzo*: Innovation and Tradition," p. 263.

14 Strauss, "Preface to *Intermezzo*," p. 102.

15 Gilliam, "Strauss's *Intermezzo*: Innovation and Tradition," p. 261.

16 Arnold Schoenberg, "On Strauss and Furtwängler (1946)," reprinted in H. H. Stuckenschmidt, *Schoenberg: His Life and Work*, trans. Humphrey Searle (London: Calder, 1977), p. 544.

17 Strauss, "Preface to *Intermezzo*" (earlier version), p. xiv.

18 Gilliam, *The Life of Richard Strauss*, p. 122.

19 See Anna Amalie Abert, *Richard Strauss: Die Opern* (Velber: Friedrich, 1972), p. 74; and esp. Walter Werbeck, "Oper und Symphonie: Zu formalen Konzeption von *Intermezzo*," *Richard Strauss-Blätter* (new series) 45 (June, 2001): 109–23.

20 Gilliam, "Strauss's *Intermezzo*: Innovation and Tradition," p. 279.

21 See Derrick Puffett, "'Lass Er die Musi, wo sie ist': Pitch Specificity in Strauss," in *Strauss and His World*, pp. 138–63 (pp. 155–6); and Gilliam, "Strauss's *Intermezzo*: Tradition and Innovation," pp. 259–83, esp. pp. 272–9, 281.

22 Strauss to Stefan Zweig, June 24, 1932, in Willi Schuh, ed., *A Confidential Matter: The Letters of Richard Strauss and Stefan Zweig, 1931–1935*, trans. Max Knight (Berkeley and Los Angeles: University of California Press, 1977), pp. 10–11.

23 Strauss to Zweig, June 17, 1935, in *ibid.*, pp. 99–100.

24 Joseph Gregor, *Richard Strauss: Der Meister der Oper* (Munich: R. Piper, 1939), pp. 246–7.

25 Strauss to Stefan Zweig, May 17, 1935, in Schuh, *A Confidential Matter*, p. 91.

26 See Bryan Gilliam, "'Friede im Innern': Strauss's Public and Private Worlds in the Mid 1930s," *Journal of the American Musicological Society* 57/3 (2004): 579–91.

27 The interpretation of *Friedenstag* (particularly its ending) has long been mired in controversy, with some commentators detecting distinctly pro-Nazi rhetoric in its dramaturgy and denouement while others claim covert resistance to the regime on the part of the work. For the most cogent expressions of the opposing camps, see Michael Steinberg, "Richard Strauss and the Question," in *Strauss and His World*, pp. 164–89 (pp. 179–80); and Pamela M. Potter, "Strauss's *Friedenstag*: A Pacifist Attempt at Political Resistance," *The Musical Quarterly* 69/3 (1983): 408–24.

28 Richard Strauss, *Friedenstag*, CD, Collegiate Chorale and Orchestra, cond. Robert Bass (Koch International, 1991), 3–7111–2; *Friedenstag*, CD, Chor der Bayerischen Staatsoper and Chor und Symphonieorchester des Bayerischen Rundfunks, cond. Wolfgang Sawallisch (EMI Classics, 1999), 7243-5-56850-2-5; *Friedenstag*, Staatskapelle Dresden, cond. Giuseppe Sinopoli (Deutsche Grammophon, 2002), 463-494-2.

29 Strauss to Joseph Gregor, September 25, 1935; October 15, 1935, in Susan Gillespie, ed. and trans., "Selections from the Strauss–Gregor Correspondence: The Genesis of *Daphne*," in *Strauss and His World*, pp. 237–70 (pp. 240, 242).

30 Quoted in Norman Del Mar, *Richard Strauss: A Critical Commentary on His Life and Works*, 3 vols., Vol. III (London: Barrie and Rockliff, 1972), p. 111.

31 Gillespie, "Selections from the Strauss–Gregor Correspondence," pp. 267–8.

32 *Ibid.*, p. 268 (emphasis in original).

33 See Bryan Gilliam, "Ariadne, Daphne, and the Problem of *Verwandlung*," *Cambridge Opera Journal* 15/1 (2003): 67–81.

34 Gilliam, *The Life of Richard Strauss*, p. 163.

35 *Ibid.*

36 See Philip Graydon, "Richard Strauss's *Die ägyptische Helena* (1927): Context and Contemporary Critical Reception" (Ph.D. diss., Queen's University Belfast, 2004), pp. 174–215.

37 Gilliam, *The Life of Richard Strauss*, p. 163.

38 Quoted in Ernst Krause, *Richard Strauss: The Man and His Music*, trans. John Coombs (London: Collett's, 1964), p. 427.

39 Strauss to Clemens Krauss, September 14, 1939, in Günter Brosche, ed., *Richard Strauss, Clemens Krauss. Briefwechsel: Gesamtausgabe* (Tutzing: Hans Schneider, 1997), p. 240; quoted in Klaus Adam, liner notes, trans. Mary Whittall, for Richard Strauss, *Capriccio*, Symphonieorchester des Bayerischen Rundfunks, cond. Karl Böhm (Deutsche Grammophon, 1972), 445–347–2, p. 16.

40 The text for the sonnet, written by the sixteenth-century poet Pierre de Ronsard (of the *Pléiade*), was found and translated by the conductor Hans Swarowsky.

41 Gilliam, *The Life of Richard Strauss*, p. 165.

42 As an instrument, the French horn held a special fascination for Strauss. Having written an early concerto for his father Franz (whom Bülow famously dubbed "the Joachim of the *Waldhorn*") in 1883, Strauss composed a second concerto for the instrument in 1942 – no doubt in remembrance of his beloved father at a time when the composer himself was in his twilight years. However, the use of the horn for the "moonlight music" in *Capriccio* and the poignant presentation of the *Tod und Verklärung* theme in "Im Abendrot" from the *Four Last Songs* (1948) seem to be on a more personal level. The air of quiet yet content resignation (particularly in the latter) is thus the obverse of the youthful exuberance encoded in the Hero's theme (for horn and strings) that opens *Ein Heldenleben*.

43 Willi Schuh, *Über Opern von Richard Strauss* (Zurich: Atlantis, 1947), p. 101.

44 See Leon Botstein, "The Enigmas of Strauss: A Revisionist View," in *Strauss and His World*, pp. 3–32 (pp. 14–32).

9 "Actually, I like my songs best": Strauss's lieder

1 Cited in Michael Kennedy, *Richard Strauss: Man, Musician, Enigma* (Cambridge: Cambridge University Press, 1999), p. 118.

2 The scholarly literature on Strauss's songs includes Alan Jefferson, *The Lieder of Richard Strauss* (London: Cassell, 1971); the invocations of Strauss throughout Edward Kravitt, *The Lied: Mirror of Late Romanticism* (New Haven and London: Yale University Press, 1996); the many discussions of songs

and poets in *Chronicle*; Suzanne Marie Lodato, "Richard Strauss and the Modernists: A Contextual Study of Strauss's Fin-de-siècle Song Style" (Ph.D. diss., Columbia University, 1999); Barbara Petersen, *"Ton und Wort": The Lieder of Richard Strauss* (Ann Arbor: UMI Research Press, 1980); Ursula Lienenlüke, *Lieder von Richard Strauss nach zeitgenössischer Lyrik* (Regensburg: Gustav Bosse Verlag, 1976); Roland Tenschert, "Verhältnis von Wort und Ton: Eine Untersuchung an dem Strauss'schen Lied 'Ich trage meine Minne,'" *Zeitschrift für Musik* 101 (1934): 591–5; Christine Getz, "The Lieder of Richard Strauss," in Mark-Daniel Schmid, ed., *The Richard Strauss Companion* (Westport, CT: Praeger, 2003), pp. 335–82; and Hans-Joachim Bracht, *Nietzsches Theorie der Lyrik und das Orchesterlied: Ästhetische und analytische Studien zu Orchesterliedern von Richard Strauss, Gustav Mahler und Arnold Schönberg* (Kassel: Bärenreiter, 1993). The sources on the *Vier letzte Lieder* are cited later in the chapter.

3 The great accompanist Graham Johnson has recorded these songs, both of them representative of earlier approaches to lied composition – "Die Drossel" vaguely reminiscent of Schumann, "Der müde Wanderer" of Schubert – with the soprano Marie McLaughlin on Hyperion's Helios series CDH55202 (1995 and 2005). The recollections of chorale, of Baroque walking bass, and of antique style in his early setting of "Lass ruh'n die Toten" on a poem by Adelbert von Chamisso are also striking; one remembers Schumann's invocation of times gone by in songs such as "Stirb, Lieb' und Freud'!", Op. 35, or "Auf einer Burg" from the Eichendorff *Liederkreis*, Op. 39. The bird-song in the piano at the beginning of "Die Drossel" would find its ultimate manifestation in "Im Abendrot" from the *Vier letzte Lieder* more than seventy years later.

4 Strauss wrote this song at the Palace Hotel in Montreux on November 23, 1948 for the great singer Maria Jeritza, his Octavian, Ariadne, and Helena. She did not allow anyone else to see it, perform it, or copy it; she did not even give Strauss a copy of his own autograph manuscript when he asked for one. Not until after her death without an heir in December, 1983 was it possible to go through her papers in search of the manuscript. Betty Wehrli-Knobel was a prolific novelist, writer about women's issues, memoirist, travel writer, and poet; her poetic anthology *Zwischen Tag und Abend* (*Between Day and Evening*) was published in Chur by Moham in 1935. Her imagery of summer flowers that blow away gently in the wind is as delicate an invocation

of death as anyone might wish it to be; no wonder Strauss was drawn to it at the close. The soprano Jessye Norman and the pianist Geoffrey Parsons were the first to record the work on *Richard Strauss: Lieder* with Philips (416–298–2) in 1985. See also J. M. Kissler, "Malven: Richard Strauss's letzte Rose!," *Tempo* 185 (1993):18–25.

5 According to Strauss, he was waiting for his wife Pauline one day in 1895 and put the twenty-minute wait to use by composing this song. See Kennedy, *Richard Strauss*, p. 92.

6 Cited in *Chronicle*, p. 455.

7 Cited in Kennedy, *Richard Strauss*, p. 23.

8 See William Wilder Colson, "Four Last Songs by Richard Strauss" (D.M.A. thesis, University of Illinois, 1975); Aubrey Garlington, Jr., "Richard Strauss's *Vier letzte Lieder*: The Ultimate Opus Ultimum," *The Musical Quarterly* 73 (1989): 79–93; Jane Strickert, "Richard Strauss's *Vier Letzte Lieder*: An Analytical Study" (Ph.D. diss., Washington University in St. Louis, 1975); and Timothy Jackson, "The Last Strauss: Studies of the *Letzte Lieder*" (Ph.D. diss., City University of New York, 1988).

9 There is, of course, a long literary and artistic tradition of comparing women to flowers; modern women might well wince at the clinging-ivy and blue-eyed-cornflower female stereotypes in Dahn's verses – this as the *Frauenbewegung* (women's movement) was already underway in Germany. But "Ach Lieb, ich muss nun scheiden" ("Oh Beloved, I Must Now Depart"), the third song in Op. 21, is a lovely thing, a latter-day *Lied im Volkston*.

10 Cited in *Chronicle*, p. 451.

11 When the eminent accompanist John Wustman in his youth asked Elisabeth Schwarzkopf to explain to him what "Zueignung" was really all about, she replied, "Nothing! It's about a high note!" Whether she meant to be dismissive about this first Strauss "chestnut" of them all or was pinpointing the source of the song's charm is not altogether clear. My thanks to John Wustman for this anecdote in an email communication.

12 Strauss wrote this in a letter from the 1930s to his librettist Joseph Gregor, a letter that is fascinating for the thumbnail critiques of Brahms, Mendelssohn, and even Schubert.

> A perfect Goethe poem doesn't need any music; precisely in the case of Goethe, music weakens and flattens the words … many songs owe their origin to the circumstance that the composer looks for a poem that will match a fine melodic idea and the poetically musical atmosphere – Brahmsian songs! If he *can't*

find a poem you get a Song *without* Words (Mendelssohn). Or the *modern* Lied: the verse gives birth to the vocal melody – not as happens so often, even in Schubert, that the melody is poured over the verse without getting the cadence of the poem quite right! (Cited in Kennedy, *Richard Strauss*, p. 118.)

13 Martina Steiger, ed., *Richard Strauss, Karl Böhm: Briefwechsel 1921–1949* (Mainz: Schott, 1999), p. 122.

14 See Kennedy, *Richard Strauss*, pp. 71, 77, 216, 234, 357.

15 The Goethe settings published in his lifetime include "Pilgers Morgenlied," Op. 33, No. 4; "Gefunden!", Op. 56, No. 1; the *Drei Lieder aus den "Büchern des Unmuts"*, Op. 67, Nos. 4–6; and "Erschaffen und Beleben," Op. 87, No. 2. The *pièces d'occasion* "Sinnspruch," "Durch allen Schall und Klang" (dedicated to Romain Rolland), "Zugemessne Rhythmen" (a thank-you gift for the musicologist Peter Raabe), and "Xenion" are in a different category from songs gathered into an opus and meant for recital performance.

16 Schoenberg might call mm. 3–4 different forms of II: a borrowed supertonic seventh chord followed by a Neapolitan seventh. Strauss, having touched on the raised IV and flatted II moves to B in a way that recalls the interaction of B and C in *Also sprach Zarathustra* (a work that also tried to be in C much as this song does). I am grateful to the *echt* Straussian Charles Youmans for pointing out the tonal kinship to the great symphonic tone poem.

17 It is no wonder that Dehmel's poetry was included in *Chorus eroticus: Neue deutsche Liebesgedichte*, ed. Karl Lerbs (Leipzig: Rainer Wunderlich, 1921). See also Fritz Horst, *Literarischer Jugendstil und Expressionismus: Zur Kunsttheorie, Dichtung und Wirkung Richard Dehmels* (Stuttgart: J. B. Metzler, 1969).

18 Richard Dehmel, *Gesammelte Werke*, 3 vols. (Berlin: Fischer, 1916), Vol. I, from the collection *Erlösungen: Gedichte und Sprüche*, pp. 40–1. The poem immediately following "Leises Lied" on p. 41 is an exercise in the same sexing-up of a traditional trope, a *Ständchen* beginning "Das Rosenstöcklein steht in Flor; / O Gärtnerin, wie blüht's empor! / Sie hat ihr Pförtlein zugemacht. / Tiefe Nacht" ("A little rosh bush is standing in bloom; / O Miss gardener, how it blooms forth! / She closed her little gate. / Deep night").

19 Dehmel, *Gesammelte Werke*, Vol. II, pp. 126–7.

20 Strauss uses F♯ major for a similar context in the "Presentation of the Rose"

("Wie himmlische, nicht irdische, wie Rosen vom hochheiligen Paradies …") in *Der Rosenkavalier*.

21 In *Richard Strauss's Orchestral Music and the German Intellectual Tradition: The Philosophical Roots of Musical Modernism* (Bloomington: Indiana University Press, 2005), Charles Youmans discusses Strauss's evolving opposition to all things metaphysical; by the time of this song's composition his spirituality was firmly based in the physical world.

22 From the Strauss–Ludwig Thuille correspondence in *Strauss and His World*, pp. 196–7 (emphasis in original).

23 Strauss's tonal shifts, carrying us from beginning to end in the most seamless manner, are roughly analogous to Dehmel's enjambments; Strauss, one notices, tracks the poem as prose and therefore locates the final return to F♯ major *after* the start of the third stanza in Dehmel's ordering.

24 Cited in *Chronicle*, p. 442.

25 Conrad Ferdinand Meyer, *Sämtliche Werke: Historisch-kritische Ausgabe*, ed. Hans Zeller and Alfred Zäch (Bern: Benteli, 1963).

26 Noting the choice of key, one remembers Strauss's letter to Clemens Krauss in 1941 regarding the newly completed *Capriccio*, his final opera: "Do you really believe that … something better or even just as good can follow? Isn't this D flat major the best conclusion to my life's work in the theater?" See Kennedy, *Richard Strauss*, pp. 334–5.

27 In *The Life of Richard Strauss* (Cambridge: Cambridge University Press, 1999), pp. 27–8, Bryan Gilliam recounts the family crisis when Strauss's mother was institutionalized in the famous sanatorium in Eglfing on April 14, 1885 and its deep effect on the young composer. Kennedy, in *Richard Strauss*, pp. 10–11, quotes Strauss's "Reminiscences of My Father" on the subject of his mother: Richard Strauss, "Reminiscences of My Father," in *Recollections*, pp. 127–33 (p. 131).

28 William Shakespeare, *Hamlet*, in *Shakespeare in deutscher Übersetzung*, trans. Karl Simrock and Ludwig Seeger, 10 vols., Vol. VI (Hildburghausen: Bibliographisches Institut, 1868).

10 Last works

1 See Bernd Gellermann, "Richard Strauss, *Die Donau*, AV 291, Symphonische Dichtung für großes Orchester, Chor und Orgel: Fragment," *Sammelblatt des historischen Vereins Ingolstadt* 90 (1981): 7–69.

2 Willi Schuh, ed., *Richard Strauss: Briefwechsel mit Willi Schuh* (Zurich: Atlantis, 1969), pp. 50ff. He expressed himself in a similar vein

in letters to Schuh of December 22, 1943 (p. 57) and November 6, 1945 (p. 87). Skat is a popular card game in Germany.

3 Strauss to his grandson, Richard Strauss, October 3, 1944, in Franz Grasberger, ed., *"Der Strom der Töne trug mich fort"*: *Die Welt um Richard Strauss in Briefen* (Tutzing: Hans Schneider, 1967), p. 428.

4 Strauss to Willi Schuh, May 1, 1944, in Schuh, *Briefwechsel mit Willi Schuh*, p. 66.

5 Strauss to Willi Schuh, May 20, 1946, in *ibid.*, p. 89 (emphasis mine).

6 Leon Botstein has made a case for incipient postmodernism in Strauss's works of the 1920s and 1930s. See Leon Botstein, "The Enigmas of Richard Strauss: A Revisionist View," in *Strauss and His World*, pp. 3–32.

7 Clemens Krauss to Richard Strauss, May 12, 1943, in Günter Brosche, ed., *Richard Strauss, Clemens Krauss. Briefwechsel: Gesamtausgabe* (Tutzing: Hans Schneider, 1997), p. 501.

8 "Have you finished the second suite for winds?" asks Willi Schuh in a letter to Strauss of May 23, 1943. Schuh, *Briefwechsel mit Willi Schuh*, p. 40.

9 Strauss to Schuh, May 31, 1943, in *ibid.*, p. 40.

10 Strauss to Schuh, May 8, 1943, in *ibid.*, p. 38.

11 Strauss to Schuh, December 22, 1943, in *ibid.*, p. 57.

12 Strauss to Krauss, March 21, 1944, in Brosche, *Richard Strauss, Clemens Krauss. Briefwechsel*, p. 517.

13 *Ibid.*, p. 516.

14 Strauss to Krauss, November 27, 1944, in *ibid.*, p. 513.

15 See, among others, Birgit Lodes, "Eine 'Urfassung' der *Metamorphosen* von Richard Strauss?," *Musica* 48 (1994): 275–9; and Birgit Lodes, "Richard Strauss' Skizzen zu den *Metamorphosen* und ihre Beziehung zu *Trauer um München*," *Musikforschung* 47/3 (1994): 234–52.

16 Jürgen May, "Bassoon's Suicide and *Quartettstyl*: Strauss's *Duet Concertino* in the Context of His Late Compositions." Lecture given at the International Conference *Strauss among the Scholars*, University of Oxford, 2007.

17 Strauss to Karl Böhm, September 30, 1944, in Martina Steiger, ed., *Richard Strauss, Karl Böhm: Briefwechsel 1921–1949* (Mainz: Schott, 1999), p. 171.

18 There is a version for seven strings that is occasionally performed and also available on CD, but, far from an *Urfassung* – as it has been referred to many times – it happens to be a

posthumous arrangement by Rudolf Leopold, the cellist of the Vienna String Sextet.

19 Strauss to Ernst Reisinger, summer, 1945, in Grasberger, *Der Strom der Töne trug mich fort*, p. 440.

20 *Die Philharmonischen Konzerte* (Program Booklet) 112, Subscription Concert 8 (Vienna, April 24, 1954), p. 242. Cited after Müller von Asow, *Richard Strauss*, 3 vols., Vol. III: *Werke ohne Opuszahlen* (Vienna: Doblinger, 1974), p. 1327.

21 Heinrich Kralik, *Richard Strauss: Weltbürger der Musik* (Vienna: Wollzeilen, 1963), p. 337.

22 See n. 16.

23 Roland Tenschert, ed., *Richard Strauss und Joseph Gregor: Briefwechsel* (Salzburg: O. Müller, 1955), pp. 136ff.

24 For instance in the slow movement of the String Quartet, Op. 18, No. 1; in the first movement of Op. 18, No. 4; or, particularly striking, in the clarinet cantilena in the second movement of the Septet, Op. 20.

25 Hector Berlioz, *Treatise on Instrumentation*, rev. and enl. Richard Strauss, trans. Theodore Front (New York: Kalmus, 1948), p. 194.

26 Hermann Hesse to Ernst Morgenthaler, February 1, 1946, in Hermann Hesse, *Musik, Betrachtungen, Gedichte, Rezensionen und Briefe: Eine Dokumentation*, ed. Volker Michels (Frankfurt am Main: Suhrkamp, 1978), pp. 178ff.

27 Photocopy of the autograph title page, Richard-Strauss-Archiv, Garmisch.

28 The change of pronoun from *das* to *dies* in the song bespeaks this personal dimension.

11 Strauss's place in the twentieth century

1 For the quoted phrases, see Richard Strauss, "Is There an Avant-Garde in Music?," in *Recollections*, pp. 12–17 (p. 12).

2 Charles Ives, *Essays before a Sonata, The Majority, and Other Writings*, ed. Howard Boatwright (New York: Norton, 1970), p. 83.

3 Aaron Copland, *Our New Music: Leading Composers in Europe and America* (New York: Whittlesey House, 1941), p. 36.

4 Igor Stravinsky and Robert Craft, *Conversations with Igor Stravinsky* (New York: Doubleday, 1959), pp. 83–4.

5 Henry-Louis de La Grange, Günther Weiss, and Knud Martner, eds., *Gustav Mahler: Letters to His Wife*, trans. Antony Beaumont (Ithaca, NY: Cornell University Press, 2004), p. 258.

6 Stephen Walsh, *Stravinsky: A Creative Spring. Russia and France, 1882–1934* (New York: Knopf, 1999), p. 194.

7 Claude Debussy, "Richard Strauss," in Debussy, *Monsieur Croche the Dilettante Hater*,

trans. B. N. Langdon Davies (New York: Dover, 1962), pp. 44–6.

8 Béla Bartók, "Autobiography," in Bartók, *Béla Bartók Essays*, ed. Benjamin Suchoff, (Lincoln, NE: University of Nebraska Press, 1992), pp. 408–11 (p. 409).

9 See especially Walter Werbeck, *Die Tondichtungen von Richard Strauss* (Tutzing: Hans Schneider, 1996); Charles Youmans, *Richard Strauss's Orchestral Music and the German Intellectual Tradition: The Philosophical Roots of Musical Modernism* (Bloomington: Indiana University Press, 2005); and Bryan Gilliam, *Richard Strauss's* Elektra (Oxford: Clarendon Press, 1991).

10 Bryan Gilliam, *The Life of Richard Strauss* (Cambridge: Cambridge University Press, 1999), p. 89.

11 Arnold Schoenberg, *Style and Idea: Selected Writings of Arnold Schoenberg*, ed. Leonard Stein, trans. Leo Black (Berkeley: University of California Press, 1984), p. 137.

12 Schoenberg to Webern, May 3, 1926, Arnold Schönberg Center, Vienna.

13 Joseph Auner, *A Schoenberg Reader: Documents of a Life* (New Haven: Yale University Press, 2003), pp. 316–17.

14 Hans Heinz Stuckenschmidt, *Arnold Schoenberg: His Life, World, and Work*, trans. Humphrey Searle (New York: Schirmer, 1978), p. 66.

15 Arnold Schoenberg, *Berliner Tagebuch* (Frankfurt: Propylaen, 1974), p. 25.

16 On *Pelleas* and other projects, see Stuckenschmidt, *Arnold Schoenberg*, pp. 61–6.

17 Walter Frisch, *The Early Works of Arnold Schoenberg, 1893–1908* (Berkeley: University of California Press, 1993), p. 222.

18 Willi Reich, *Schoenberg: A Critical Biography*, trans. Leo Black (New York: Praeger, 1971), p. 25. Schoenberg's copy of the vocal score of *Salome* can be seen at the Arnold Schönberg Center in Vienna; the first five pages are missing. There are several precise corrections of minor mistakes, suggesting that Schoenberg went through the score thoroughly.

19 See "Fremden-Liste," *Grazer Tagespost* (May 18, 1906). Out of Schoenberg's pupils at this time, only Webern and Egon Wellesz were unaccounted for. Webern could not make the trip because he was studying for his oral examinations at the University of Vienna; Wellesz seems to have gone to England in the summer of 1906.

20 Susan Gillespie, ed. and trans., "Selections from the Strauss–Thuille Correspondence: A Glimpse of Strauss during His Formative Years," in *Strauss and His World*, pp. 193–326 (p. 214).

21 Maurice Ravel, "An Interview with Ravel," in Arbie Orenstein, ed., *A Ravel Reader* (New York: Columbia University Press, 1990), pp. 470–1 (p. 470).

22 Richard Taruskin, *The Oxford History of Western Music*, 6 vols., Vol. IV: *Music in the Early Twentieth Century* (Oxford: Oxford University Press, 2005), p. 48.

23 Stuckenschmidt, *Arnold Schoenberg*, p. 525.

24 MS 77, III. Skizzenbuch, Sk 212, Arnold Schönberg Center, Vienna.

25 Remarkably, Egon Wellesz's 1921 book *Arnold Schönberg* (Leipzig: E. P. Tal, 1921; reprinted Wilhelmshaven: Heinrichshofen's Verlag, 1985) claims that it was *Strauss* who picked up the flutter-tonguing effect from Schoenberg, saying that *Die Frau ohne Schatten* showed the influence of Schoenberg's *Five Pieces* (see p. 122).

26 Glenn Gould, "Strauss and the Electronic Future," in Gould, *The Glenn Gould Reader*, ed. Tim Page (New York: Knopf, 1984), pp. 92–9 (p. 98).

27 Tethys Carpenter, "The Musical Language of *Elektra*," in Derrick Puffett, ed., *Richard Strauss*: Elektra (Cambridge: Cambridge University Press, 1989), pp. 74–106.

28 George Perle, *The Operas of Alban Berg*, 2 vols., Vol. II: *Lulu* (Berkeley: University of California Press, 1985), p. 94.

29 Stuckenschmidt, *Arnold Schoenberg*, p. 71.

30 For Erwin Stein's involvement, see Stein to Alma Mahler, March 28, 1914, in the Mahler–Werfel Papers, University of Pennsylvania.

31 Schoenberg to unknown correspondent, April 22, 1914, in Arnold Schoenberg, *Arnold Schoenberg: Letters*, ed. Erwin Stein, trans. Eithne Wilkins and Ernst Kaiser (Berkeley: University of California Press, 1987), pp. 50–1.

32 Leon Botstein, "Strauss and Twentieth-Century Modernity: A Reassessment of the Man and His Work," in Bernd Edelmann, Birgit Lodes, and Reinhold Schlötterer, eds., *Richard Strauss und die Moderne* (Berlin: Henschel Verlag, 2001), pp. 113–37 (p. 119).

33 See Anne Shreffler, "The Coloratura's Voice: Another Look at Zerbinetta's Aria from *Ariadne auf Naxos*," in Edelmann, Lodes, and Schlötterer, *Richard Strauss und die Moderne*, pp. 361–90.

34 Richard Taruskin, *Stravinsky and the Russian Traditions: A Biography of the Works through* Mavra" (Berkeley: University of California Press, 1996), pp. 255–306.

35 Vera Stravinsky and Robert Craft, *Stravinsky in Pictures and Documents* (New York: Simon and Schuster, 1978), p. 90.

36 I. Stravinsky and Craft, *Conversations with Igor Stravinsky*, p. 83.

37 Sylvia Kahan, *Music's Modern Muse: A Life of Winnaretta Singer, Princesse de Polignac* (Rochester: University of Rochester Press, 2003), pp. 177–8.

38 For an excellent discussion of "Das Lied des Steinklopfers," see Walter Frisch, *German Modernism: Music and the Arts* (Berkeley: University of California Press, 2005), pp. 59–62.

39 Joan Peyser, *Boulez: Composer, Conductor, Enigma* (New York: Schirmer, 1976), p. 1.

40 Gabriele Strauss and Monika Reger, eds., *Ihr aufrichtig Ergebener: Richard Strauss im Briefwechsel mit zeitgenössischen Komponisten und Dirigenten* (Berlin: Henschel Verlag, 1998), p. 285.

41 Gould, "Strauss and the Electronic Future," p. 99.

42 Copland, *Our New Music*, p. 35.

43 Robin Holloway, *On Music: Essays and Diversions* (New York: Continuum, 2008), p. 380.

44 Hans Werner Henze, *Bohemian Fifths: An Autobiography*, trans. Stewart Spencer (Princeton: Princeton University Press, 1999), p. 208.

45 Helmut Lachenmann, "Richard Strauss, *Eine Alpensinfonie–Ausklang*," essay included with the Ensemble Modern recording of Strauss's *Alpensinfonie* and Lachenmann's *Ausklang* (Ensemble Modern Medien, 2005), EMCD-003.

12 Musical quotations and allusions in the works of Richard Strauss

1 Strauss to Willi Schuh, January 23, 1944, in Willi Schuh, ed., *Richard Strauss: Briefwechsel mit Willi Schuh* (Zurich: Atlantis, 1969), p. 61.

2 Roland Tenschert, "Musikalische Entlehnungen, Zitate und Selbstzitate," in Tenschert, *Musikerbrevier* (Vienna: Wilhelm Frick Verlag, 1940), p. 211.

3 *Ibid.*, p. 214.

4 Günter von Noé, *Die Musik kommt mir äußerst bekannt vor: Wege und Abwege der Entlehnung* (Vienna: Doblinger, 1985), p. 78.

5 The word appears at rehearsal no. 60.

6 William Mann, *Richard Strauss: A Critical Study of the Operas* (London: Cassell, 1964), p. 202.

7 Act II, rehearsal no. 10.

8 One m. after rehearsal no. 11.

9 Measures 3–5 after rehearsal no. 36

10 Rehearsal no. 37.

11 One m. after rehearsal no. 12

12 Noé, *Die Musik kommt mir äußerst bekannt vor*, p. 65.

13 Trans. Peggie Cochrane, reproduced in liner notes for Richard Strauss, *Ariadne auf Naxos*, Wiener Philharmoniker, cond. Erich Leinsdorf (Decca, 1958), 443–675–2, p. 50.

14 *Ibid.*

15 After Denza filed a lawsuit protesting this unauthorized use, Strauss paid a royalty each time the work was performed.

16 *Ibid.*, p. 77.

17 *Strauss/Hofmannsthal*, p. 30.

18 *Ibid.*, pp. 486–7 (translation modified).

19 Rehearsal no. 59; the published score gives no indication of the source.

20 Five mm. after rehearsal no. 34.

21 Günter Brosche, ed., *Richard Strauss, Clemens Krauss. Briefwechsel: Gesamtausgabe* (Tutzing: Hans Schneider, 1997), p. 240.

22 Reinhold Schlötterer, "Ironic Allusions to Italian Opera in the Musical Comedies of Richard Strauss," in *New Perspectives*, pp. 77–91.

23 Giangiorgio Satragni, "Das 'Lied des Piemontesers' in der Oper *Friedenstag*," in *Richard-Strauss-Blätter* (new series) 59 (June, 2008): 32–67.

24 Schlötterer, "Ironic Allusions to Italian Opera," pp. 77–8.

25 *Ibid.*, p. 89.

26 Willi Schuh, ed., *Richard Strauss: Briefe an die Eltern 1882–1906* (Zurich and Freiburg: Atlantis, 1954).

27 Noé, *Die Musik kommt mir äußerst bekannt vor*, p. 81.

28 Willi Schuh, "Richard Strauss und 'Freut euch des Lebens,'" in Schuh, *Straussiana aus vier Jahrzehnten* (Tutzing: Hans Schneider, 1981), pp. 9ff.

29 See n. 1.

30 Richard Specht, *Richard Strauss und sein Werk*, 2 vols., Vol. I: *Der Künstler und sein Weg: Der Instrumentalkomponist* (Leipzig, Vienna, and Zurich: E. P. Thal and Co., 1921), pp. 338ff.

31 Rehearsal no. 46.

32 Ernst Krause, *Richard Strauss: Gestalt und Werk*, 5th edn. (Leipzig: Breitkopf and Härtel, 1975), p. 490.

33 Willi Schuh, ed., *Richard Strauss, Stefan Zweig: Briefwechsel* (Frankfurt: Fischer, 1957), p. 128.

34 Measure 32 in the horn.

35 Measures 86–8, 93–5 in the organ.

36 Jürgen May, "Hugo von Hofmannsthals und Richard Strauss' Festspiel *Die Ruinen von Athen* nach Ludwig van Beethoven: Mehr als ein Kuriosum?," in May, *Richard Strauss und das Musiktheater: Bericht über die Internationale Fachkonferenz Bochum, 14. bis 17. November 2001*, ed. Julia Liebscher (Berlin: Henschel, 2005), pp. 45–60 (p. 55).

37 Noé, *Die Musik kommt mir äußerst bekannt vor*, p. 56.

38 Laurenz Lütteken, *"Eine 3,000 jährige Kulturentwicklung abgeschlossen": Biographie und Geschichte in den Metamorphosen von Richard Strauss* (Winterthur: Amadeus, 2004), p. 14.

39 *Ibid.*

40 *Ibid.*

13 Strauss in the Third Reich

1 Strauss to Lionel Barrymore, January 1, 1947, in O. Rathkolb, *Führertreu und gottbegnadet: Künstlereliten im Dritten Reich* (Vienna: Österreichischer Bundesverlag, 1991), pp. 179–80.

2 Pamela M. Potter, "Strauss and the National Socialists: The Debate and Its Relevance," in *New Perspectives*, p. 111. See also Bryan Gilliam, "'Friede im Innern': Strauss's Public and Private Worlds in the Mid 1930s," *Journal of the American Musicological Society* 57/3 (2004): 565–97.

3 See, for instance, Gerhard Splitt, *Richard Strauss 1933–1935: Ästhetik und Musikpolitik zu Beginn der nationalsozialistischen Herrschaft* (Pfaffenweiler: Centaurus, 1987), pp. 21–41; and Potter, "Strauss and the National Socialists."

4 Potter, "Strauss and the National Socialists," pp. 110–11.

5 Strauss to Hugo von Hofmannsthal, August 5, 1918, in *Strauss/Hofmannsthal*, pp. 310–11.

6 See Michael Walter, *Richard Strauss und seine Zeit* (Laaber: Laaber Verlag, 2000), pp. 323–44.

7 Strauss to Stefan Zweig, June 17, 1935, in Willi Schuh, ed., *Richard Strauss, Stefan Zweig: Briefwechsel* (Frankfurt am Main: Fischer, 1957), p. 142.

8 Splitt, *Richard Strauss 1933–1935*, p. 81.

9 Strauss to his father, March 17, 1901, in Willi Schuh, ed., *Richard Strauss: Briefe an die Eltern 1882–1906* (Zurich and Freiburg: Atlantis, 1954), p. 242.

10 The publisher Hase in this case; see *ibid.*, pp. 244–5.

11 Michael H. Kater, *Composers of the Nazi Era: Eight Portraits* (New York and Oxford: Oxford University Press, 2000), p. 251.

12 Werner Egk, *Die Zeit wartet nicht: Künstlerisches, Zeitgeschichtliches, Privates aus meinem Leben*, rev. edn. (Munich: Goldmann, 1981), p. 342.

13 See Walter, *Richard Strauss und seine Zeit*, pp. 73–83.

14 See Friedrich von Schuch, *Richard Strauss, Ernst von Schuch und Dresdens Oper* (Dresden: Verlag der Kunst, n.d. [1952]), p. 143.

15 Strauss to Stefan Zweig, June 17, 1935, in Splitt, *Richard Strauss 1933–1935*, p. 219.

16 Strauss to Clemens Krauss, December 16, 1932, in Günter Brosche, ed., *Richard Strauss, Clemens Krauss. Briefwechsel: Gesamtausgabe* (Tutzing: Hans Schneider, 1997), p. 112.

17 Strauss to Clemens Krauss, March 30, 1934, in *ibid.*, p. 157. After becoming an Austrian citizen in 1910, Bruno Walter had his birth name "Schlesinger" officially deleted.

18 Franz Schalk to Strauss, November 9, 1922, in Günter Brosche, ed., *Richard Strauss, Franz Schalk: Ein Briefwechsel*, (Tutzing: Hans Schneider, 1983), p. 334.

19 Strauss to Schalk, January 4, 1922, *ibid.*, p. 267

20 Strauss to Schalk, January 4, 1919, *ibid.*, p. 84. Even here, Strauss misjudged the political implications. The difficulties in engaging Szell resulted from his being Hungarian rather than his Jewishness.

21 Diary entry by Rolland of May 28, 1907, in M. Hülle-Keeding, ed., *Richard Strauss, Romain Rolland: Briefwechsel und Tagebuchnotizen* (Berlin: Henschel, 1994), p. 187.

22 Matthew Boyden, *Richard Strauss: Die Biographie* (Munich: Europa, 1999), p. 489. Pauline Strauss remarked in the same conversation with Klemperer that, when the Nazis went after him, he should just come to her: she would set the gentlemen "straight." Strauss himself continued: "This would be the right moment to show support for the Jews!" Pauline's remark shows that she clearly overestimated her husband's position during the National Socialist regime; Strauss's follow-up is typical of his political opportunism.

23 The original is in the archive of the Institute for Musicology at the Karl-Franzens-Universität Graz (Mojsisovics folder).

24 Strauss to Anton Kippenberg, March 29, 1933, in Willi Schuh, ed., "Richard Strauss and Anton Kippenberg: Briefwechsel," *Richard Strauss Jahrbuch* (1959–60): 114–46.

25 Egk, *Die Zeit wartet nicht*, p. 343.

26 Potter, "Strauss and the National Socialists," p. 110.

27 See Kater, *Composers of the Nazi Era*, pp. 220ff.

28 *Völkischer Beobachter*, March 19–20, 1933, in Splitt, *Richard Strauss 1933–1935*, p. 45.

29 In an article in the *Völkischer Beobachter*, quoted in Klaus K. Hübler, "Protest der Richard-Wagner-Stadt München: Ein Pamphlet und seine Folgen," *Klangspuren* 2 (1989): 6.

30 *Ibid.*, p. 15.

31 See also Walter, *Richard Strauss und seine Zeit*, pp. 363–4.

32 Strauss to Zweig, June 17, 1935, in Schuh, *Richard Strauss, Stefan Zweig: Briefwechsel,* p. 142.

33 Richard Strauss, "Ansprache anlässlich der Eröffnung der ersten Arbeitstagung der RMK," in *Kultur, Wirtschaft, Recht und die Zukunft des deutschen Musiklebens: Vorträge und Reden von der ersten Arbeitstagung der Reichsmusikkammer,* ed. Presseamt der Reichsmusikkammer (Berlin: Parrhysius, 1934), pp. 9ff.

34 Splitt, *Richard Strauss 1933–1935,* pp. 97ff.

35 Personal note, September 24, 1935, in Hartmut Schaefer, ed., *Richard Strauss, Autographen, Porträts, Bühnenbilder: Ausstellung zum 50. Todestag* (Munich: Bayerische Staatsbibliothek, 1999), p. 154. (This exhibition was a collaboration of the Richard-Strauss-Archiv, Garmisch; the Theater Collection of the University of Cologne; and the Theater Museum, Munich.)

36 Strauss to Zweig, June 17, 1935, in Schuh, *Richard Strauss, Stefan Zweig: Briefwechsel,* p. 142.

37 Splitt, *Richard Strauss 1933–1935,* p. 190.

38 Strauss to Gustav Havemann, February 23, 1934, in Franz Grasberger, ed., *"Der Strom der Töne trug mich fort": Die Welt um Richard Strauss in Briefen* (Tutzing: Hans Schneider, 1967), p. 352.

39 Strauss to Bruno von Nissen, June 11, 1935, in *ibid.,* p. 366.

40 *Ibid.*

41 Strauss to Julius Kopsch, October 4, 1934, in Splitt, *Richard Strauss 1933–1935,* p. 135.

42 Strauss to Wilhelm Furtwängler, December 27, 1933, in Grasberger, *Der Strom der Töne,* p. 349.

43 Heinz Ihlert to Hans Hinkel, the managing chair of the RMK, May 22, 1935, in Splitt, *Richard Strauss 1933–1935,* pp. 209ff.

44 Strauss to unknown recipient, April 30, 1935, in Schaefer, *Richard Strauss, Autographen, Porträts, Bühnenbilder,* p. 154.

45 Splitt, *Richard Strauss 1933–1935,* p. 160.

46 See *ibid.,* p. 212.

47 See Rosenberg's letter to Goebbels regarding this issue (B. Drewniak, *Das Theater im NS-Staat: Szenarium deutscher Zeitgeschichte 1933–1945* [Düsseldorf: Droste, 1983], pp. 291ff); and Bernhard Adamy, "Richard Strauss im Dritten Reich: Randbemerkungen zum Thema bei Kurt Wilhelm," in *Richard Strauss-Blätter* (new series) 14 (1985): 34–42 (p. 39).

48 Splitt, *Richard Strauss 1933–1935,* p. 175.

49 Maria Publig, *Richard Strauss: Bürger, Künstler, Rebell – Eine historische Annäherung* (Graz: Styria, 1999), p. 213.

50 Strauss to Manfred Mautner Markhof, November 24, 1944, in Alice Strauss, ed., "Richard Strauss, Manfred Mautner Markhof: Briefwechsel," *Richard Strauss-Blätter* (new series) 5 (1981): 5–23.

51 Strauss to Rudolf Hartmann, June 7, 1945, in Roswitha Schlötterer, ed., *Richard Strauss, Rudolf Hartmann: Ein Briefwechsel mit Aufsätzen und Regiearbeiten von R. Hartmann* (Tutzing: Hans Schneider, 1984), pp. 46–7.

52 With the quotation Strauss refers to Winston Churchill's address to the academic youth, given at the University of Zurich on September 19, 1946. The speech has become famous because Churchill promoted the idea of a European Union. The passage to which Strauss alluded read as follows: "The first step in the recreation of the European family must be a partnership between France and Germany. In this way only can France recover the moral and cultural leadership of Europe. There can be no revival of Europe without a spiritually great France and a spiritually great Germany." Winston Churchill, "The Tragedy of Europe," in Churchill, *His Complete Speeches 1897–1963,* 8 vols., Vol. VII, ed. Robert Rhodes James (New York: Chelsea House, 1974), pp. 7379–82 (p. 7381). (In the German translation "spiritually" became *geistig,* which is the term Strauss used.) Strauss to Hartmann, November 12, 1946, in Schlötterer, *Richard Strauss, Rudolf Hartmann,* pp. 73–4.

14 Strauss and the business of music

1 Quoted in Nicolas Slonimsky, *Lexicon of Musical Invective: Critical Assaults on Composers since Beethoven's Time* (New York: W. W. Norton, 2000), p. 195.

2 Theodor W. Adorno, "Richard Strauss: Born June 11, 1864," trans. Samuel and Shierry Weber, *Perspectives of New Music* 3 (1964): 14–32 (p. 14).

3 Christopher Reynolds, "Musical Careers, Ecclesiastical Benefices, and the Example of Johannes Brunet," *Journal of the American Musicological Society* 37 (1984): 49–97.

4 Lewis Lockwood, *Music in Renaissance Ferrara 1450–1505* (Cambridge, MA: Harvard University Press, 1984), pp. 203–4.

5 See Bach's letter (No. 152) to Georg Erdmann in Hans T. David and Arthur Mendel, *The New Bach Reader: A Life of Johann Sebastian Bach in Letters and Documents,* rev. and enlarged by Christoph Wolff (New York: W. W. Norton, 1998), pp. 151–2.

6 Neal Zaslaw, "Mozart as a Working Stiff," in James M. Morris, ed., *On Mozart* (Washington: Woodrow Wilson Center Press; New York: Cambridge University Press, 1994), pp. 102–12.

7 William Drabkin, *Beethoven*: Missa Solemnis (Cambridge: Cambridge University Press, 1991), esp. Chapter 2: "Composition, Performance and Publication History," pp. 11–18.

8 Jeffrey Kallberg, "Chopin in the Marketplace. Aspects of the International Music Publishing Industry in the First Half of the Nineteenth Century: France and England," *Notes* 39 (1983): 535–69; and "Chopin in the Marketplace. Aspects of the International Music Publishing Industry in the First Half of the Nineteenth Century: The German-Speaking Lands," *Notes* 39 (1983): 795–824.

9 Mosco Carner, *Puccini: A Critical Biography* (New York: Alfred Knopf, 1968), p. 225; and Julian Budden, *Puccini: His Life and Works* (Oxford: Oxford University Press, 2002), p. 475.

10 Michael Walsh, *Andrew Lloyd Webber: His Life and Works* (New York: Abrams, 1989), pp. 111–12; and John Snelson, *Andrew Lloyd Webber*, Yale Broadway Masters (New Haven: Yale University Press, 2004), pp. 14–15, 18, *passim*.

11 Alfred Kalisch, "Richard Strauss: The Man," in Ernest Newman, *Richard Strauss* (Freeport, NY: Books for Libraries Press, 1969), pp. xvii–xx. Kalisch's essay has been reprinted in Bryan Gilliam, ed., *Richard Strauss and His World* (Princeton: Princeton University Press, 1992), pp. 273–9.

12 Ernst Roth, *The Business of Music: Reflections of a Music Publisher* (New York: Oxford University Press, 1969), p. 181.

13 See Mark-Daniel Schmid, "The Tone Poems of Richard Strauss and Their Reception History from 1887–1908" (Ph.D. diss., Northwestern University, 1997), for the most extensive study of the critical reception of Strauss's orchestral music in that era. Only two small items, both from after 1900, attack Strauss for his supposed interest in earning money. The earlier was a review by Paul Hiller of a 1901 performance of *Aus Italien* that appeared in the *Neue Zeitschrift für Musik* on January 22, 1902 (*ibid.*, p. 76), and the latter item was a general article on Strauss by Richard Batka that appeared in his column "Der Monatsplauderer" in the *Neue Musik-Zeitung* 28/17 (1907): 372 (Schmid, "The Tone Poems of Richard Strauss," pp. 438–9).

14 Richard Strauss, "Reminiscences of My Father," in *Recollections*, pp. 127–33 (p. 131).

15 *Chronicle*, p. 7.

16 See *ibid.*, pp. 49–53, on these and other early public performances of Strauss's works.

17 Franz Trenner, "Richard Strauss und die 'Wilde Gung'l,'" *Schweizerische Musikzeitung* 90 (1950): 403–5.

18 See the facsimile edition: Richard Strauss, *Aus alter Zeit: Gavotte*, ed. with an introduction by Stephan Kohler (Tutzing: Hans Schneider, 1985).

19 Erich H. Mueller von Asow, *Richard Strauss: Thematisches Verzeichnis*, 3 vols., Vol. I (Vienna: Doblinger Verlag, 1959), pp. 4–5.

20 For an overview of Strauss's relationship with Aibl Verlag, see Alfons Ott, "Richard Strauss und sein Verlegerfreund Eugen Spitzweg," in Richard Baum and Wolfgang Rehm, *Musik und Verlag: Karl Vötterle zum 65. Geburtstag am 12. April 1968* (Kassel: Bärenreiter, 1968), pp. 466–75.

21 In addition to his fame as a horn player, Franz Strauss was a capable composer of solo pieces for his instrument, and also of marches, waltzes, and other simple dance pieces. Interestingly, one of the elder Strauss's first two publications was issued in 1844 by Aibl Verlag, while the other appeared that same year in the catalogue of Falter und Sohn. Presumably, Falter und Sohn offered the better terms, since Franz Strauss did not deal again with Aibl until 1880, when he offered that publisher two light orchestral pieces. It seems curious that the elder Strauss turned to Aibl after a thirty-six-year hiatus, and also that he offered up dance pieces, a genre in which he had never published. Thus, Franz Strauss's two marches may have been a small offering to Eduard Spitzweg as a means of opening the door for Richard's music. On Franz Strauss's compositions and publications, see Franz Trenner, "Franz Strauss (1822–1905)," in Willi Schuh, ed., *Richard Strauss Jahrbuch 1959/60* (Bonn: Boosey & Hawkes, 1960), pp. 33, 40–1.

22 See *Chronicle*, Chapter 3: "The Berlin Winter, 1883–84," pp. 62–87, for a synopsis of this time, while Strauss's letters to his parents (Willi Schuh, ed., *Richard Strauss: Briefe an die Eltern, 1882–1906* [Zurich and Freiburg: Atlantis, 1954], pp. 22–54) recount his Berlin activities in detail.

23 Schuh, *Eltern*, pp. 53–4. The letter is dated March 26, 1884.

24 Hans von Bülow, *Briefe und Schriften*, ed. Marie von Bülow (Leipzig: Breitkopf and Härtel, 1907), 8 vols., Vol. VII, pp. 287–8. (Also identified as *Briefe, VI. Band. Meiningen 1880–1886*.) "Reveal nothing to him of his market value up to now," advised Bülow.

25 Franz Grasberger, ed., *"Der Strom der Töne trug mich fort": Die Welt um Richard Strauss in Briefen* (Tutzing: Hans Schneider, 1967), p. 19.

26 *Recollections*, p. 135.

27 See Richard Strauss, *Betrachtungen und Erinnerungen*, ed. Willi Schuh (Zurich and Freiburg: Atlantis, 1949), p. 163, for Strauss's own mention of the fees for his earliest works. This specific paragraph was excised when the English-language translation was issued four years later. See *Recollections*, p. 135 for the location of the excision.

28 See Grasberger, *Der Strom der Töne*, pp. 49–50, for Strauss's offer in a letter of December 7, 1889 to Spitzweg. Additionally, see Scott Warfield, "The Genesis of Richard Strauss's *Macbeth*" (Ph.D. diss., University of North Carolina at Chapel Hill, 1995), pp. 147–222, for a detailed account of these negotiations, including English translations of all letters and other documents.

29 See, for example, the letter of December 20, 1889, from Strauss's boyhood friend and fellow composer Ludwig Thuille (Franz Trenner, ed., *Richard Strauss, Ludwig Thuille: Ein Briefwechsel* [Tutzing: Hans Schneider, 1980], p. 106); and Strauss's own unpublished letter of December 31, 1889, to his family (Munich, Bayerische Staatsbibliothek, ANA 330, I, Strauss, no. 168), both of which are translated in Warfield, "Genesis," pp. 162–3.

30 Strauss's unpublished letter to Abraham and the reply are both held in the Leipzig Staatsarchiv, while English translations of both are in Warfield, "Genesis," pp. 175–6.

31 Strauss to Spitzweg, September 23 and October 23, 1890 (Munich, Städtische Bibliothek, Sammelstücke Nos. 40 and 39, respectively).

32 Strauss to Spitzweg, November 19, 1890, in Grasberger, *Der Strom der Töne*, pp. 55–6.

33 On the importance of piano reductions in general, see Helmut Loos, *Zur Klavierübertragung von Werken für und mit Orchester des 19. und 20. Jahrhunderts* (München: Katzbichler, 1980), as well as the extensive lists of such arrangements in Marc André Roberge, "From Orchestra to Piano: Major Composers as Authors of Piano Reductions of Other Composers' Works," *Notes* 49 (1993): 925–36.

34 Mueller von Asow, *Richard Strauss*, Vol. I, pp. 83–4.

35 Strauss surely knew this, and one should remember that his offer of *Macbeth* to Max Abraham included both the full score and a piano reduction that the composer himself had already prepared.

36 Strauss to Thuille, April 4, 1890, in Trenner, ed., *Strauss, Thuille: Briefwechsel*, p. 113. Thuille was not the first person to discover this problem with Strauss's scores. An earlier review of the four-hand piano reduction of

Aus Italien noted that the arrangement did not sound very good because the mass of lower voices overwhelmed the melismatic upper lines (*Allgemeine Musik-Zeitung* 21/23 [June 7, 1889]: 238).

37 See the display ad for Aibl Verlag, *Musikalisches Wochenblatt* 22 (April 16, 1891): 230.

38 *Musikalisches Wochenblatt* 26 (September 19, 1895): 497.

39 See the list of performances of Strauss's orchestral music in Warfield, *Genesis*, Appendix B, pp. 451–66.

40 See n. 27 above for Strauss's comments on his own fees. For an example of the writing on the business aspects of Strauss's career, see Barbara A. Petersen, "*Die Händler und die Kunst*: Richard Strauss as Composers' Advocate," in *New Perspectives*, pp. 115–32.

41 *Chronicle*, pp. 93, 473.

42 Raymond Holden has written the most frequently about Strauss as a conductor, but has focussed primarily on his interpretations and repertoire, and the numbers of concerts, operas, recordings, and other appearances, without saying anything about fees. See Raymond Holden, *The Virtuoso Conductors: The Central European Tradition from Wagner to Karajan* (New Haven and London: Yale University Press, 2005), Chapter 3: "Richard III: Richard Strauss," pp. 119–42, and the bibliography, which lists many of Holden's other writings on the topic.

43 The *Schreibkalender* have sometimes been described erroneously as Strauss's diaries, when in fact they are datebooks that Strauss used to record appointments, conducting engagements, and occasionally personal notes to himself. The first was given to him by his bride Pauline as a wedding present. The originals remain in the Strauss villa in Garmisch-Partenkirchen, while microfilm copies are held by the music department of the Bayerische Staatsbibliothek.

44 Schuh, *Eltern*, pp. 270–3.

45 *Ibid.*, pp. 210–11.

46 Pauline Strauss to Richard Strauss and his response (September 1 and 3, 1897, respectively). See the original texts in Grasberger, *Der Strom der Töne*, pp. 106–8; and English translations in *Chronicle*, pp. 465–8. Note, also, that the couple's only child, Franz, had been born just a few months earlier on April 12, 1897.

47 Strauss's *Schreibkalender* for 1898 notes a royalty payment from Spitzweg after the twenty-fifth performance of *Don Quixote*. Later that same year, it includes a careful comparison of two competing offers for *Ein*

Heldenleben. The publishers Forberg and Fürstner each offered a different cash payment up-front, one including and the other without the performing rights, but, more importantly, each offered a different percentage of the performance royalties after a varying number of performances.

48 For example, both Matthew Boyden and Ernst Krause treat Sommer as almost an afterthought, which then inflates Strauss's role in the initiation of this cause. See Matthew Boyden, *Richard Strauss* (Boston: Northeastern University Press, 1999), especially Chapter 14: "Protecting the Merchandise," pp. 136–9; and Ernst Krause, *Richard Strauss: The Man and His Work* (Boston: Crescendo Publishing, 1969), pp. 47ff.

49 For the most accurate and detailed account of the struggle to found a society for the protection of composers' rights in Germany, see Hans-Christoph Mauruschat, "The Appreciation of Music" (Parts 1–7), *GEMA News* (December, 1999–November, 2002): 160–6. Also see *Chronicle*, pp. 488–93, for an overview of the matter and extracts from many of Strauss's letters related to the issue.

50 The full text of Strauss's letter (in translation) is in *Chronicle*, pp. 488–91. Irina Kaminiarz, *Richard Strauss Briefe aus dem Archiv des Allgemeinen Deutschen Musikvereins (1888–1909)* (Weimar: Böhlau Verlag, 1995), pp. 112–17, gives a German text of the letter based on a copy in the archives of the *Allgemeiner Deutscher Musikverein* that includes some handwritten alterations.

51 *Chronicle*, pp. 489–90.

52 Peter Franklin, "Richard Strauss and His Contemporaries," in Mark-Daniel Schmid, ed., *The Richard Strauss Companion* (Westport, CT: Praeger, 2003), pp. 45–6. On Strauss's well-known support of Schoenberg, see Günter Brosche, "Richard Strauss und Arnold Schoenberg," *Richard Strauss-Blätter* (new series) 2 (1979): 21–8.

53 See Lynda L. Tyler, "'Commerce and Poetry Hand in Hand': Music in American Department Stores, 1880–1930," *Journal of the American Musicological Society* 45 (1992): 80–1 for one brief account of Strauss's performances in department stores.

54 Willi Schuh, ed., *A Confidential Matter: The Letters of Richard Strauss and Stefan Zweig, 1931–1935*, trans. Max Knight (Berkeley and Los Angeles: University of California Press, 1977), pp. 99–100.

55 *Ibid.*, pp. 118–19.

56 See Michael H. Kater, *Composers of the Nazi Era: Eight Portraits* (New York and Oxford: Oxford University Press,

2000), Chapter 8: "Richard Strauss: Jupiter Compromised," pp. 211–63, esp. pp. 216–19, 230–1, for Strauss's goals for copyright reform and the promotion of serious music during his term as president of the *Reichsmusikkammer*.

57 Among the more obvious acts was Strauss's conducting of the Berlin Philharmonic on March 20, 1933 in place of the deposed Bruno Walter. Strauss took to the podium only when he was convinced that the financially strapped orchestra would suffer further losses, and only on the condition that his fee would go directly to the orchestra. See Schuh, *A Confidential Matter*, p. 119; Kater, *Composers of the Nazi Era*, pp. 220–1; and Erik Ryding and Rebecca Pechefsky, *Bruno Walter: A World Elsewhere* (New Haven: Yale University Press, 2001), pp. 221–3, for varying accounts of the events surrounding that concert and its subsequent place in history.

58 Günter Brosche, ed., *Richard Strauss, Franz Schalk: Ein Briefwechsel* (Tutzing: Hans Schneider, 1983), p. 205. Also quoted in a slightly abbreviated form and different translations in Kurt Wilhelm, *Richard Strauss: An Intimate Portrait*, trans. Mary Whittall (New York: Rizzoli, 1989), p. 161; and Michael Kennedy, *Richard Strauss: Man, Musician, Enigma* (Cambridge: Cambridge University Press, 1999), pp. 216–17.

59 Richard Strauss, Igor Stravinsky, and Zoltan Kodály, "Correspondence with Dr. Roth," *Tempo* 98 (1972): 9–17.

60 Roth, *Business*, p. 182.

61 The three items that this previously unnoticed exchange comprises are held by the US Library of Congress, call no. ML 95.S968. Felix Greissle, Director of Publications for Edward B. Marks Music, wrote first from New York on September 21, 1948; Strauss responded from Montreux on October 16, 1948; and Greissle rejected Strauss's offer on November 3, 1948.

62 The official rates of conversion for post-war Deutschmarks were DM3.33 to the US dollar and DM13.4 to the British pound, making the British film offer worth DM268,000 and Strauss's requested honorarium worth DM33,300. See "Historical Dollar-to-Marks Currency Conversion Page," www.history.ucsb.edu/faculty/marcuse/projects/currency.htm (accessed December 1, 2009).

15 Kapellmeister Strauss

1 Franz Strauss was born in Parkstein in 1822 and died in Munich in 1905.

2 Felix Weingartner, *Über das Dirigieren* (1895), trans. Ernest Newman as *On Conducting* (London: Breitkopf and Härtel, 1906), p. 12.

3 Levi conducted the Symphony in D minor on March 30, 1881 and the Concert Overture in C minor on November 28, 1883 at the Munich Odeonssaal.

4 Richard Strauss, "Reminiscences of Hans von Bülow," in *Recollections*, pp. 118–26 (p. 119). The Odeonssaal was opened in 1828 and was one of Munich's principal concert halls. It was destroyed during World War II.

5 *Ibid.*, p. 119.

6 *Ibid.*, p. 120.

7 Strauss wrote his own cadenzas for the Mozart concerto at Munich in 1885 but they are now lost.

8 *Ibid.*, p. 118.

9 Strauss removed the trombones from both the *Lacrimosa* and *Quam olim Abrahae* in the Requiem; see Strauss's letter to his father, November 7, 1885, in Willi Schuh, ed., *Richard Strauss: Briefe an die Eltern 1882–1906* (Zurich and Freiburg: Atlantis, 1954), p. 69.

10 Letter from Strauss to his father, January 31, 1886, in *ibid.*, p. 85.

11 Strauss conducted *Così fan tutte* on November 12 and 17, 1886.

12 Alexander Ritter (1833–96), Estonian-born violinist and composer.

13 Franz Fischer (1849–1918), German conductor. After a brief period as Hofkapellmeister at Mannheim (1877–9), Fischer joined the staff of the Munich Hofoper, where he worked until his retirement in 1912.

14 Richard Strauss, "Reminiscences of My Father," in *Recollections*, pp. 127–33 (pp. 130–1).

15 Information concerning Strauss's Weimar period was kindly provided by Kenneth Birkin. For a detailed study of his activities in Weimar see Birkin, "Richard Strauss in Weimar," *Richard Strauss-Blätter* (new series) 33 (June, 1995): 3–36; 34 (December, 1995): 3–56.

16 Hans Bronsart von Schellendorf (1830–1915), German pianist, conductor, composer, and administrator, gave the premiere of Liszt's Piano Concerto No. 2, of which he is the dedicatee. He was Intendant at Weimar between 1888 and 1895. Eduard Lassen (1830–1904) was a Danish-born German composer, pianist, and conductor.

17 The statistic of sixteen subscription concerts does not include the concerts that Strauss directed for the Liszt Stiftung nor those that he performed on behalf of the Hofkapelle's fund for widows and orphans.

18 At Weimar, Strauss conducted Mozart's Symphony No. 41 ("Jupiter") on January 12, 1891. This was of particular significance because it was his first of a symphony by that composer and the first of a work with which he would later be closely associated.

19 See Raymond Holden, "Richard Strauss: The *Don Juan* Recordings," *Richard Strauss-Blätter* (new series) 40 (December, 1998): 52–70. Strauss conducted the premiere of *Don Juan* on November 11, 1889; the first performances of his tone poems *Macbeth* (first version) and *Tod und Verklärung* were on October 13, 1890 and January 12, 1891 respectively; a second reading of *Don Juan* on January 11, 1892; and a performance of his symphonic fantasy, *Aus Italien*, on December 4, 1893.

20 Operas that were conducted by Strauss as part of a double-bill have been counted separately.

21 Strauss conducted the world premiere of Humperdinck's *Hänsel und Gretel* on December 23, 1893.

22 Strauss conducted *Wem die Krone?* and *Der faule Hans* on June 8, 10 and 17, 1890. The world premiere of *Guntram*, under Strauss's direction, took place on May 10, 1894.

23 Richard Strauss, "Reminiscences of the First Performance of My Operas," in *Recollections*, pp. 146–67 (p. 148); Kurt Wilhelm, *Richard Strauss: An Intimate Portrait*, trans. Mary Whittall (New York: Rizzoli, 1989), p. 56.

24 Ernst von Possart (1841–1921) was a German actor and theater manager. He was manager of the Munich Theater from 1875 and Intendant of the Royal Theaters from 1895 to 1905. Strauss composed the melodramas *Enoch Arden* and *Das Schloss am Meere* for Possart, which they premiered at Munich and Berlin on March 24, 1897 and March 23, 1899 respectively.

25 Strauss conducted the premiere of the new production of *Don Giovanni* on May 29, 1896. He had conducted two performances of an earlier production on December 12 and 26, 1895.

26 The basis for these reforms was set out in Possart's 1896 article, *Ueber die Neueinstudierung und Neuinszenierung des Mozart'schen* Don Giovanni (Don Juan*) auf dem kgl. Residenztheater zu München* (*On the New Preparation and Production of Mozart's* Don Giovanni *at the Royal Residenztheater, Munich*).

27 By performing the Prague version of *Don Giovanni*, Strauss and Possart reinstated the epilogue, which had fallen from favour during the nineteenth century.

28 Richard Strauss, "On the Munich Opera," in *Recollections*, p. 80 (translation modified).

29 At Berlin, Strauss conducted Wagner's *Der Ring des Nibelungen* for the first time. He

performed *Das Rheingold* on June 19, 1899; *Die Walküre* on June 20, 1899; *Siegfried* on June 22, 1899; and *Götterdämmerung* on June 24, 1899.

30 Julius Kapp, *Richard Strauss und die Berliner Oper* (Berlin-Halensee: M. Hesse, 1939), p. 39.

31 Strauss conducted *Guntram* at Weimar on May 10, 15, and 24, and June 1, 1894; and at Munich on November 16, 1895.

32 Some years later, Strauss erected a memorial to *Guntram* in his garden. The inscription leaves no doubt that the opera was, at least in Strauss's mind, "horribly slain," by "the symphony orchestra of his own father." A photograph of this marker can be found in Wilhelm, *An Intimate Portrait*, p. 56.

33 After the fall of Kaiser Wilhelm II at the end of World War I, the Berlin Hofkapelle became known as the Berlin Staatskapelle.

34 This figure excludes the performances in which Strauss programmed his tone poems in the same evening as either *Elektra* or *Salome* but includes the *Sonderkonzerte* (special events).

35 At Berlin, Strauss also conducted the Berlin Tonkünstler-Orchester between October, 1901 and April, 1903. With that orchestra, he gave a number of contemporary works.

36 Hofmannsthal to Strauss, August 1, 1918, in *Strauss/Hofmannsthal*, pp. 307–9.

37 *Ibid.*

38 Strauss to Hofmannsthal, August 5, 1918, in *ibid.*, pp. 309–11.

39 *Ibid.*

40 *Ibid.*

41 *Salome* received its premiere at Dresden on December 9, 1905.

42 Player pianos could reproduce the duration of the notes with relative accuracy but could not replicate the player's articulation and dynamics fully.

43 Strauss was in the recording studio on December 5, 6, 13, 15, and 20, 1916; Franz Trenner, *Richard Strauss: Chronik zu Leben und Werk*, ed. Florian Trenner (Vienna: Dr. Richard Strauss, 2000), pp. 379–80.

44 Only sides 3 and 4 were recorded by Strauss. Sides 1 and 2 were recorded by his assistant, Georg (George) Szell, later famous as conductor of the Cleveland Orchestra.

45 On the labels of the 1921 gramophone recordings, the orchestra is anonymous. Strauss's 1921–2 tour of the United States was the third of his four visits to that country. His other tours of North America were in 1904, 1920, and 1923. In 1921, Strauss also made his first recordings as an accompanist. In Berlin, he recorded some of his songs with the tenor, Robert Hutt, and the baritone, Heinrich

Schlusnus, for Deutsche Grammophon. During Strauss's 1921–2 tour of the United States, he recorded the accompaniments to "Zueignung," "Allerseelen," and "Traum durch die Dämmerung" in December, 1921 on piano-rolls for the Ampico company. The accompaniments were intended for amateur singers, whose desire to be accompanied by the composer could be fulfilled in the comfort of their parlor. Each accompaniment was recorded twice in different keys.

46 Strauss conducted the last concert of his 1921–2 tour at the Hippodrome, New York, on January 1, 1922. The program included Beethoven's Symphony No. 5, Wagner's Overture to *Tannhäuser*, and his own *Till Eulenspiegel*.

47 Strauss recorded Beethoven's Symphonies Nos. 5 and 7 with the Berlin Staatskapelle in 1928 and 1926 respectively. He also documented Wagner's Overture to *Der fliegende Holländer* and the Prelude to Act I of *Tristan und Isolde*, Weber's Overture to *Euryanthe*, Gluck's Overture to *Iphigénie en Aulide* (ed. Wagner), and Cornelius's Overture to *Der Barbier von Bagdad* for Deutsche Grammophon in 1928.

48 Strauss had recorded *Ein Heldenleben* and *Tod und Verklärung* with the Berlin Staatskapelle in 1926.

49 Between 1942 and 1943, Austrian Radio also recorded Strauss accompanying some forty of his songs with leading singers from the Vienna Staatsoper.

50 Strauss and his cousin, the violinist Benno Walter, gave the premiere of his Violin Concerto at the Bösendorfersaal, Vienna, on December 5, 1882. For that performance, Strauss accompanied Walter at the piano.

51 Strauss conducted the Vienna Philharmonic on December 16, 1906; March 3 and December 1, 1907; and March 8, 1908.

52 The works that Strauss recorded with the Vienna Philharmonic in 1944 were *Also Sprach Zarathustra*, the suite from *Der Bürger als Edelmann*, *Don Juan*, *Ein Heldenleben*, *Symphonia domestica*, *Till Eulenspiegel*, and *Tod und Verklärung*. Along with his own works, Strauss recorded Wagner's Overture to *Die Meistersinger von Nürnberg* with the orchestra that year. He regularly recorded his music for broadcast during the Third Reich. Many of these recordings have been released on CD.

53 Franz Strauss to his son, October 26, 1885, in Schuh, *Eltern*, p. 64.

54 Strauss, "On Conducting Classical Masterpieces," in *Recollections*, p. 44.

55 *Ibid.*

56 *Ibid.*

57 As found in *Recollections*, p. 38.

58 The present author has written extensively on Strauss's activities as a performer, and much of that research has been published in the *Richard Strauss-Blätter*, the journal of the *Internationale Richard Strauss-Gesellschaft* (Vienna). The present author is also preparing a book for Yale University Press on Strauss's work as an executant musician.

16 Strauss and the sexual body: the erotics of humor, philosophy, and ego-assertion

1 *Chronicle*, pp. 312–13.

2 Paul Bekker, *Das Musikdrama der Gegenwart: Studien und Charakteristiken* (Stuttgart: Streker and Schröder, 1909), p. 36. Translations are mine unless otherwise indicated.

3 Arthur Schopenhauer, *The World as Will and Representation*, trans. E. F. J. Payne (New York: Dover Publications, 1969), pp. 326–7.

4 "Of the Despisers of the Body" is the title of Part I, Chapter 4 of *Also sprach Zarathustra*; Friedrich Nietzsche, *Also sprach Zarathustra*, ed. Giorgio Colli and Mazzini Montinari (Munich: Deutscher Taschenbuch Verlag and de Gruyter, 1993), p. 39.

5 Arthur Seidl, "Richard Strauß: Eine Charakterskizze" [1896], in Siedl, *Straußiana: Aufsätze zur Richard Strauß-Frage aus drei Jahrzehnten* (Regensburg: Gustav Bosse, 1913), pp. 11–66 (p. 54).

6 Ernst Bloch, who once declared Strauss's "brilliant hollowness" and "profound superficiality," confessed, in his later years, to being duped by Strauss as a young philosopher. In a later conversation with literary critic, Marcel Reich-Ranicki, Bloch, in his seventies, described an evening with Strauss in Berlin (November, 1911). He told Reich-Ranicki that the two "spoke about *Elektra*, but Bloch did most of the talking while Strauss, who ate dumplings and drank beer, remained silent. Only once in a while did he mumble something in agreement. Bloch said it became a 'horrible' evening. He was suddenly struck by terrible thoughts: this Strauss, this Bavarian beer drinker, he did not at all understand the subtle, exquisite, wonderful music of *Elektra*. As [Bloch] thought about it, he laughed cheerfully – surely at himself" (Marcel Reich-Ranicki, *Mein Leben* [Stuttgart: Deutsche Verlags-Antalt, 1999], p. 342).

7 Nietzsche, *Also sprach Zarathustra*, p. 49.

8 Richard Strauss, "On Johann Strauss," in *Recollections*, p. 77.

9 Given the fragmentary nature of Strauss's scenario, discovered after the composer's death, it is not clear whether the work was to be one act or two; Seidl ("Richard Strauß," p. 51) suggested that it was intended to be a two-act work.

10 Charles Youmans, *Richard Strauss's Orchestral Music and the German Intellectual Tradition: The Philosophical Roots of Musical Modernism* (Bloomington: Indiana University Press, 2005), p. 184.

11 James Hepokoski, "Framing Till Eulenspiegel," *19th-Century Music* 30/1 (2006): 4–43 (p. 9). Walter Werbeck, *Die Tondichtungen von Richard Strauss* (Tutzing: Hans Schneider, 1996), p. 128.

12 Ernst von Wolzogen to Strauss, March 18, 1899, in Franz Grasberger, ed., *"Der Strom der Töne trug mich fort": Die Welt um Richard Strauss in Briefen* (Tutzing: Hans Schneider, 1967), pp. 120–1. The setting was changed to legendary timelessness (though a medieval setting, much like *Meistersinger*, is clearly stated in the stage directions).

13 Ernst von Wolzogen, *Wie ich mich ums Leben brachte* (Braunschweig: Georg Westermann, 1922), p. 147.

14 *Chronicle*, pp. 312–13.

15 Theodor W. Adorno, "Richard Strauss: Born June 11, 1864," trans. Samuel and Shierry Weber, *Perspectives of New Music* 3 (1964): 14–32 (p. 24).

16 Richard Strauss, "Letzte Aufzeichnung," in *Betrachtungen und Erinnerungen*, 2nd edn., ed. Willi Schuh (Zurich: Atlantis, 1957), p. 182.

17 Franz Trenner, ed., *Cosima Wagner, Richard Strauss: Ein Briefwechsel*, ed. with the assistance of Gabriele Strauss (Tutzing: Hans Schneider, 1978), p. 255 n. 5.

18 Cosima Wagner to Strauss, February 25, 1890, in *ibid.*, p. 26.

19 Catharina von Pommer-Esche, "Siegfried Wagner gegen Richard Strauss," *Der Turm* (October 16, 1911).

20 *Ibid.* The copyright stipulated that *Parsifal* could only be performed in Bayreuth, curiously a stipulation that Strauss supported all his life and was successful in extending through persistent personal lobbying.

21 Joris-Karl Huysman, *A rebours*, trans. Margaret Mauldon (Oxford: Oxford University Press, 1998), p. 45.

22 Oscar Wilde, *De profundis* (1909), in Wilde, *The Picture of Dorian Gray and Other Writings* (New York: Simon and Schuster, 2005), pp. 261–364 (p. 318).

23 Strauss to Stefan Zweig, May 5, 1935, in Willi Schuh, ed., *A Confidential Matter: The Letters of Richard Strauss and Stefan Zweig, 1931–1935*, trans. Max Knight (Berkeley and

Los Angeles: University of California Press, 1977), p. 90.

24 Bekker, *Das Musikdrama der Gegenwart*, p. 44.

25 Alfred Heuss, review of the premiere of *Salome*, *Zeitschrift der Internationalen Musikgesellschaft* (Leipzig) 7 (1906): 426–8.

26 Gustave Samazeuilh, "Richard Strauss as I Knew Him," trans. Robert L. Henderson, *Tempo* 69 (Summer, 1964): 14–17 (p. 16).

27 Strauss, "Reminiscences of the First Performance of My Operas," in *Recollections*, pp. 146–67 (p. 154).

28 He served as director from 1910 until his death two years later.

29 Ernst Kris, review of *Freudianism and the Literary Mind*, by Frederick J. Hoffman, *Psychoanalytic Quarterly* 15 (1946): 226.

30 Philip Ward, *Hofmannsthal and Greek Myth: Expression and Performance* (Bern: Peter Lang, 2002), pp. 63, 94.

31 Strauss, "Recollections of the First Performance of My Operas," p. 155 (translation modified).

17 Strauss and the nature of music

1 Cosima Wagner to Strauss, February 25, 1890; Strauss to Cosima Wagner, March 3, 1890. In Franz Trenner, ed., *Cosima Wagner, Richard Strauss: Ein Briefwechsel*, ed. with the assistance of Gabriele Strauss (Tutzing: Hans Schneider, 1978), pp. 26–9.

2 On Strauss's parodic treatment of Jochanaan, see Bryan Gilliam's comments above, pp. 276–7. The modernist dimension of historical elements in *Der Rosenkavalier* is treated in Gilliam, *The Life of Richard Strauss* (Cambridge: Cambridge University Press, 1999), p. 89; and Lewis Lockwood, "The Element of Time in *Der Rosenkavalier*," in *New Perspectives*, pp. 243–55. The classic treatment of incipient postmodernism in Strauss is Leon Botstein, "The Enigmas of Richard Strauss: A Revisionist View," in *Strauss and His World*, pp. 3–32. James Hepokoski has offered a series of essays on formal deformation in Strauss's tone poems, most notably "Fiery-Pulsed Libertine or Domestic Hero? Strauss's *Don Juan* Reinvestigated," in *New Perspectives*, pp. 135–75; and "Framing Till Eulenspiegel," *19th-Century Music* 30/1 (2006): 4–43.

3 The most extensive scholarly treatment of *Musik über Musik* in Strauss is Anette Unger, *Welt, Leben und Kunst als Themen der "Zarathustra Kompositionen" von Richard Strauss und Gustav Mahler* (Frankfurt am Main: Peter Lang, 1992), pp. 20–1, 132–43.

4 Ernst Otto Nodnagel, *Jenseits von Wagner und Liszt* (Königsberg: Druck und Verlag der Ostpreußischen Druckerei und Verlagsanstalt, 1902), pp. 78–9; see the discussion by Morten Kristiansen in this volume, p. 112. Theodor Adorno, "Richard Strauss at Sixty," in *Strauss and His World*, p. 414.

5 The most important recent studies of *Metamorphosen* are Timothy L. Jackson, "The Metamorphosis of the *Metamorphosen*: New Analytical and Source-Critical Discoveries," in *New Perspectives*, pp. 193–241; and Laurenz Lütteken, *"Eine 3,000-jährige Kulturentwicklung abgeschlossen": Biographie und Geschichte in den* Metamorphosen *von Richard Strauss* (Winterthur: Amadeus, 2004). On the last songs see Jackson's "The Last Strauss: Studies of the *Letzte Lieder*" (Ph.D. diss., City University of New York, 1988).

6 Strauss's youthful appropriations of other composers' music is treated in R. Larry Todd, "Strauss before Liszt and Wagner: Some Observations," in *New Perspectives*, pp. 3–40.

7 Walter Werbeck, Preface to *Richard Strauss Edition*, 30 vols., Vol. XXVII: *Werke für kleinere Ensembles* (Vienna: Dr. Richard Strauss, 1999), p. xii.

8 A concise summary without oversimplification can be found in Hepokoski, "Framing Till Eulenspiegel," pp. 4–8. For a more extended treatment see Charles Youmans, *Richard Strauss's Orchestral Music and the German Intellectual Tradition: The Philosophical Roots of Musical Modernism* (Bloomington: Indiana University Press, 2005), pp. 29–113.

9 Jackson, "Metamorphosis," pp. 198–202.

10 Engagement with Beethoven's Fifth and *Tod und Verklärung* begins with large-scale tonal structure (C minor to C major) and its programmatic implications (especially considering the music's collapse back onto C minor in *Metamorphosen*). The textural and harmonic idiom, on the other hand, are clearly drawn from *Tristan*, as though the Beethovenian precedent were being reprocessed by Wagner's counterpoint. The most obvious allusion to *Heldenleben* is a negative one: the precedent of the Funeral March from the *Eroica* was deliberately avoided in the tone poem. On the latter point see Walter Werbeck, *Die Tondichtungen von Richard Strauss* (Tutzing: Hans Schneider, 1996), p. 158.

11 Charles Youmans, "The Twentieth-Century Symphonies of Richard Strauss," *The Musical Quarterly* 84 (2000): 238–58.

12 See Gilliam's remarks on dance and gesture above, p. 271.

13 Richard Strauss, "On Inspiration in Music," in *Recollections*, pp. 112–17 (p. 116).

14 *Ibid.*

15 Alex Ross, *The Rest Is Noise: Listening to the Twentieth Century* (New York: Farrar, Straus, and Giroux, 2007), p. 8.

16 The earliest source of this claim is an interview related in Henry T. Finck, *Richard Strauss: The Man and His Work* (Boston: Little, Brown, 1917), p. 181.

17 On Strauss's reading of Nietzsche before and during the genesis of the tone poem *Also sprach Zarathustra*, see Charles Youmans, "The Role of Nietzsche in Richard Strauss's Artistic Development," *Journal of Musicology* 21/3 (2004): 309–42.

18 Friedrich Nietzsche, *Also sprach Zarathustra*, ed. Giorgio Colli and Mazzino Montinari (Munich: Deutscher Taschenbuch Verlag and de Gruyter, 1993), pp. 274–5.

19 Normal Del Mar describes the musical connection, but passes over its dramatic significance, in *Richard Strauss: A Critical Commentary on His Life and Works*, 3 vols., Vol. I (London: Barrie and Rockliff, 1962), p. 409.

20 The parallels between the Marschallin and Hans Sachs, dramatically and in their emergence as central characters during the compositional process, are discussed by Del Mar, *ibid.*, p. 338.

21 Hugo von Hofmannsthal to Strauss, April 24, 1909, in *Strauss/Hofmannsthal*, p. 30 (translation modified).

22 On this contrast see David Murray, "*Ariadne auf Naxos* (ii)," in *The New Grove Dictionary of Opera*, ed. Stanley Sadie, *Grove Music Online, Oxford Music Online*, www.oxfordmusiconline.com/subscriber/article/grove/music/O900173 (accessed November 11, 2009).

23 On stylistic heterogeneity in *Feuersnot*, see Morten Kristiansen, "Richard Strauss, *Die Moderne*, and the Concept of *Stilkunst*," *The Musical Quarterly* 86/4 (Winter, 2002): 689–749.

24 Werbeck demonstrates exhaustively that Strauss often adapted the programs of his tone poems to suit his evolving musical ideas during the compositional process. See Werbeck, *Tondichtungen*, pp. 103–207. Regarding the libretto of *Capriccio*, Strauss of course collaborated with Clemens Krauss, though as in *Guntram* the ultimate responsibility for the text was his.

25 The Sextet had an independent premiere of sorts, on May 7, 1942 in the Vienna home of Baldur von Schirach, the city's Gauleiter; Michael Kennedy, *Richard Strauss: Man, Musician, Enigma* (Cambridge: Cambridge University Press, 1999), p. 340.

26 On the filmic qualities of *Intermezzo* see Bryan Gilliam, "Strauss's *Intermezzo*: Innovation and Tradition," in *New Perspectives*, pp. 259–83 (pp. 266–7).

27 Programmatic annotations in the sketches of this passage (*träumerisch* at m. 5; *es geht nicht weiter* at m. 11) are discussed in Werbeck, *Tondichtungen*, p. 179.

28 Arnold Schoenberg, "On Those who Stayed in Germany" (1946), in Joseph Auner, ed., *A Schoenberg Reader: Documents of a Life* (New Haven: Yale University Press, 2003), pp. 315–16 (p. 316).

29 In Hanslick's criticism it is easy to find passages such as this one on Brahms's First Symphony: "In the first movement, the listener is held by fervent emotional expression, by Faustian conflicts"; Eduard Hanslick, *Music Criticisms, 1846–99*, trans. and ed. Henry Pleasants (Baltimore: Penguin, 1950), p. 126. Alexander Ritter published his reductive reading of Hanslick's aesthetics in the satirical essay "Vom Spanisch-Schönen," *Allgemeine Musikzeitung* 18/10 (1891): 128–9.

30 Strauss to Hans von Bülow, August 24, 1888, in Gabriele Strauss, ed., *Lieber Collega! Richard Strauss im Briefwechsel mit zeitgenössischen Komponisten und Dirigenten* (Berlin: Henschel, 1996), p. 82.

31 Hepokoski, "Framing Till Eulenspiegel," pp. 7–8.

32 For an introduction to Hepokoski's concept of sonata deformation, a practice widely applied in the music of the late nineteenth century, see James Hepokoski and Warren Darcy, *Elements of Sonata Theory: Norms, Types and Deformations in the Late-Eighteenth-Century Sonata* (Oxford: Oxford University Press, 2006), pp. 614–21.

33 Hepokoski, "Framing Till Eulenspiegel," pp. 28, 30–4.

34 Charles Youmans, "The Private Intellectual Context of Richard Strauss's *Also sprach Zarathustra*, *19th-Century Music* 22/2 (1998): 101–26 (pp. 119–20).

35 Strauss to Stefan Zweig, May 5, 1935, in Willi Schuh, ed., *A Confidential Matter: The Letters of Richard Strauss and Stefan Zweig, 1931–1935*, trans. Max Knight (Berkeley: University of California Press, 1977), p. 90 (translation modified).

Select bibliography

Abert, Anna Amalie. *Richard Strauss: Die Opern*. Velber: Friedrich, 1972.

Adorno, Theodor W. "Richard Strauss: Born June 11, 1864." Trans. Samuel and Shierry Weber. *Perspectives of New Music* 3 (1964), 14–32; 4 (1965), 113–29.

Bie, Oscar. *Die moderne Musik und Richard Strauss*. Berlin: Bard Marquardt, 1906.

Birkin, Kenneth. "Richard Strauss in Weimar." *Richard Strauss-Blätter* (new series) 33 (June, 1995), 3–36; 34 (December, 1995), 3–56.

Blaukopf, Herta, ed. *Gustav Mahler–Richard Strauss: Correspondence 1888–1911*. Trans. Edmund Jephcott. Chicago: University of Chicago Press, 1984.

Botstein, Leon. "The Enigmas of Richard Strauss: A Revisionist View." In *Strauss and His World*, pp. 3–32.

Bracht, Hans-Joachim. *Nietzsches Theorie der Lyrik und das Orchesterlied: Ästhetische und analytische Studien zu Orchesterliedern von Richard Strauss, Gustav Mahler und Arnold Schönberg*. Kassel: Bärenreiter, 1993.

Brecher, Gustav. *Richard Strauss: Eine monographische Skizze*. Leipzig: Hermann Seemann Nachfolger, n.d. [1900].

Brosche, Günter, ed. *Richard Strauss, Clemens Krauss. Briefwechsel: Gesamtausgabe*. Tutzing: Hans Schneider, 1997.

Richard Strauss, Franz Schalk: Ein Briefwechsel. Tutzing: Hans Schneider, 1983.

Del Mar, Norman. *Richard Strauss: A Critical Commentary on His Life and Works*. 3 vols. Ithaca, NY: Cornell University Press, 1986.

Edelmann, Bernd, Birgit Lodes, and Reinhold Schlötterer, eds. *Richard Strauss und die Moderne*. Berlin: Henschel, 2001.

Erwin, Charlotte E. "Richard Strauss's Presketch Planning for *Ariadne auf Naxos*." *Musical Quarterly* 47 (1981), 348–65.

Frisch, Walter. *German Modernism: Music and the Arts*. Berkeley: University of California Press, 2005.

Getz, Christine. "The Lieder of Richard Strauss." In Schmid, *The Richard Strauss Companion*, pp. 335–382.

Gillespie, Susan, ed. and trans. "Selections from the Strauss–Thuille Correspondence: A Glimpse of Strauss during His Formative Years." In *Strauss and His World*, pp. 193–236.

Gilliam, Bryan. "Ariadne, Daphne, and the Problem of *Verwandlung*." *Cambridge Opera Journal* 15/1 (2003), 67–81.

"'Friede im Innern': Strauss's Public and Private Worlds in the Mid 1930s." *Journal of the American Musicological Society* 57/3 (2004), 565–97.

The Life of Richard Strauss. Cambridge: Cambridge University Press, 1999.

"Richard Strauss's *Intermezzo*: Innovation and Tradition." In *New Perspectives*, pp. 259–83.

"Strauss's Preliminary Opera Sketches: Thematic Fragments and Symphonic Continuity." *19th-Century Music* 9 (1985–6), 176–88.

Gilliam, Bryan, ed. *Richard Strauss and His World*. Princeton: Princeton University Press, 1992.

ed. *Richard Strauss: New Perspectives on the Composer and His Work*. Durham, NC: Duke University Press, 1992.

Gilman, Lawrence. "Strauss's *Salome*: Its Art and Its Morals." In Gilman, *Aspects of Modern Opera*. New York: John Lane, 1909, pp. 65–106.

Gould, Glenn. "An Argument for Richard Strauss." In Gould, *The Glenn Gould Reader*, ed. Tim Page. New York: Knopf, 1984, pp. 84–92.

Grasberger, Franz, ed. *"Der Strom der Töne trug mich fort": Die Welt um Richard Strauss in Briefen*. Tutzing: Hans Schneider, 1967.

Grasberger, Franz, and Franz Hadamowsky, eds. *Richard Strauss-Ausstellung zum 100. Geburtstag*. Vienna: Österreichische Nationalbibliothek, 1964.

Graydon, Philip. "Richard Strauss's *Die ägyptische Helena* (1927): Context and Contemporary Critical Reception." Ph.D. diss., Queen's University Belfast, 2004.

Gregor, Joseph. *Richard Strauss: Der Meister der Oper*. Munich: R. Piper, 1939.

Hansen, Mathias. *Richard Strauss: Die Sinfonischen Dichtungen*. Kassel: Bärenreiter, 2003.

Heisler, Wayne, Jr. *The Ballet Collaborations of Richard Strauss*. Eastman Studies in Music. Rochester, NY: University of Rochester Press, 2009.

Heisler, Wayne "Kitsch and the Ballet *Schlagobers*." *The Opera Quarterly* 22/1 (Winter, 2006), 38–64.

"'To drive away all cloudy thoughts': Heinrich Kröller's and Richard Strauss's 1923 *Ballettsoirée* and Interwar Viennese Cultural Politics." *The Musical Quarterly* 88/4 (Winter, 2005), 594–629.

Hepokoski, James. "Fiery-Pulsed Libertine or Domestic Hero? Strauss's *Don Juan* Reinvestigated." In *New Perspectives*, pp. 135–75.

"Framing Till Eulenspiegel." *19th-Century Music* 30/1 (2006), 4–43.

Review of Walter Werbeck, *Die Tondichtungen von Richard Strauss*. *Journal of the American Musicological Society* 51 (1998), 603–25.

"Structure and Program in *Macbeth*: A Proposed Reading of Strauss's First Symphonic Poem." In *Strauss and His World*, pp. 67–89.

Hepokoski, James, and Warren Darcy. *Elements of Sonata Theory: Norms, Types and Deformations in the Late-Eighteenth-Century Sonata*. Oxford: Oxford University Press, 2006.

Holden, Raymond. "Richard Strauss: The *Don Juan* Recordings." *Richard Strauss-Blätter* (new series) 40 (December, 1998), 52–70.

Hutcheon, Linda, and Michael Hutcheon. "Staging the Female Body: Richard Strauss's *Salome*." In Mary Ann Smart, ed., *Siren Songs*. Princeton: Princeton University Press, 2000, pp. 204–21.

Jackson, Timothy. "The Last Strauss: Studies of the *Letzte Lieder*." Ph.D. diss., City University of New York, 1988.

Jefferson, Alan. *The Lieder of Richard Strauss*. London: Cassell, 1971.

Kapp, Julius. *Richard Strauss und die Berliner Oper*. Berlin-Halensee: M. Hesse, 1939.

Kater, Michael H. *Composers of the Nazi Era: Eight Portraits*. New York and
   Oxford: Oxford University Press, 2000.
Kennedy, Michael. *Richard Strauss: Man, Musician, Enigma*. Cambridge:
   Cambridge University Press, 1999.
Kissler, J. M. "Malven: Richard Strauss's letzte Rose!" *Tempo* 185 (1993), 18–25.
Knaus, Gabriella Hanke, ed. *Richard Strauss, Ernst von Schuch: Ein Briefwechsel*.
   Berlin: Henschel, 1999.
Kohler, Stefan. Preface to Richard Strauss, *Trio Nr. 1 A-Dur für Klavier, Violine und
   Violoncello*, 1st edn. New York: Schott, 1996.
Konrad, Ulrich. "Die Deutsche Motette op. 62 von Richard Strauss: Entstehung,
   Form, Gehalt." In Edelmann, Lodes, and Schlötterer, *Richard Strauss und die
   Moderne*, pp. 283–310.
Kramer, Lawrence. "Modernity's Cutting Edge: The Salome Complex." In Kramer,
   Opera and Modern Culture: Wagner and Strauss. Berkeley: University of
   California Press, 2004, pp. 128–66.
Krause, Ernst. *Richard Strauss: The Man and His Music*. Trans. John Coombs.
   London: Collett's, 1964.
Kristiansen, Morten. "Richard Strauss before *Salome*: The Early Operas and
   Unfinished Stage Works," In Schmid, *The Richard Strauss Companion*,
   pp. 245–73.
   "Richard Strauss, *Die Moderne*, and the Concept of *Stilkunst*." *The Musical
   Quarterly* 86/4 (Winter, 2002), 689–749.
   "Richard Strauss's *Feuersnot* in Its Aesthetic and Cultural Context: A Modernist
   Critique of Musical Idealism." Ph.D. diss., Yale University, 2000.
   "Strauss's First Librettist: Ernst von Wolzogen beyond *Überbrettl*." *Richard
   Strauss-Blätter* (new series) 59 (June, 2008), 75–116.
Larkin, David. "*Aus Italien*: Retracing Strauss's Journeys." *The Musical Quarterly* 92
   (2009), 70–117
   "Reshaping the Liszt–Wagner Legacy: Intertextual Dynamics in Strauss's Tone
   Poems." Ph.D. diss., University of Cambridge, 2006.
Lienenlüke, Ursula. *Lieder von Richard Strauss nach zeitgenössischer Lyrik*.
   Regensburg: Gustav Bosse Verlag, 1976.
Lodato, Suzanne Marie. "Richard Strauss and the Modernists: A Contextual Study
   of Strauss's Fin-de-siècle Song Style." Ph.D. diss., Columbia University,
   1999.
Lodes, Birgit. "Richard Strauss' Skizzen zu den *Metamorphosen* und ihre
   Beziehung zu *Trauer um München*." *Musikforschung* 47/3 (1994), 234–52.
Louis, Rudolf. *Die deutsche Musik der Gegenwart*. Munich and Leipzig: Georg
   Müller, 1909.
Lütteken, Laurenz. *"Eine 3,000 jährige Kulturentwicklung abgeschlos-
   sen": Biographie und Geschichte in den* Metamorphosen *von Richard Strauss*.
   Winterthur: Amadeus, 2004.
Merian, Hans. *Richard Strauß' Tondichtung* Also sprach Zarathustra: *Eine Studie
   über die moderne Programmsymphonie*. Leipzig: Carl Meyer, 1899.
Messmer, Franzpeter, ed. *Kritiken zu den Uraufführungen der Bühnenwerke von
   Richard Strauss*. Pfaffenhofen: W. Ludwig, 1989.

Myers, Rollo, ed. and trans. *Richard Strauss and Romain Rolland: Correspondence, together with Fragments from the Diary of Romain Rolland and Other Essays.* London: Calder and Boyars, 1968.

Newman, Ernest. *Richard Strauss.* Freeport, NY: Books for Libraries Press, 1969.

Nodnagel, Ernst Otto. *Jenseits von Wagner und Liszt.* Königsberg: Druck und Verlag der Ostpreußischen Druckerei und Verlagsanstalt, 1902.

Orel, Dobroslav. *Ján Levoslav Bella: k. 80. narozeninám seniora slovenské hudby.* Bratislava: Philosophy Faculty of the Comenius University of Bratislava, 1924.

Petersen, Barbara. *"Ton und Wort": The Lieder of Richard Strauss.* Ann Arbor: UMI Research Press, 1980.

Pfister, Kurt. *Richard Strauss: Weg, Gestalt, Denkmal.* Vaduz: Liechtenstein Verlag, 1950.

Potter, Pamela M. "Strauss and the National Socialists: The Debate and Its Relevance." In *New Perspectives*, pp. 93–113.

"Strauss's *Friedenstag*: A Pacifist Attempt at Political Resistance." *The Musical Quarterly* 69/3 (1983): 408–24.

Phipps, Graham. "The Logic of Tonality in Strauss's *Don Quixote*: A Schoenbergian Evaluation." *19th-Century Music* 9 (1986), 189–205.

Publig, Maria. *Richard Strauss: Bürger, Künstler, Rebell – Eine historische Annäherung.* Graz: Styria, 1999.

Puffett, Derrick. "'*Lass Er die Musi, wo sie ist*': Pitch Specificity in Strauss." In *Strauss and His World*, pp. 138–63.

Puffett, Derrick ed. *Richard Strauss*: Elektra. Cambridge: Cambridge University Press, 1989.

Richard Strauss: Salome. Cambridge: Cambridge University Press, 1989.

Richard Strauss: Autographen, Porträts, Bühnenbilder. Ausstellung zum 50. Todestag. Munich: Bayerische Staatsbibliothek, 1999.

Roese, Otto. *Richard Strauss*: Salome. Berlin: Bard, Marquardt and Co., 1906.

Schaarwächter, Jürgen. *Richard Strauss und die Sinfonie.* Cologne: Verlag Christoph Dohr, 1994.

Schlötterer, Reinhold. "Ironic Allusions to Italian Opera in the Musical Comedies of Richard Strauss." In *New Perspectives*, pp. 77–91.

Schmid, Mark-Daniel, ed. *The Richard Strauss Companion.* Westport, CT: Praeger, 2003.

Schmid, Mark-Daniel, "The Tone Poems of Richard Strauss and Their Reception History from 1887–1908." Ph.D. diss., Northwestern University, 1997.

Schmitz, Eugen. *Richard Strauss als Musikdramatiker.* Munich: Dr. Henrich Löwe, 1907.

Schuch, Friedrich von. *Richard Strauss, Ernst von Schuch und Dresdens Oper.* Dresden: Verlag der Kunst, n.d. [1952].

Schuh, Willi. *Richard Strauss: Briefe an die Eltern 1882–1906.* Zurich and Freiburg: Atlantis, 1954.

Richard Strauss: Briefwechsel mit Willi Schuh. Zurich: Atlantis, 1969.

Richard Strauss: A Chronicle of the Early Years 1864–1898. Trans. Mary Whittall. Cambridge: Cambridge University Press, 1982.

Straussiana aus vier Jahrzehnten. Tutzing: Hans Schneider, 1981.

Über Opern von Richard Strauss. Zurich: Atlantis, 1947.

Schuh, Willi, ed. *A Confidential Matter: The Letters of Richard Strauss and Stefan Zweig, 1931–1935.* Trans. Max Knight. Berkeley and Los Angeles: University of California Press, 1977.

Schuh, Willi and Franz Trenner, eds. *Correspondence of Hans von Bülow and Richard Strauss.* Trans. Anthony Gishford. London: Boosey and Hawkes, 1955.

Shreffler, Anne. "The Coloratura's Voice: Another Look at Zerbinetta's Aria from *Ariadne auf Naxos.*" In Edelmann, Lodes, and Schlötterer, *Richard Strauss und die Moderne,* pp. 361–90.

Seidl, Arthur. "Richard Strauß: Eine Charakterskizze" [1896]. In Seidl, *Straußiana: Aufsätze zur Richard Strauß-Frage aus drei Jahrzehnten.* Regensburg: Gustav Bosse, 1913, pp. 11–66.

Specht, Richard. Preface to Richard Strauss, *Aus Italien, sinfonische Fantasie für grosses Orchester, G dur, op. 16.* Vienna: Universal Edition, 1904.

Richard Strauss und sein Werk. 2 vols. Leipzig: E. P. Tal, 1921.

Splitt, Gerhard. *Richard Strauss 1933–1935: Ästhetik und Musikpolitik zu Beginn der nationalsozialistischen Herrschaft.* Pfaffenweiler: Centaurus, 1987.

Steiger, Martina, ed. *Richard Strauss, Karl Böhm: Briefwechsel 1921–1949.* Mainz: Schott, 1999.

Steinberg, Michael. "Richard Strauss and the Question." In *Strauss and His World,* pp. 164–89.

Steinitzer, Max. *Richard Strauss 1. bis 4. Aufl.* Berlin: Schuster and Loeffler, 1911.

"Richard Strauss' Werke für Klavier." *Die Musik* 24/2 (November, 1931), 105–9.

Strauss, Franz and Alice, eds. *The Correspondence between Richard Strauss and Hugo von Hofmannsthal.* Arr. Willi Schuh. Trans. Hanns Hammelmann and Ewald Osers. Cambridge: Cambridge University Press, 1980.

Strauss, Gabriele, ed. *Lieber Collega! Richard Strauss im Briefwechsel mit zeitgenössischen Komponisten und Dirigenten.* Berlin: Henschel, 1996.

Strauss, Gabriele, and Monika Reger, eds. *Ihr aufrichtig Ergebener: Richard Strauss im Briefwechsel mit zeitgenössischen Komponisten und Dirigenten.* Berlin: Henschel Verlag, 1998.

Strauss, Richard. "*Aus Italien*: Analyse vom Komponisten." *Allgemeine Musikzeitung* 16/26 (June 28, 1889), 263–6.

Strauss, Richard *Betrachtungen und Erinnerungen.* 3rd edn. Ed. Willi Schuh. Zurich: Atlantis, 1981.

"Is There an Avant-Garde in Music?" In *Recollections,* pp. 12–17.

"On Inspiration in Music." In *Recollections,* pp. 112–17.

Recollections and Reflections. Ed. Willi Schuh. Trans. L. J. Lawrence. London: Boosey and Hawkes, 1953.

"Recollections of My Youth and Years of Apprenticeship." In *Recollections,* pp. 134–45.

"Reminiscences of Hans von Bülow." In *Recollections,* pp. 118–26.

"Reminiscences of My Father." In *Recollections,* pp. 127–33.

"Reminiscences of the First Performance of My Operas." In *Recollections,* pp. 146–67.

"Ten Golden Rules for the Album of a Young Conductor." In *Recollections*, pp. 38.

Tod und Verklärung, op. 24: Faksimile-Reproduktion der Handschrift. Vienna: Universal Edition, 1923.

Tenschert, Roland. *Straussiana aus vier Jahrzehnten.* Ed. Jürgen Schaarwächter. Tutzing: Hans Schneider, 1994.

Todd, R. Larry. "Strauss before Liszt and Wagner: Some Observations." In *New Perspectives*, pp. 3–40.

Trenner, Franz. *Richard Strauss: Chronik zu Leben und Werk.* Ed. Florian Trenner. Vienna: Dr. Richard Strauss, 2000.

Richard Strauss: Werkverzeichnis (TrV). 2nd edn. Vienna: Dr. Richard Strauss, 1999.

Die Skizzenbücher von Richard Strauss aus dem Richard-Strauss-Archiv in Garmisch. Tutzing: Hans Schneider, 1977.

Trenner, Franz, ed. *Cosima Wagner, Richard Strauss: Ein Briefwechsel.* Ed. with the assistance of Gabriele Strauss. Tutzing: Hans Schneider, 1978.

ed. *Richard Strauss, Ludwig Thuille: Ein Briefwechsel.* Tutzing: Hans Schneider, 1980.

Urban, Erich. *Richard Strauss.* Berlin: Gose and Tetzlaff, 1901.

Wajemann, Heiner. *Die Chorkompositionen von Richard Strauss.* Tutzing: Hans Schneider, 1986.

Walden, Herwarth, ed. *Richard Strauss: Symphonien und Tondichtungen.* Meisterführer 6. Berlin: Schlesinger, n.d. [*c.* 1908].

Walter, Michael. *Richard Strauss und seine Zeit.* Laaber: Laaber Verlag, 2000.

Warfield, Scott. "Friedrich Wilhelm Meyer (1818–1893): Some Biographical Notes on Richard Strauss's Composition Teacher." *Richard Strauss-Blätter*, new series 37 (June, 1997), 54–74.

"The Genesis of Richard Strauss's *Macbeth*." Ph.D. diss., University of North Carolina at Chapel Hill, 1995.

Werbeck, Walter. "Oper und Symphonie: Zu formalen Konzeption von *Intermezzo*." *Richard Strauss-Blätter* (new series) 45 (June, 2001), 111–23.

Die Tondichtungen von Richard Strauss. Tutzing: Hans Schneider, 1996.

Wilhelm, Kurt. *Richard Strauss: An Intimate Portrait.* Trans. Mary Whittall. New York: Rizzoli, 1989.

Williamson, John. *Strauss: Also sprach Zarathustra.* Cambridge: Cambridge University Press, 1993.

Youmans, Charles. "The Private Intellectual Context of Richard Strauss's *Also sprach Zarathustra*." *19th-Century Music* 22/2 (1998), 101–26.

Richard Strauss's Orchestral Music and the German Intellectual Tradition: The Philosophical Roots of Musical Modernism, Bloomington: Indiana University Press, 2005.

"The Role of Nietzsche in Richard Strauss's Artistic Development." *Journal of Musicology* 21/3 (2004), 309–42.

Index

Cambridge Companions to Music

The Cambridge Companion to Schoenberg
Edited by Jennifer Shaw and Joseph Auner

The Cambridge Companion to Schubert
Edited by Christopher Gibbs

The Cambridge Companion to Schumann
Edited by Beate Perrey

The Cambridge Companion to Shostakovich
Edited by Pauline Fairclough and David Fanning

The Cambridge Companion to Sibelius
Edited by Daniel M. Grimley

The Cambridge Companion to Richard Strauss
Edited by Charles Youmans

The Cambridge Companion to Verdi
Edited by Scott L. Balthazar

Instruments

The Cambridge Companion to Brass Instruments
Edited by Trevor Herbert and John Wallace

The Cambridge Companion to the Cello
Edited by Robin Stowell

The Cambridge Companion to the Clarinet
Edited by Colin Lawson

The Cambridge Companion to the Guitar
Edited by Victor Coelho

The Cambridge Companion to the Organ
Edited by Nicholas Thistlethwaite and Geoffrey Webber

The Cambridge Companion to the Piano
Edited by David Rowland

The Cambridge Companion to the Recorder
Edited by John Mansfield Thomson

The Cambridge Companion to the Saxophone
Edited by Richard Ingham

The Cambridge Companion to Singing
Edited by John Potter

The Cambridge Companion to the Violin
Edited by Robin Stowell